MOMENTS OF MEANING-MAKING

MOMENTS OF MEANING-MAKING
On Anachronism, Becoming, and Conceptualizing

Mieke Bal

Photography by
Lena Verhoeff

Valiz, Amsterdam

CONTENTS

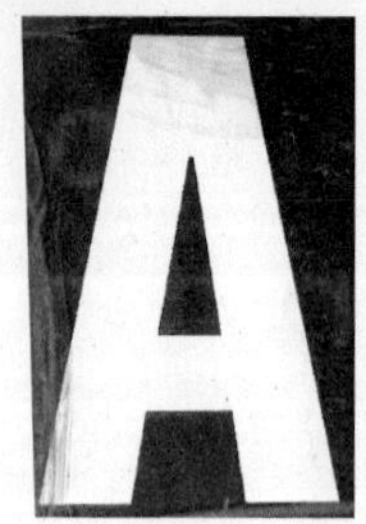

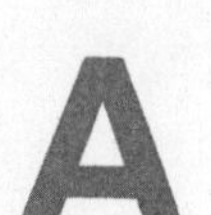

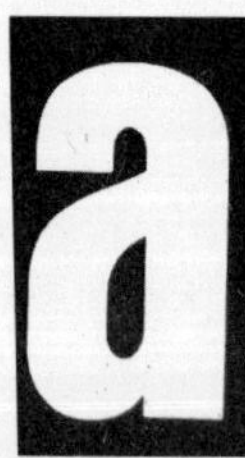

CONTENTS

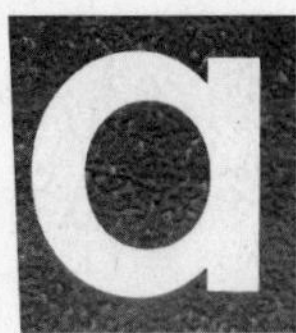

CONTENTS

CONTENTS

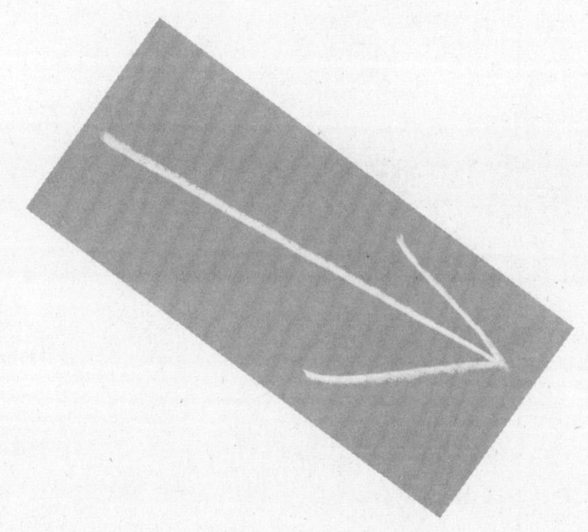

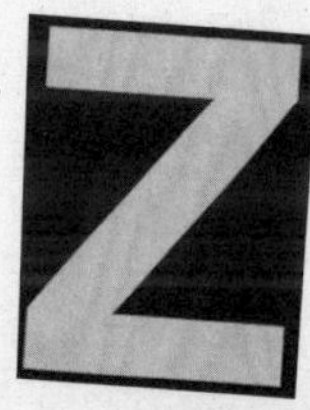

Introduction

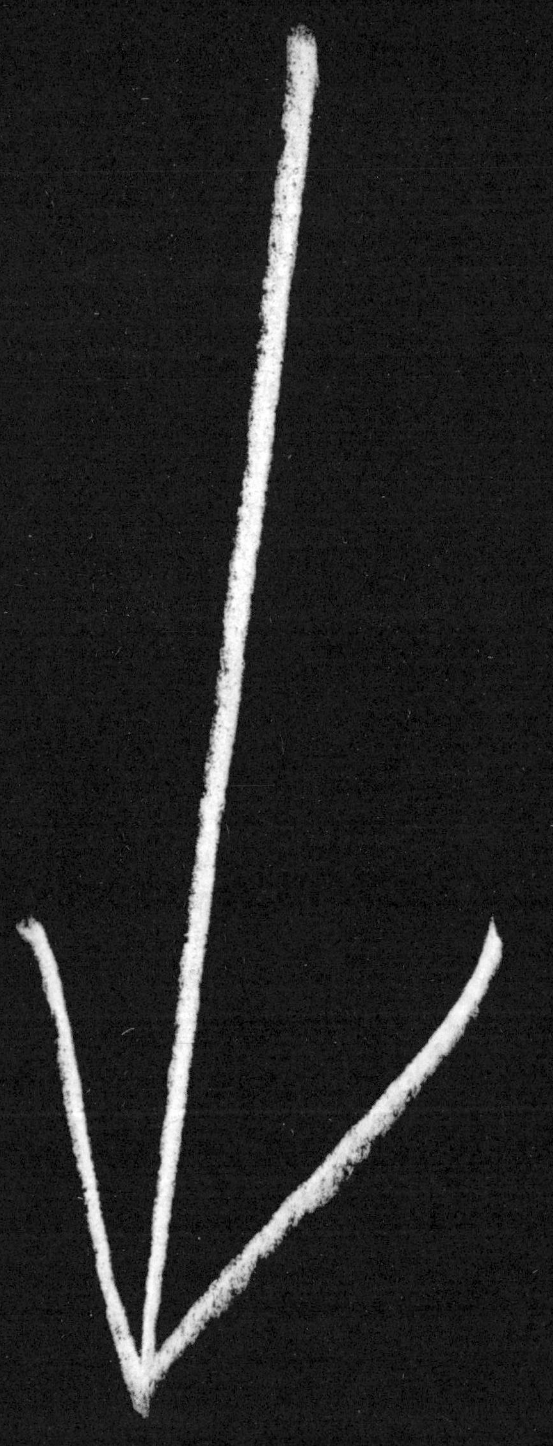

That dinner, at the Clark Art Institute in Williamstown, Massachusetts, where I had a residency in 2016, after a lecture by one of the fellows: I will never forget it. It was my first conscious moment of deep emotional ambivalence. This is how I felt. The lecture had been very exciting, and I was completely involved, asked questions, and liked the speaker very much. But on the back of my mind was a dark, almost tangible shadow. I can still feel it. I knew that the next day I was going to hear from the neurologist who had done an MRI and an EEG after my last episode of losing consciousness, what I was dying of and at what pace: a brain tumour, Alzheimer, or Parkinson. That evening, the only time when I felt this, my imminent death seemed a certainty. But of course, I didn't talk about this with the colleagues on that nice social occasion. Sitting next to me was a literary agent of non-fiction. She kept nudging me that I should write my memoirs. The dark expectation of the moment suddenly made it seem like an urgent but also a fun thing to do. To leave behind a memory, a trace, after I had departed, and also to have something exciting to do during the waiting.

Just recently, I had pushed a friend who was dying of ALS to finish the book he had almost completed, and offered to help him editing the drafts. On the back of my mind had been the wish to give him something to get up for in the morning, in his horrible situation. He died some time later, and he did finish the book to a degree that we, his friends, could complete it and get it published. My next day after that dinner at the Clark was better than his had been, the day after he had been diagnosed. It turned out that I had none of the above-mentioned diseases. I had just been given the wrong medication. The relief came with a new desire. The idea that you can write memory stories, episodes from your life, mixing work-related academic incidents with personal memories, whether or not they end up being published, made me consider if I should do it anyway. The memory of the anxiety merged with the intellectual discussions and sociality of that evening enticed me to do it.

But how? I don't like biographical criticism, never did; and I loathe the intellectual laziness of critics who revert to the artists and ask for their intentions, what they mean to say with their art, and just write it down, as if under dictation.

My view of the point of criticism was different. My resistance to biography in art writing has been with me for as long as I can remember. And some artists, the most intelligent ones I think, agree with me. Belgian artist Lili Dujourie chose me among a range of potential catalogue contributors, to write about her work after, and because, I had declined to meet her until I would have finished writing the essay. I expressed this refusal in spite of the exhibition's curator's wish, since he had proposed that the artist and I should meet. I was ever so happy that the artist agreed with me. When we met later on, the conversation with her confirmed our intuitive choice. The title of the book about her work, *Hovering between Thing and Event: Encounters with Lili Dujourie*, which appeared in 1998, expresses quite clearly what mattered to her and me both. Here is one of her more recent works, *Dolores*, from 2001. (see fig. 1)

Similarly, but in a different spirit, I had declined to meet Louise Bourgeois when I was asked to write about her work, which I admired immensely. I'd like to meet her after the writing, I said. I assume Louise wasn't too happy when I declined her invitation; generally, most critics of her work said that she tended to say in an imposing tone, almost dictating, what her art meant. For her, the biographical content, especially her relationship with her mother, mattered a lot. Which was, of course, the primary reason for my rejection of the proposal we meet. I regretted it a bit when she passed away before I got around to attend one of her Sunday salons later on. But I am glad that I got to write the book, *Louise Bourgeois' Spider: The Architecture of Art-writing,* on my own. No, not quite; of course, I talked with a lot of Bourgeois connoisseurs, read about her work, and discussed her work with students and PhD candidates, and colleagues. But at least, the personal distance from her enabled me to do the thinking and interpreting separated from the artist and her stated intentions. (see fig. 2) For me this was and is a condition *sine qua non* to write about art. This resistance stems from my conviction that I do such writing as a mediator, but not one between artist and public, but instead, between the art, the work it does, and its 'second persons'.

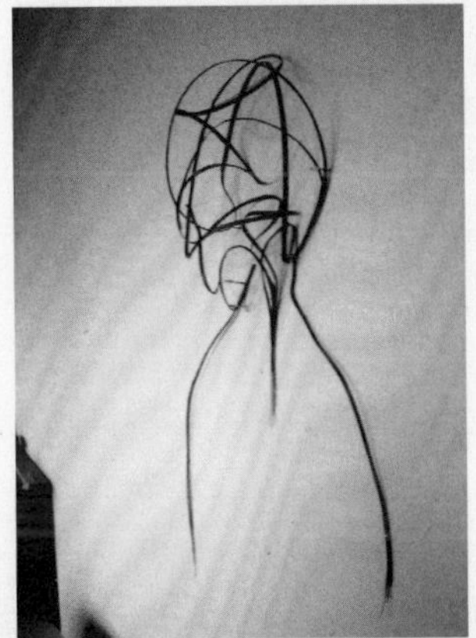

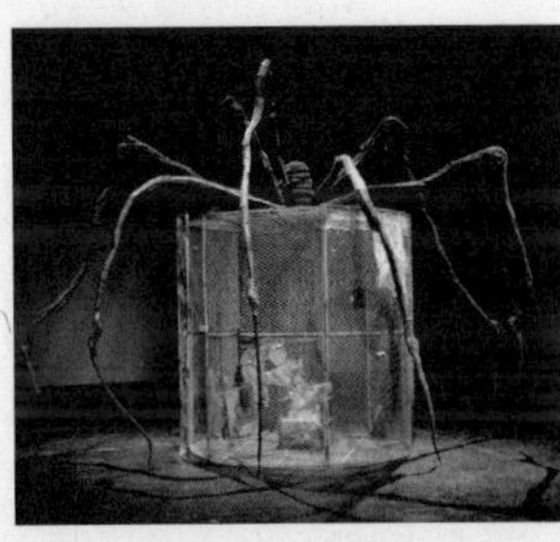

That would be those people who feel addressed by the work; feeling they can respond, and thus become first persons.[1]

Biography is particularly problematic in the case of artists who are no longer alive, since it is impossible to ask questions and verify if your interpretation of their art is correct. But this is where I part ways with the tradition of art criticism. For, even living artists are not the masters of the meanings of their work, since meaning emerges in the 'I'–'you' interaction. These interactions are the kind of moments of meaning-making referred to in the title of this book. This is the first and strongest principle in what I do. The members of the public are the 'second persons' to whom the art is addressed; to whom it speaks. But according to the theory of language from which the notions of first, second, and third person are derived—for me, the primary source was French linguist Émile Benveniste (1902–1976)—the 'I' and the 'you' exchange their positions, while the third person, the 'he', 'she', or 'them', remains outside; the object 'about' whom the first and second person communicate. They cannot participate in the conversation. In contrast, as soon as the addressed, second person responds to the first person's address, they become a first person, if only temporarily. The address is what empowers the second person to take up the voice, to speak up, to say 'I'. Only then can the encounter with art become a dialogue.[2]

Meaning emerges, producing what we can see as events. The tools of meaning-making are not simply a solid knowledge of the language in which we communicate. They involve activities such as listening, dialogue, and the temporal aspect of looking back, as well as the creativity of imagining other possibilities. Meaning occurs in encounters. This is why meaning is occasioned, why it happens, instead of being rigidly fixed, ready for eternalization in textbooks, dictionaries, and encyclopaedias, useful as such publications may be when the meaning depends on communicating in a certain language. But it cannot really be fixed. This is why, in this book, I decline the

---

1 *Louise Bourgeois' Spider: The Architecture of Art-writing* appeared in 2001. Just recently in 2024, at the initiative of an Italian publisher I didn't know, a bilingual edition of a short book on Bourgeois appeared that I had composed out of fragments of my various articles on this artist.

2 More on this idea of 'the work of art' rather than the 'artwork' under W.

chronological approach to the life story and instead connect childhood and youth memories from arbitrarily ordered moments, determined by the instants they come into my mind, make me think, create meaning. Travelling through time, I associate these memories and the meanings they generate with the future elaboration of concepts. Those concepts I later deploy to analyze artworks, in the 'I'–'you' exchange between the art, my own memories, and the possibility to inspire other people to do that, too. If there are connections, it is not between the critic/theorist and the artist, but between remembrances and what, later, we can derive from these when confronted with, and responding to, the 'work' of art. The life stories and the understanding of the art later on are not causally linked, but neither are they unrelated. They cannot be, since the subject of understanding lives in the afterlife of that which she remembers, however much she and her life have changed since the memorial moment. But the order is more or less arbitrary, since it is connected to the everyday life of the subject of the acts of memory.[3]

My decision to shape this book as an alphabet is meant to enhance that temporal arbitrariness, the rejection of linear chronology. For, although every life is temporally framed and limited, the moments when something meaningful happens, those moments of meaning-making, cannot be fixated in linear time. Hence the title of this book. As the entries or vignettes of which this book consists will demonstrate, some of such events are punctual, other are enduring, habitual, subject to routine. The punctual ones may go by in a flash, or take some more time. For, even within a temporally limited moment, the moment can be shorter or longer. The alphabet is the shape I gave to the non-linearity, the rejection of chronology in favour of mutuality between past and present, as I have argued in my 1999 book *Quoting Caravaggio*. The point is not time, duration, or rhythm, but the occurrence; the way meaning emerges out of an experience, making an event, in a social framework, in

---

3 On memory as an act, see my introduction 'Memories in the Museum' to the collective volume from 1999.

connection to other people. The entries here will make that clear.[4]

Just one quick, informal, and even banal example. Years ago, I visited the office of the bank that managed my account, to settle some minor things. I had to wait a bit. Before me were two Arabic-looking men. They did their business, speaking Dutch with a strong accent, and when they left they said, in a tone that sounded a bit dry or grumpy, to the woman that she had helped them okay. They used the informal *je* form of the second person, instead of the polite *U* one. After they left, the woman started to scold them, complaining about that use of *je*, saying some negative things about foreigners being rude. I told her something I just happened to know from an Arabic friend, that the Arabic language did not have that distinction between the two forms of the second person, no more than English. She looked at me intensely, then smiled. 'Oh, thank you for setting me straight.' I was jubilant. I had helped, if only in a small way, to change her attitude towards foreigners. This, I immediately realized, was a moment of meaning-making, of meaning-changing. If only I could do such things more often!
It would help against the reigning xenophobia. This was when the phrase 'moments of meaning-making' occurred to me.

This is not the first time I deploy an alphabetic (non-) order. At the request of my favourite editor at the University of Chicago Press, Susan Bielstein, in 2008 I published a book about an artist's work, in dialogue with the artist, John Sparagana, from Houston, Texas, a faculty member at Rice University. No, I didn't know him; to this day I have not even met him. I was asked to respond to his work, which I decided to do according to an alphabet of mostly verbs and adjectives; very few nouns. The dialogue consists simply of alternations of his (photography-based) artworks with my comments on these. Having to think about the art with a particular letter as my guideline was a way of enhancing the refusal to take the artist's own statements for a standard. The artist gladly collaborated with this idea. And I learned enormously from his near-abstract photographic work. The book has been beautifully designed

---

4 My resistance against linear time is theorized in *Quoting Caravaggio* (1999) as an instance of baroque thinking. The term I came up with was 'pre-posterous history'. The book was my reply to criticisms of my earlier book on Rembrandt for being 'ahistorical', which it is not. More on this under A.

and produced, as a true artbook. But in distinction from that genre, there is no biographical information other than a single sentence for each of us, in a small typeface in the colophon. The arbitrary order allows reading also in arbitrary order. And sometimes, ideas are repeated; if that hinders you, it may be simply due to that lack of (chrono-)logic.

The idea of the alphabet did not quite come out of the blue. It was inspired earlier on by a book I read in 2002, in which the entire content is alphabetically ordered. Nanna Verhoeff's book, titled *After the Beginning: Westerns Before 1915* (Amsterdam University Press) emerged immediately as an alphabet once she began to develop the letter A in the sense of *after*, while remaining focused on the earliest stages of cinema culture; the beginning *after* which the genre she studied emerged. The temporality was paradoxical from the beginning. Her book is inspiring as an instance of a non-linear, non-chronological study of culture, even if it is delimited in time, between the invention of cinema and the year 1915. It is a work of history, but not in the traditional sense. It is no coincidence that her first entry is 'after the beginning', and my first one here is 'anachronism'.

In the present book, there is a visual aspect to this. My twenty-six entries, which I term 'vignettes', are accompanied by photographs made by a young artist, who has a brilliant creative imagination. This enabled her imaginative responses to the texts I proposed she read. Later in the course of the process, she and I made a film together (*Refugeedom*, 2023). To tacitly demonstrate the contrast, only in the first two entries have I done the more usual thing: include and discuss some artworks from museums. After due reflection, I decided to keep those in, to make readers feel comfortable through recognition. I did this to demonstrate the difference between art used more or less as 'illustrations', which is the traditional way of combining writing with visual art, and the black-and-white photographs that seriously respond to the ideas brought up. These cannot be considered illustrations, since they do not bring in evidence of the 'truth' of the writing. Instead, they propose a response,

an interpretation, of the content of the memories and the subsequent concepts. Sometimes they are almost abstract. It takes
some effort to get the point of those images. That task for the
readers is meant to activate their imagination, to almost turn
them into artists, but at least, into second persons becoming
first persons for a moment.

This book is not meant as a textbook or theoretical or
historical treatise, nor as an overview of my life. Instead, the
'auto'-aspect of the vignettes serves a few purposes for the
reader. One is to suggest the possibility to reflect on your own
life without turning it into a narcissistic navel-gazing exercise.
More importantly, I seek to encourage 'thinking back', to allude
to the more common idea of 'speaking back'. I was considering
ways of making 'acts of memory' useful for later skills and
practices. Part of this wish was also, to take children seriously
as interlocutors, to heed their incipient insights, their early
wisdom. No hierarchy between children and adults can be
assumed. The merging of memories with intellectual developments is also a way of being loyal to our lives. But that merging
is not automatic. It is itself an act, producing an event, of
meaning-making in a different moment. And when the connections between the memories and the conceptual developments
seem convincing, we learn something important about intellectual work, about thinking. This insight discourages the 'dryness'
of what we call 'science'. Instead, it allows taking the emotional
aspects on board in our intellectual efforts to contribute to
knowledge. I believe in the relevance of the emotional, indeed,
affective side of thought for the creation of a more integrated,
richer view of the world to which knowledge must contribute.

This book, thus, proposes a different mode of laying out
thoughts, ideas, in relation to history, to art, and connect them,
in a productive merging, to personal experiences. Each letter is
bound to a primary word, then to adjacent laterally associated
words. The attempt is to make such academic routines more
alive, inspiring, due to their 'live' framings. Framing is the act
we perform when we make, suggest, propose relationships
between cultural artefacts, moments, occurrences, at particular
moments. We *make* meaning, in specific moments. The

meanings we then make and, in our first-person voice, propose, give life meaning, make it meaningful. Culture works that way. Hence, the cultural artefacts, 'things', or rather, events are of crucial importance for the sociality within which we live. Whether these events are artistic, literary, or otherwise praiseworthy or not, is not my primary interest. It is how they solicit responses and thereby make people endorse first-personhood for a moment, longer or forever, that makes the happening of art worthwhile. If the vignettes here inspire people to do that, my goal will have been achieved.

Anachronism

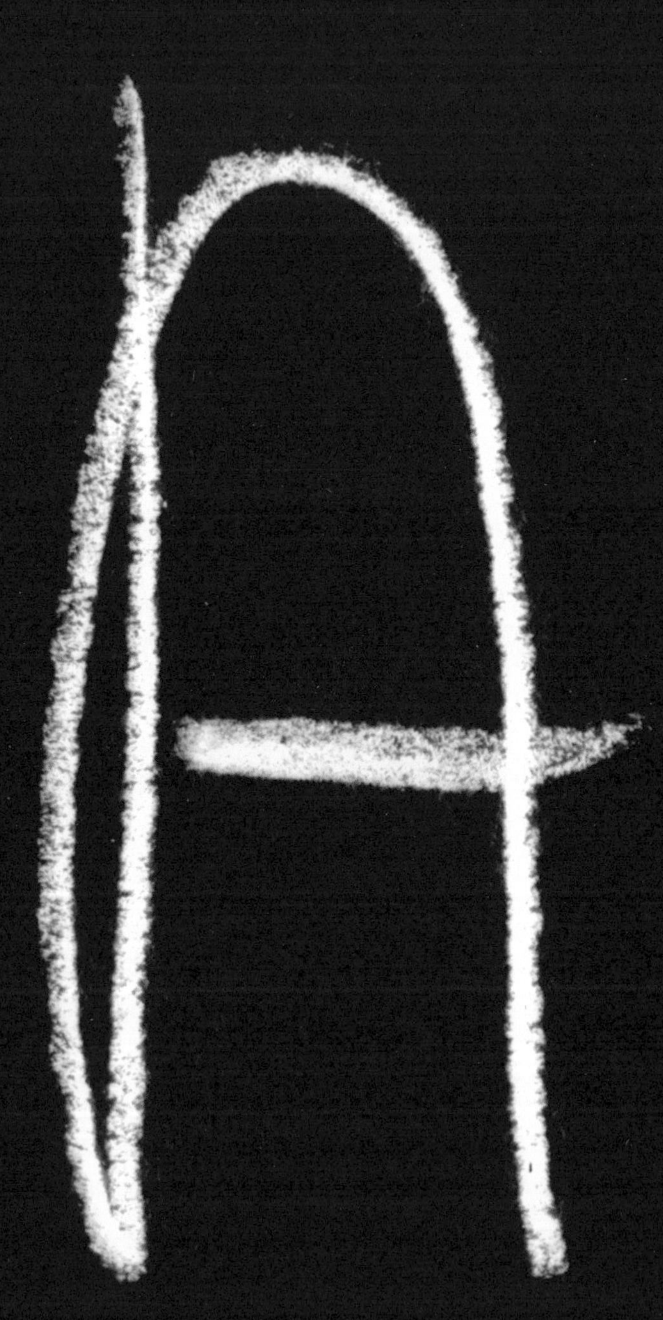

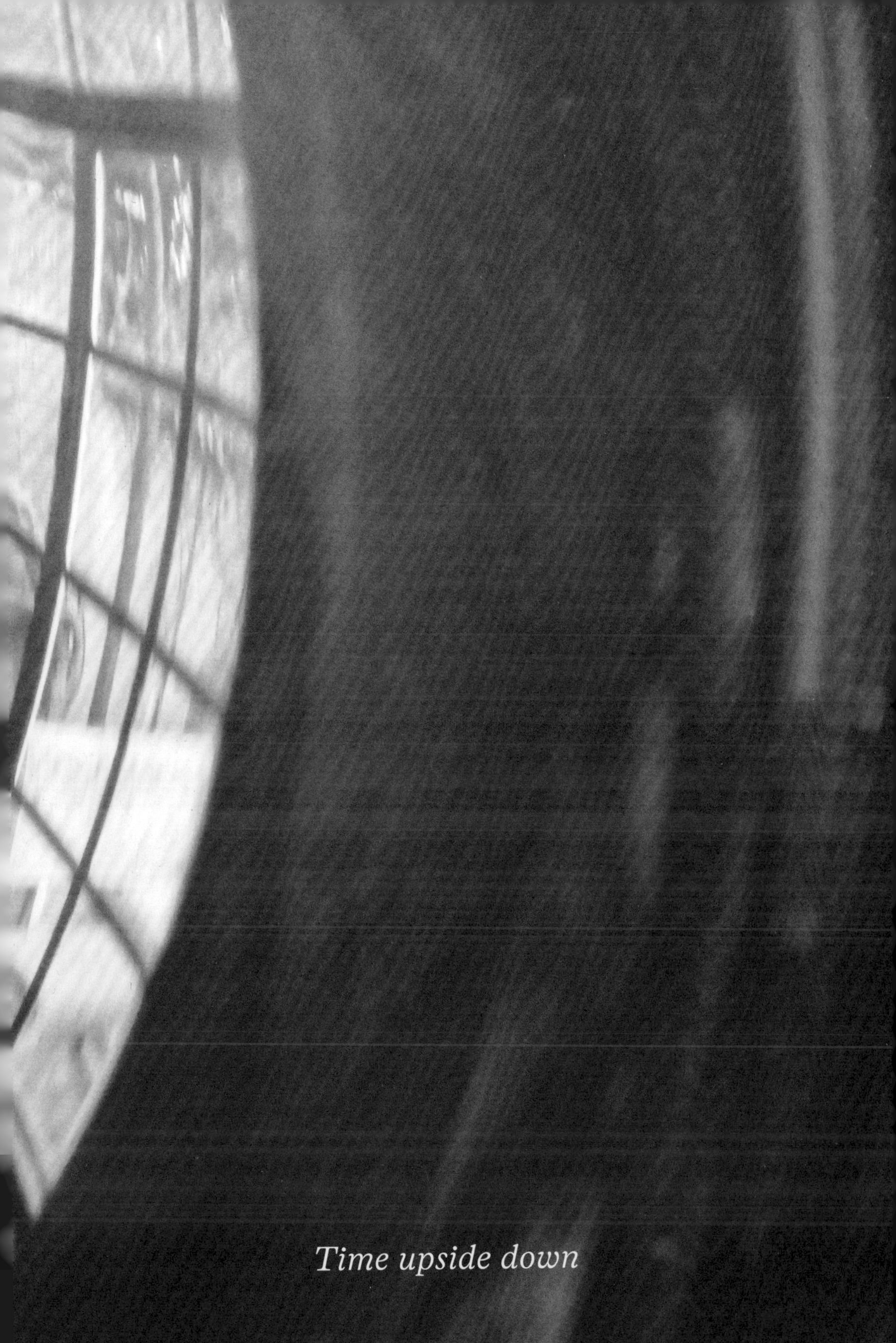

Time upside down

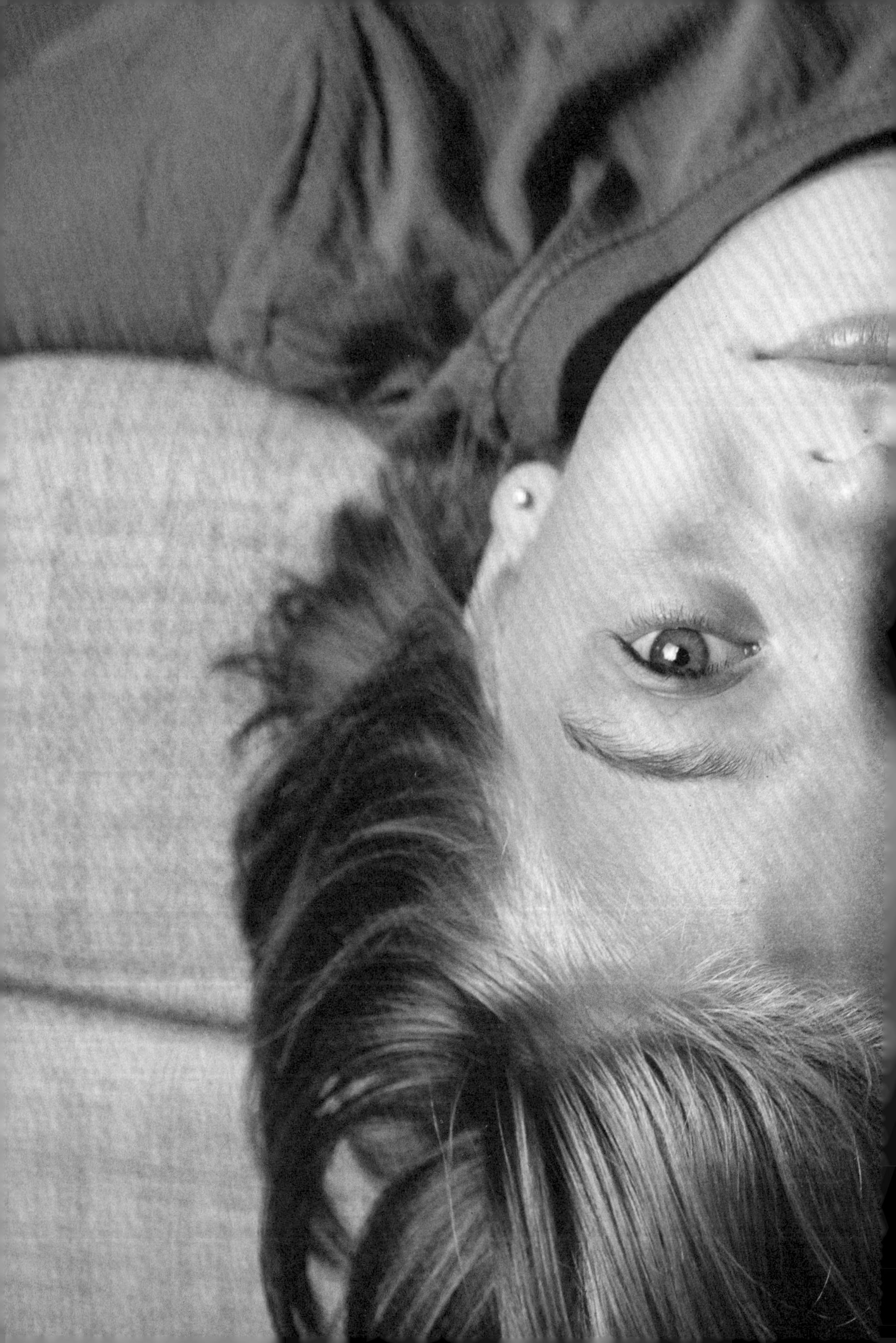

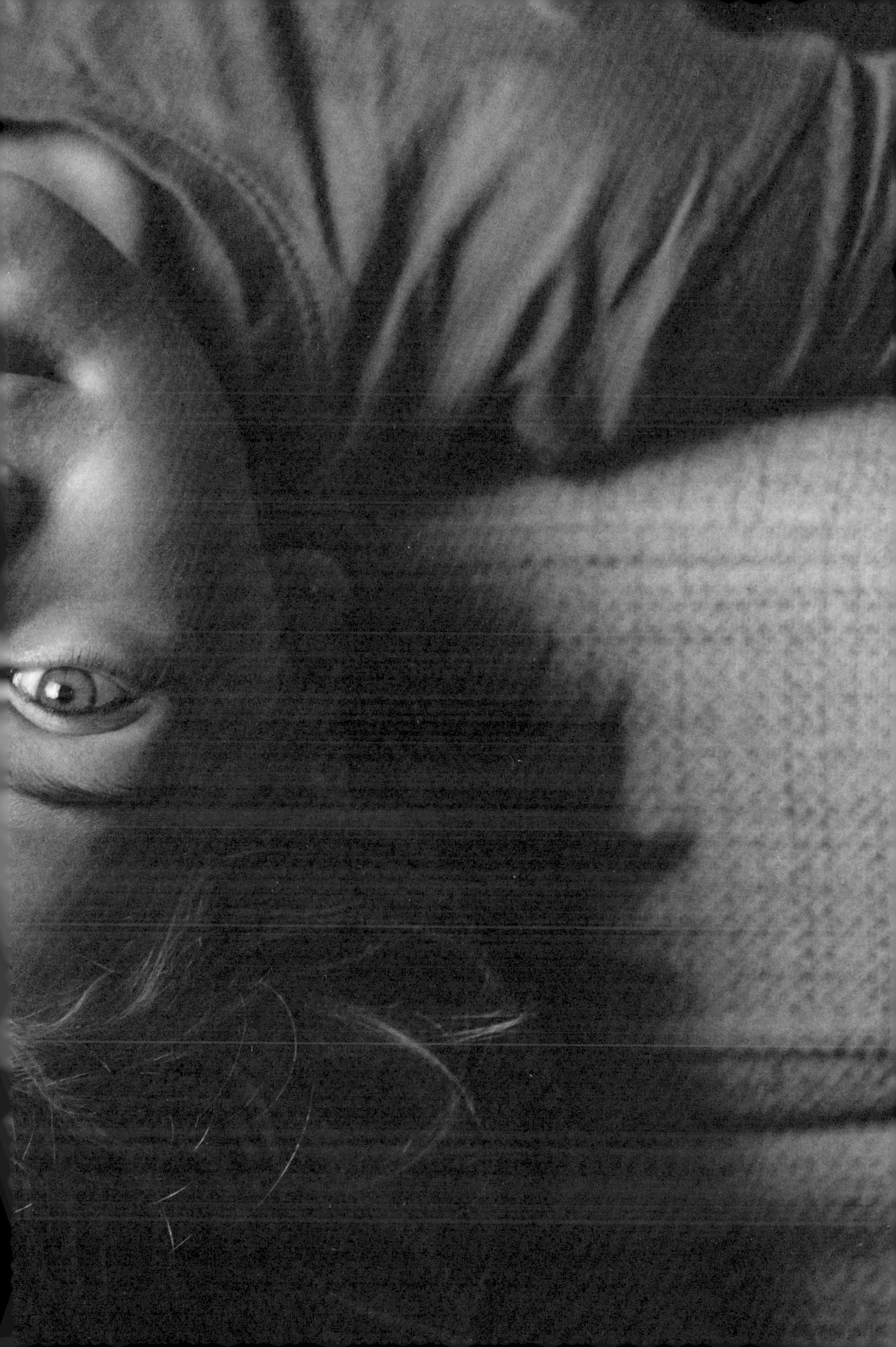

I like to think that history is not a past we can reconstruct or know. Nor can we isolate it within a different time. It is part of the present. Otherwise, why would we be interested in it? Writing about my own life cannot be a chronological, linear account of what happened from year to year; that would be tedious. Nor would I be able to put such an account forward, since it cannot become a coherent whole. Instead, I think of history, including my own, as that past we cannot see otherwise than through the lens of the present, through a screen that hangs between the present where we are and that past long gone; and in fragments. Only retrospectively, putting what came before ('pre-') *after* what is now ('post-') can we assess what is important in what respect and why it is important, and call on the past on behalf of the present, so that a liveable future may come. The temporality of these three dimensions together is best captured in the word—verb, qualifier, noun all at once—of 'becoming'. This is a process, not a thing or state. The next vignette is devoted to that verb. The German painter Max Beckmann could not know, in 1950, how his painting *Falling Man* would later be seen as predictive, prophetic. (see fig. 3)

    We cannot see it without a flash of 9/11 passing by. It is not just the motif of a man falling out of a burning high-rise, or the biographical fact that Beckmann was in New York when he made the painting, in the last year of his life. The details of the painting contribute retrospectively, or anachronistically, to what we can now call 'the 9/11 effect'. I coin this term in analogy with Ernst van Alphen's 'Holocaust effect', in the subtitle of his book *Caught by History: Holocaust Effects in Contemporary Art, Literature and Theory*, from 1997.

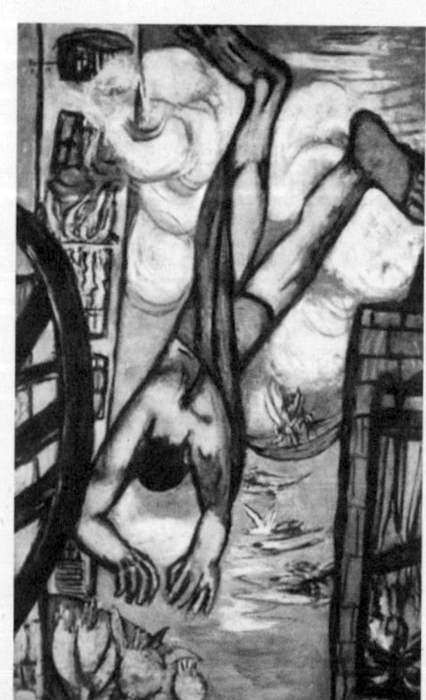

What do we make of the very different dwelling on the right side, which looks more like a shed in an agricultural environment that looks like it is not made of stone or brick but of wood? Or consider the cactuses flowering on the window sill, which effectively bring us

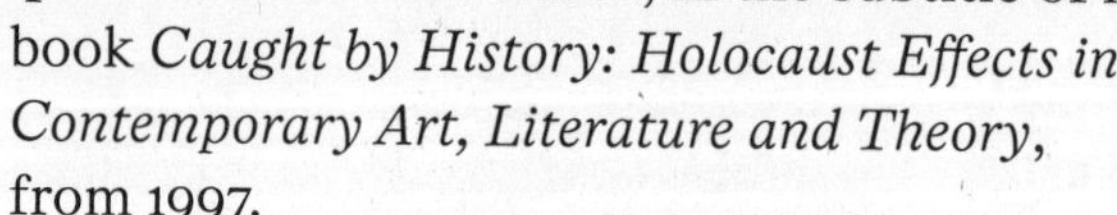

to other geographical areas such as, perhaps then, Mexico, but now, rather, the Middle East. Such details make the painting vibrant with contemporary associations, in spite of the decades that have passed on since Beckmann made it. And then there is the cropping of the feet that tells us that the event evoked is larger than the canvas and the artist can encompass. It all heightens the effect of an overwhelming catastrophe. But most of all, it is our present, with the memory of the attacks still vivid, the fear never really dissipated, that puts that past of the act of painting *after* the present in which we see it.

When Beckmann painted *Falling Man*, he had long since fled from Germany, the country for which he had fought in WWI, only then to be labelled by Adolf Hitler a 'cultural Bolshevik' whose works were displayed at the 'Degenerate Art' exhibition in 1937 in Munich. He couldn't have known that his voluntary exile from those horrors, first to the Netherlands, then to the US, was about to end in his own fall, coming in the form of a fatal heart attack on the streets of New York, when he was on his way to an exhibition of his own paintings, in that same year he painted this falling man, 1950. Doesn't this convergence echo in some fashion with our contemporary view, in which 9/11 is already some 25 years past and still so vivid, constantly extending onto other scenes of horror, some of which must have been playing through Beckmann's artist mind as well? I realize that historians will consider such a view 'preposterous'; which is why, in 1999, I coined that qualifier, tongue-in-cheek, to signify otherwise: pre-posterous, with a hyphen. I used it in the subtitle of a book on the Italian Baroque painter, Caravaggio, and contemporary art, or, I should say, contemporary art and Caravaggio. Since then, this conception of history as reimagined through the lens of the present has become more acceptable under the name, equally a kind of rebellious one, of 'anachronism'. Still, when I talk about artworks through this collapsing of chronology and the inter-temporal dialogue that is its substitute, I am accustomed to people attached to historical thinking, protesting: 'But that's preposterous!' All I then need to say is, 'Indeed'. Tongue-in-cheek, and amused. Endorsing what is meant as an insult is something I got used to and enjoy.

BRIEFLY

My eager concession that 'indeed' such a commentary is preposterous, usually catches people off-guard, forcing them to think more deeply about the meaning of that word. This single word has the power to alter understanding, to add a layer of meaning to the original meaning. It is its brevity that surprises; the need it produces to rethink the meaning of the previous comment. It also enforces a realization of that constant inter-play of what we tend to distinguish as 'literal' and 'figurative' meanings. I propose to let go of that distinction and, instead, open our minds up to the multiple possibilities words and other signs offer. In the present vignette, my examples demonstrate the turns and revisions words can have, due to the very short-ness, even curtness, of one-word answers. Indeed![5]

The way meaning is shaped through past and present, through a palimpsest of words and histories and moods, extends to the future. There too, a single word can make a situation assume an entirely new meaning. Not that long ago, a film I made on madness together with British artist Michelle Williams Gamaker, was accepted in a festival on Madness & Art. We had shown it to the festival director when it was almost, but not quite finished. Not that anything ever is, but the film did need some crucial work, and the time was tight. During those last weeks before the deadline I had a routine dental check-up and, it turned out, I needed to have a tooth pulled. No big deal.

But the pain of the extraction continued and increased for days following, and I could sense something growing in my throat. My partner insisted we go to a hospital to have it looked at, despite my resistance, worried as I was about the deadline for those finishing touches to the film. The young surgeon took one look, immediately called his assistant and told her to cancel his appointments for the day, and to prepare the operating room for immediate surgery. 'Oh no!' I said. 'I have a deadline!' Finishing the film for the festival was foremost on my mind. The doctor looked me in the eyes and said, after a dramatic

---

[5] The binary opposition between literal and figurative has been definitively undermined by many, of whom Lyotard's theorizing of 'the figural' stands out (1971). See also Rajchman, 'Another View of Abstraction' and his book *Constructions* (1998).

second of silence: 'You do indeed.'

When my children visited me in the hospital the next day,
I heard the surgeon tell them, 'We are optimistic, but we are not
there yet.' Optimistic, but? Shocked by these two words, I asked
what he meant. All he said was, 'I wanted you to hear this.'
He had quickly recognized my stubborn tendency of putting
work above all else, even my own health. Later, I learned that
a colleague of mine had died after walking around with the
same infection for 24 hours. I had survived 48 hours before
treatment. It took ten days in the hospital to recover, giving
me plenty of time to think about the literal sense of that word
'dead-line'. This surgeon saved my life, gave me my future back
when I had been about to squander it. He also taught me a
lesson about priorities, and about meaning—not only of words.
We are all faced with deadlines, and one hopes to have the
wisdom to react appropriately to those that are more urgent,
those that are more literally *dead*-lines. Never again have I
panicked in the same way as I then did towards any other form
of less-critical deadlines. The word became literal, and the
meaning consequential.

SHIFTING

Such brief events of meaning-making occur frequently.
Another one, more recently, happened when I was showing my
'preposterous' film on René Descartes and Queen Kristina, at a
film festival in Kraków, Poland. During the discussion someone
asked a question, which he began by saying he was not at all
disturbed by the anachronisms, for which I had given a justifi-
cation in the introductory talk, but by the empathetic approach.
Why, for heaven's sake, he asked, had I bothered making a film
about someone everybody dislikes? For it is true; Descartes
is generally hated, loathed, for what is (wrongly) seen as an
excessive rationalism and for promoting a mind-body split,
according to the misreading of his slogan. Now trained in such
situations, and with my dental surgeon still on my retina and

the indignant historian's complaints still ringing in my ears, my answer was: 'That's why.'

This was not about a simple word, nor about the question if words have a literal meaning, such as 'pre-posterous', which proposes to swap what comes before with what comes after, or a word the figurative meaning of which can be complemented by a literal one, and which gets priority, as it was with 'dead-line'. It was about other forms of meaning-making, including opinion-shaking, ideology-breaking, bringing the intellect together with affect, and claiming to be right when it matters, without defensiveness or inhibitions. I wouldn't have bothered to make a film, always a long and expensive process, indeed, if it was to confirm prejudices and cry with the wolves that Descartes is a bad guy. Instead, I wanted to convey the value of some of Descartes' ideas for today, in our precarious present, so that with their help, we might allow a future to be possible. A bit more reasonableness in today's world doesn't seem to be so pointless, does it? 'That's why' is a simple and clear answer to the question 'why?' But I shifted it from his question to his certainty. I took up the second part of his statement that was not a question, but the self-evident one, 'someone everybody dislikes'. My 'that's why' meant to critique the self-evidence as such, and the loss this entails for the life of the world. I wanted to shake his certainty. I don't mind hyperboles, but that's for another time. I do mind wholesale condemnations, reiterated clichés, and the refusal to think anew; I mind stating something as a natural truth in the guise of a question. After my brief answer, he scratched his chin. I knew he was thinking about it. Goal achieved!

I had, among other motivations, a justice-seeking desire to redress a wrong, because simplistic view of an important contributor from the past. So, by answering 'that's why' I was able not only to say that I made the film precisely to end the self- evidence of that general dislike, but also to imply that the man asking that question was himself colluding with that prejudice. There was no need to add all the things that matter in filmmaking: such as that I therefore had wanted to present a Descartes who would at least hold the viewer's attention for the duration. This required an ambivalence, allowing, besides criticism, also empathy, understanding, and at times, compassion, without enforcing these sentiments through tear-jerking sentimentality. In common parlance, it's called 'human interest'. This was the brief I had given myself, and the meandering itinerary through historical documents, writings, biographies, and if required, also, fiction. These were the implications of my 'that's why'.

In scholarship, it is no coincidence that the best book on this much-written-about philosopher is Kyoo Lee's masterly *Reading Descartes Otherwise: Blind, Mad, Dreamy, and Bad*. She is one of very few contemporary scholars who see value in all those moments of 'mad' or 'bad' thinking in Descartes' work. Too bad, that in another, small moment of 'preposterousness', I encountered that book only after finishing the film. But no; that retrospective coincidence of our views was a fantastic confirmation, rather than a shameful scholarly omission, which, of course, it also was, or could be considered as such. My mistake, or omission, turned out to be a confirmation of both our views.

This calling on fiction to flesh out the characters, more than the anachronistic approach, which seemingly 'only' entailed historically-irresponsible costumes and settings, was the pre-posterous aspect; and still, the qualifying double meaning I have given to that qualifying word came along. How dare I, who had never even met the figures, present them as living human beings with their dreams, anxieties, and impatience? How could I oppose or at least nuance the firmly established historical accounts of Descartes and Kristina as insufferable, stubborn, arrogant people? Well, first of all, it is the people who hold them to the accumulated knowledge that has come to parade as the truth about them, who are perpetrating the sin of anachronism, rather than I; but then, without knowing it. For it is their own, contemporary account that they hold to be the historical truth, and that they project on figures who, without such views, might have something meaningful to say. Hence, I needed the fictional moments to flesh out the complexity that would partly answer the question: why were and are these two people so unpopular?

FACT AND FICTION

This requires some basis in facts—as far as anything is ever a fact, but I'll just use that word for what passes as truthful history. It didn't take me long to make historical facts congeal in a network where they were the knots, and fiction the threads. To give just one example: the historical *fact* is that both Descartes and Kristina were more or less orphaned from early childhood on, losing one parent to death and the other to neglect. Once that fact was connected to a certain arrogance, also a fact but never considered together with the early orphaning, I could come up with a fiction of anxiety and insecurity. This made it possible to suggest for them, pre-posterously, now in the sense of historical reversal, a psychoanalytical idea, namely an 'abandonment complex'. This concept holds that those who have been abandoned as a child tend to experience difficulty later on to affectively bond with others. As a result, out of fear of a repetition of the abandonment, they prefer to do the abandoning. This is another, important mode of meaning-making no theory of meaning will be able to accommodate smoothly. It is literally pre-posterous.[6]

Of course, there is no historical evidence of that for our two figures, other than that they remained single, and that their writings and the witnesses of their time criticized their behaviour. And psychoanalysis had not yet been invented, the abandonment complex not yet thought out. Therefore, the suggestion is blatantly preposterous in the popular sense. But it does help make them more humane and agreeable, while the historical fact of their wish but inability to get along, is made understandable. Understanding, in turn, can lead to empathy, even to recognition in oneself or one's environment of similar tendencies. This is how the life of meaning impacts on the meaning of life. It is what makes history relevant for today, by means of fiction. And don't be fooled: all historians, biographers, and other story-tellers do this. No story can be told without fiction, nor is any fiction cut off from reality.

<hr>

6 On this 'abandonment complex', see Verhoeff, *'Adolphe' et Constant* (1976).

Becoming

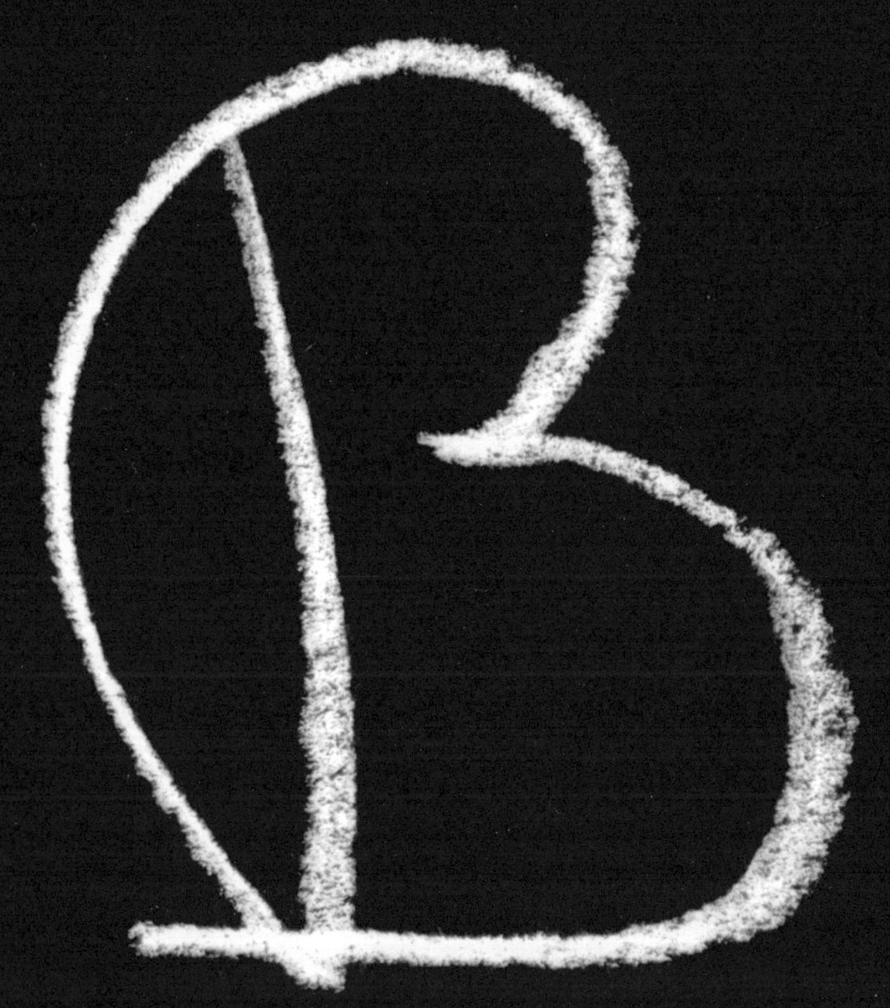

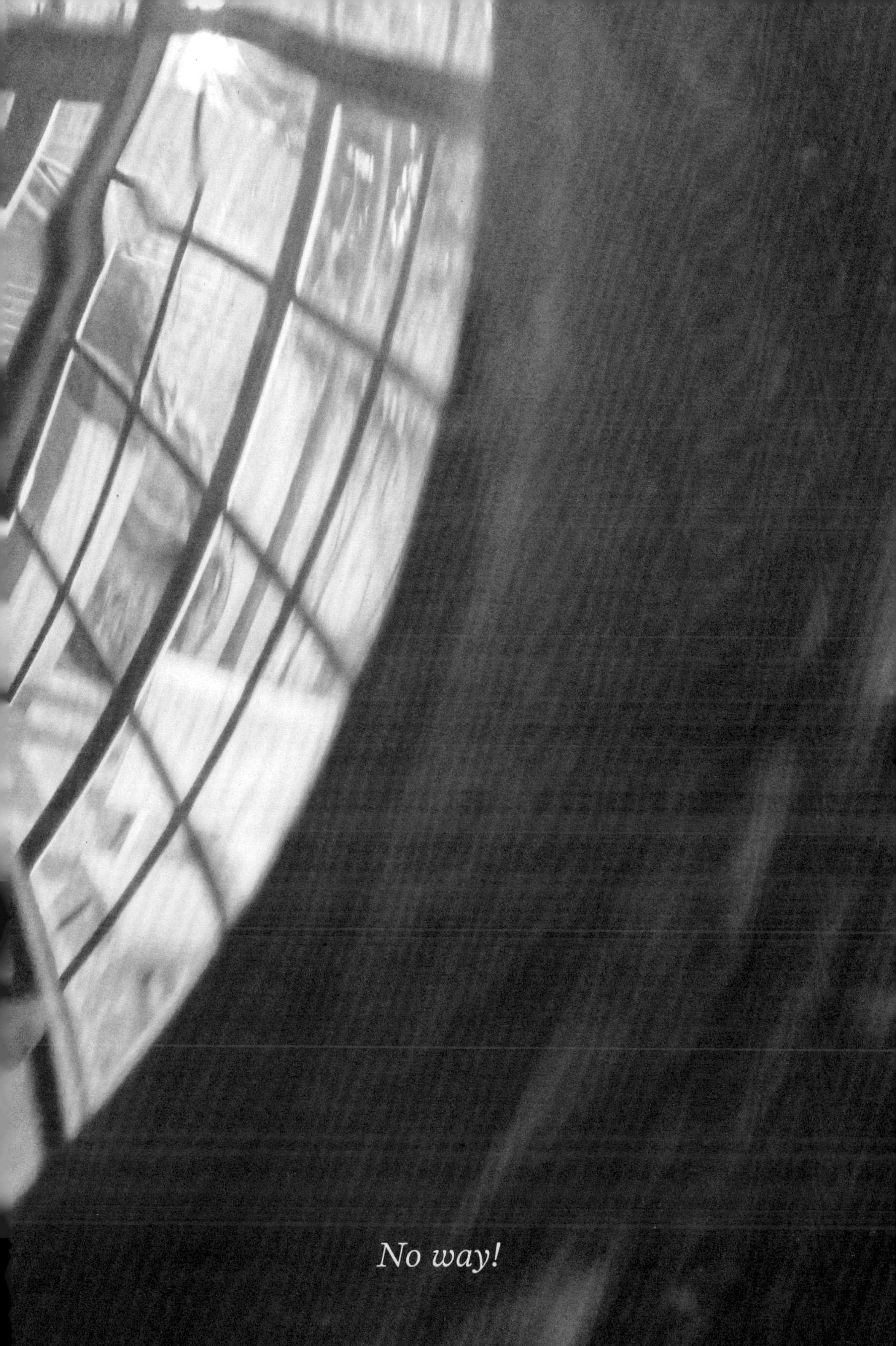

No way!

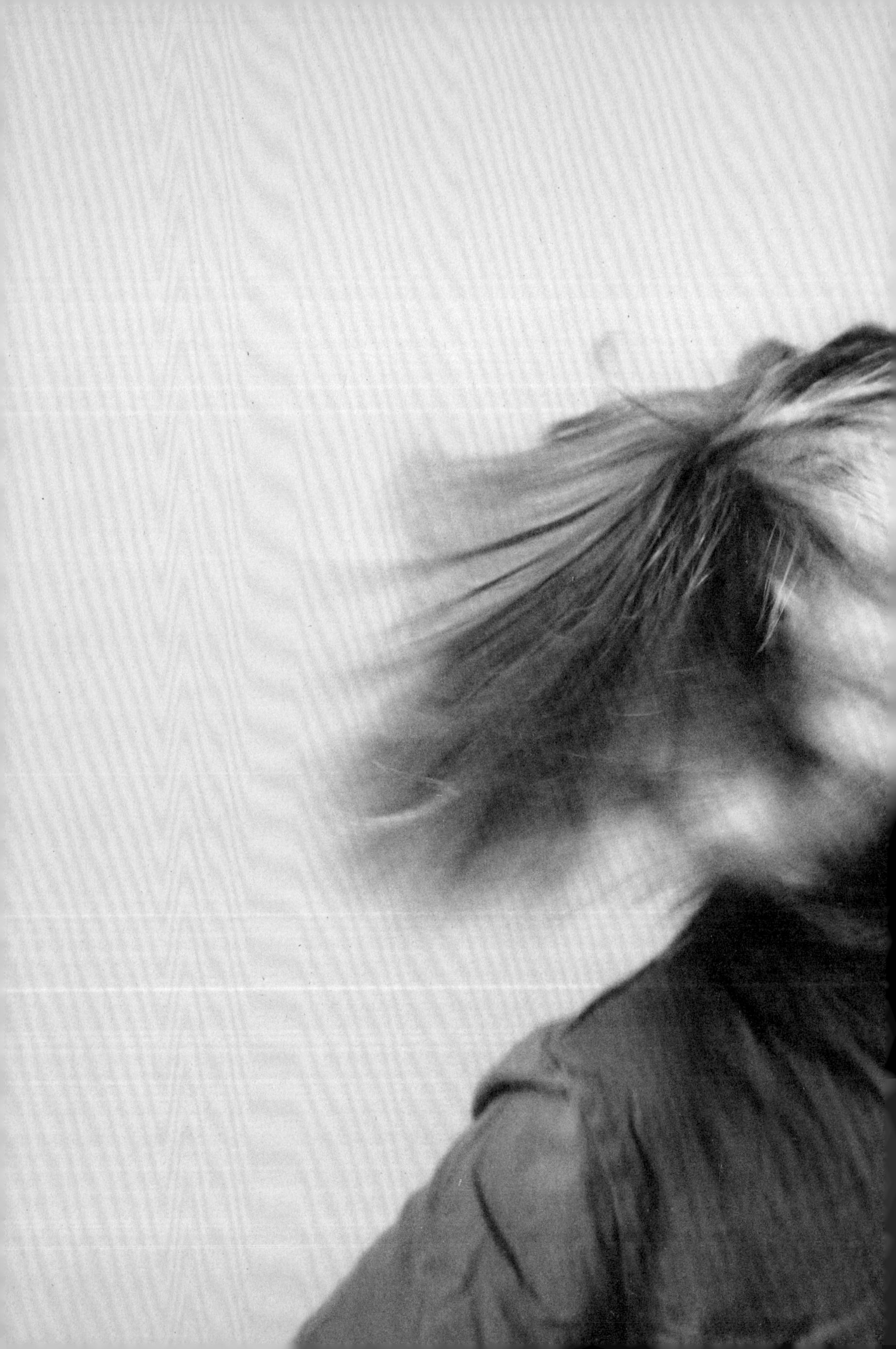

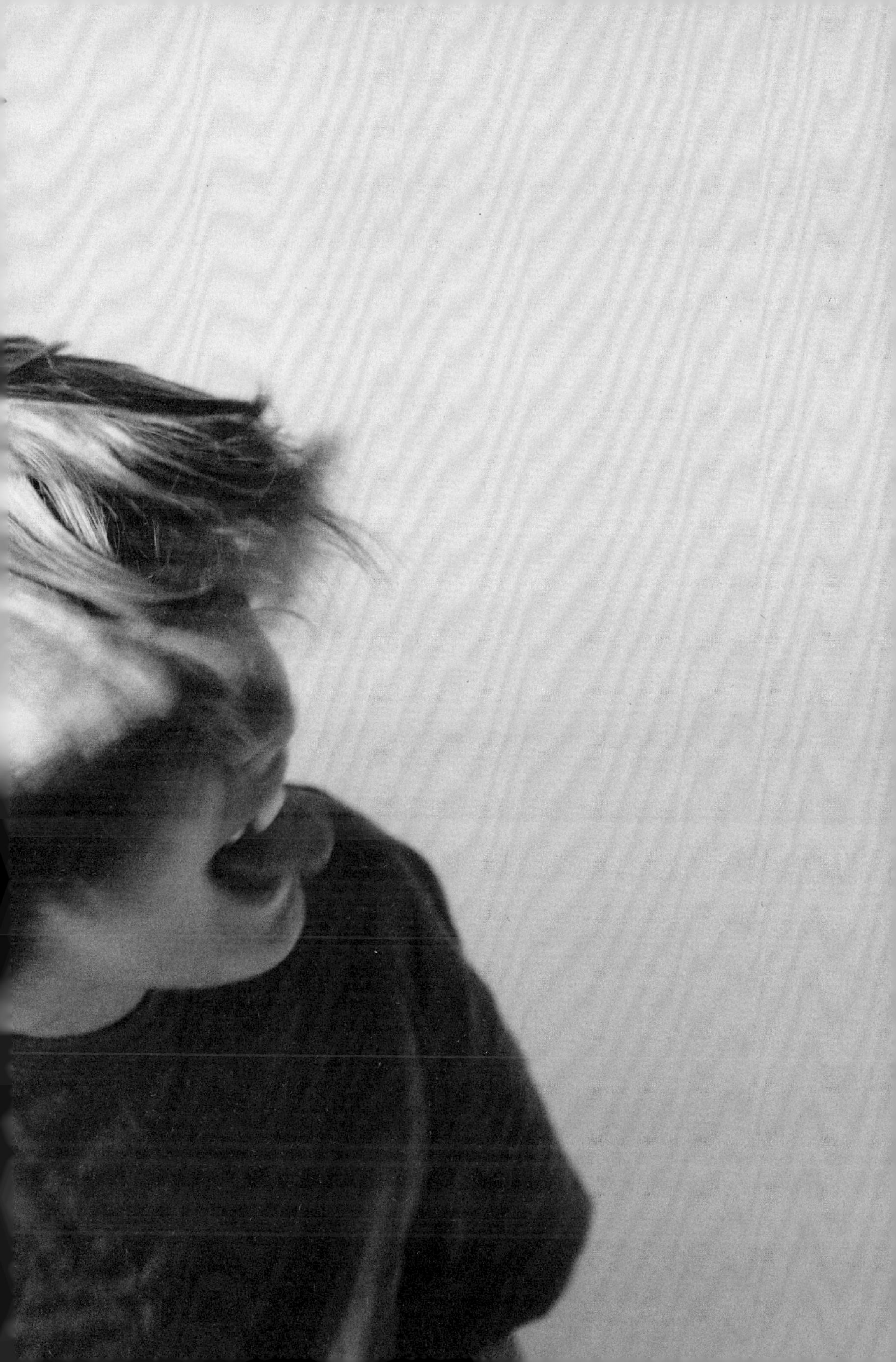

The first time I heard the word 'feminist' coming from the outside world with reference to myself was after I had published my first international book. One critic, herself a noted feminist writer, ended her review of the book with the remark that I must be a feminist because all novels I had discussed were either written by a woman or had a woman protagonist; and because the last word of my book was 'death'. It has always intrigued me that she added that final remark. What does death have to do with feminism? I never got the chance to ask her. I don't even remember in what context I used the word, and it had not occurred to me until I read in that review that it was my final word. But recently, upon reworking, for the umpteenth time, my life-long companion novel, Flaubert's *Madame Bovary*, this time in view of a film I wanted to make, suddenly it made sense, in a sad, upsetting way. Feminism became a polemical, antagonistic position, nourished by a sentiment I didn't like. I never had the slightest regret of being a woman. Just discontent, anger, sometimes fury at what was made of that gender, according to experiences. Some of these go back to my earliest memories. That is where my 'becoming' began.[7]

I remember when I was four years old, overhearing my father say: 'I am so happy to have many daughters; they are such wonderful homemakers!' Perhaps I was five, I don't quite remember, but not much older. It is among my earliest memories, perhaps *the* earliest. Also, it may have been my mother repeating what my father had said to her. Hearsay, or a true memory? Father's words or mother's inflection of them, doubtlessly sarcastic, or upsettingly genuine? All I know with certainty is the mental headshake in response to the sentiment the good man expressed: no way! I can still feel the headshake in the turning of my neck, even though it was only mental. That rejection I do remember, as clearly as if it was yesterday. The time of the memory, the source of the words: it matters, but not a whole lot. It would matter if I were trying to write the true history of my parents, but this is not my endeavour. I do have the memory, I cherish it, and it belongs to the box 'memories of Father', even if it may have been my mother who conveyed it to me. A homemaker? *No way.* I knew at that young age that this

---

7 I don't remember the name of the reviewer nor the publication details. The book she reviewed was the book version of my PhD dissertation (1977).

was not my goal in life. It was enough to witness what being a homemaker had done to my mother. And I always juxtapose it with that other story about my father.

BEING NOTICED

I was even smaller, probably three, for I cannot even remember the drowning doll, nor its name. We were playing in the garden; it was small, but to us it seemed large enough. It had a huge (in our eyes) apple tree, with a trunk large enough to hide behind. Later, once I was able to read, I used to climb into that tree on Wednesday afternoons with a book and a pillow, and spend hours reading, hopefully unseen. Further down, at the bottom of the garden was a canal, or ditch, its water covered by duckweed. There was a fence between our garden and the ditch, but not one that would keep us safe if needed. We climbed over it all the time, challenging that dangerous water. We also knew it was not very deep. That day we were playing outside. My two older siblings suddenly went inside and screamed: 'Mieke fell into the water!' I was accidentally behind the apple tree, so father didn't see me when he ran out, shook off his jacket, and with shoes and all, dived into the shallow, dirty water. He came up and asked: where? And my siblings pointed to my sister's doll, also called 'Mieke', as I was told later. I didn't see, or don't remember his face. I don't remember the doll either; probably it belonged to my older sister who had named it after me when I was born. What I remember is my father's determined dive.

A few years ago, this memory came back to me because I became involved with the paintings of Edvard Munch, in view of an exhibition the Munch Museum had invited me to curate. When going through the impressive four-volume catalogue raisonné of his work, I came upon a painting that made my eyes sting a little. It took me a split second to understand why. Before seeing the title—*The Drowning Child*—I looked, riveted, at that helpless child in a red dress, with a lump next to her that must hint at a doll. And of the men and women walking on the pier, no one paying any attention. (see fig. 4)

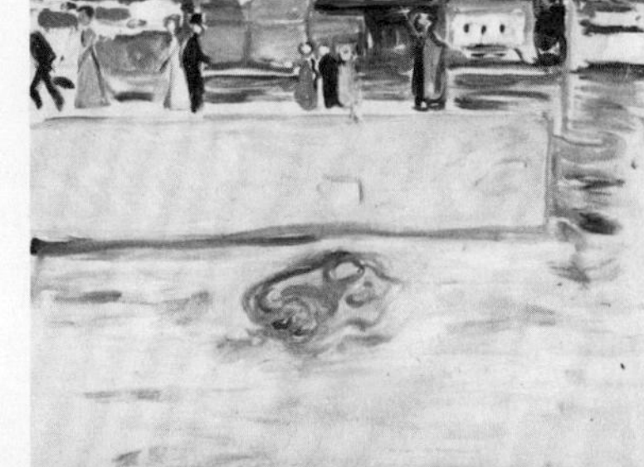

FIG. 4 Edvard Munch, *The Drowning Child*, 1904 (?)

That breathtaking moment when the dress fills up, with still air in it so that the child still floats, then slowly becoming soaked and drawing the child under, is painted in a sketchy, almost childish brushstroke. The scale says it all: the child is larger than any of the adults. They are just unseeing puppets, worldly creatures idling away their lives. In contrast, she is drowning; this makes her important, so that she is awarded with the larger scale. And that the surface of that part of the painting looks so flat is a way to preserve, for just a split second, some hope. She is floating—still.

A red dress visually interrupting a monochromatic field: for me it recalls the girl in a red coat in Steven Spielberg's 1993 film *Schindler's List*. That Holocaust film is about saving people; an action the main character undertakes once he has *noticed* what is happening to the Jews. In the black-and-white images, several times a little girl is singled out, becomes visible as one among the many, thanks to her red coat. Towards the end, Schindler watches the smoking ovens, the busy carts transporting dead bodies to mass graves, and again the red coat comes into view. The little girl has not been saved. But at least, the man who tried to save Jews had seen her, noticed her. The association works through visibility; in *The Drowning Child* it works through the difference between that blue-outlined shape and the red of the dress, curved and oblique in the horizontal monochrome plane. The image states: visibility as a pictorial condition is not enough; saving requires active seeing on the part of witnesses who are getting ready to act. This is a statement about the socio-political importance of seeing, as an act. An act that, as all acts do, has, or can have, consequences.

That childishly-drawn helplessness of the unnoticed child and her doll brought back the story of my father. In the painting, the child can still be saved, if only one of those people would dive, fully dressed, as he had done. But not only does no one dive; that simple act of looking and seeing; of noticing and paying attention; then deciding and doing: none of it occurs to anyone. They are all too busy with themselves. A child can be so alone, not only in tragic situations such as the one depicted in the Munch painting and Spielberg's film, but always, when no one pays attention. I have often felt that lack of attentiveness. As the third child, I sensed that my two older siblings got all the attention there was to spare. Perhaps escaping into the apple tree was a way of precluding the lack of care, the oversight of me, by preventing care's possibility. If I was invisible, I was unnoticeable of my own volition, so that no one could demonstrate their lack of thoughtfulness and interest in me.

My oldest brother was my parents' pride; smart and handsome, and carrying my father's names, all three of them. The sister who followed made herself a 'difficult' child, which was an effective way of getting attention, even if negative. I was the reasonably well-behaved, probably a trifle mousy one. The brother after me was extremely difficult. As a result, when my mother inherited a Steinway piano from an aunt, the two older ones got piano lessons, and the brother after me too. The oldest ones because they were the oldest—my turn would come—the younger one to keep him off the street. I begged, but got no for an answer, without an explanation that I could accept. But by hiding in the tree, I made myself complicit of their lack of attention to me.

Somehow, from the mixture of memories from my early childhood I got a sense of ambivalence. 'No way!', yet daddy loved me. He did, I am sure of it. In case of doubt: he ruined his clothes and shoes to save me from drowning. He was not even angry, only relieved, when the mystery was cleared, and I came forward from behind the tree. And the doll? Probably it was left there, perhaps not. No matter.

NO-WAY
AS A WAY OF LIFE

He loved me as a girl, and he liked girls. That is where the incipient feeling of discontent began. Because he loved me and was a loving although understated man, I never made a fuss about those words of happy satisfaction with his homemaker daughters. I kept my 'no way!' to myself, but I kept it alive, always. Later, it came in good stead. For example, when my

parents were talking about our futures, the high cost of education with so many children—we ended up nine siblings—and
what to do about it, the phrase recurred. Father worked very
hard, first as a high-school teacher, then as a school director,
and taught evening classes four days a week to earn extra, year
after year, meanwhile also writing two PhD dissertations. The
first, when he had just finished it, became useless when another
dissertation appeared just then, on the exact same topic. Those
were the days only the truth counted; differences in interpretation wouldn't help poor daddy. So, he started all over, on a
topic somewhat more open to interpretive difference. It didn't
help my parents' marriage, but it does explain his concerns
about money. They were not talking trifles. But the idea was
clear, of the no-way kind. Having two boys and seven girls, they
discussed how they could send only the boys to university when
the time came. The girls should marry well. This they discussed
openly; I heard it.

We were all considered intelligent. Once the man who
came to wallpaper the living room said to my mother: 'I hear
your children are doing well in school; they must have inherited
the brains of their father.' Needless to say, my mother, who
had grown up a girl, too, fumed inside but didn't say anything.
When she repeated this to us children it pained me deeply; we
laughed wholeheartedly at so much stupidity. But it wasn't stupid. Somehow, I felt it was a kind of truth, in the social sense.
I knew even then that Mother was just as smart as Father was.
Just the wrong sex, then. I didn't think it in those words, but
felt something to that effect.

So, how to reconcile our intelligence with our fate and
Dad's wallet? We, the girls, who were equally smart, should
work well in school, especially in foreign language classes, we
were told. That way, we would be well educated, and could
perhaps net a valuable husband; for example, a prestigious
doctor, who would have foreign friends visiting. Said totally
imaginary husband could then count on his wife to both speak
intelligently with the guests, entertaining them, and cook
sophisticated dinners for them. All this would help his career.
Hence, for us girls, it would be best to have a short pre-nuptial

stint in nursing. That's always useful for a mother, was taught in a state-sponsored programme, and offered the best opportunity to find, attract, and marry such a husband.

I heard it all, and my mental headshake became a permanent feature of my mind. Although I was what they called lazy, spending most of my time reading novels rather than memorizing words and grammatical rules, I did quite well in school, and so, logically, I went to the Latin and Greek curriculum. My parents were quick to find out that such over-qualification would not prohibit me from entering the nursing school. And by the time my career choice became an issue, some of my sisters had already obeyed the unspoken wish and taken the slightly lower-level curriculum, thus having also more time for fun. So, the terror about costs was a bit mitigated. By that time, also, I had amply earned the nickname they gave me, 'Miss know-it-all'—the one who always spoke back and argued, who never accepted wishes for rules and rules for the law, and discussed instead of obeyed. I can partly understand that it irritated the hell out of my parents, and when they were fed up with my voice, they simply shut me up, as we will see under S. I would then continue the discussion silently, imagining what they would answer to my new, utterly convincing arguments. But I was too cowardly to brave their attitude of silencing me, and speak up. So, I swallowed it.

NOTICED!

Much later, when I had earned my stripes on my own and ignored the sneers, especially coming from my mother, that being ambitious was 'elbowing' and morally as well as socially despicable. I ignored that moralistic sneer, because I didn't see myself as ambitious, only curious, as I explain under N. Later, I got another inside view of my father. He was kind enough to proofread my first articles and my dissertation, which was hard on him because I wrote in French. When I got my PhD he seemed to be moderately proud, but didn't shout about it. Mother was furious; my older brother should not be outshone, and when I got my first academic position her response was: 'Your brother got an offer like that also, but he declined.' The look on her face told me she found me 'elbowing'.

The real awareness of Father's attitude towards me came after his death. When we went through his meagre belongings, we found a book of clippings. Everything I had ever published, journalistic or academic, was there. He had never expressed his pride in me—Mother would have been miffed, and I can't tell what my brother would have thought but I fear the worst. However, here it was: his pride evidenced by his clip book. It was not the pride I rejoiced in, but the attention. He had seen me, after all. I knew it from his dive, but it was comforting to realize he had continued to notice me.

It would be two decades after being 'Miss know-it-all', then stopping to accept that title, before I first heard the word 'feminist'. But the persuasion, indeed, the feeling had been with me all my life, ever since that mental headshake. Once I could express the feeling, I saw nothing special about it, and was amazed at how many young women didn't find it necessary to call themselves feminists. I couldn't understand nor accept the argument that they did not suffer from the patriarchal social fabric. Of course they did. Moreover, it is not about an individual person's chance circumstances. You don't become a feminist only because something awful happens, changing your identity. If you had a relatively good deal in life, count yourself lucky and become concerned about the less lucky. Solidarity became the first rule of thumb. Not that it went very far, because there was so little one could do; the social worlds of each of us were so small. But after all my silently swallowed no-way! headshakes, talking about these things with others did me a world of good. Finally, I was no longer alone; the days of being called Miss know-it-all were over, and I became normal again—almost. Aloneness, like the child in the Munch painting, was replaced with being able to turn the silent headshake into an outspoken one.

Nowadays, the time when women—and some men—were proud to call themselves feminists is long gone. Now, I frequently have to explain why this qualifier is 'still relevant'.

Some even dare to speak of 'post-feminism'—to which my silent
and sometimes spoken reply is: when rape is over, feminism
may be over; not a day sooner. The hated noun 'rape' gets added
meanings. It becomes an allegory of all injustices, all inflictions
of pain, mainly but not exclusively aimed specifically at women.
The word is shorthand for the horrors of the world. Not only,
I now know, will my feminist sense of identity never vanish.
I also become more loquacious in explaining why feminism
is and continues to be not only necessary for all humans; it is
the only way of scratching the surface of the hypocrisy under
which the ingrained selfishness must be laid bare. By the way,
I use the word 'feminist' as a qualifier, rather than a noun,
because I cannot limit my identity to it; and that qualifier
indicates an ongoing process, rather than a state. Hence,
this vignette's title, 'becoming feminist'. Identity as a notion
wrongly suggests unity and continuity; both restrict. And if
there is one thing I am fed up with, it is restriction.

Criticism

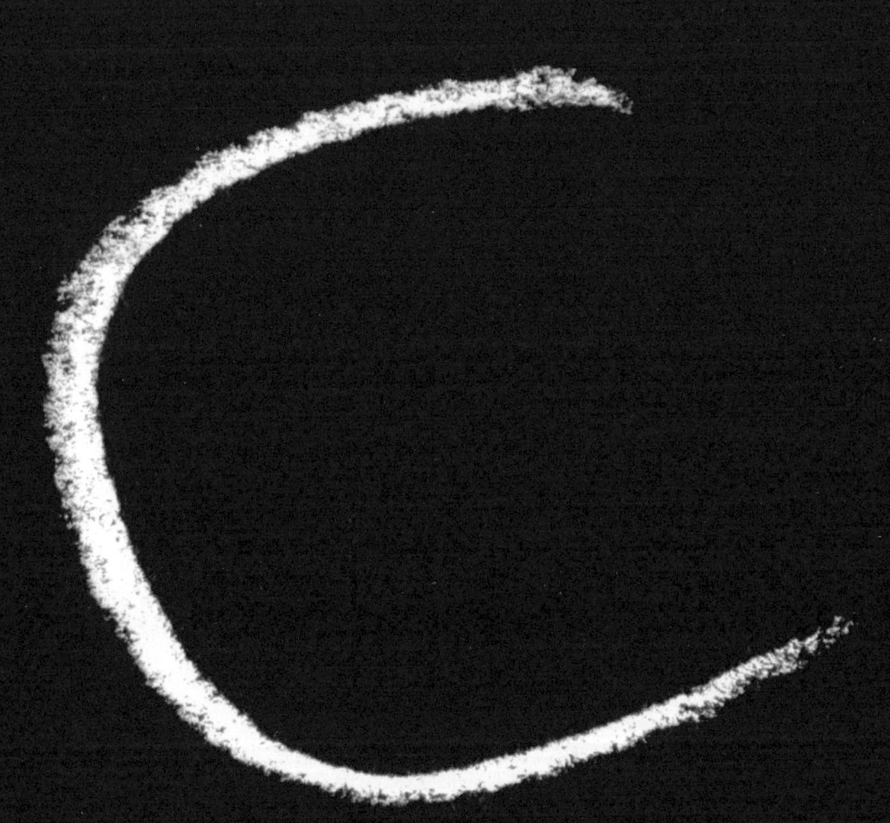

Criticism

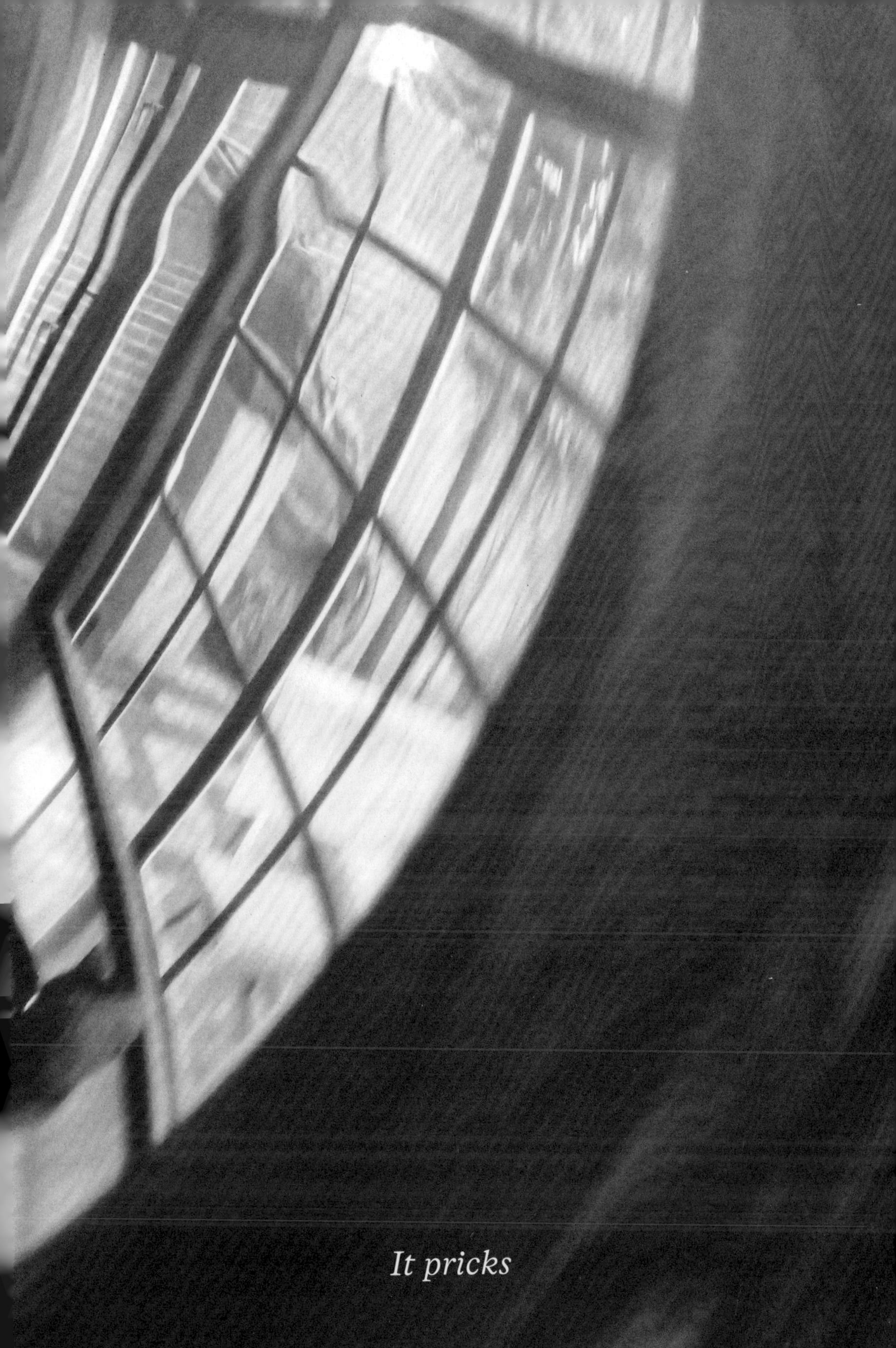
It pricks

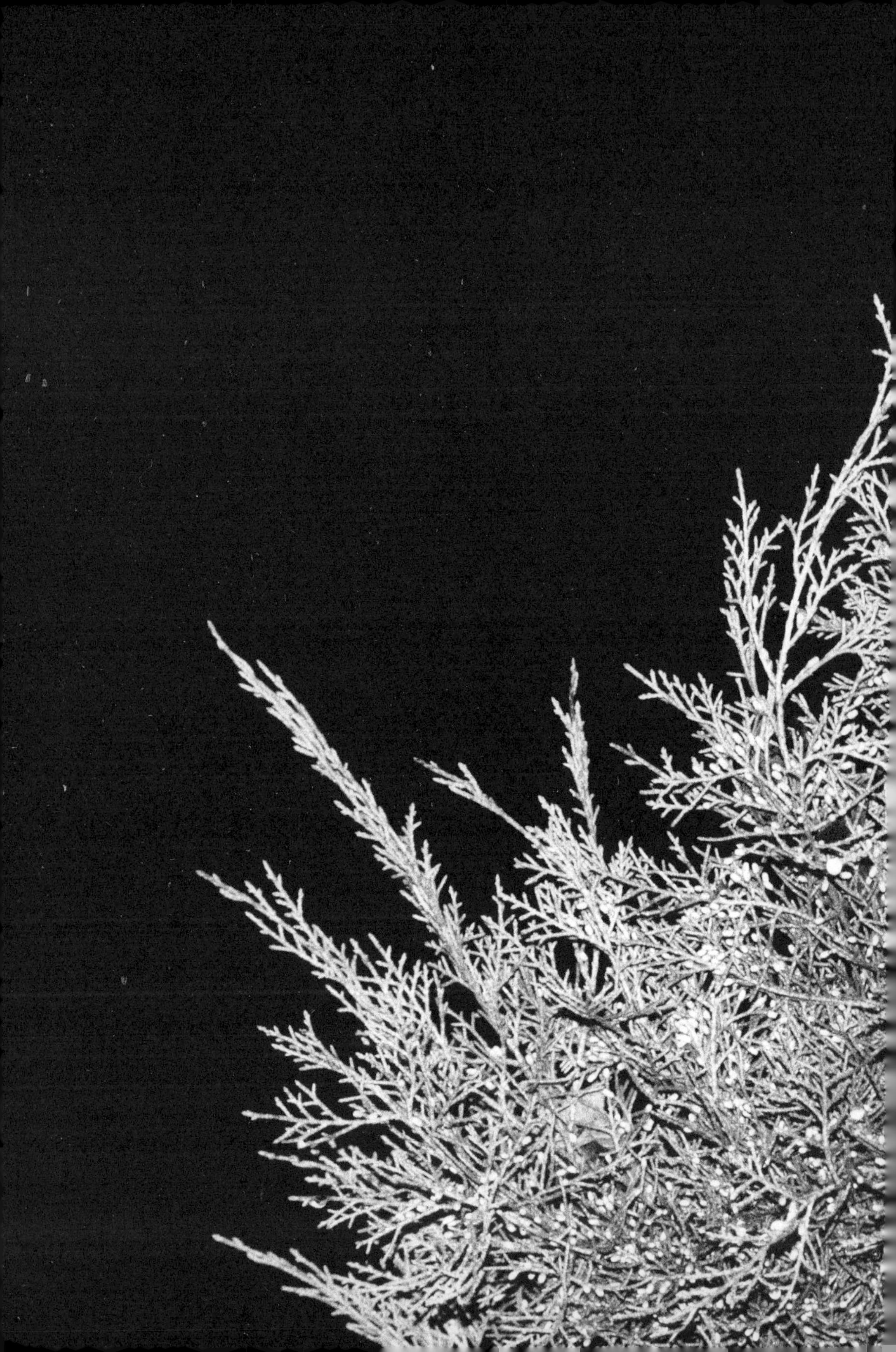

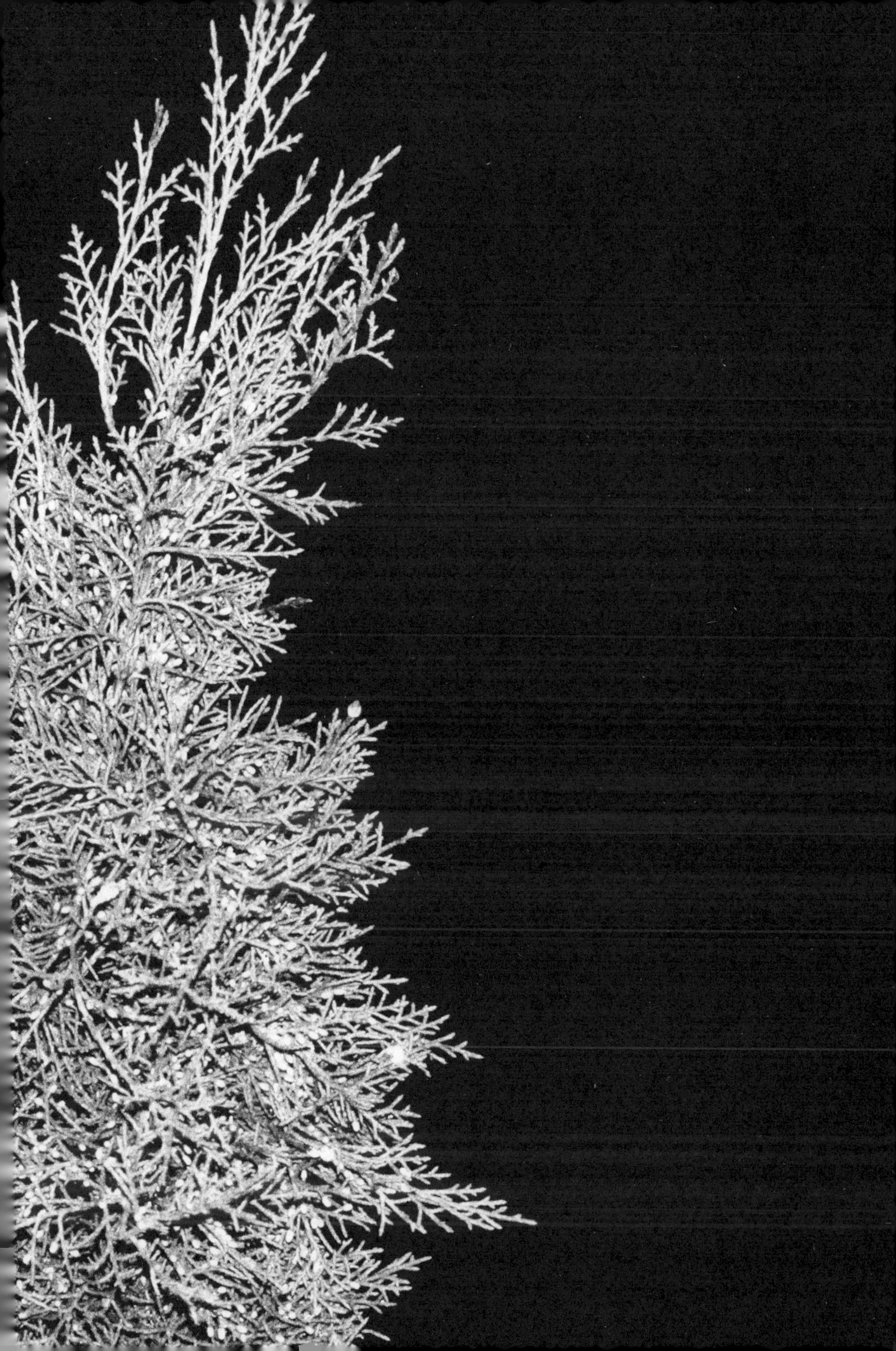

When I gave birth, I realized I had been midwifing all my life without knowing it. My first child was born when I was barely nineteen. A beginning student, my parents had withdrawn financial support, minimal as it was, as soon as they found out I was pregnant. Never mind that I advanced the lame argument that accidents can happen. So, I could not afford a proper doctor and hence, fell back on the cheapest way of giving birth: a midwife, and a home delivery. The small apartment where I lived briefly with the person at the other side of that accidentally getting-together had no hot water and no telephone. But the midwife lived not very far from us, and the father of the child was able to claim priority at the over-crowded neighbourhood phone booth to call her. Once it was clear I was in labour, he went out to make the call, after having put a large pot of water on the stove. When the midwife arrived, she praised his foresight. Meanwhile, I was experiencing the worst pain ever in my life. But the pain vanished for a moment when the midwife put hot water in the hot-water bottle and put the tiniest white shirt around it, to warm it up. A living being I had never met before, whom I had carried but not seen, was about to appear, her gesture told me. My tears of pain became tears of emotion.

The midwife was clearly there to help. I didn't know her, other than from a few clinical visits, but at that moment she became both the good mother I didn't feel I had, and the best friend I had lost. Calming me when the pain hit, and when the man by my side said I should squeeze his hand, she became critical. She said 'No!' The opposite; I should relax, not squeeze. The advice did wonders. And then, after the worst pangs and some pushing, it was over; in the sudden way ordinary pain never is. From one instant to the next it was gone. He was there, the new person. The woman was radiant, as if she had done it. Well, in a sense she had. She had helped me do what I needed to do but didn't think I could. That's what it is to be a midwife. And the miracle continued. The next morning, I woke up to a change in the rhythm of the breathing of that tiny new human being whom I knew I'd love, feel bound to, depend on, and would never entirely break free from. He was about to wake up, but not yet. The change in breathing woke me, and I waited until, a few moments later, his tiny voice made itself heard. That waking up because of the changed respiration of someone else is the fine-tuned mediation between one person who needs help and another one who would not bear to not give it. That, too, is midwifing.

THE SHADOW OF AUTHORITY

I also experienced the opposite. When I became an academic, a teacher, and researcher, I got the privilege of advising PhD candidates. These beginning scholars, most but not all young and just out of their more limited tasks of earning an MA, were both craving and dreading the lonely task of writing their own book. It is daunting indeed. How do you turn an idea into the skeleton of a book, divide it up in logically connected sub-ideas, bring these together to cultural objects such as novels, stories, poems, films? The sheer enormity of the task makes it appealing to some to adhere to a collective programme where a chief researcher has divided his idea up, and distributes the pieces like candy to the eager young beavers. They are not only given the scholarship to write a dissertation in three years, but also the subject. And since the chief had devised the topic, he knew where he wanted it to go, and so, all the student had to do was follow his lead.

This was not how I saw the thought-nurturing work of an advisor. I don't think I would have been able, even if I had wanted to do it, to be so directive. I couldn't believe how this was possible: to think someone else's thoughts. I once took over advising one of such 'followers' as I secretly called them, when she fell out with the chief because she wasn't obedient enough. Used as she was to having to obey, it took a while to settle into a relationship of both trust and autonomy with me. Her work took a very different direction from the group that had informally formed, and then she changed direction again. Not knowing quite how to leave her free yet give her guidance, my concern remained to keep her closely engaged with the object of her choice: a photography album.

Knowing how delicate the relationship was, due to the huge inequality in status, power, and expertise, I kept simultaneously close, checking that she was not getting stuck, and distant, avoiding to impose. That was when I thought of the midwife again. Just being there, helping when needed, staying not as a shadow of authority looming over her shoulder but as a silent support system she could fall back on. Her draft chapters were uneven; some required serious rewriting, even reconceptualizing, and some just needed some light editing. At one point she had written a draft that was so problematic that I felt a strong intervention was called for. She had more or less neglected the photos that were her object of analysis, the context—the catholic church in the 1950s—as well as the theoretical approach she had developed, step by step, over the past chapters. I was so committed to her success that I wrote a new outline for her, in some detail, with sources and references she needed to consult. I gave it to her, thinking of it as a gift. To my utter dismay, she became angry. She felt overruled, overpowered, and said it was not up to me to think for her. That was a blow, which turned into an illumination once I reflected on the task of the teacher.[8]

She was right, of course. It didn't take me long to see it. Thinking *with* her, yes; not *for* her. So, we separated ways for a bit, until she came back with a new draft. Who else could she turn to, in order to make progress? I felt a bit bad as clearly, she came back because she needed me, not out of her own volition. But I was also very happy that she had not given up, and that her criticizing me for my interference had, in the end, helped her. This draft did not resemble her old one, nor in the least my proposed alternative outline. I lavishly praised her for having solved the problem on her own. This repaired our precarious relationship, and I felt she trusted me again. But I had walked a very fine line indeed. From midwife I had, for a brief moment, threatened to become a shadow, looming over her, suffocating her thinking. Shadows are dangerous to thought. For, thought needs autonomy, even if it is also inevitably social. To put it more strongly: only with recognition of the social nature of thought, and in interaction with others, is the autonomy of thought possible.

Decades later, when I made the film on Descartes

---

8 This reflection is further developed in the book of interviews with Jeroen Lutters, *The Trade of the Teacher* (2018).

mentioned before, I realized this social side of thought and
developed it with fiery conviction. But looking back, I can
see that the experience with that early student who had been
a reject of a leader who thought others could think for him,
taught me a lesson that was easy enough to understand even
if sometimes hard to put into practice. Thinking is social, but
social implies mutual. Although the formal-institutional relationship is terribly unequal, hierarchal, and a breeding ground
for dependency and slavish discipleship, the actual process can
break that mould, and reverse the relationship of need into an
interactive relationship between two autonomous thinkers,
who each have a stake, an interest, in the success of the work.
The teacher-advisor needs the student to succeed as much as
the student needs a helping hand to do *her* (not my) thinking.
This made me reconsider the idea of shadows. It became my
principal idea about teaching.

THOUGHT-MIDWIFERY

A midwife as I experienced it at age nineteen is the opposite
of a shadow. The midwifing consists in nurturing the
thoughts when they seem to go towards more insight, and
asking constructive questions when you see a problem the
apprentice-thinker is heading for. Not judge and condemn but
probe how much further she can go in that direction without
hitting a brick wall. And if the brick wall came around, make
her discover it herself. When that happened, in the case I just
evoked, she was actually pleased to have avoided the dangerous
cliff. No need to tell her I had warned her, softly and implicitly.
I had, but at that point she could not yet hear the midwifery in
the criticism, and thought that, like others, I was just criticizing
her in a negative sense, as the usual sense of criticism has it.
Instead, the near-crash and then avoidance of the brick wall
made her proud, and her pride in herself empowered her, which
would improve the quality of her work, and hence, make mine
easier. Criticism needs to be of this kind: thought-midwifery
instead of a darkening shadow. Hence the phrase 'constructive

criticism'. I have seen more of the opposite, destructive criticism, than I like to remember. Papers marked with exclamation marks in red, staining the paper and making it illegible.

This insight came in handy when, years later, I had a student who was intellectually hampered for a while, to the point of being handicapped, by his justified anger. He had chosen to write about a historical trauma in his country. So, he was, willy-nilly, doing 'preposterous history'. I tend to encourage people to study what they feel is important, and I value subjects with a political angle, even if the work of academic analysis becomes more challenging because of it. But in his case, I discovered that this closeness can lead to serious affective overloads that make the work near-impossible. A repetitive lament over the suffering of his people was not, I knew, going to fly high with the academic judges who were only interested in the quality of his sources, his reasoning, and his analysis. But these judges are not the only ones of his readers who mattered. I also doubted it would work for his larger intended audience. For some time, all I could do was ask him to structure the drafts more clearly, so that others who were not so versed in the history of his country could follow the arguments. In other words, I tried to persuade him to open up to the non- or not-yet-converted instead of keeping preaching to the converted. Only then, I told him, could he make new 'converts'—in other words, persuade people to share his point of view instead of rejecting it as overly political.

It worked. This candidate did well and since all is well that ends well, the fact that he is now a respected colleague retrospectively (pre-posterously, perhaps) vindicates my concerns of those earlier days. This candidate was by far not the only one with this too-closeness problem. But the more the relationship between the researcher and his or her chosen topic is close, intense, the more it can become a paralyzing handicap, not only for the researcher but also for the advisor. Calling out caution can be perceived as indifference, even offensive disagreement. Here, the criticizing as midwifing experience becomes crucial again. Seeing the pain of the other as inevitable, perhaps even valuable, productive, and trying to help where criticism can help, is the only possible way out of such impasses. To not take 'failure' as an option but do what it takes, always through empowering the other, is an attitude that midwives are bound to practice. This insight turned midwifery into my guideline for teaching and advising; the model for criticism.[9]

9 The successful dissertation by Palestinian Ihab Saloul appeared in print in 2012, and a second edition in 2018. In 2020, he published the crucial article 'Postmemory and Oral History' on memory in exile.

Details
(that Matter)

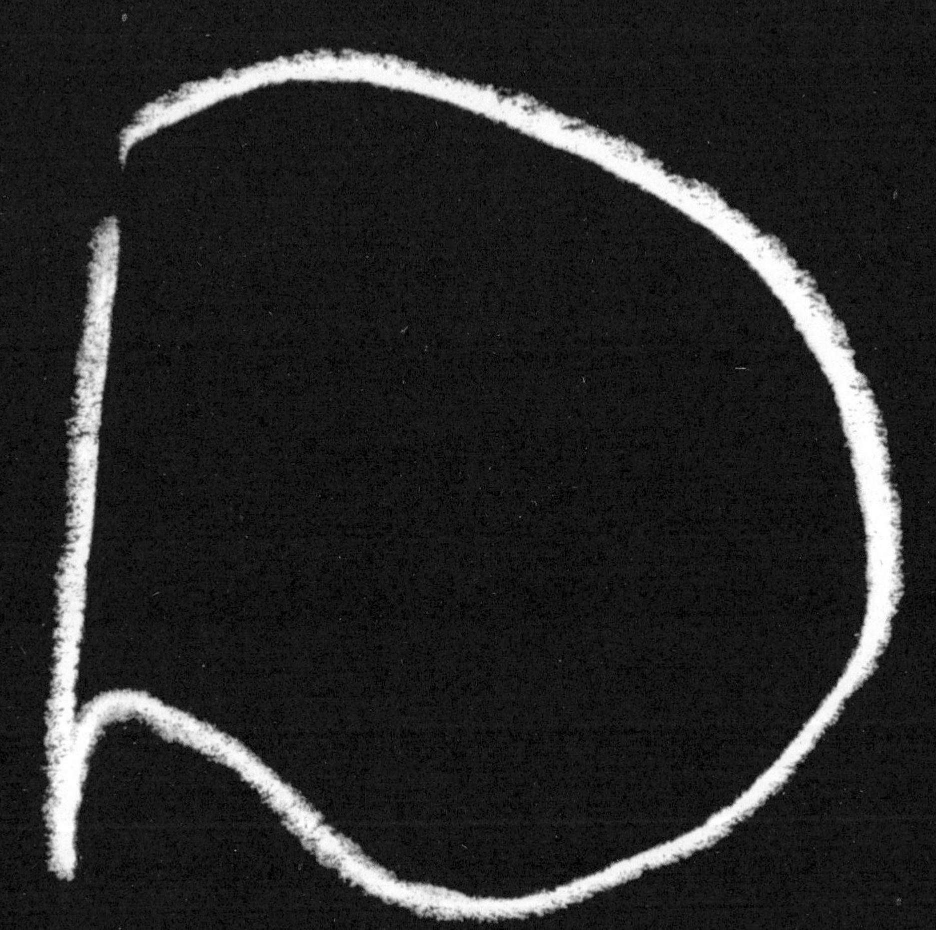

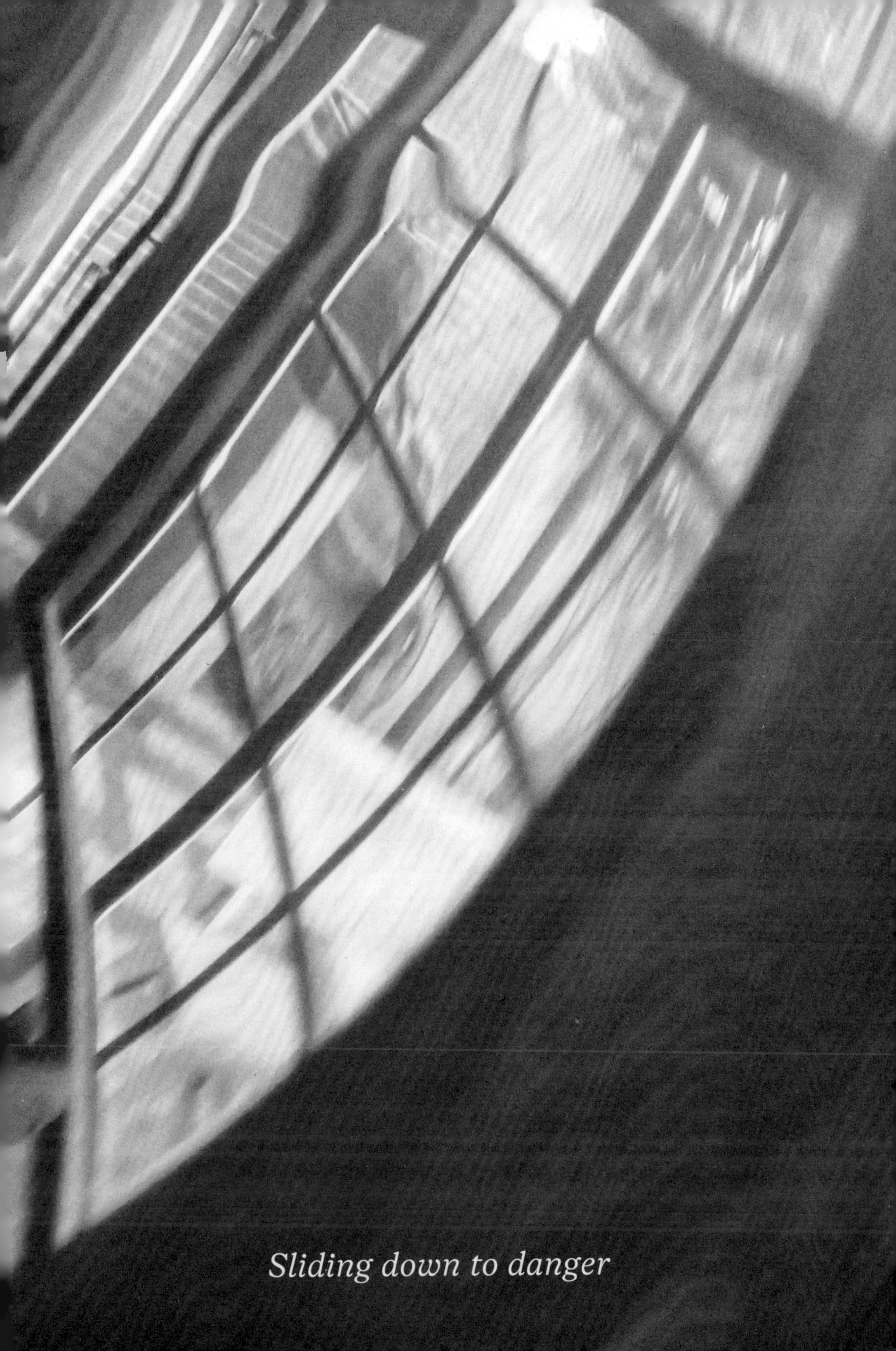

Sliding down to danger

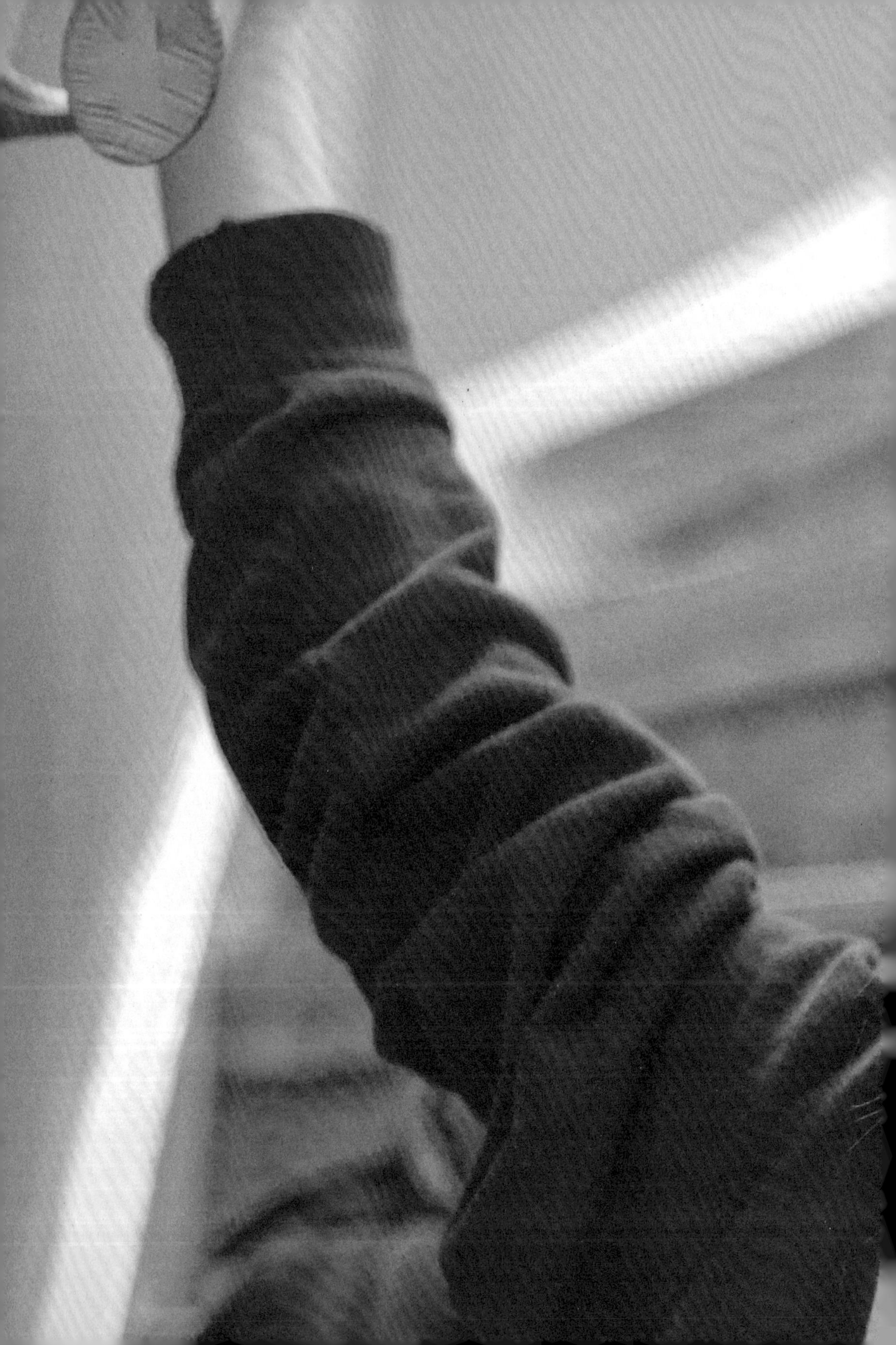

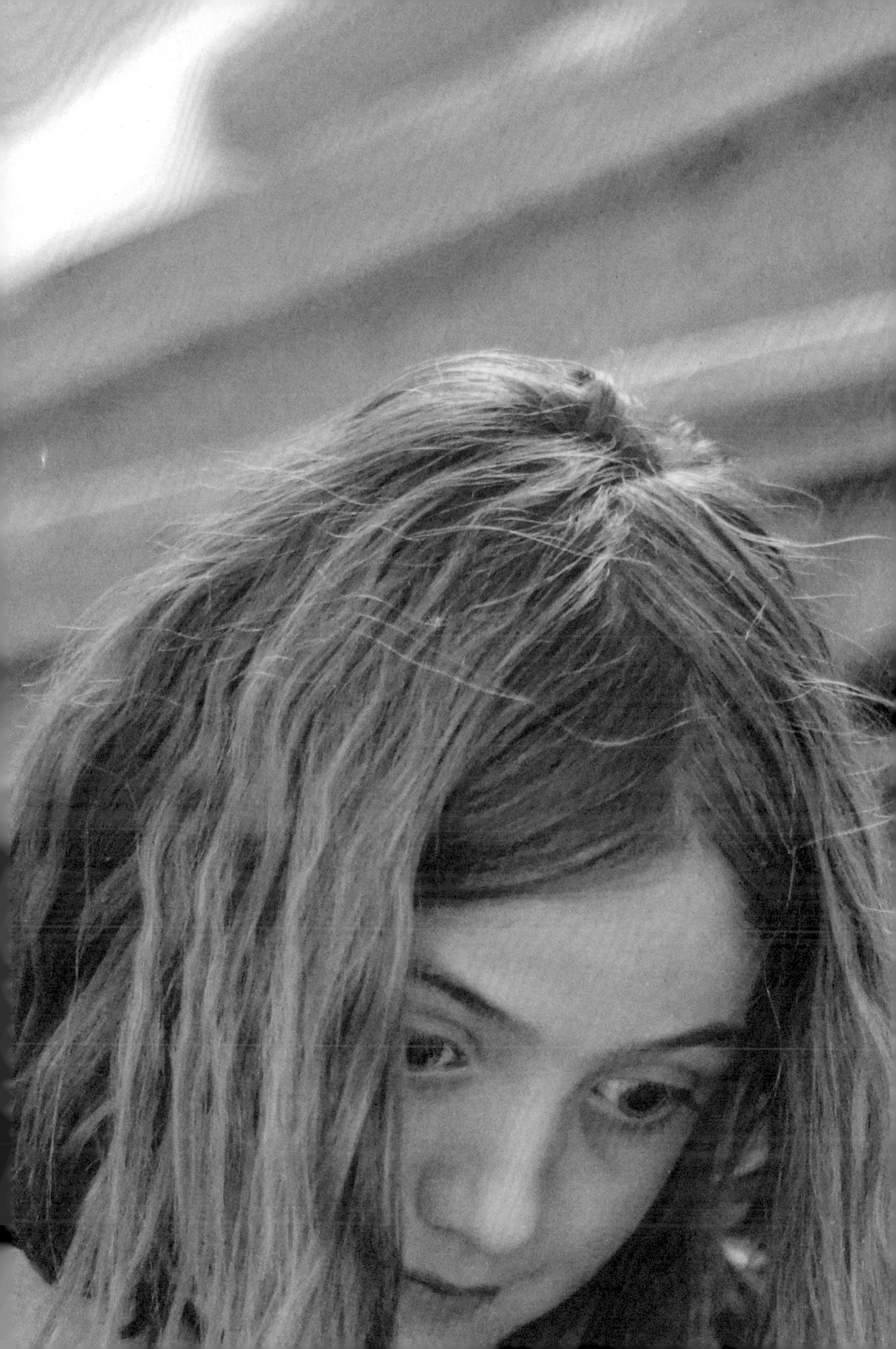

Meaning is pervasive. The world around us habitually means something, but we don't realize, question, or are even aware of it. We live by semantic routine. The unthinking attribution of meaning to what we see, hear, smell, and feel around us, is necessary; it saves us from constant chaos, concern, confusion. Sometimes, however, the routine makes us miss moments of delightful wonder. Not-understanding can be an exciting experience. Seeing what is perhaps so routine as to be invisible, can become a moment of meaning-making when unexpectedly it connects to you; when you are its 'second person'. Second-personhood, combined with the multi-sensorial nature of all perceptions, compels a questioning of all certainty about meaning. That certainty comes from not questioning it, from taking it for granted.

A good example of that need for routine is language. Language can only function as a means of communication if the participants in its game all know the rules, don't question these, and thus free themselves from thinking about the medium, so that they can just use it. This explains why repetition is so important, both in the language acquisition of children and in entering into a new, foreign linguistic community. Many have experienced this, I suppose: when learning a foreign language, a moment comes that the preoccupation with that difficult task, the concentration on the learning, leads to dreaming in that language. That occurs at a moment when the foreign language becomes less foreign, and the learner almost reaches a level of knowing the language; a level near to routine. But not quite; for the constant concern with that other language keeps it so close to our subconsciousness that in sleep it pops up.

When studying French, I had that dreaming experience. But I also had moments, wide-awake, when the language struck me, as if protesting against the way I took my access to it for granted. I learned that the word for 'love', *amour*, well-known and cliché as it is, has an anomaly, like some other words or phrases do. Mostly, these come from a time long gone, and the etymology—the origin and history of words—has only been continued because of the routine necessary for languages to function. *Amour* is masculine in the singular and feminine in the plural. Easy enough to remember. It took my feminist inclination to realize that this anomaly, even if just inherited from the long-gone past, has been preserved in contemporary French for a reason. That reason is simple: it confirms and reconfirms a perennial gender bias. A woman has 'un grand amour' for life. A man can have many loves, mostly clandestine, unknown to the one woman whose 'grand amour' he is. The linguistic anomaly has been perpetuated because it has long become, and stayed, simply normal. It fits the traditional gender ideology that still reigns. The force of routine showed when I began to run this insight by my French friends, most of whom are convinced feminists. They had never thought about this. None of them was persuaded; they could not believe there was anything other than history and routine involved. Shrugging it off was what they did.

Much later in life, I took up learning Spanish, at first because I was going to spend a semester in New York City and, I felt, Spanish was necessary there. At some point, I struggled with the difficult distinction, for the two versions of the verb 'to be', between *ser* and *estar*. Among other differences, basically put, the former verb denotes permanent features, the latter temporary states. When I was more or less able to read, I enjoyed the semi-automatism that reading helps to acquire; not having to look up several words a page. But perplexity came to me—if only for the briefest moment—when I stumbled upon a sentence that used *estar* to say that someone was dead, and had been for years. Had I misunderstood the distinction? But no, I soon got it. This language, which I love very much, is not only embedded in a catholic culture; it *is* catholic, as a language. *Estar* is 'logical' if you believe that death is temporary, followed by resurrection and afterlife. Even languages as a whole cannot be isolated from other ways of meaning production in the culture where they originated, grew, and still function.

This realization, then, retrospectively, illuminated earlier moments of meaning-making where an initial confusion or perplexity led to an insight I was jubilant to acquire. In general terms, this particular insight concerns the understanding of odd, awkward, incongruous details in texts or visual images; things that don't quite match the overall picture. Such details

de-automatize the perception of the whole. They are not, as
is traditionally, and mostly rightly, assumed in hermeneutical
philosophy, entrances into the whole we are looking at. True, I
have often enjoyed such 'hermeneutical circles', from whole to
detail, then back to the whole with a more complex or subtle
understanding. It offers an effective pathway to interpretation.
The analysis the Austrian Romanist Leo Spitzer wrote on
Racine's 1677 tragedy *Phèdre*, for example, helped me grasp, not
just how the tragedy worked, but also what the text's details did
to make that working possible. Nevertheless, the not-fitting
details, the bizarre ones, can produce an effect of wonderment
that does not lead to a better understanding of the whole, but
instead, undermines what the whole seemed to say, turning
it on its head, and deviates, destroys, decomposes, or decon-
structs the assumed overall meaning.[10]

DISCOVERING DARKNESS

As a child I was very afraid of the dark. I have often wondered
why, other than simply not being able to see. Two memories
help understand this phobia. They don't explain it all, but they
add to the normal anxiety this special aspect of terror induces.
One comes from having been raised with the cherished
tradition of Sinterklaas, the 6th of December celebration of the
birthday of Saint Nicholas. A few weeks before that date, he
enters the city on a white horse, as becomes fairy-tale figures,
but also sometimes, dictators—apparently, North-Korean Kim
Jong-Un also rides a white horse. The white-bearded Saint
was surrounded by colourfully-dressed black-faced clowns,
all called Zwarte Piet (Black Pete). Festive, funny, and full of
surprises, they turn the boring, grey, early-winter days into
a period of partying. They knock on windows, while inside,
near the hearth, children sing the season's songs. Sometimes,
without anyone leaving the room, the door opens a notch and
a handful of candies are thrown in. The Black Petes used to
threaten and shake their birch branches, but these days they

10 Spitzer (1887–1960), a pioneer in detailed interpretations according to the
'hermeneutic circle', from the entire text to details, then bringing these back to
the whole, published the article 'Sur Racine's Phèdre' (1948). See Spitzer, *Le récit
de Théramène* (1983).

mainly reassure kids by giving them candy. Reassurance is called for. This alone is what deserves attention.[11]

I remember that the season when this happened did increase my fear of darkness. Then, one day during that time, when I was aware that these slightly scary Black Petes were roaming the streets, I suddenly saw a figure scarier than the festive clowns: a really Black man walked through our street. Not dressed as a clown; just a normal man. I must have been four or five years old. All I remember is the terror I felt. I ran home, crying. Then my mother explained that this is simply a person who, like most people in Africa, is black by nature. As usual, it took a while for the terror to leave me, my body. And then came the guilt, the uneasy feeling I had been 'bad', unfair. Fascination and reassurance—hence, a play with anxiety—are what underlies this Dutch tradition. It seems to me to be a typical cultural configuration of sentiments towards 'race' and other differences among people as they are instilled in children. These days, there are many protests against this tradition, but just as many people protest against the protests, which allegedly hurt Dutch cultural custom.

But the de-automatization of this perception of blackness—the transformation of fear into guilt, and more importantly, ongoing reflection—turned me into a fierce anti-racist, just as my father's thought that girls were meant to become homemakers had turned me into a fierce feminist. The experience also taught me to distinguish better between forms of darkness. Dark skin is nothing to be afraid of, I learned, an insight I owe to my anti-racist parents. Black-faced clowns are not scary, they won't really abduct you in their burlap sacks. But they are portrayed as servants, a class derogation for which seventeenth-century paintings had set the example. And they are being ridiculed. It was soon clear to me that this tradition was problematic; deeply so.

Then came the second, totally different experience of the fear of darkness, this time in summer. It had nothing to do with people. The ditch near our house with duckweed-covered water had a semi-steep bank. In summer, the duckweed was

---

11 In 1999, I wrote the article 'Zwarte Piet's *Bal Masqué*' about this problematic tradition, in relation to an artwork by British artist Anna Fox. This has made a huge impact and was republished many times.

so dense that it almost looked like a lawn you could walk on, and it looked totally dry. When I saw that, and stopped taking for granted that the duckweed was always just that: duckweed, my innate curiosity got the better of me and made me want to check out if this was true. The ambiguity between solid and yielding, dry and wet, surface and volume was incomprehensible to me. I must have been around six, which was the age at which I was allowed to play outside alone. What I did was lay down on my belly, at the top of the bank, and slowly let myself slide downwards, until I could reach the duckweed with my hands. Then came the scary moment of darkness.

I had slid just a bit too far. Now I could test the surface, but I couldn't get back up. Slowly, now involuntarily, I slithered downwards. Irreversibly, sluggishly, not I but the ground under me pushed me downwards, to the surface that now that I had touched it revealed the blackness of the water underneath. The realization that I was going to drown, to die in that darkness, made my heart stop. Fortunately, I had enough resistance in me to think of a way to save myself. And with utmost carefulness but filled with fear I managed somehow to slowly get back to the top, crawling sideways. But I never forgot that darkness of the water ready to swallow me. The effect of de-automatizing perception is the long duration of the sensation the moment produces. At that young age I was beginning to realize this. Later in life, it stood me in good stead.

And while I was trembling with fear, desperately trying to get back up, I suddenly remembered that I had learned something about darkness that would have been life-saving. When ice-skating, I had been told, if I ever got into a hole in the ice and slid under the layer of ice, what I ought to look for was the darkest place. That is where the road to safety was. Dark meant the hole, light would be the unbreakable ice, and I would drown. This insight helped me to drop the panic and simply work hard to get back to the edge of the slope. I keep remembering this, and thinking: nothing is automatic.

DEFEATING VOYEURISM

One such experience produced an integration of several attitudes to perception. It brought together my own view already
formed, the novelty of the de-automated perception, and the
widely circulating commonplace considered 'knowledge'. It was
when, some thirty-five years ago, I had begun to look a bit more
closely at Rembrandt, an artist so 'typically Dutch' that I had
never bothered with his art. Now my curiosity had been triggered in view of an image I was considering to put on the cover
of a book of feminist-literary interpretations of ancient, mostly
biblical stories. I was still totally into literary studies. Even my
work on the Bible was frowned upon by some colleagues, who
considered the Bible 'not literature'. In this case, my experience
had a profound impact on my professional life. For, much later,
the moment of meaning-making described below would lead to
the book *Reading Rembrandt* that so helpfully established my
controversial, deeply ambivalent reputation in art history.

What counts for this entry on de-automated meaning-making is *how* it happened. During a long-term stay in
the USA I had gone to Washington DC to look at some of
Rembrandt's paintings, with my newly triggered interest. I had
no professional (art-historical) interest, let alone knowledge, yet
at all. I only wanted to get a better grasp of this artist's work.
For reasons of subject matter—my interest in the problem of
rape, part of my feminist persuasion—I especially wanted to
see Rembrandt's 1664 painting of the suicide of Lucretia in the
National Gallery of Art. My young adolescent daughter was
with me, so I knew I would have to spare her impatience and
be quick. While I was looking at the Rembrandts, she took a
look around the gallery, where Rembrandt was neighbouring
Vermeer.

Because of this mother-daughter outing, I was planning
to let her set the pace of the visit, accepting that I had no time
to really study the painting; just take a look and think about
it later. To my utter perplexity, the painting was missing from
the rich and famous gallery, officially called Northern Baroque.
That seemed impossible; there was no sign saying it was on

loan. I asked the guard on duty, who said he would call someone to inquire, and asked my name. And—after the painful missing of the painting, the second perplexity of the day, this time positive—a few minutes later appeared the chief curator of the department, Professor Arthur Wheelock. He apologized for the absence of the painting, and explained that it was undergoing a cleaning. I was utterly surprised when he proposed to take me to the workshop in the basement where this was happening.

We descended into the august vault. For my daughter, this privilege was rather exciting. 'Mum, there is a fake Vermeer there!' she exclaimed, as soon as we reached the lower floor, pointing at a painting hanging to the side. And yes, there was a discarded Van Meegeren—the (in)famous Vermeer-falsifier. It was such a successful imitation that the museum had acquired it as a Vermeer. Quite embarrassing, for such an eminent museum. And here was that thirteen-year-old who had not been to museums much, and she saw it right away. To my growing excitement, triggered by the curator's generous willingness to take the time for this excursion, a feeling of pride in my girl was added. So, my state of mind was already quite shaken. And then came the moment. Among some disorderly items stood an easel, covered by a dirty-looking cloth. 'Here she is!' said the smiling curator, taking the cloth away in one swift gesture. What I saw—and I swear I really *saw* it—was *movement*. The woman in the painting moved her head, to the right, as if to avoid looking these curious viewers, or voyeurs, in the face. That movement and its meaning is what I saw. I know it wasn't possible, and didn't fit what my routine dictated me to see: a still painting. The divorce between seeing and knowing was flabbergasting.

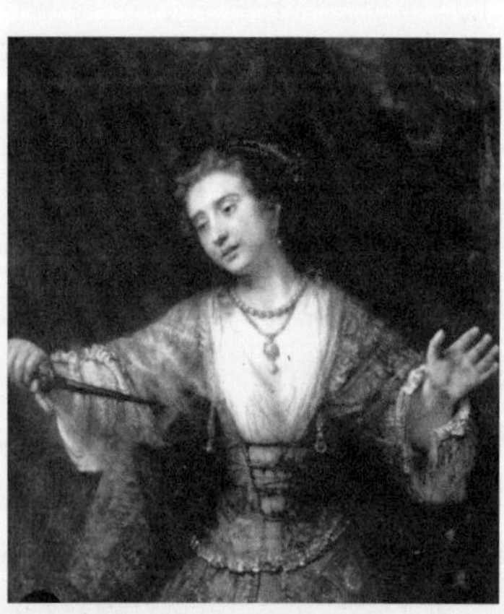

FIG. 5 Rembrandt van Rijn, *Lucretia*, 1664

The perplexity of that sensation stretched out the moment. It is still with me. It took me some time to connect to what Professor Wheelock said: that despite her deadly pallor, the cleaning had brought her back to life. I never forgot those words. Only later, and in front of colour copies of the painting in the library, did I see the detail that had 'caused' the movement; a tiny, seemingly irrelevant one. It was the earring on Lucretia's left ear, which was not hanging straight down. Its oblique presentation made the movement of the head visible. True, her hands had come forward, emphasizing the force and the surprise of her act of suicide, literally self-killing. The subject of the chaste Roman Lucretia who stabbed herself in the presence of her husband and father after her husband's fellow-soldier had raped her, was familiar in Rembrandt's time. It would lead to a routine act of recognition: oh yes, this is Lucretia, a commonplace topic at the time. Thanks to the cleaning, also, her hands had come forward, emphasizing the force and the surprise of her act of suicide. All this suggests movement, and the presence of others. But what I saw was less immediately the hand, the blurred sleeve, and the dagger significantly doubled by a shadow, all elements that present the figure as moving, but that earring. This tiniest of objects persisted in telling me that the deadly-white face, the head, was what was moving primarily, not the act of the hand with the dagger.

Aware, with my routine knowledge, that the victim of rape killed herself in the presence of her father and her husband whose boasting about her beauty to a fellow soldier had triggered intermale rivalry leading to the rape, my feminist responsiveness was already in place before I got to see the painting. There are a lot of details in this painting that can guide viewers to gaze through the lens of a feminist rhetorical and iconographical mode of looking. But that the oblique-hanging earring became for me the visual event, the moment that undermined everything else, was due to the doubling of the men in the story watching her commit suicide, with my own sense of indiscretion, verging on voyeurism. In an iconographic reading, this averted gaze would simply indicate her modesty, her refusal to return the gaze of the viewer, and thus her refusal to acknowledge the latter's naturalized right to witness her plight by visually taking her in. To my knowledge, no art-historical commentary, of which I later read a lot, mentions that earring.

Reading the painting narratively, 'for the plot', we would interpret Lucretia's movement as a consequence of the presence of the men. Father and husband are trying to comfort her when suddenly she kills herself, pre-empting their futile comforting attempt. For she has to act swiftly before they can restrain her. Such a reading is realistic in its argument. It is an explanation of the detail in terms of the 'real' story, taking the motivations from the story rather than from the scene as it is depicted. It is also verbal in the traditional sense, since it super-imposes on the painting an 'underlying' verbal story that the painting is then supposed to 'illustrate'. But no man is present in the scene as the painting presents it. The appeal to such a realistic reading demonstrates how much even traditional art interpretation owes to the relations between visual and verbal texts.

The frontal light becomes significant. The woman—the subject, or rather, the object of the presentation—stands right in the middle of the canvas. Her body is turned directly toward the spectators. So is her bodice which, closed beneath the bosom, has an opened 'lock'. This opened closure refers rhetorically to the violent opening of Lucretia, to her simulta-neous rape and her display, with the latter coming to stand for the former. The chaste Lucretia has become public property through her rape. The visual presentation of the woman at the moment of her self-killing partakes of this 'publication'. In accordance with the culture, Lucretia is put on display for the eyes of the indiscreet onlookers. Critiquing that same culture, she turns her head away in order to break contact with the spectators, preferring isolation to remaining an object of their voyeuristic gaze. The figure, in the democratic space of an exhibition, would actively reject the traditional modes of looking, encouraging instead a polemical disagreement. This moment of seeing her head turn away, a movement signified by the oblique-hanging earring, is a visual event of meaning-mak-ing properly speaking.

In its wake, but only as such an after-effect, her raised left hand comes to signify resistance to that gaze, a request to the viewer to turn away. Denying contact with others, in this final moment of death at her own hand, she seems to say that she alone can perform it. Even the pitying, sympathizing onlookers are, at this moment, indiscreet and superfluous. This interpretation is, of course, *pre-posterous* in the sense I have brought up under A. It is not premised on the historical *reconstruction* of the work, allegedly as the artist *intended* it, nor on the autonomy of the *work of art* from its messy embeddedness in the web of cultural signification, including its after-effect, its *work*. All these attributions of meaning are undermined.

Instead, unlike iconographic readings, which would explain it through the pre-texts and the pre-images, this reading forcefully explains that one tiny detail, which, for me, constitutes its secret. The earring that doesn't hang straight, its oblique position that accounts for the sense I had when it was, literally, unveiled to me: that Lucretia actually moved, that she was still alive, and that she swiftly turned her head away from me. It was the work's *work*: its power to strike over four centuries and reach us today, compelling us to ask questions that have routinely been smoothed over. The narrativity of this work is played out between the painting and today's viewers. This is what I got, like a gift, from the moment of meaning-making that was going to have a lasting impact on my approach to visual art, the visual imagination, or the art of *imaging*.[12]

---

12 For a detailed analysis of this painting, see *Reading 'Rembrandt'* (1991), 64–86.

Envy

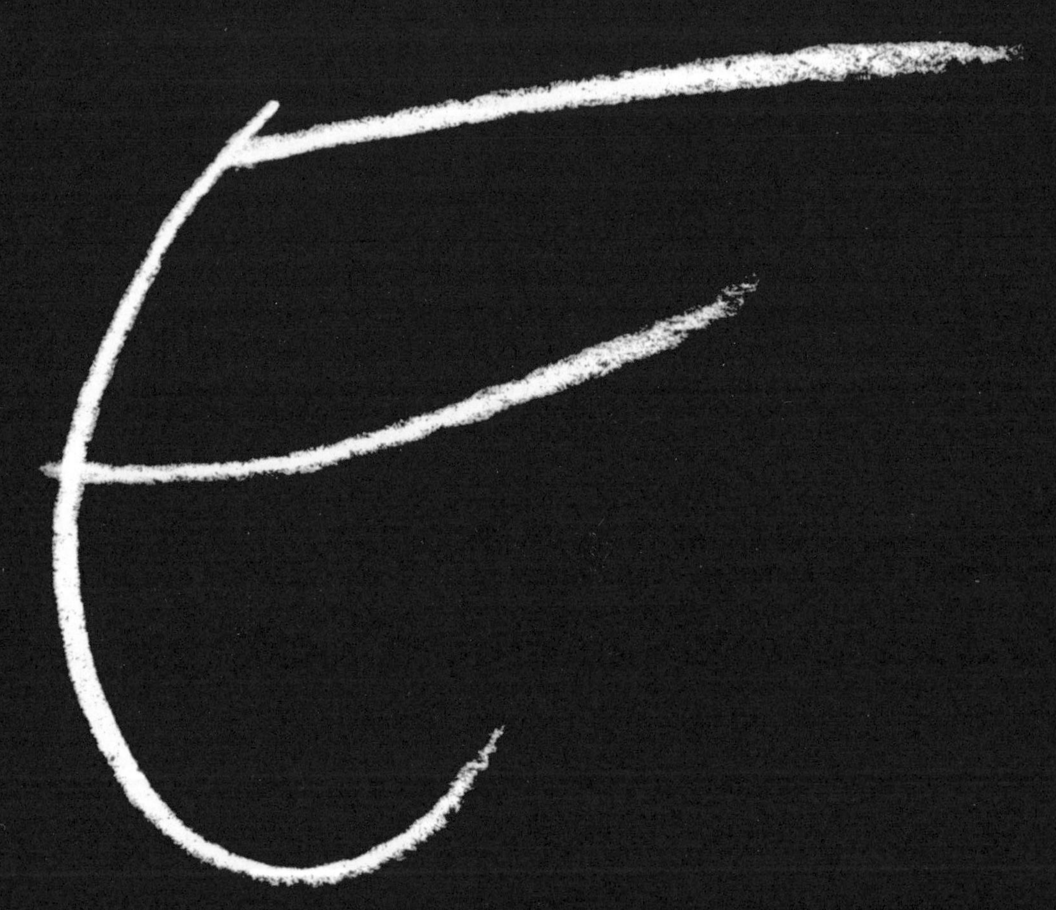

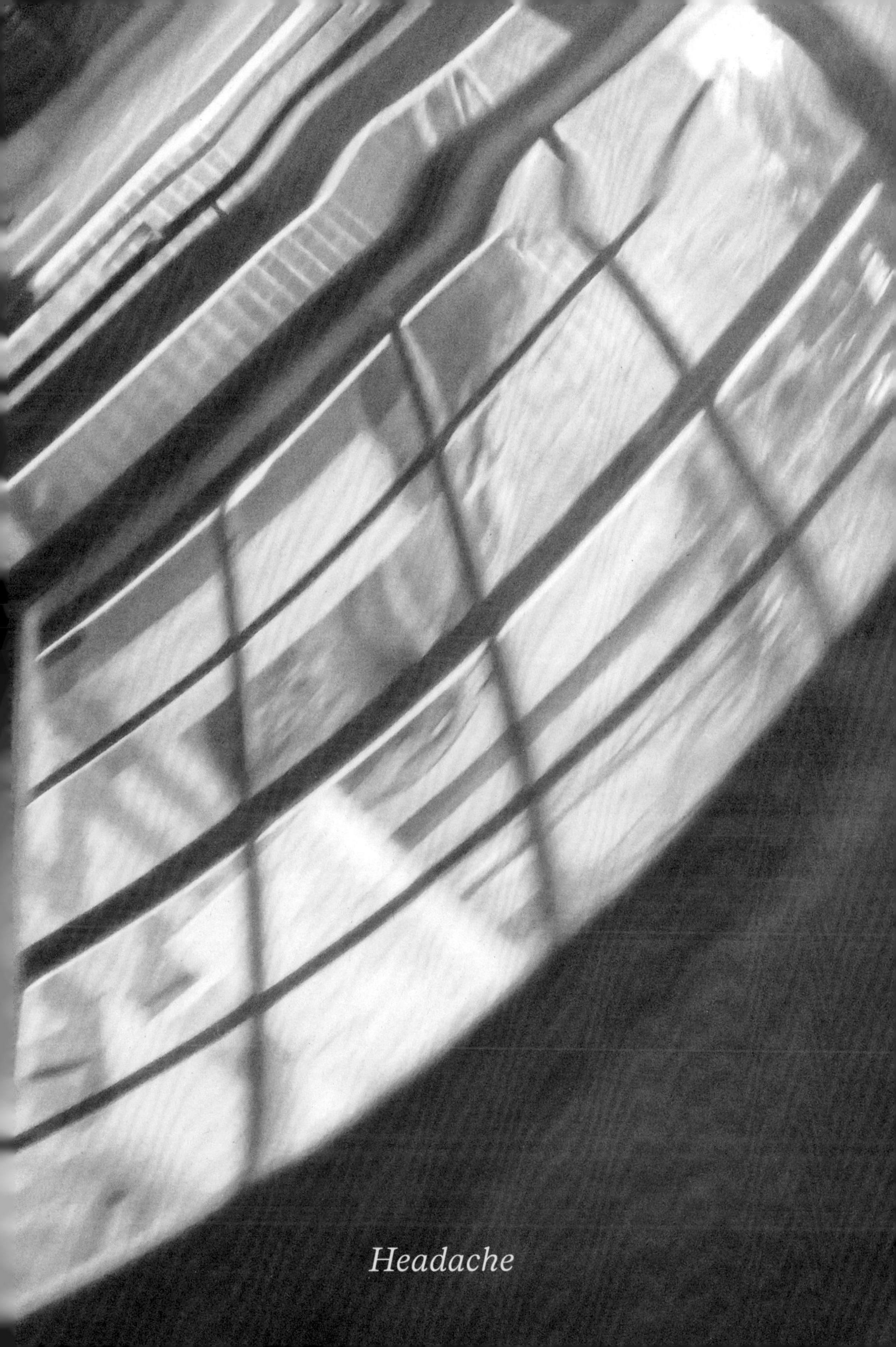

Headache

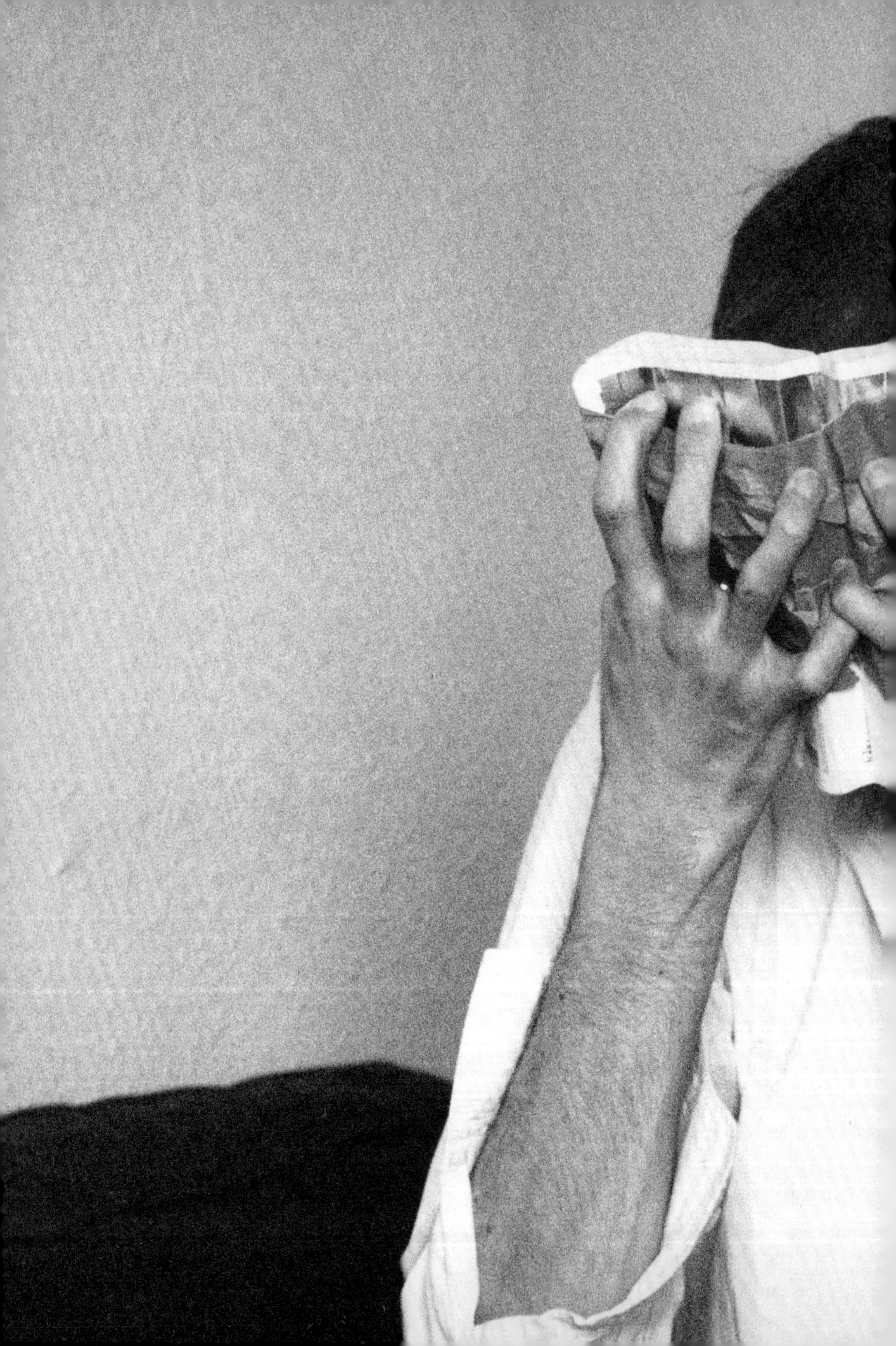

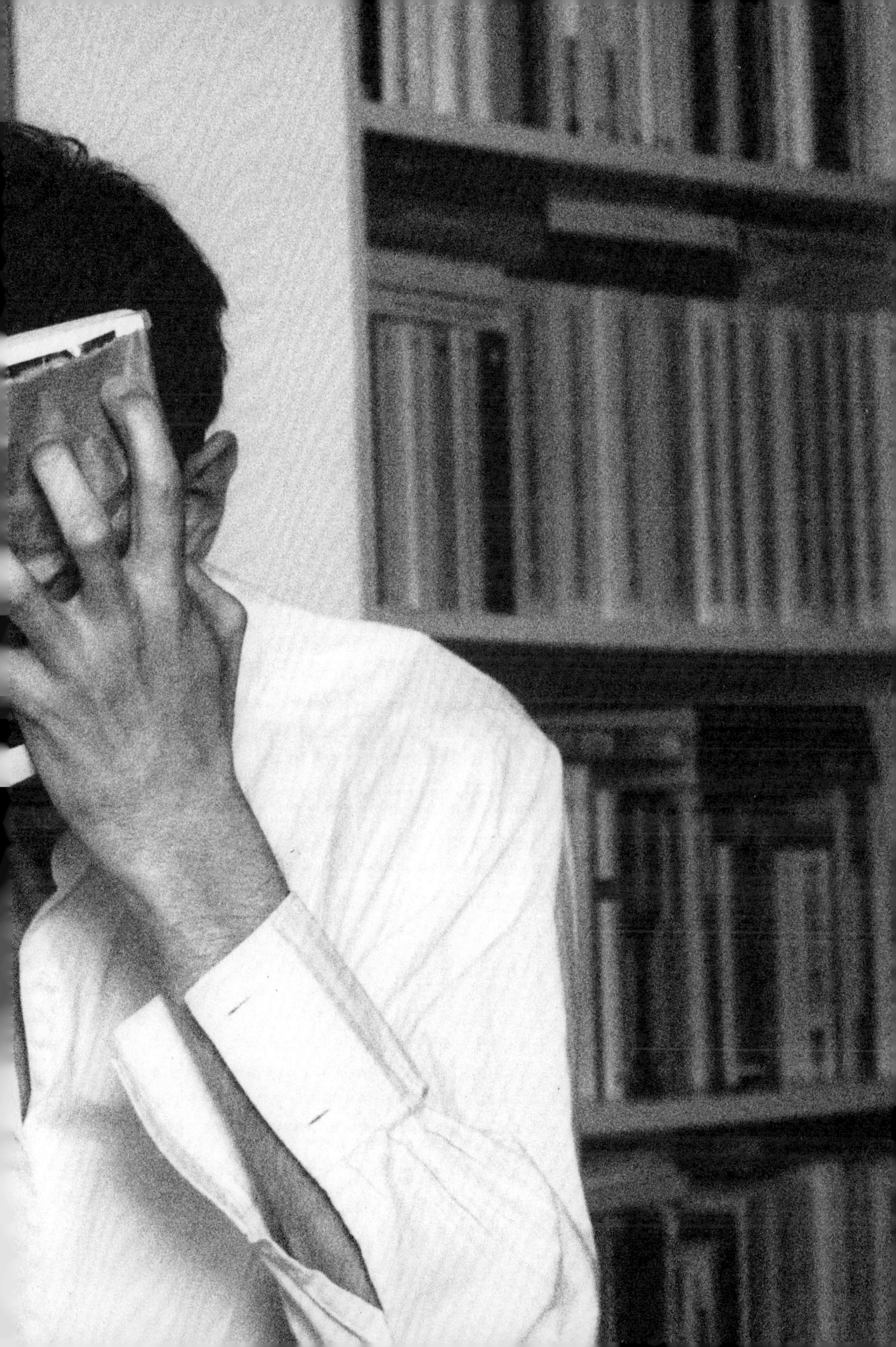

Envy is an emotion; a very special, significant one. Emotions pertain to the private domain, or so they say. Any strong emotion from my past I can evoke here would sound banal; we all have such emotional moments, between calm and hysterical fits; between indifference and strongly falling in love; between happiness and anxiety; between friendliness and anger. What is less well-known is the odd mixture of professionalism and emotion on the work floor, and within the limits of my knowledge, especially in the academy—that hornets' nest of ambitions crossing swords. Even if the so-called neoliberal regime had not already practically destroyed universities around the world, the remaining hard-working people whose intellectual curiosity is their primary drive, can sometimes be hard-hit by the way jealousy can morph into envy.

We all know, experience, and feel jealousy in life, whether we like it or not, either accept and acknowledge it, or repress it. Jealousy is an understandable emotion that emerges when someone else has what we don't: beauty, success, money to spare, love, a beautiful home, and what have you. Jealousy makes us want to have what they have. But envy is a different emotion. Envy is not desiring to acquire but to destroy. The mentality that makes people not just craving to have it, too, but to be so angry of the ones who have it that they want to demolish those others. I have, sadly, been the target of envy in my professional life, in ways that have made clear to me what the difference between these two emotions is. Envy can become superimposed on, or merge with, political or intellectual disagreement, but it can also be 'pure', when the envious person simply cannot bear to see a colleague do or be well.

A HEADACHE

In the early years of primary school, I had a classmate, a friend, called Lucy. We were sitting next to each other in class. She had thin, straight dark hair. I had a head full of silvery curls. I hated the curls; they hurt when my mother insisted on combing them, and they made me stand out, a difference I did not like. I was quite jealous of Lucy's easy coiffure. Combing did not hurt her. But as it turned out, she was jealous of my curls, and liked the very blond colour of my hair. Lucy came from a wealthier family than ours was. She often brought candy to school, and was practically constantly chewing gum, while I only got 'school milk', which tasted horribly. I was jealous of her endless supply of candy and chewing gum, too. I regularly asked her to give me some gum but she always refused. I never understood why; she had her pockets full of it. Then, one day, she was irritated by my asking. She took the fully chewed wad out of her mouth and stuck it firmly onto my head, sticking it onto the curls. It took me a while to understand what she was doing. Then the teacher came in and the lesson began. I forgot about the gum in my hair.

Until I came home. My mother saw it, and was horrified. She tried to wash it out, but failed. It had hardened, cementing my curls to the skin of my head. Then Mother did the only possible thing: she took a pair of scissors and cut the locks that were glued together. It took some time, for the gum was entangled through a large patch of my head. It also hurt terribly. When I looked in the mirror, it was my turn to be horrified. A patch of several square inches of my head was basically bold, as if I had just had surgery. What a headache! Appalled, I realized what Lucy had done, what her goal had been. She had not simply been annoyed by my begging for chewing gum. She had wanted to destroy what she—not me—considered my beauty asset: my blond curls. And she had succeeded. It took weeks, if not months, for the hair to grow back. And all that time I had to explain to people who asked if I was ill, or what else was the matter with my head, not daring to mention the aggression in her act. I was never bold (or angry) enough to betray Lucy. Instead, I came up with lame excuses that no one really believed. The reason I never came forward about her hostility was that I understood that she was not just jealous, but envious. Without knowing the word, I learned its meaning, and felt the danger in it.

INTELLECTUAL OWNERSHIP

I have had to confront envy quite often in my professional life. After my studies, I began working. First as a high school teacher. For more or less arbitrary reasons I had studied French, specializing in narrative literature. A few years later I managed, not without difficulty, to secure a job at a university. I ended up in a relatively small department of Comparative Literature. We were about seven faculty members. At the time, we had regular meetings, where we discussed the teaching programme, our publication achievements, and also, invitations abroad. For these we needed to obtain the agreement of the entire department. During the years that I was the youngest department member, I struggled with the jealousy of my colleagues. I was somewhat more prolific than most. One year, the annual report was embarrassing. On a total of twelve publications, six were mine, the other six by the rest of the department. Unforgivable, especially since I was the only woman, apart from an older one about to retire. That's where the trouble began. I became the target of painful gestures of envy, taking all kinds of shapes.

One colleague openly began to protest that I should spend more time cooking and doing other household chores. I did not belong in a faculty. I just laughed it off. This colleague also began to leave semi-pornographic cartoons in my mailbox. I recognized the typeface of his typewriter. I shrugged this off, too; just despised him for it. But then, one day, another colleague showed his envious hand. I received an invitation to China, for a lecture tour. I was quite excited. It would be for two weeks, and my then-partner was willing to take his turn in childcare. But when I brought it up in the department meeting, in order to secure the colleagues' permission, one of these, who had done a stint of diplomacy in China before earning his PhD, almost screamed: 'No! China is mine!'

This is a literal quote; I'll never forget it, coming out of his mouth, distorted by anger. My jaw dropped. The others looked embarrassed, studying their nails. The chair decided a written vote was called for. But when it came to it, the unanimous result was 'no'. I could not go. This was one of those moments that the noun 'envy' acquired its sharp, destructive actuality. What did anyone have to lose if I went off for two weeks, making sure I would catch up with the missed classes? Of course, the classes where not the issue; no one cared. But without a doubt, they already dreaded the next annual report of our output. The year after, I omitted some publications from my list. It seemed to help a bit; no screaming matches this time. But the cordiality was lukewarm.

As feminism became stronger in my awareness, small incidents irritated me, but nothing was really dramatic. For some time, I got along quite well with a colleague in a different department, French, where I sometimes did substitutions. This man had small children and was very excited about them. But no one was interested. He just counted on me, given my gender. So, every time we met, he began the conversation talking about children, asking about mine, boasting about his. This became a kind of secret conversation no one else participated in. At some point I got fed up with it. Why would I always, and only, talk about children? Stupidly and tactlessly, I said so. He turned around, and we never spoke again. I suppose the friendliness was halted by his insight that I did have a point. Retrospectively, I consider his obsessive talking about (mostly his) children a way of keeping me out of the intellectual discussion; of diminishing my interest in front of the others. I was the woman with a family. Not really an intellectual. Was this behaviour fed by envy? I am not sure, I cannot tell, but it did bother me.

ENVYING SIMILARITY

An area in the current regime where envy gets to roam freely is the so-called 'peer review system'. Since reviews are anonymous, this solicits the two sides of the ills that compelled the creation of the system: what is called the 'Old-Boys network', where approval is based on friendship and other forms of closeness; and the intolerance of dissenting views. The author whose article or book is negatively reviewed will not know who caused the rejection of the manuscript; hence, nastiness remains unnoticed and unpunished. When the argumentation is elaborate enough, an author gets the opportunity to contradict the review. But disingenuous intellectual arguments can hide such simple emotions as envy: rationalizing, justifying, defending, all academic qualities, can obscure for the scholar their own emotions. The rejection is not even based on disagreement—problematic but understandable, and contradictable when well-argued—but on not bearing the productivity, success, or even opportunity to get a promotion or a better job, of someone else. This can extend to strife between the reviewer and the candidate-victim's sponsor or supervisor. Well-meant originally, the system is deeply unfair in practice.[13]

I have witnessed as well as been targeted by the destructive role of envy in that anonymity, which demonstrates that envy tends to come in, in a merger with other emotions and concerns. One day I was asked by a friendly acquisition editor with whom I had published with great pleasure, to review a book manuscript. I accepted, and although I wasn't too thrilled by it, I thought of it as publishable, so I recommended it. The book had an experimental side to it; what we now call inter-disciplinarity. It didn't do much with it, but at least there was something. And clearly, the editor liked it, or/and the author, and I liked the editor. I know these are the wrong reasons—precisely the reasons the system had been invented to counter. But if, even without knowing the author, and being un-thrilled by the book, I felt compelled to recommend it, I knew there was something wrong with the system as such. I knew myself as incorruptible, and yet, this came too close to corruption for comfort.

It got a lot worse. When, sometime later, I submitted a book to the same press, hence, through the same editor, it made sense that she would ask that author to review mine, trusting he would be positive. I never knew for sure, factually, that it was him, but to this day I am convinced it was. For one, his field and mine, although not identical, were congenial enough to trust he would be sufficiently knowledgeable to be expected to make

---

13 See my article 'Abolish the Peer Review System' (2018) in which I critique this system, which was immediately translated and published into Italian. Clearly, I am not the only opponent.

a fair assessment. No one else came close, as close as he and I seemed to be. Already before the review process got started the editor wrote to me that she loved the book, 'every word of it'. So, I thought I had nothing to worry about. Little did she know that envy, competitiveness, and even total hatred of those who dare do something a little too similar to what you did, would overrule both her sense of expertise and of fairness. Neither did I know how far envy would carry. When I saw his review, I immediately got it, an insight nourished by my experience with my classmate-friend Lucy and her use of chewing gum as a weapon.

How do I know it was this same 'peer' who had reviewed my manuscript? Because I had read his book, I recognized some of the arguments he brought up against mine, enough to identify who he was, in spite of the anonymous procedure. To say he trashed it is an understatement. He completely destroyed it. And due to the congenial interdisciplinarity between his book and my manuscript, the editor had no other choice than to believe him, and reject, or at least suspend publication of my book. I could not and did not blame her for this disaster; it was the system, qua system, and how it promoted the emergence of—yes: envy. I swallowed my pride and anger, and did an obedient revision, as much as I could without betraying my own thoughts. Still not good enough. Three rounds were necessary. It took a year, almost, until he grumpily accepted it was good enough. By then, I had almost finished the next book, and asked the editor if the same delay would hold up that next one. The editor said she could not do anything against the 'peer-review system'. At that point, feeling disconsolate enough, I had already found another publisher. To this day I regret the loss of regular contact with that brilliant and lovely editor. But I remain astounded by the destructive role of envy in this process.

Of course, as usual in this system, a second 'peer' had been asked to review my manuscript. That could have saved me, had it been as jubilantly positive as it could and should have been. Again, I could guess who it was. This time, I was more deeply devastated. For this reviewer was a friend—a personal, close friend. This is why, I surmise, she didn't dare write it down, knowing I would recognize her arguments, style, and wording. She just called the editor on the phone, who then wrote to me telling more or less what the reviewer had said. She had trashed it in the most condescending terms—'not ready', 'immature'. Nothing more specific than that. This double trashing had a huge impact on the rest of my publishing history. Two people who could and should have at least read the manuscript with a constructively critical mindset, for different reasons, both tried to destroy it/me, because I came too close to what they did. Only one conclusion was possible. The peer-review system breeds envy as the motor of academic life.

This experience had a huge impact on my sense of self as an academic. They envied, I speculated, my ease with boundary-crossing, my ingrained interdisciplinary mindset. The woman I considered a friend, and whose work I admire immensely, declined to write a report—most likely, she feared I would be able to guess who she was, which I did anyway. This moment, also and even more than the previous one done by that guy I didn't particularly care for, changed my life.

ENVY AS THREATENING

Let me end this reminiscence with an earlier experience—something between the primary school one and the publishing disaster. When I had written and defended my PhD thesis, I got invited to participate in a discussion of, as it turned out, several PhD theses/books on a similar topic: narrative theory, or as we began to call it, 'Narratology'. This term ended up as the title of my book. I read the most directly competing book. Never mind what I thought of it. It is hardly surprising that I considered mine better, more systematic, and more convincing than his. But I barely knew the author and had no grudge against him. When the discussion afternoon came, I had a spontaneous flash: knowing that I had developed a good skill in replying to criticism, I asked the chair to be allowed to speak last; not to 'have the last word' but to be able to defend myself against the attacks I was expecting. This was one of my best intuitions. It was just an intellectual debate. I knew I would have to defend myself against a more traditional view of the field. I also knew I could do it.

Things proceeded as I expected. My colleague/rival spent his speaking time, not arguing for what was best about his own theory, but trashing mine. I immediately knew this was to his detriment. This was a great opportunity for me. I had an easy time refuting his arguments, and the right to speak last helped a lot. So far, there is nothing in this account that would bring up 'envy'. I just went home happy that I had been able to swing the debate in my direction. However, little did I know at that time that envy is unforgiving to the point it turned out to be. This colleague was going to take a nasty revenge. And he did; in a way I considered and still consider as being on the verge of criminal.

This was his revenge. Sometime later—perhaps a year or two, I can't date the event—both he and I were participating in a conference abroad. For three days we were politely nodding to each other and avoiding to talk. He gave his lecture, I gave mine. All seemed quiet at the horizon. Until I left, a bit before the end of the conference. Then, when I had the train to catch in the evening, something happened that gave the word 'envy' additional, threatening weight. I walked to the station. At the front, there was too much traffic, so I went to the back of the station. And here he was, with some mates, ready to pounce. I have seldomly been so scared in my life. He was shouting, screaming, and running after me, like an ordinary thug. What had I done wrong, other than being intellectually right when he was wrong? Why is it so important to win or lose a debate? My conclusion is clear. Envy can breed violence. Out of breath, I made it into the train, which left on time. Safe.

Friendship

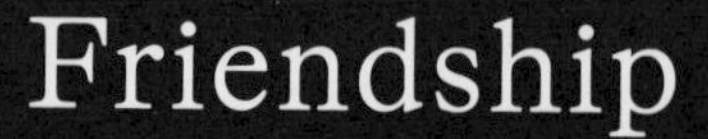

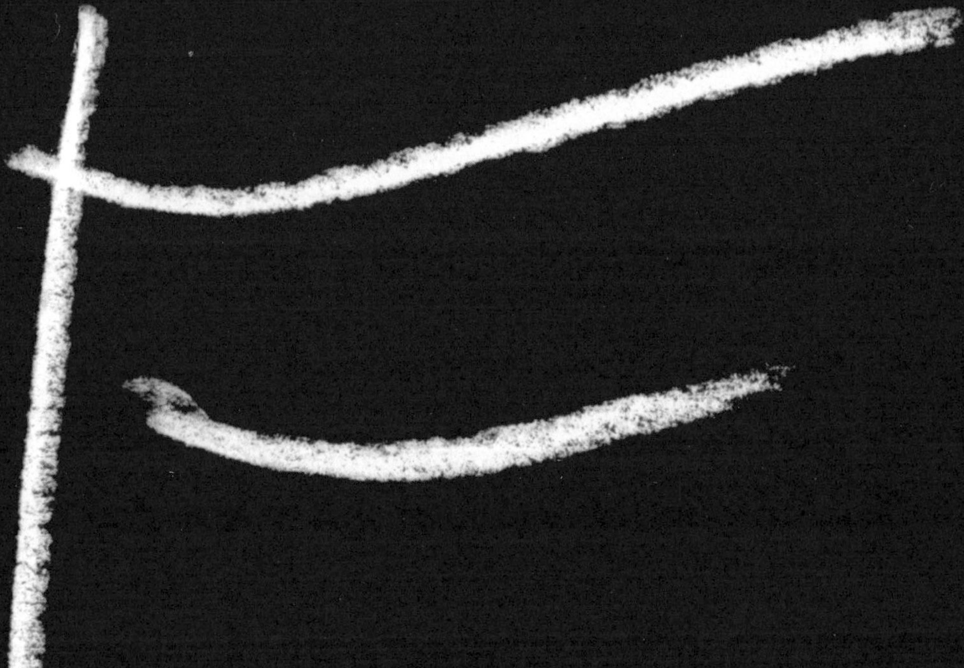

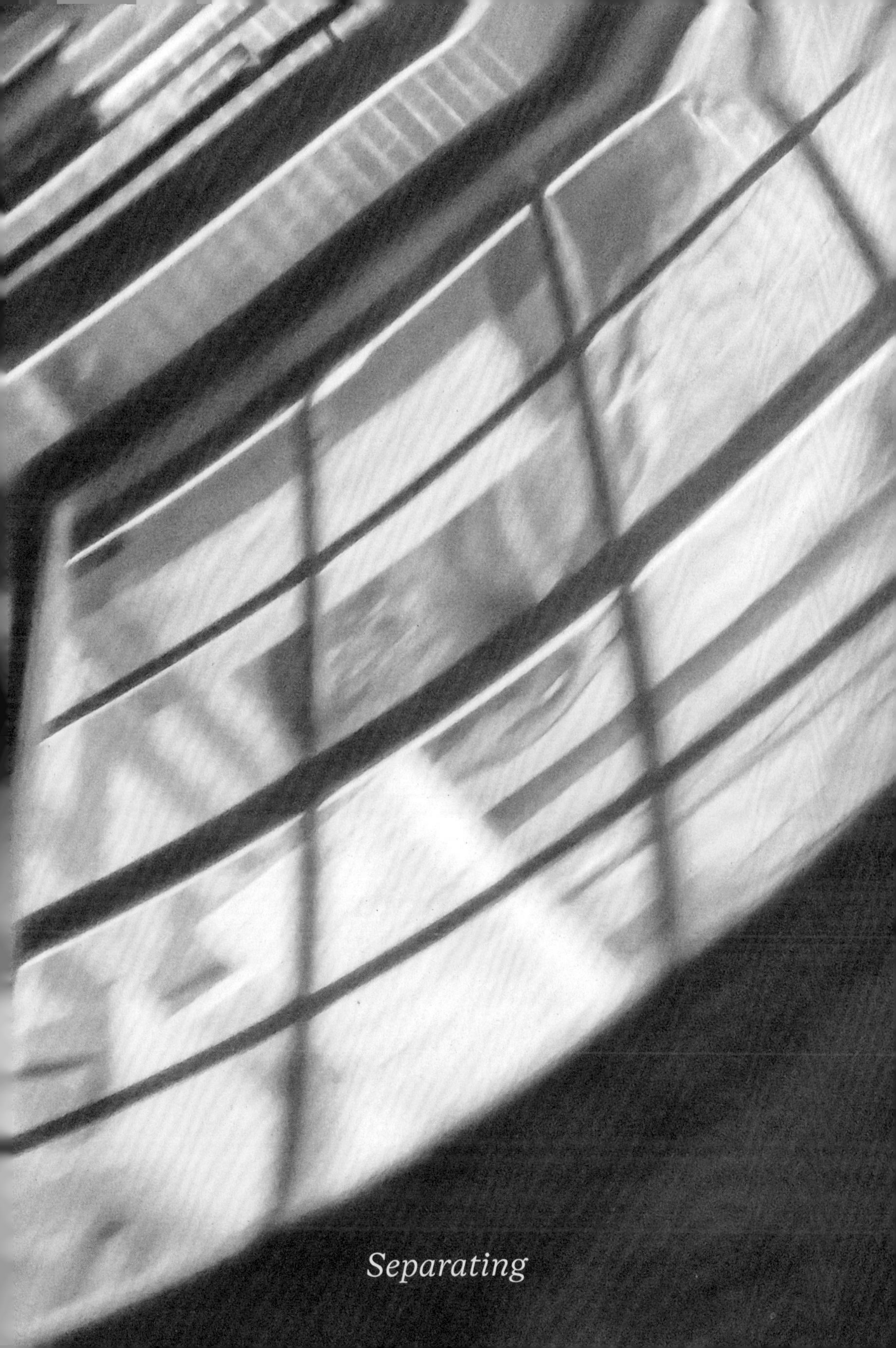

Separating

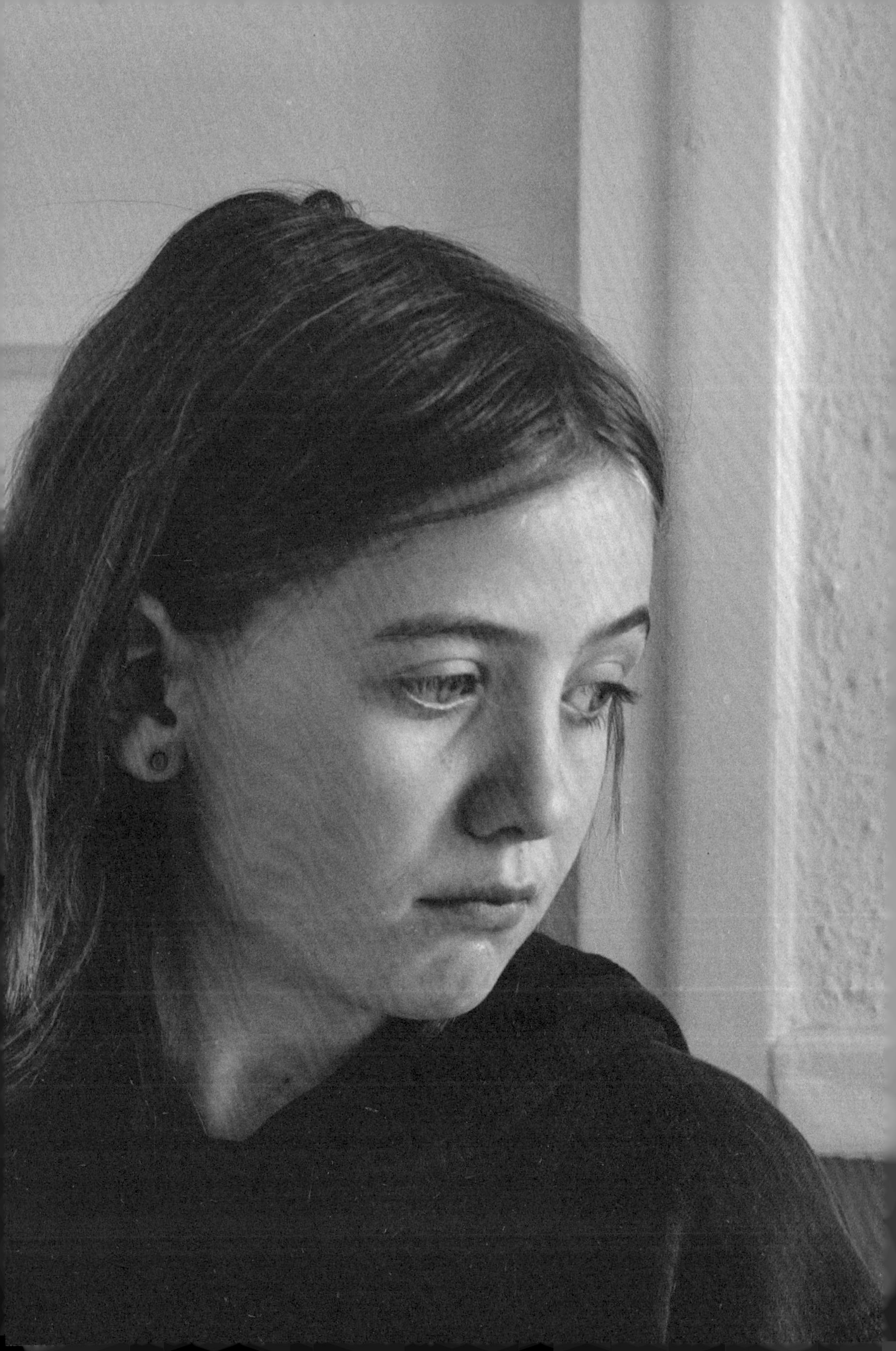

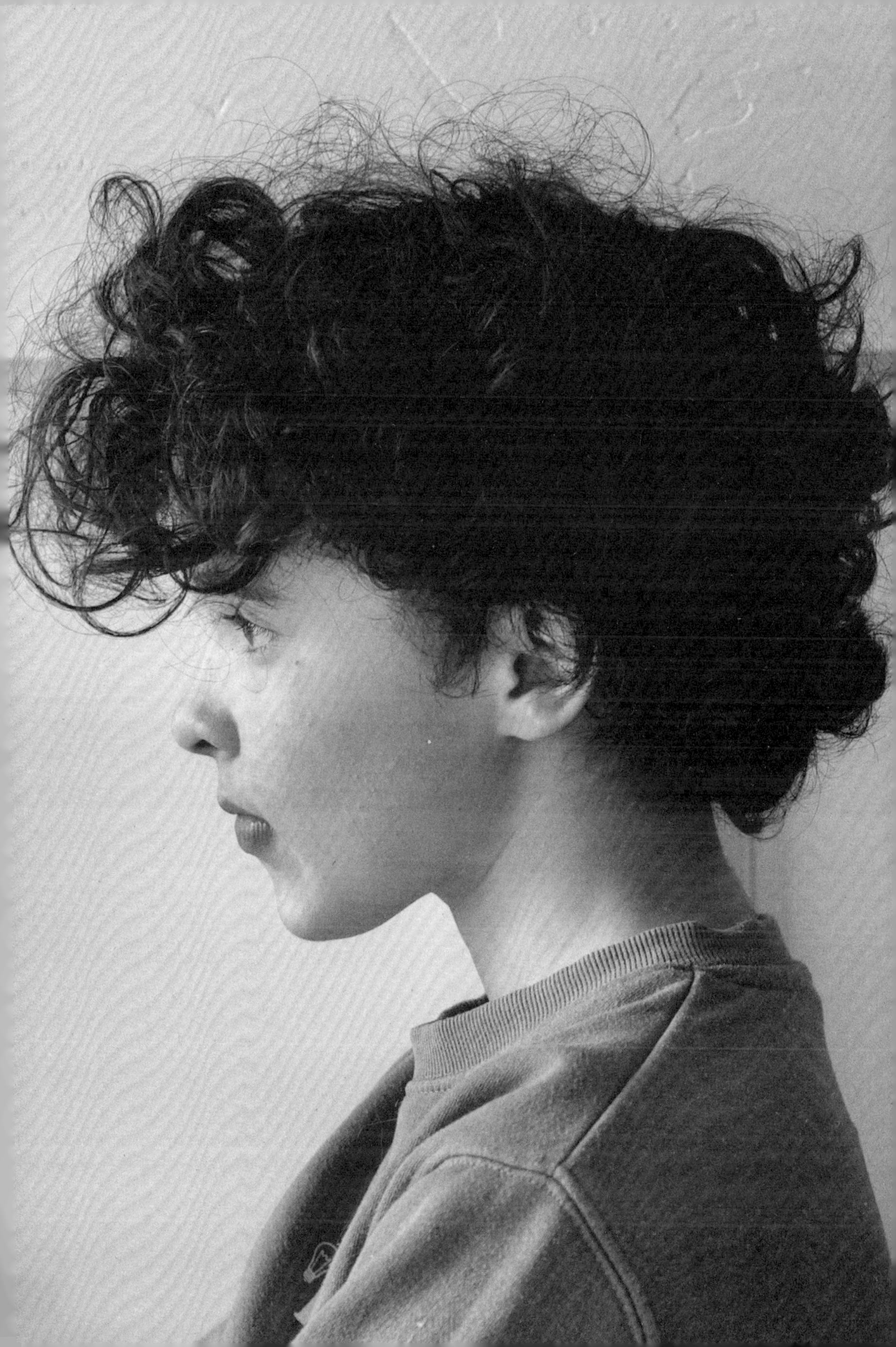

When I think back to my childhood friendships, all I can remember is their coincidental emergence and disappearance. I would befriend the girl sitting next to me in the classroom; or the nearest child in the neighbourhood where we lived; the cousins we visited with our parents; the children of my parents' friends. I cannot remember any other beginning of friendship. But only when a friendship was lost did it became clear that this was, had been, a friendship. Losing a friend was dramatic. Once, I lost a friend of several years—having been sitting next to each other in class for years. Her name was Marion. We soon visited each other's homes. She had a twin sister, in another class, and I befriended her as well, although never as intensively. The difference was subtle. It had nothing to do with liking one better than the other; just, I assumed, with the frequency of seeing each other. In the early years of high school, during breaks Marion and I would simply walk rounds together in the schoolyard, and talk.

But the dramatic turn-around that happened was when she had to double a class. She stayed in fourth grade. It became a bit more difficult to see each other. And then one day she said: we cannot be friends anymore. True, I had also felt a bit of distancing between us. Nevertheless, I was devastated. I even cycled the twenty or so miles to see a friend of my parents who was a parish priest in a village. My mother tended to consult him when she had problems (she always did) and spoke highly of his wisdom, his insight in the psyche. So, I went, pretended to want to confess, and in the confessional, I burst out in tears. I asked him how to persuade my friend to stay friends. He gave me some advice, I don't remember what exactly, but it did comfort me to think that there was an attempt I could make. It didn't work, not really, but by then I was more or less over my grief.

This moment of mourning was, I think, the beginning of my feeling, my experience, of what friendship is, beyond playing with other children, which was the socializing of my earliest years. Much, much later I began to reflect on it; on the value of friendship. By then, Marion and I had completely lost sight of each other. This reflecting began when I took seriously, literally, and concretely, the personifying metaphor that ancient philosophers invoked as a figure for philosophy itself. Here, my thinking came close to wondering where all this hanging out, talking, discussing may possibly end up. Having meanwhile become a teacher, and feeling passionately about the teacher-student relationship, my everyday life contained a measure of what I kept considering as friendship. This was not bound to friends I knew, but to the sense of the work in which I was involved. Perhaps it was time to decide who these students were, and what a (future) teacher was. This is where friendship became a concept, a metaphor, for the integration of my professional and social life.

Deleuze and Guattari invoke a conceptual persona (*personnage conceptuel*) from Greek philosophy: the teacher. In the face of *that* tradition, I end on a figure of the teacher that is both a traditionalist and a theatrical gesture. In philosophy, this figure is usually the lover. We know how this metaphoric conception of the teacher-student relationship was exclusively something among men and boys, and often has led to abusive situations. None of that could have anything to do with me. In her book *What Can She Know? Feminist Epistemology and the Construction of Knowledge*, the Canadian philosopher Lorraine Code takes this tradition up and turns it around. For Code, the concept-metaphor that best embodies her ideal is the friend, not the lover. That distinction became the motor of my thinking. The conceptual persona of the friend—the model of friendship—is not embedded in a definition of philosophy but of knowledge. This suits me very well; I am not a philosopher. My professional self-definition, now, is as a 'cultural analyst', but before that, I considered literature, and the theory of it, as my field. I specialized in narrative and its theory—narratology.[14]

---

14 Code's crucial book, to which I will return, is *What Can She Know?* (1991).

But with an in-born tendency to be always curious of
what lies around the corner, I had very early on begun to also
consider narrativity in other texts, such as journalistic ones, and
other media, such as painting. The definition of friendship as a
pathway to knowledge is necessarily one that takes knowledge
as provisional. If the authority of the author/artist, as well
as that of the teacher, is unfixed, then the place it vacates
can be occupied by *theory*. The literary theorist Paul de Man
(1919–1983) defined theory long ago as 'a controlled reflection
on the formation of method'. The teacher, then, no longer holds
the authority to dictate the method; her task is to facilitate a
reflection—both individual and collective—that is ongoing, and
necessarily interactive. Method is and remains in formation—it
is never finished. Knowledge is knowing that reflection cannot
be terminated, as both Sigmund Freud and the Yale-based literary scholar Shoshana Felman (1942) have asserted. Moreover,
to use Felman's super-useful phrase, knowledge is not to learn
something *about* but to learn something *from*. Knowledge, not
as a substance or content out there waiting to be appropriated
but as a 'how-to' aspect, bears on such learning *from* the
practice of interdisciplinary cultural analysis. Again much later,
when I began for various reasons to make video art, I learned
that what matters is to learn from art what matters in it.[15]

FRIENDSHIP VS LOVE: LEARNING

Within the framework of Felman's description of teaching
as facilitating the *condition* of knowledge, Code's apparently
small shift from lover to friend is, at least provisionally, a way
out of the philosophy/humanities misfit. If I now have had the
privilege to first publish these reflections on meaning-making
in a philosophical journal, the title of which evokes friendship
(philo-) and women (SOFIA), it must be due to that overcoming
of what, before, I had never been able to reconcile. Friendship
is a paradigm for knowledge production, the traditional task

15 Paul de Man's book, *The Resistance to Theory*, that opens with this phrase
was published posthumously in 1986. Of Felman's many important publications,
I refer here specifically to two articles; 'To Open the Question' (1977) and
'Psychoanalysis and Education' (1982).

of the humanities, but then production as an interminable
process, not as preface to a product. Code lists the features
of friendship, as opposed to the lover's passion, as productive
analogies for knowledge production. I have cited her list many
times, and each time it inspires new thoughts. In the context of
the present reflection, it helps me understand, retrospectively,
what friendship is, or what it means.

First of all, such knowledge is not achieved at once, but
rather, it develops. For knowledge, this is quite obvious, as I
write under K. But reversing the analogy, I had never realized
that friendship, too, although sometimes emerging in a flash—
like falling in love 'at first sight', an idea that has always seemed
quite mythical to me—develops slowly. Each time we walked and
talked, Marion and I were, unknowingly, involved in developing
the intimacy of friendship. This also raised the question of what
the friendship is, what we know of each other, what we like more
or like less about the other person. For, as distinct from passion,
friendship is open to interpretation at different levels. It is not
something I constantly thought of, or named. 'This is my best
friend' was not something I would say, or even think. It was
simply a matter of course.

As long as it lasts, you barely dare question the totality of a
love relationship. In contrast, friendship admits degrees, without leading to a relativizing awareness. It is not something you
think about. Irritations, suspicions, boredom, even contempt,
are as easily absorbed in friendship as excitement, compassion,
and esteem. It changes all the time, and those changes are not
even worth thinking about. It is part of friendship's nature. But
what really matters most, and distinguishes friendship from
passion, is the horizontality of the relationship. This is what
the peer review system was meant to nurture (peerage) but so
utterly failed to accomplish. And what the word 'colleague' as
co- (together) in the same -league, falsely suggests. This is, also,
how friendship and knowledge are analogous, as the subject
and object positions in the process of knowledge construction
are reversible. This was an insight the experience of teaching
made clear to me. The student was an equal, regardless of the

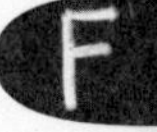

discrepancy in age, experience, and years of learning.

The excitement of teaching is in the learning, on both sides. 'If you don't learn from your students, you are a bad teacher': this is a slogan I came up with, and firmly believe in. Since it is a never-accomplished constant process, the 'more-or-lessness' of the knowledge affirms the need to reserve and revise judgement. This is why you keep learning, always, from the interaction with students, with friends, with others, and also with objects. As a consequence, what we call objects, such as artworks, texts, films, are never objects in the sense of being objectifiable. They are not mute things. They become subjects, speaking back to us. Another of my academic slogans is: 'The object always speaks back.' If you allow it, if you listen to it, as it is becoming between friends. This analysis of friendship and/as knowledge production helps to distinguish between philosophy in the narrow sense, as a discipline or potential inter-discipline, and the humanities as a more general field, 'rhizomatically' organized according to a dynamic interdisciplinary *practice*.[16]

Philosophy creates, analyzes, and offers concepts. Analysis, in pursuing its goal—which is to articulate the best (most effective, reliable, useful) way to do, to perform, the pursuit of knowledge—puts them together with potential objects that we wish to get to know. Disciplines use these ways of doing analysis called methods, apply and deploy them, in interaction with an object, in the pursuit of specialized knowledge. But, in the best of situations, this division of tasks does not imply a rigid division of people or groups of people along the lines of disciplines or departments. For such a division deprives all participants of the key to a genuine practice of cultural analysis: a sensitivity to the provisional nature of concepts considered as friends. Without claiming to know it all, each participant learns to move about, between these areas of activity. In our everyday practice of teaching, learning, interacting, unwittingly we constantly negotiate these differences.

16 For the concept of 'rhizome' and the adverb I derive from it here, see Deleuze and Guattari, *Rhizome* (1976).

FRIENDSHIP AS READING, WITH CRITICAL INTIMACY

The fundamental equality of friendship does not mean similarity. Friends must be different enough to remain what is called, with a rather empty, meaningless word, 'interesting'. This word, interestingly, has two very different, meanings, as I discovered, also a bit late in life. These meanings are even opposed, according to their contexts. To take an interest is, let's say, the opposite of indifference. Between friends, it is a given that they take an interest in each other. But in the sense derived from the German, it comes closer to the financial term 'interest'. Then, it has to do with self-interest, with the expectancy of financial gain. This is radically opposite to friendship. You don't become friends as an investment.

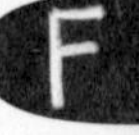

This is a good lesson for learning, which happens a bit between these two meanings. You learn better when you are interested in the material; when you find it 'interesting'. That is also why learning is exciting, fun. But you also decide to learn, or our parents compel us to, as an investment in your future. That may be less fun, but is considered useful. The best of the two worlds is when both meanings are valid. Sometimes, they waver. You pick up a book, because of the title or subject matter appeals to you, but then it becomes hard to read; you feel you don't understand it well enough. What is lacking, then, is the analogue of friendship; instead, you feel repulsed. True, readability is an irritating but indispensable concept. In the contact with cultural artifacts, one is frequently confronted with the question of readability, and with the doubt as to how to impute unreadability. Is it one's own lack of fluency with another field, or is the writer at fault? I have often found myself too stupid, or insufficiently prepared, to read something. But I have also found reviewers totally impatient and un-understanding, trashing a book simply because they, the reviewers, failed to understand it. It is not easy to acknowledge publicly that one finds a particular reading difficult, so it is easier to attribute the difficulty to the object. However, for a teacher, something important can be gained if one challenges a convention born out of intimidation.

Reading is a practice of intimacy, not of love or passion, nor of hatred or irritation. It is an activity in which friendship is the motor of response. The same with looking, which is a two-way act. I have attempted to foreground that mutuality in my video installations. And this is where the model of friendship becomes key. Friends, more easily than lovers, can be critical of each other. Rather than taking offense when you are being criticized, you can be grateful, appreciative of the trouble and the risk your friend takes to explain to you where and how you are wrong, so that you can learn from the criticism without losing the friendship. The trust between friends is crucial for this. No two friendships are identical. But all are forms of what Gayatri Spivak called in her discussion of the ideas of Kant, 'critical intimacy'. Let me be clear here. What is unreadable should not be read; it is a waste of time and effort. In contrast, what is difficult may be worth exploring, in order to understand what kind of readability is involved in reading it. Degree and mode of readability are not unrelated, but they are discontinuous. Friendship is like that, too. This is why the loss of Marion's friendship, painful as it was back then, was not a tragedy. Neither she nor I became different persons. And we both developed other friendships, with different modes of critical intimacy.[17]

One trusts a friend. When you have a good friend, it is in your interest not to lose them. You discuss what appears painful, or problematic. You are eager to hear an explanation that makes the problematic element more acceptable. Or not; you can forgive a slip. Why would you do that? Because—and this is the important pedagogical moment—once the problem is explained as fully as possible, you can recognize in yourself similar sentiments, or slips. This is the moment when critical intimacy teaches. You learn. For learning is always, also, learning something about yourself and the *hic-et-nunc* in which you live.

---

17 'Critical Intimacy' is the title and central topic of a chapter (I think the final one) of Gayatri Spivak's very important and brilliant book *A Critique of Postcolonial Reason* (1999). I devoted the final chapter of my book *Travelling Concepts* (2002) to this crucial concept.

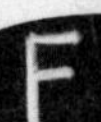

Generosity

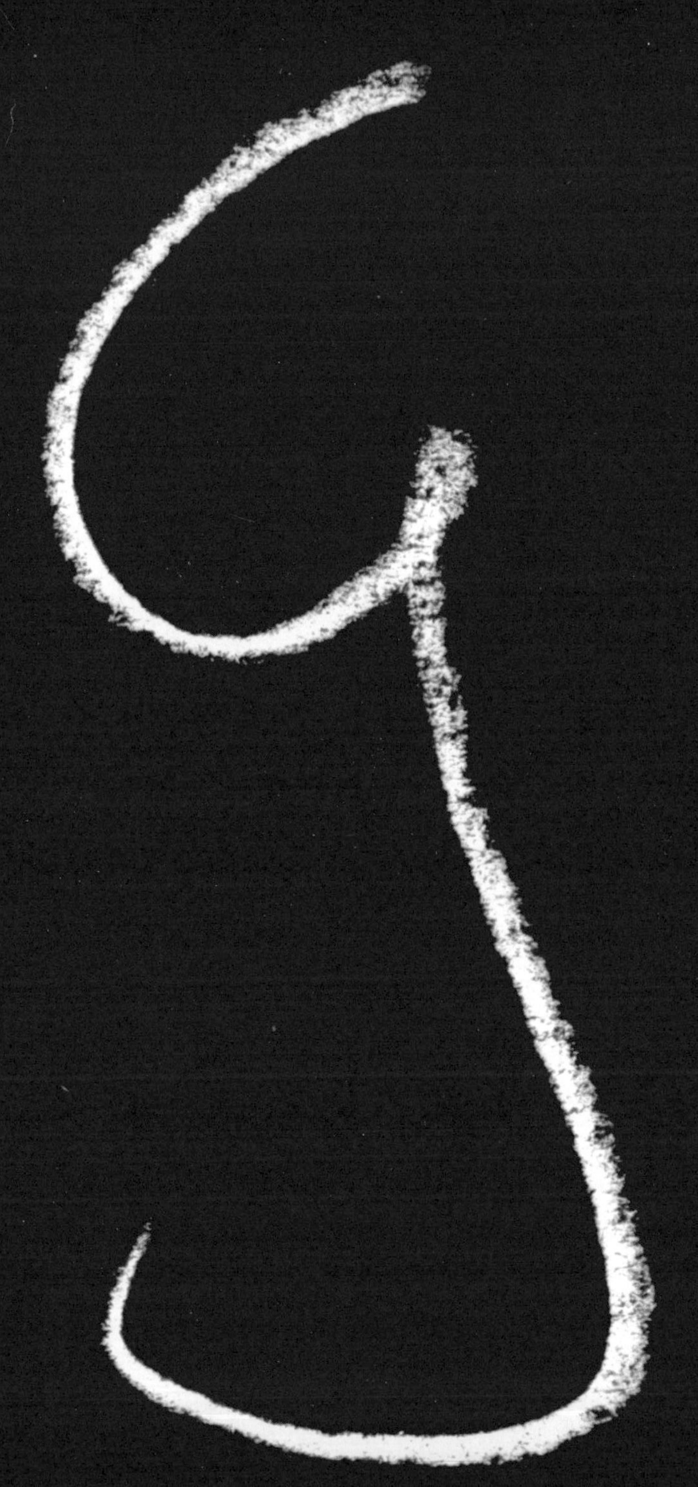

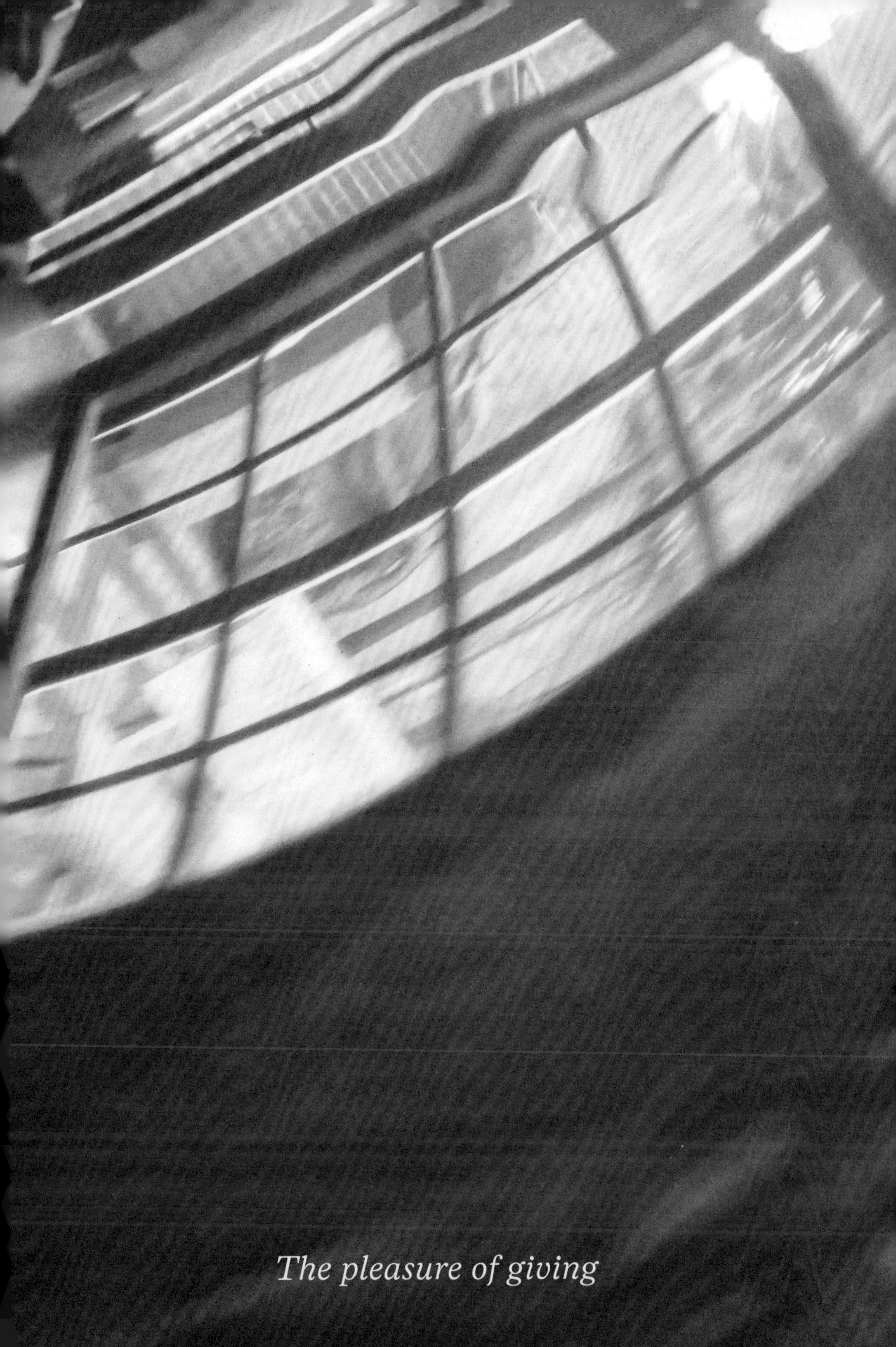

The pleasure of giving

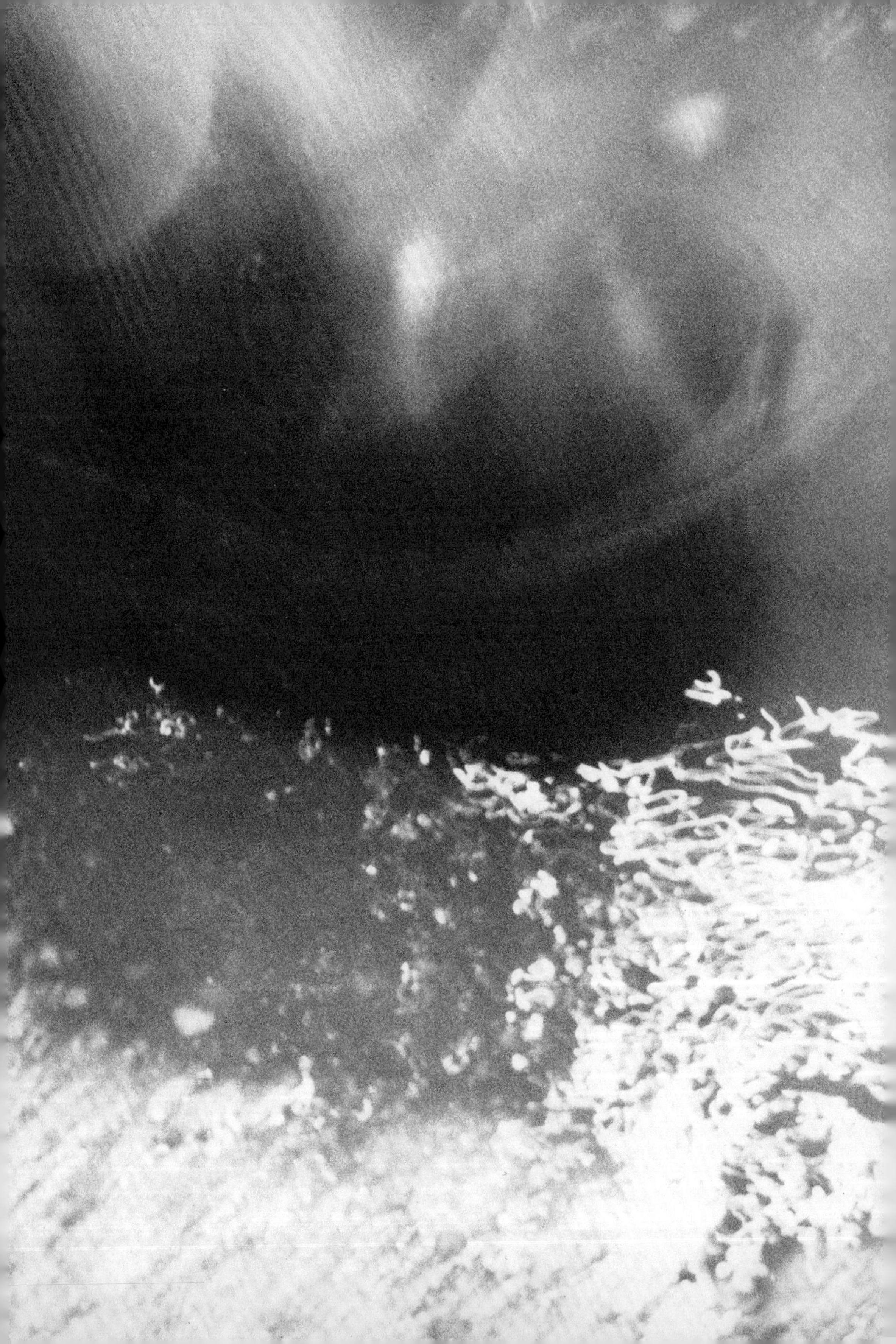

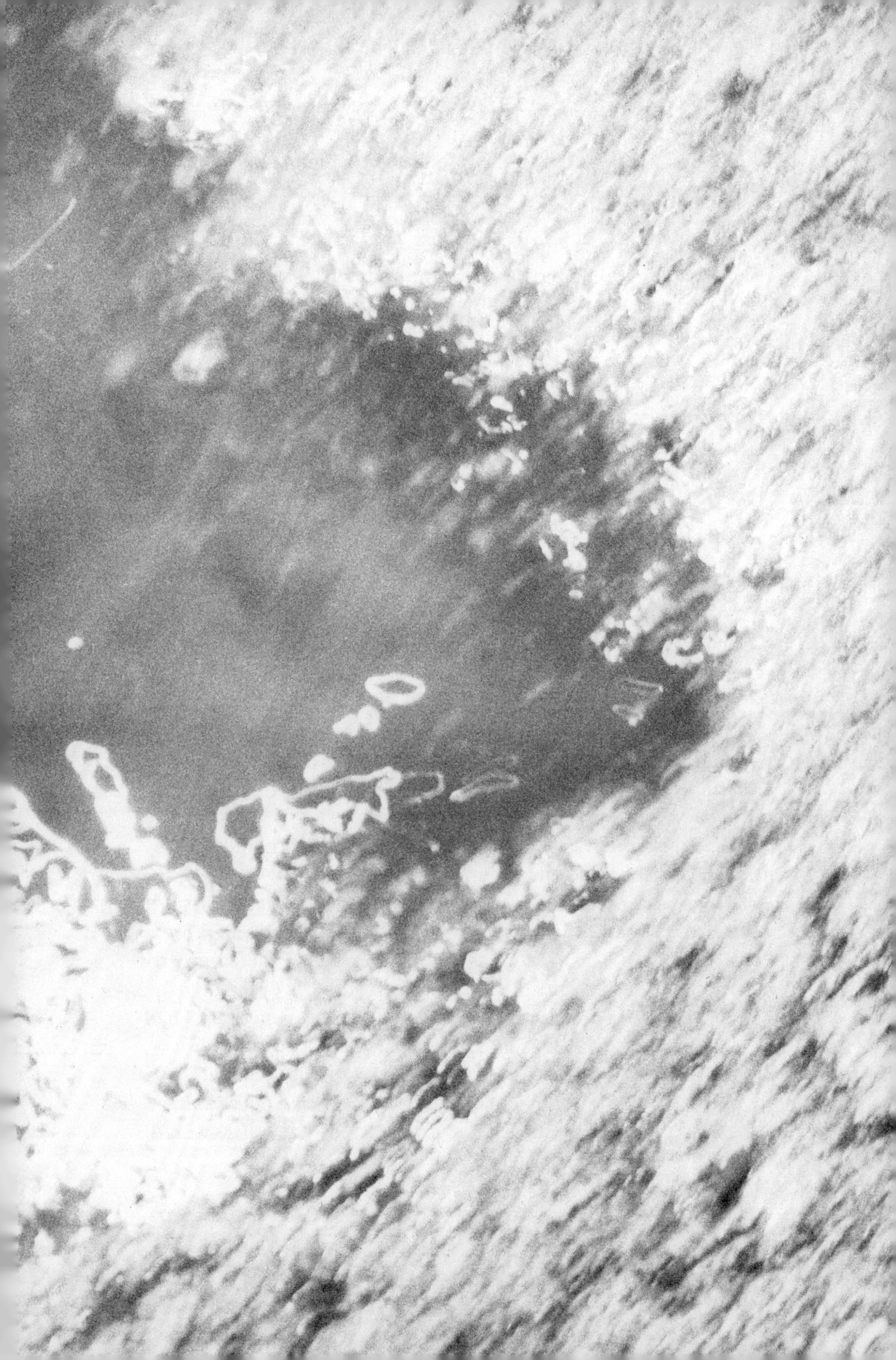

Here is a word that I had probably heard but never bothered to understand. Until, in the first year of high school, a teacher whose name and discipline I don't even remember, devoted a class to the question of values. He began by asking each of us to state and explain to our neighbour in class what we considered the most important value. This was his way of making us reflect on, and understand the importance of such an idea, or concept, as a 'value'. Even that word had little specific meaning to me. Just something positive, abstract, and general. The girl sitting next to me, called Yvonne, seemed quite excited about the assignment. She proposed we should each write our value down, then explain to each other why it was important. Writing it down would help to stick to our guns. I chose 'honesty', she chose 'generosity'. My turn to explain it was first.

I wasn't sure which of the two meanings of the word 'honesty', sincerity as the opposite of lying, or decency, I had in mind. I soon discovered that it was precisely the ambiguity of the word that appealed to me. This is a tendency that has stayed with me: a keen interest, even excitement, not in lack of clarity as in vagueness, but in multiple possibilities words can harbour. So, Yvonne and I discussed the potential and implications of honesty at some length. To my satisfaction, I began to see how the two meanings are related. To put it simply: to tell the truth is decent behaviour. Lying is at the detriment of the other, and therefore, not polite, not respectful. I had learned something, and was very happy about that.

But more was to come. Yvonne, with a big, friendly smile, said that we could add a third meaning of honesty: to speak up, speak your mind, express your opinions, even at the risk of disapproval by others. My heart flipped. This was something that tended to be my supposedly worst behavioural feature: to speak up. My parents often found me stubborn, even conceited. Suddenly, this bad feature became not simply something I had the right to, as I had seen it until then, but part of my most cherished value. If I didn't speak up, I would be dishonest, secretive. I felt so grateful to Yvonne. From now on, with her blessing, I could speak up freely, no matter what others would think. This value stayed with me all my life.

When it was her turn, I said, blushing, that I had no clue what her value word meant. Instead of laughing at me, she smiled again, and this time, too, it didn't feel offensive. On the contrary: the warmth of her smile was a gift. She bent over her bag, and took out a bar of chocolate. She simply gave it to me, shifting it from her side of the desk to mine. She didn't say a word. My jaw dropped. I asked her: is generosity giving something? She explained: it doesn't have to be something, a thing, like the cholate, but it can be immaterial. To praise a fellow student who had made progress, for example. That would help that peer to do better, work harder, and become a more successful student. I realized, as my first insight into the meaning of 'generosity', that it was a systemic opposite of envy and jealousy. Without thinking, I broke the chocolate bar in half and gave her one half. This seemed quite normal, obvious politeness, but now I saw there is a little more to such small gestures. It brings people together, improves relationships, and can, in fact, become a crucial social thread. Yvonne's choice, and sharing, of the value of generosity was a very generous thing to do.

BONDING

Much later I experienced how far this can go, socially, and also, intellectually. Twice I experienced generosity in a big way, and both people became lifelong friends as a result. The first time was at a moment when I was quite desperate, on the verge of a nervous breakdown. My personal (non-)relationship was falling apart, and I felt I had to get out before I'd go mad. But I had a two-year old child, no income, and no place to live. I was still an undergraduate student. And neither the guy I wanted to leave nor my parents were willing or able to help. So, for a while I felt stuck, and more: I felt imprisoned and about to lose my mind. In that extremely difficult period, for reasons I cannot imagine in retrospect, on a Friday evening I went to a student party. Probably the need to get out and meet up with normalcy had driven me. I had gone there walking, although I usually biked. At some point, not very late, my then-usual exhaustion got the better of me, and I decided to go home. A guy I had not even talked to during the party left at the same time, and offered me a ride. Only upon entering his car we introduced ourselves to each other. His name was Bram.

That offer to drive me home was already a nice gesture, falling under the category of generosity. I was grateful. Little did I know what was to come. During the ride, he glanced at me and said: 'I have a feeling that you are troubled. Is something the matter?' I explained as briefly as I possibly could what the problem was: I had to leave my partner, take my child with me, and I had no place to go. Uhm... he was silent, did some thinking, and then said he was on the board of the student union. Perhaps he could look into the housing possibilities, talk to some fellow board-members. I thanked him, but didn't expect much. Knowing of the housing shortage in the city, how could he help? I was frankly flabbergasted when the following Monday morning at 9 a.m. I received a phone call, from the office of the student housing bureau. Would I care to come and look at a flat? She had heard I was in need of one. Of course, I went right away.

Two hours later I had signed a low-rent contract for a great apartment in a student housing facility, smack downtown in the city, on a beautiful canal. Early that afternoon I had been able to enlist a friend with a driver's license (which I did not have) to rent a small van, come to my house, and move the indispensable pieces of furniture that my cynical partner was willing to let go. Then we went to a carpentry shop, I bought a few planks and some screws, and put together a semblance of a bed. Before dinner, I had picked up my son and explained to him that we were going to live somewhere else. From feeling tortured, I was walking on clouds. Meanwhile, I kept wondering: why had Bram done this? What buttons had he had to push to get this done so immediately? There was no self-interest whatsoever involved. He had not made the slightest move on me. I could only conclude that this was an instance of generosity in its purest form. He had seen someone in need, so he had acted. I didn't even have his address.

I never saw him again. But since we both published, in different fields but also sometimes in newspapers, his name had passed by some times. And I always thought back to that totally selfless, for me life-saving gesture, which remained with me through the decades. Then, forty years later, at a reception of the university, I heard his name, turned around, and yes, it seemed to be the same guy. I barely recognized him. I asked simply: are you Bram? and he said yes, looking puzzled. I said my name and then he nodded, and apologized for not recognizing me. I asked him if he remembered what he had done for me, how he had saved me. He did not remember, not at all. He frowned, shook his head, then smiled, introduced his partner, and we chatted a bit, about how we had sometimes read each other's writings in the newspapers. He was, typically as it turned out, on his way to a demonstration against the rampant Islamophobia, which was surging in the city in the wake of the Charlie Hebdo attack in Paris.

When we parted, he said we should see each other again, have a drink, and we made an appointment for the next Monday. This was the beginning of an enduring friendship, which is ongoing to this day. As it turned out, we also shared intellectual interests, and above all, political ones. So, we began to read each other's work, and had long discussions about the issues that mattered most to both of us, without those issues being exactly the same. A social as well as intellectual bonding resulted. The generosity of that totally selfless gesture of all those years ago had not only saved my life, or at least my sanity, at the time. It had also enriched my life. In my appreciation of that enrichment, I often think of my classmate Yvonne, her proposal of generosity as her favourite value, and the lasting consequences such gifts produce.

HELPING OUT OF THE BLUE

What Bram had done to help me had come out of the blue. Since then, I recognized generosity when I saw it, and tried to practice it as much as possible. The second time was quite similar in situation, except that I was in much better shape when it happened. I had graduated, and written my PhD thesis that was such a stake of contention mentioned under E. I began to go to conferences, which I was told was the best way for a beginning scholar to make contacts, and a name for oneself. For me, it was also a nice social occasion. There were roughly two types of conferences: large ones, organized by professional organizations, where you had to pay to be admitted and pay more to be scheduled as a speaker; and smaller, more 'elite' ones, where speakers were invited rather than having to apply. At a very early moment in my itinerary, prematurely you could say, I happened to be at one of the very first super-fancy academic conferences of the latter type where I had been invited, due to a generous nomination by someone I had just met at another, less prestigious conference of the former type.

The conference was devoted to my field of specialization, the theory of narrative, and this was a time when many scholars were designing such theories. The majority of the speakers were specialists of worldwide renown, and the sheer fact of being there already made me feel very satisfied, grateful, and hopeful for my career that was just beginning. But I also felt intimidated. My opportunity was a problem, too; a double one. First of all, at that point in time I was very shy, and had never yet spoken at a conference. I was determined that this had to change. I felt compelled to overcome this handicap by raising my hand right after the first lecture. The speaker was a noted scholar in the field, one of the organizers of the conference, and I had read some of his work, so I knew I could and should do this. I just had to come up with a good question. That was not so hard; there is always some quibble to find. The second difficulty, which I had not foreseen, was that the conference had been announced as bilingual, French and English. Since French had been my first field of study, I had written my paper in French and was all set to ask my question also in that language.

Trembling, blushing, and fearful, I did raise my hand as soon as he was finished. I had been able to scribble down my question, and I thought it was a good enough one to not be ridiculous asking it. So, I did; in French. But as soon as I had begun, I saw on his face that he had no French; he didn't have a clue what I was going on about. I felt so awful. Nothing I could do, but stumble an apology. But no need. A man sitting two seats away from me, whom I had never seen before, raised his hand, and before having been given the floor, started to speak. Let me help, he said. Then he said who I was, that I had published a very important article in the prestigious journal *Poétique*, and that just a few months back, Jacques Derrida had told him this was an excellent intervention in the field. Then he explained, succinctly and clearly, what my main argument in that article was. So, coming from there, he then added, her question to you today is this. And he explained my question, totally adequately. The speaker was thus enabled to answer it. I felt I was going straight from hell to heaven.

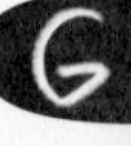

Almost moved to tears, I asked the woman sitting next to me: 'Who is this incredible guy?' Smiling, she said: 'That's my husband, Jonathan.' Again, my jaw dropped. The man who had, out of the blue, spoken up for me, generously helping both me and the speaker, and all those present, was someone whose every book I had read. His reputation was according to the kind and quality of his books. He had been described to me just the evening before as 'the most generous of literary critics'. How right that description was! His books tend to explain difficult theoretical and philosophical ideas and concepts without oversimplifying, bringing them to the reach of the many others who feel intimidated by such 'high theory'. He did that for the benefit of others, colleagues and students, as a gesture of generosity. I had learned from him more than from anyone else. Of course, after the session ended, I went up to him and profusely thanked him. He shrugged it off, said that it was worth it, that he had liked my article very much. I answered that he still had been under no obligation to do this, so it was a gift. No, it's out of a kind of obligation, it's my duty, he replied. Just to make the conference better, and make the participants feel better. Again, as with Bram, this was pure generosity. The friendship that resulted is, again, enduring. For life.

GOOD SPORTS

These are two examples of huge, life-changing acts of generosity. There are also small ones, and those can also be memorable. I consider someone who is a 'good sport' when being criticized, willing and able to reply, and rightly or wrongly winning the debate, also as generous. In this sense, generosity is an intellectual gain, helping the community of scholars to make progress, rather than everyone earning their own stripes. At the same conference, one such a small act of generosity occurred. On the evening of arrival, during the welcoming reception, I had seen an older man carrying my book, then just fresh from the press, which had made me feel deeply ambivalent: proud that he knew of it and had purchased it, and fearful at the same time. Did he intend to call me on the carpet? The fear temporarily won over when I saw in the conference programme that someone else, the only other Dutch participant, was going to give a lecture titled 'A Critique of Mieke Bal's Theory'. This was a full professor at another university. I had recently applied for a job at his department, and had been declined. So, adding insult to injury, he was going to publicly trash me, at my first prestigious conference!

Luck was again on my side. I happened to be the speaker after him. So, during that opening reception, when I saw his title, I went up to him and asked if I could read his paper, to be a bit prepared for the second day. He could barely refuse, and gave me a carbon copy; not too happy, if his facial expression was any indication. I spent the night, giving up on sleep, reading and marking the copy, and, for the first time ever, hand-writing a reply in English. It was quite extensive, since his critique was very detailed. Then the next day, after the great event I just mentioned, I went to the table of the organizers with a copy of my paper in French. This was before computers. I told them I had the impression that not everyone in the conference understood French, in spite of the announcement that the conference was going to be bilingual. So, would they please make a stack of copies of my paper, so that the French readers could have it, and I could improvise in English? They gracefully did.

So, the next morning, this man whom I considered a colleague because we both did narrative theory—he was a full professor, I an aspiring, still jobless assistant professor who had been turned down by this very same man—gave his talk. For thirty minutes, he talked about my book, and all the things I had wrong. In my biased eyes, his facial expression and tone seemed a bit smug. He didn't apologize for (ab)using his speaking time at an international conference to trash the work of a totally unknown and jobless junior person from his own country. So, in the beginning I was furious, as I would later be with that other colleague whose envious misbehaviour I have described under E. I could see that the audience was a bit puzzled, since they didn't know me or my theoretical views, other than what they had heard, thanks to Jonathan, that most generous theorist, the previous morning from the brief exchange after the opening lecture. 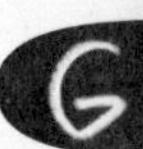

When my turn came, I said that I understood there might be a need for a reply, and that I had written my own paper in French. I explained its main points in five minutes and invited people who read French to take a copy. I then replied to the 'attack', as I called it to my inner self. Politely but pointedly, I refuted all his criticisms and explained why my theory was more adequate than his. I saw my critic's face: to my amazement, he looked no longer smug but, instead, kept nodding his head, suggesting that he finally 'got it'. After the session, which ended with a thundering applause, he came to me, in front of the audience who were beginning to gather their papers and go to lunch, shook my hand and said with a big smile: 'Congratulations. You won!' The simplest, briefest acknowledgement of a good sport.

I thanked him, and added that perhaps he had in fact done me a favour, unwittingly. And true enough: during the remaining days of that conference, people kept referring to our debate. It, hence I, became something of a reference point, and in all honesty: the event made my career. I began to be internationally invited quite frequently right after this. This was, of course, not something he had done wilfully. But the fact that he didn't mind, and conceded I was more or less right, made for a tone of debate, rather than strife. That he had been not only generous but also honest, was proven by the invitation to visit him at his home, to come for dinner. We became long-term friends. Again, the classroom conversation with Yvonne came back. That teacher who had paired us up to discuss values had generated a moment of meaning-making: generosity and honesty, both with multiple nuances, together are wholesome for the improvement of the social fabric.

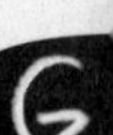

Home, or Horror?

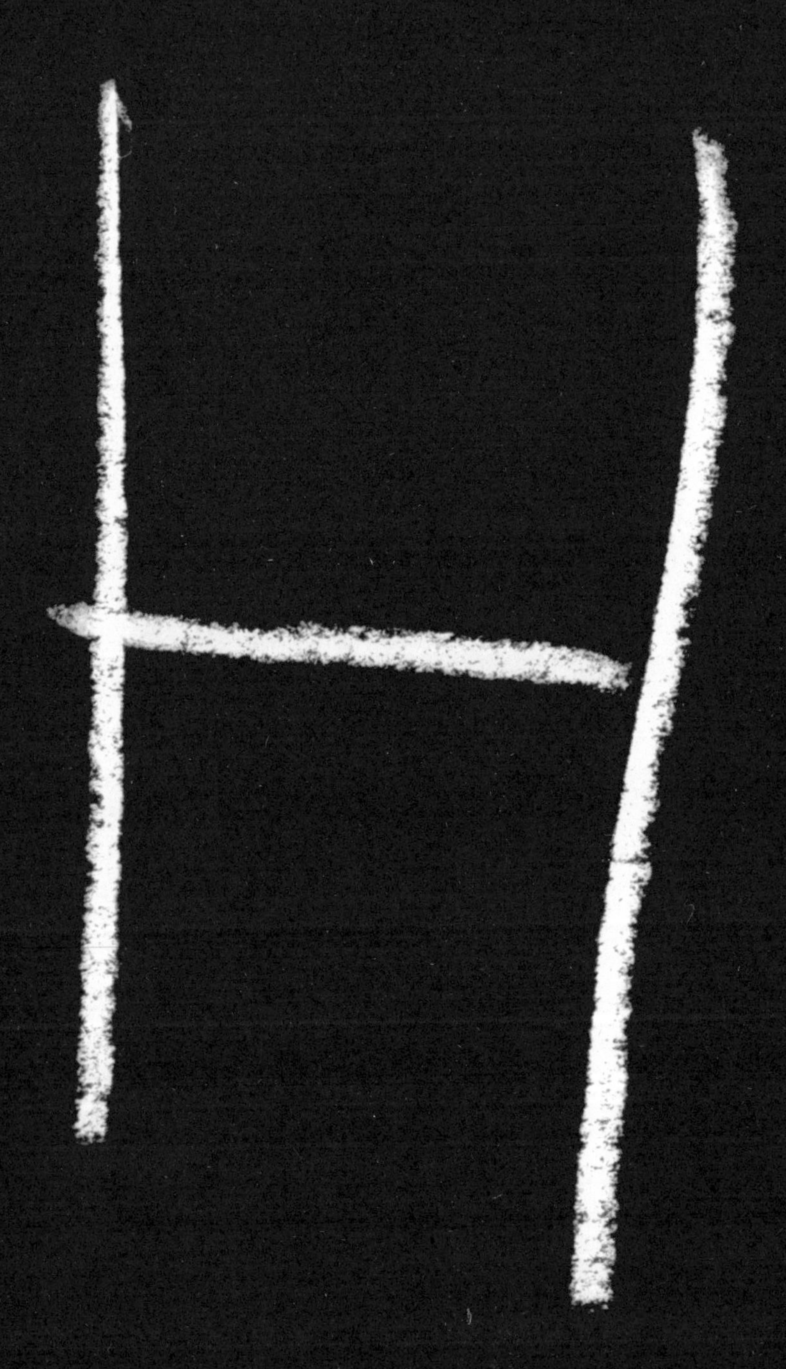

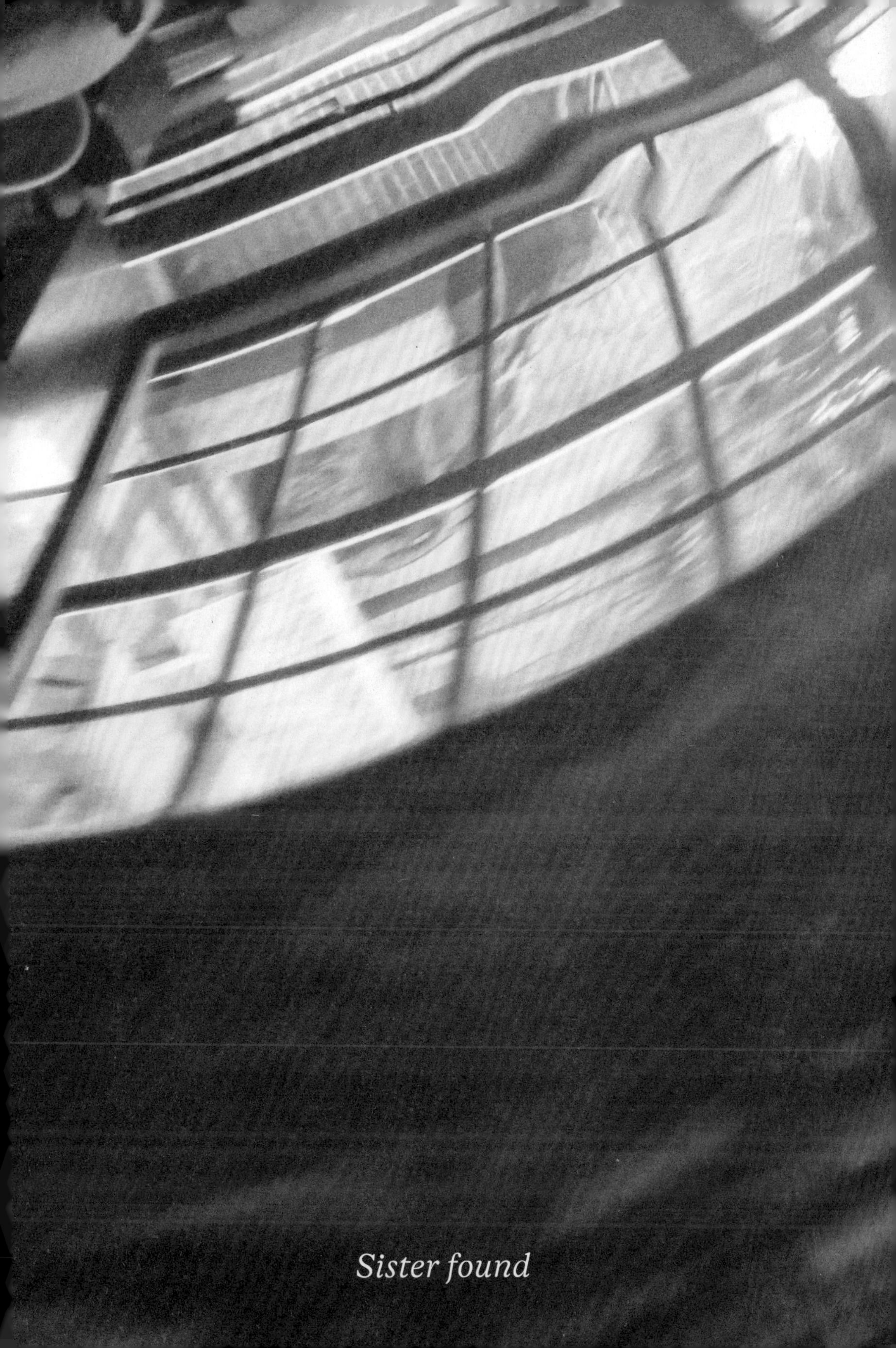

Sister found

HOMEY VS, OR ENTANGLED WITH HOMELY?

Home: it sounds so homey, which is reassuringly comfortable, cozy, relaxed. It is where you belong, the place to which you always return, where you feel safe and loved. If only... But then there is the word 'homely', which suggests unattractive, uninviting, plain. Who would want to have that as the basis of life? Both words have the root of 'home', which means domesticity, family; the basis of life, at least according to prevailing ideology. As a note of caution, the confusing similarity between 'homey' and 'homely' also invokes Freud's notion of 'unheimlich', where the same root of 'Heim', German for home, is subject to conversion into horror. As the inventor of psychoanalysis explained, the horror comes from the recognition, the familiarity, when it meets strangeness, the threatening unknown things. It is that encounter between 'home' and strange, new, unknown that produces the creepy feeling he called 'unheimlich'.

As a child, of course I knew nothing of this kind of thinking. But I had a home that was both homey and homely. Perhaps I didn't know but I did feel it. Against the homeliness, I escaped in reading. When I was in primary school, I walked home after classes, and was bound to get there on time; the rules were strict. Yet, I never hurried. I walked with a book in my hands, and read during the half-hour walk. I was addicted to reading in a way that has neither completely left me, nor remained the same once I had home responsibilities of my own and my reading habits transformed into what we call 'close reading': focusing on details, reading more slowly. The family had a subscription to the local library, where I went constantly to find new books. The lust for reading, in Dutch alliterating nicely: *LeesLust*, became my way of life. And since it was a quiet occupation, it was not countered. This *modus vivendi* has often protected me from the over-crowded household that was my family: nine siblings and two parents made up a household of eleven. That makes for a lot of talking, screaming, rowing. So, I was the mousy one, and they never understood that I had my own turmoil in my head, from imagining the situations I read about, and thinking these through.

Imagine the noisy, busy situation, with always something to do to help out an over-worked mother, who mobilized her children to do everything, from cooking to cleaning. Through my own fault, I was especially targeted. For, the parents said, I was so 'handy'. This is not quite true. It was a sense of despair, of need, that made me undertake tasks I now think I should better have left alone. That might have saved me a lot of aggravation later in life as well as then. But it was impossible. The table needed setting, the beds making, the laundry doing, the dishes washing and drying. In such a large household, there is never a moment that it is all done.

The problem was that Mother couldn't cope. There was too much work to do, she was constantly either pregnant or breast-feeding or both, and so tired she had to take afternoon naps. And with my father's single salary as a high school teacher, there was not enough money for adequate help. I was the third child. As I later learned from my current partner, who is a third child himself, there is a special role for the first three children. The oldest is a good, obedient one, the second one revolts, and the third one tries to reconcile, and calm the constantly threatening tensions by helping out. The fourth one escapes, falls by the wayside, doesn't really count. It may be a stereotype, but in my case, it seemed to fit. Rather than having screaming and crying going on, I tried to solve the practical problems. All I could do was self-learning by trial and error. (This is probably why later in life I took Karl Popper's ideas on methodology seriously.) I did not take it on as severely as some colleagues did, who used it to militate against everything I came up with, such as interpretation, inventive models for analysis, and what was dismissed as 'formalism'—attention to what made texts into literature and images into art.[18]

The strategy of trial-and-error has, I speculate, helped me greatly in my later research work. It kept me on my toes, made me inventive, bold, and unorthodox, because if I tried, I could learn new things, and if it turned out bad, I was in error and would try again. In my teaching this came in good stead as well. I was never afraid of being wrong, nor of admitting it to my students, who tended to follow the example and also tried, erred, and admitted defeat when necessary. This attitude is the 'self' part of learning. The result is a dialogic situation, rather than a

18 On Popper's methodological reflections, see especially his book *The Logic of Scientific Discover* (1968). His 'trial-and-error' (falsification) strategy was very impactful.

hierarchical teaching-learning dichotomy based on monologue.

I don't think I was handier than the other siblings, but it was, I later learned, my role as the third child to clean up the mess left by the other two. And the six children that followed were too little; they needed care and protection, not tasks. I felt that, if I didn't do something about it, disaster threatened: parents divorcing, Mother going mad and having to be institutionalized: all catastrophes I had read about in the many books I read on my way home from school. Through the reading I had learned a lot, including things I recognized at home. So, during Mother's naps I tried out things I knew needed doing. This was my itinerary from feeling-knowing to taking responsibility, and from trying out to developing skills. After folding the stuff, I put the endless stacks of laundry where they belonged in the many different cupboards. What needed ironing, I ironed. And the day my parents bought an 'ironing machine', I used one of those napping hours to learn how to use it. So, when Mother woke up, I was machine-ironing. Quick as a flash, she complimented me, then heaped more clean but un-ironed linen in the basket, and so I could iron on for a few hours more.

Something similar happened with cooking. I don't quite remember when and how it started, but I do know that even before the age of ten, I cooked daily. The meals were not very sophisticated, so there was not much to learn. I had the authority to ask/require the boys—the oldest was a boy, and the one after me, too—to peel potatoes. That, and shining shoes, was considered boys' work; gender roles came on early as well. And peeling potatoes for eleven eaters when not much else was on the menu, apart from vegetables and on Fridays, some fish, and in the weekend, a bit of meat, meant peeling a lot of potatoes. I sometimes went with Mother to the market to buy potatoes and vegetables. They were heaped into a handcart, and at home were thrown into the basement through a chute. But just as my knowledge gleaned from reading made me trip into the development of a home-sociality, where fear as much as responsibility played their part, with the cooking it was my taste for food that made me more and more ambitious to make it taste better. So, I developed the skill to fry onions, add spices and other tricks to enhance the taste. Father complimented me when it was a bit better-tasting than usual. And so, I became ambitious, that is, motivated to do the best I could, in this area, too.

I also experimented making puddings of all sorts, combining my lust for good things with practical curiosity: how to make puddings that would stand up? I learned about jelly, gelatin, and other goodies. When the end-of-the-year season approached, and I learned how to make and bake deep-fried donut balls, and apple slices dipped in the fluid dough, producing my favourites, apple turnovers, again I painted myself into a corner. I was excited to see the off-white dough turn a golden brown in no time, and to see the plates fill to a high stack, which I arranged as pretty towers. But there was an element of time involved in this. To bake these for eleven people, sometimes with a few added visitors, and in numbers sufficient not as dessert but to replace the meal, meant that for hours I was in the kitchen, bending over the pot, breathing in oily air. I never gave this a thought, until, after all that work, when the time came to eat them, I was nauseous from all the oil I had been inhaling, and had to go to bed. This was a revolting experience. And in the homey-homely tension, I felt unsafe having to go upstairs, with the vague murmur of the family around the table contrasting painfully with my loneliness mounting the stairs in the dark. Sick, excluded, and scared.

This must have been before I was ten. Hence, I can honestly say that before the age of ten, I was an expert cook. I know this because at ten, we moved to another city, and the visitors we had come over before that to share the New Year's Eve, were priests coming from the local seminary in the village where I spent the first ten years of my life. This ten-years divide of my youth dates my memories. Retrospectively, I allocate them to childhood versus youth. I now think that I could never really be a child. I developed a sense of responsibility too early, with the weight of the fear of family disasters as a negative motivation. My parents, understandably given how heavy their lives were, gave me more and more tasks, reckoning that I, the handy one, was able and willing to do them. So, during the summer holidays, I spent the entire day cleaning—the annual big cleaning, which in most households was done in the spring, was postponed until I was available. If we were lucky, we did get to go out for a swim, but not every day. My older sister was set to work as well, but she didn't contribute much, for, just as I had protected myself by reading, she had built a protection pretending she was slow, a bit of a half-wit. Totally untrue, but it worked: she got the reputation of being clumsy, whereas I was handy. Both labels were induced by our own self-protecting lies.

OUTSIDE THE HOME

During those first ten years my entire life took place inside. Apart from those precious moments of walking to and from school, and to and from the library, I had insufficient experience outside the home. I did try to hide in the garden behind or in the apple tree, or in the attic if it was bright enough to not be frightened of the dark, always with a book. We were too numerous to go out as a family more than once a year, to the beach, the zoo, or to visit Schiphol Airport and watch airplanes. Until rather late, we had no car. All outings had to be managed on the two bicycles: Father with one child in front and two on the back on the luggage rack, while he also pushed one or two on a scooter; Mother with at least two more on hers. I loved school, not only for the few hours of a different life, and then the half-hour reading while walking. But also, to feed my curiosity. But on the whole, life was at home.

As a consequence, this strange mixture of responsibility and fear stuck to my skin. Once I realized it, I developed an anger against that 'cosmic responsibility' I felt. On the one hand it was a sincere feeling, probably combined with a sense of my own importance, which had been so strongly overruled by being an almost anonymous member of the crowd in the home. This is why it remained important to make sure I wasn't a social wallflower. On the other hand, I felt it had been imposed. That reputation of handiness had cost me my freedom. Later, motherhood became the second-degree trap. I learned how responsible mothers were, for everything that could possibly go wrong in the home. So, I blamed it on motherhood, as an oppressive institution. Then, in my professional life, it stuck to me as well. At that time, I blamed it on femininity, and the reigning sexism in the work place. For, in spite of the Netherlands' reputation of progressiveness in issues of gender, in my experience, the academic scene at least was more behind than in advance, compared to other countries. At least in my department. But this, I must admit, came from a mixture of their old-fashioned habits and my own over-the-top sense of being, always and everywhere, responsible, and wronged.

My colleagues must have learned quickly that putting the coffee tray in front of me would only lead to my shifting it to the next person. But when, during a meeting, a problem came up for which a volunteer was required, I still feel the anxiety when I looked around the table and no hand was being raised. So, since the problem needed solving or the task performing, what else could I do than volunteer, if no one else did? And so, this quickly became a bad habit, too. How convenient, if one colleague felt the slot needed filling. Just sit tight and it will be done. I am sure none of them consciously thought about this. But I did, although not deeply and critically enough. Until my boss willy-nilly set me straight. On responsibility, hierarchy, and priorities.

One day my little son was ill. I couldn't rely on his father to take him to the doctor. That was simply out of the question. So, I was nervous, eager to get away to do that share of my responsibility which, at home, was as 'total' as everywhere because it felt to me like that. But I had to wait, leave him with kind neighbours, until the meeting was over. I was sick with worry. But then the unexpected happened. The last item on the agenda had to be postponed. The reason? My boss had to leave early, for his dog was ill. He had to take his dog to the vet. Never mind he had a wife at home—a so-called 'housewife'. But, he explained, she didn't dare go to the vet. She was afraid of the other animals in the waiting room. So, I was lucky, got out earlier than foreseen, and could take the boy to the doctor before the end of consultation hours. To my relief, he had nothing serious, and the doctor gave something against the fever and the pain. But it was a great moment at which meaning-making happened. If his dog was more important than my son, something was wrong. I became aware of the different sense of responsibility involved; the odd mixture of it with hierarchy, and I back-projected that on the power my parents had exercised in making me believe I was handy, and that my handiness was a good thing. I realized the hierarchy that allowed the department head to decide to take leave on account of his feeling responsible, but not me.

It helped me to understand the mixed meanings of these concepts, but not to change my habit of endorsing duties that I should have placed elsewhere. Slowly, and after changing partners and making enough headway in my work to get at least some collaboration at home, I developed the ability, if not to shed that feeling of responsibility, but at least to either discuss it at home or prioritize my occupations a bit differently. I discovered I was also responsible for myself, and for my work, my students, and my writing. And although I could never place a child behind a deadline on my inner list, the complexity of the life I was leading made it possible, even necessary, to not always, invariably, put the home first, and make everything else unimportant.

In the second half of my youth, as I mentioned, we had moved to a different city, and the house in which we lived for some years was huge. This made it scarier sometimes. In the attic were what we called 'secret corridors', in which I could hide, but which were too dark to be comfortable, let alone to allow reading. The little ones, as we, the four oldest, called the younger siblings—all five girls—needed care, and the house was impossible to keep orderly and clean. It was in those two years when I was still in primary school that I frequently had to stay home to help, rather than go to school. After we moved, Mother got pregnant one last time, and of course, she was totally exhausted. I hated to be deprived of my school hours, which felt so liberating, but in spite of my secret anger, I did not even protest, empathizing with that mother doomed to being a permanent Mother. It was clear there was no other solution.

I remember one incident, when 'home' got a different meaning. One of the little ones suddenly seemed to be missing. The house was big enough, she could have been anywhere. But since there was a canal nearby, a bit farther away and larger and deeper than the one behind my first home, I was shocked into dread. Whereas the fear seemed to paralyze the others who were present, I alone ran outside, towards the canal, called out her name, and couldn't find her. I'll never forget the terror. I simply assumed she was already dead, drowned, sunken, and invisible below the duckweed. I burst into tears and went home reluctantly, sobbing. My parents and the older siblings were gathered in the living room, all looking gloomy. And then I saw it.

Behind the thick curtain that went from ceiling to floor, I suddenly noticed the fronts of two small shoes. I pulled the curtain open and there she was. Standing, smiling. Unaware of the panic she had unwittingly sown. For her it was probably a little game, playing hide-and-seek with herself. I will never know, we didn't ask. I am not even sure she knew we were looking for her, worried about her. She was too little for that, perhaps two years old. No one was angry with her and no one protested. Just a wave of relief. This was a moment when I realized that fear can actually also have a positive effect. I remember it made me feel closer to that little sister, and so happy that the dread had come to an end. After fear, relief is a source of joy. I felt like celebrating, which, in the economically tight family budget, did not seem possible. No matter, she was alive, she was home. And my other fears—of the darkness, of unknown places, of strangers and strange things—vanished, compared to the horror of real loss and the relief when it was over. 'Home' got an added meaning: not-horror.

Inventiveness

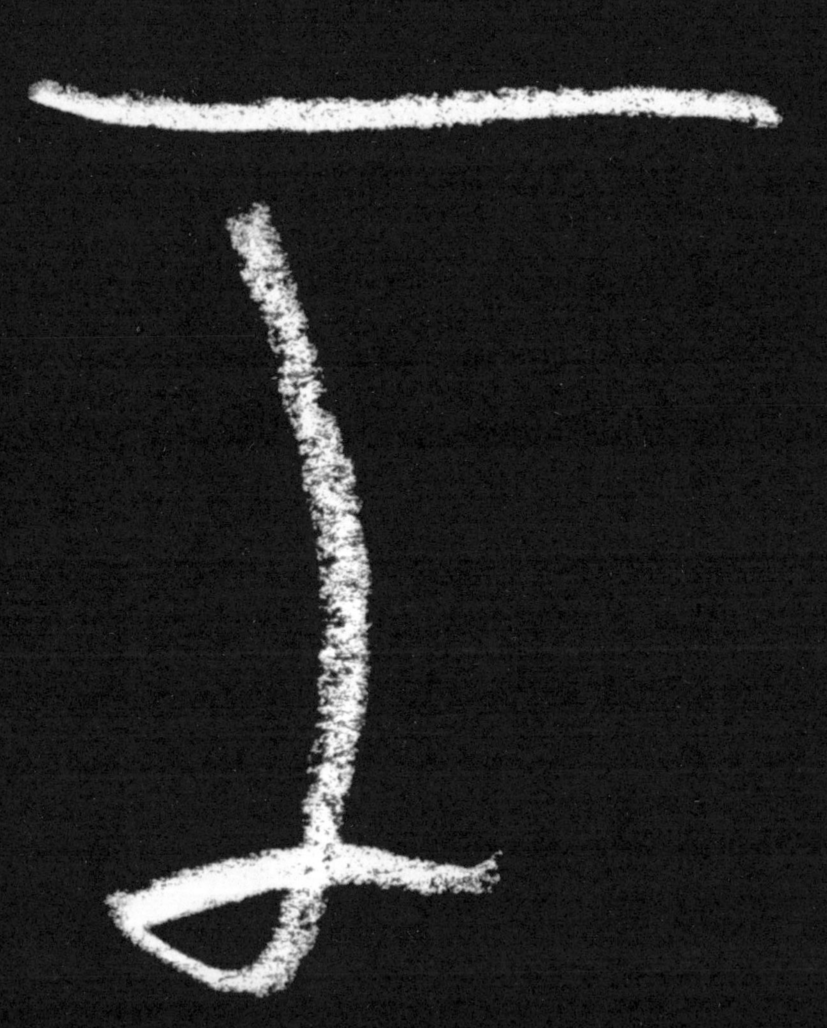

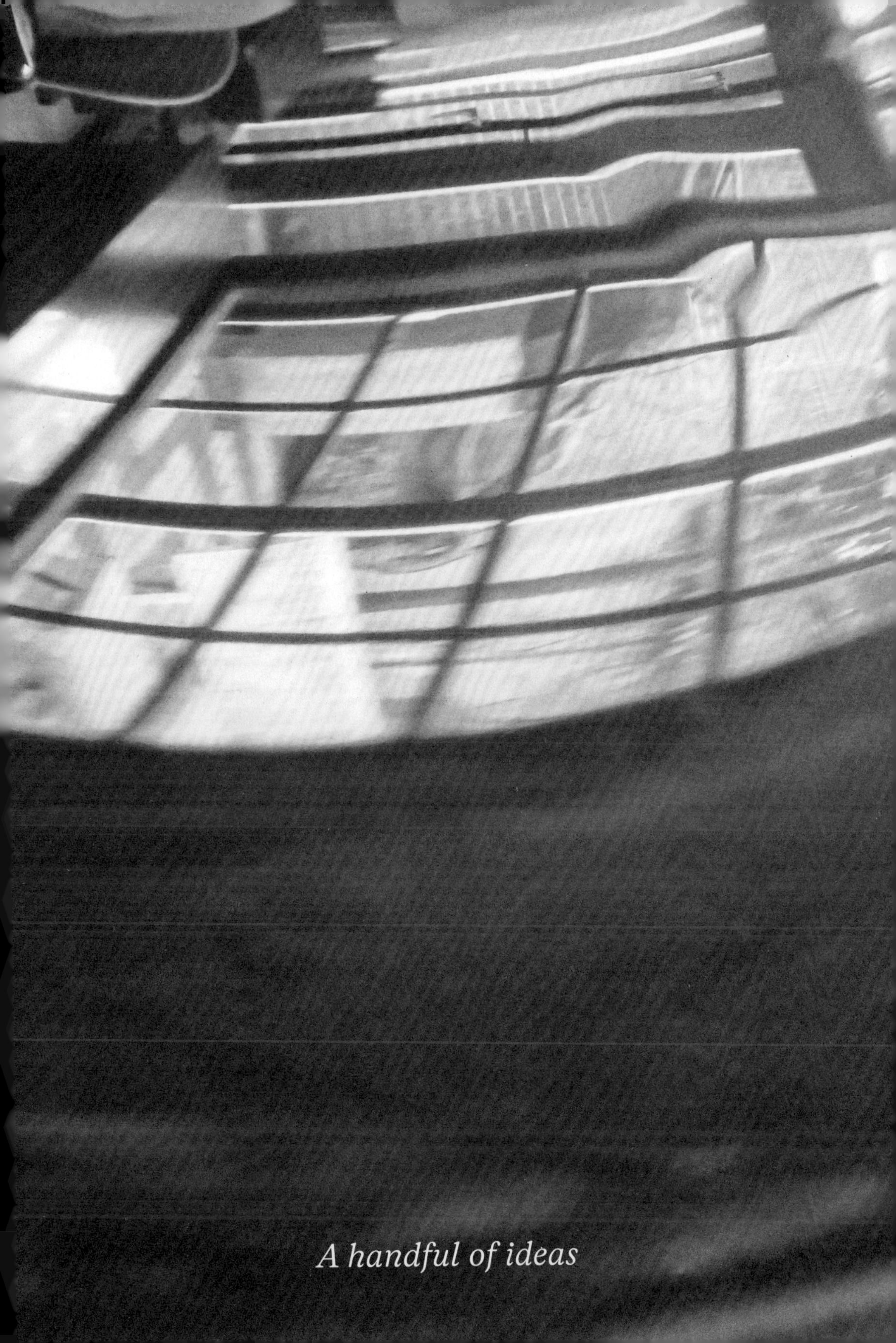

A handful of ideas

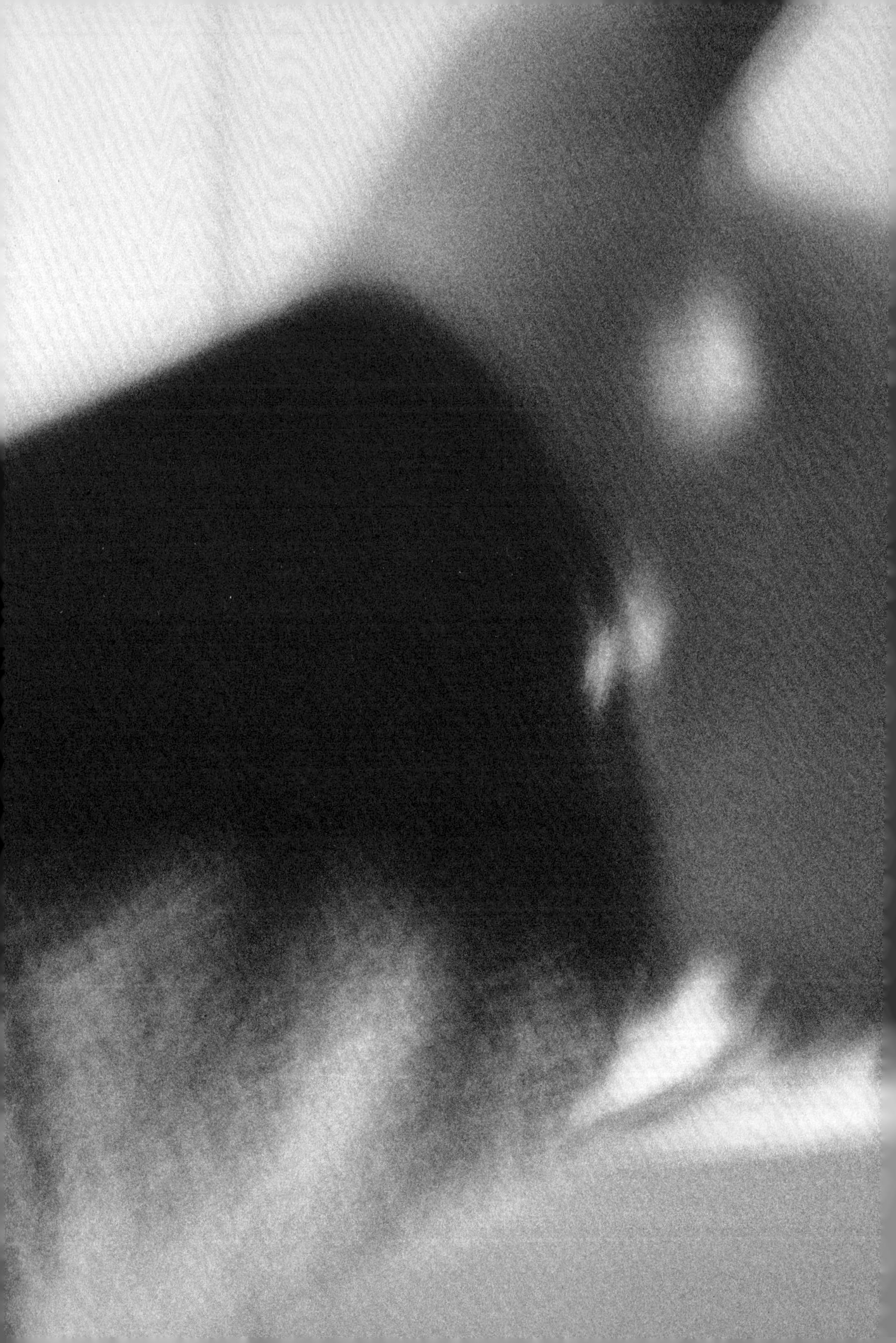

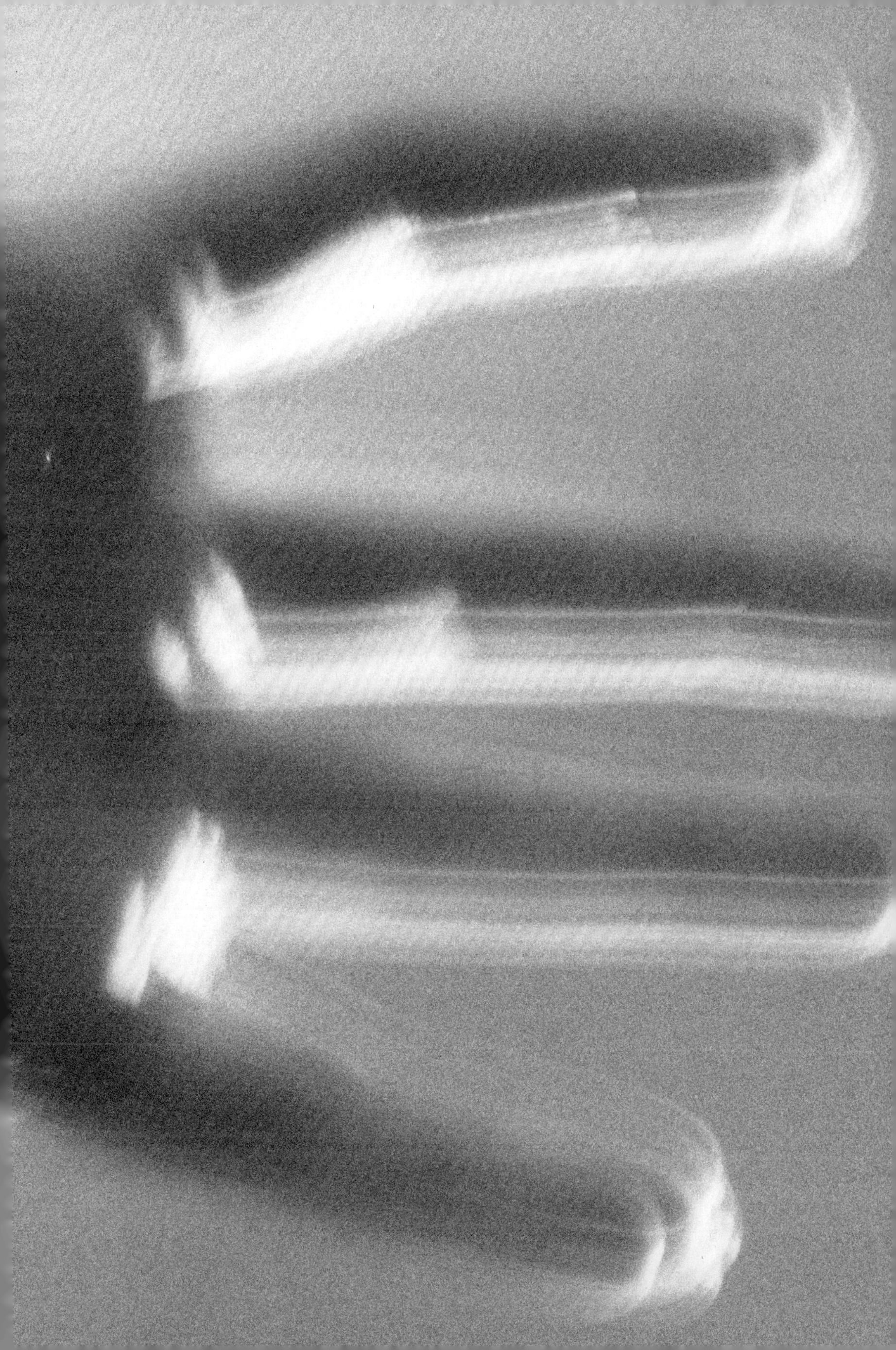

Some would call it creativity: to let the mind spark freely. Perhaps that's what it is. But for me that sounds too close to artistic, and thereby, a bit too special—both specialized, restricted to a particular domain, and special in the sense of elitist. I am not talking about a special talent but rather an attitude. What I remember and want to reflect on in this entry are moments when a problem needed solving, and an idea would pop up in my mind. A kind of 'trial and error' as brought in under H, a certain boldness in thinking that we need in order to be able to come up with solutions, imaginative things, novelties, in order to contribute to thought and to the fabric of social life. In childhood, I was often criticized for being imaginative. They—primarily my parents—said I had too much imagination, as a friendly way of saying I was lying, or fantasizing; a bit mad. I frequently was, I am sure of it now. But they were also appreciative when I came up with a helpful suggestion for solving some housekeeping problem.

Once, perhaps I was four or five, I saw that on the balcony a hose on the tap was leaking while they were watering the plants in the garden. Since they were always going on about the household budget never stretching far enough, my first association was with the waste of water this meant. I thought it might help to put a container underneath the tap where the hose was attached, and capture the water that was leaking. So, I went to the shed and fetched a bucket, which I placed under the leaking joint. I remember the zinc bucket was almost too large and too heavy for me; hence my estimated age. Now I realize the futility of this; just a few cups of water saved, on an entire garden watering. Nevertheless, Mother praised me and even gave me five cents as a reward, to demonstrate the tight bond between housekeeping, economy, and inventiveness. Many other small occurrences happened, when I had a sudden idea for solving a problem, blurted it out, and it was enough of a reward for me that my proposal was applied. It was a way of feeling I was being taken seriously, which I was so rarely.

Sometimes I vaguely felt my parents were lacking such inventiveness, complying too closely to the common habits. When I was about eight, they took me, and probably some of the siblings, to the Rijksmuseum in Amsterdam. We went through the Golden Age galleries, and I was slightly bored; not by what I saw but by what I heard. When facing Rembrandt's painting of his wife Saskia as Flora, my mother said: 'He must have loved that woman so very much.' I didn't see what she could possibly see. Just a woman, with flowers. The woman was not particularly beautiful, according to my twentieth-century taste. A bit later, she remarked on the lemon peels in a still life painting. 'How real it looks! Do you see it? Almost like real lemons, with the pores of the skin visible.' Suddenly I felt the ground of my boredom. Why go to a museum to see a 'real' woman 'being loved', and lemon peels with pores? Just look at the stalls in the market for the latter, and try to be loved yourself for the former.

The still life and her comments stopped me in my tracks, however. What bothered me was precisely that: something for which I had no words, but what I now call 'realism'. I simply discarded from my mind the comment on Rembrandt's love for his wife. Living in a household where love was not an obvious sentiment, I just shrugged it off. Instead, I started to fantasize about the difference between real lemons and these depicted lemon peels, of which the skilled painter had been able to show both sides. And things began to make sense, in a very different way from my mother's comments, although these did have the effect that I looked again, this time more attentively. And the boredom disappeared; I felt excitement. At that time, I had no words, no tools to articulate what my emotion was about. But the memory of the excitement and its intensity never left me.

The point was not the reality-like quality of the painting, but on the contrary: how it was possible to make us think these were real, while in fact, it was 'only' a flat square with yellow paint on it; for me, from my child's limited height, only to be seen with distortion. The depicted objects, the lemon peels, faded away. And I began to imagine what those dark portions meant, what those parts where nothing could be seen, had to do with the bright yellow ones. Suddenly the knife, precariously balanced at the edge of the table, acquired a sense of danger— that slightly threatening feeling that gave me goosebumps for no reason anyone else could see. But danger because the knife could become a weapon, or danger for it, or that it could get damaged when falling on the stone floor. The tabletop on which the jar with flowers and the basket with lemons stood, was leaning a bit forward. As if it might fall. In other words, I saw, I discovered perspective, depth of field, and the incipient movement immanent in the still image—all words I can now bring in, but not then; only the sensation. Little did I know that decades later, this 'event' of seeing something new, would become my professional specialization.

IMAGINATION

What happened that day in the Rijksmuseum was an unsolicited, spontaneous act of imagination. My parents were right, perhaps, that I 'had' or did too much of that. I suppose my constant reading had opened up my mind to thinking up, seeing, discovering, uncommon things. But also the thinking and daydreaming I developed, the habit of doing in order to carve out a space for myself in the turmoil of the family-crowd, facilitated this. In the end, what I saw was not only strange 'things'—the knife, the dark background, the tilting table top—but what I later understood to be the secret, the system, of depiction: of presenting something that was not, but could be. This was how flatness and volume could interact, as did still and moving. This inter-action was making the impossible possible; the invention of ambiguity. It was no longer simply solving a problem, but deploying the imagination to see things, including solutions to problems, but much more.

Later I became aware that I had moments where I made meaning in my sleep. I remember in 1972, for Christmas a French friend gave me Gérard Genette's book *Figures III*, that had just appeared. I didn't know how formative that book was going to be for the rest of my working life. I had not yet even heard the name of the author, whose entire oeuvre I would later devour. What made that book so important was the in-depth readings of Proust integrated with original, relevant theoretical reflections. Not only would I, much later, write a book about/ with Proust myself, but it was through reading Genette that I acquired the habit of integrating theory with detailed reading, and on that basis, later developed 'cultural analysis' as a field of study. Now I realize that Genette's book titles were not really titles: *Figures*, *Figures II* and *Figures III*, but instead announced a programme that he did not quite develop, of keenly looking for visuality in literature; for how words could turn into figures.

There was something that bothered me about Genette's book, however. I didn't know what it was, but I did know that I had to find it, put my finger on it, if the book was ever going to really help me in my own thinking. To do Genette's book justice I had to critique it, going further, in line with vignette C. This, too, became a mantra in my work. And then I had a dream. The 'day rest' as Freud would call it, that bit of recent experience that became the motor of the dream, was the slight sense of bother upon what I saw as the author halting his own thought. What I found exciting about the book's theoretical tenor was the distinction he made between narration and focalization. The latter he had gleaned from Henry James' prefaces, and, for me more significantly, from the English author's 1897 novel *What Maisie Knew*. In spite of its title, this novel is about, tells us, what the child Maisie did *not* know, but saw. Perhaps identifying with the little daughter of unhappy parents, I dreamt— there is no other word for it; it really happened during my sleep—about that act of seeing. The child saw, but did not know, did not understand, some act that we would call 'adulterous', happen before her eyes. And then I 'knew' or rather, mentally saw what had bothered me about Genette's theory. He did make the distinction between narration and focalization, but didn't take the step that Maisie could have suggested to him: to distinguish between subject and object of these two activities, so that different acts of focalizing would be seen in their differences: the child's act of seeing, and the adult reader's understanding of what she saw. The discrepancy between seeing and knowing is the central issue at stake in that novel. I woke in the morning, and sat down to write up my critique of Genette, which became the launching of my work as a 'narratologist'.

This was also the first time I experienced how 'seeing' something in the imagination can facilitate and speed up writing. Of course, as is normal with dreams, once I woke up the actual vision had disappeared, but I remembered enough to be able to turn it into an intellectual argument. I was not a very experienced writer yet, but I had enough practice from writing in the high school journal *Bliko* to know the sluggish slowness when thinking runs ahead and the words take more time to come. However, this piece, the critique and revision of Genette's theory, almost wrote itself, simply because I had seen it, in my dream. Not only the vision of seeing without knowing, but also the structure of the argument had outlined itself in my dream. After writing it as an article, in a mere few days, I sent it to Genette, who answered immediately: 'This is precisely the kind of constructive criticism I had been hoping for!' And he added he would publish it in the journal he edited, *Poétique*. That journal was the one I avidly read, each time it came out. The best in the business. And he did; within a few months it appeared. This promise made my day, or rather, my career, as the tales under G already made clear. Thanks to my dream, I jumped from a totally unknown beginner to someone people knew about; and from monologuing to being able to discuss my ideas.

Since then, I have been more alert to the role of the imagination in thinking, shedding the defensiveness that stern colleagues had instilled in me. Many memories from childhood experiences are based on it, either combined or not with problem-solving. One more, early example. During those first ten years we had neighbours, a friendly elderly couple. We lived as Roman Catholics in a predominantly protestant town, and when I was about six I learned that these neighbours were protestants. Having been raised as a Roman Catholic, I thought that was bad. I pitied them; they would not go to heaven after dying, while they were so friendly. Here was a problem to solve. How could I help them? So, during the winter season, while washing the dishes after the evening meal, my sister and I sang Christmas carols, as loudly as we could. This was a campaign, and I really believed it would help. 'Telling' these kind people about the birth of Jesus, I thought, would perhaps entice them to convert to the right religion. Well, sorry; I was only six.

Later, in high school, I came up with another solution to the problem of carving out time for myself. I imagined I had a boyfriend, gave him a name, and told my mother about it/him. The poor guy never existed, but for a while, it was accepted that I came home from school a few hours later, because I had meetings with him. I had to promise we would just take a stroll, never go to his house. I spent the time thus earned roaming around town and sitting on a bench with a book. It was all part of my tactics for escape, for being allowed to be alone with my imagination. But sometimes, my mother asked about him, what he looked like, if he was handsome, where he went to school. Fortunately, she never suggested I invite him to visit at home. My mother completely bought the story. But that was also where the danger of a home invitation lurked. So, at some point I had to tell her we had had a row, disagreed strongly on something important, and it was finished. I can still see in my mind the boy I had made up and described.

And then, again much later, I began to realize the importance of vision in the imagination. It is even inside the word itself: *imag*-ination. This had been 'there' all along, I now think, but I came to articulate this only once I began to make films and felt compelled to justify that this was not just a hobby on the side, but a further development and deepening of my thinking. It was only then that I didn't think my parents were wrong in saying I had too much imagination. The standard of 'too much' eluded me, but yes, I had a lot of it, and I slowly began to value the imagination. And I realized how many childhood and youth occurrences had the imagination as their motor. Seeing things had been the substance and joy of my life, all along. And if literature had been my first focus, it was through focalization as seeing that I studied it. That this interest got me to enter the domain of visual art seems retrospectively the most self-evident, 'natural' development, even if it was through anecdotes that it happened.

IMAGING

After that confrontation with a seventeenth-century still life and its lemon peels, I did not become an art buff. Museums were at most a once-a-year outing. And cinema was out of the question; no money, and too dangerous morally. But mercifully, the mind doesn't cost a penny, and as long as I could organize my life so as to keep some time to myself, I could 'image'. Imaging is not only seeing images but also 'making' them. Not in a material sense; I have never been good at drawing or painting, even if I sometimes had bouts of desiring to do it. I tried, but it came to naught. No talent there. I remember once in high school, the art teacher seemed to fall for an abstract sheet I had made. By lack of drawing skills, I had just filled a sheet with all kind of colours, totally arbitrarily distributed. Then I had covered those colours with black crayon. With a needle or the point of a knife, I subsequently made a very rough drawing by scraping away the black. Just scratching a bit. It felt like the right thing to do, in the absence of talent. But the teacher, I still don't quite understand why, liked it. He gave me a bit of suggestions for further improvement, and then when I declared it 'finished' he asked if I was convinced by it. With my innate lack of self-confidence and trained modesty, I just shrugged. Then he gave me a decent grade, but added that he would have given a higher grade if I had been convinced by it myself.

At first, I was a bit taken aback. Did the drawing change according to what I thought of it? Later I began to see his point. I had not even dared look at it, but now I understood several things about it. It was different, even what people call 'original'. It integrated colour and black. The needle or knife point made the lines fine. It was what I now call abstract, not a depiction of anything but the production of emerging new forms. I couldn't understand these aspects, however, because I had refused to look the work into the face and take it seriously. Without explaining it, the art teacher taught me that day the important, if fine line, between seeing an image in the mind and seeing it come into existence outside; two subsequent steps in imaging. I never took on drawing or painting, but I now think

my filmmaking, the desire, even craving to do it, came out of
the seed that the art teacher had sewn that Friday morning
by punishing me for my refusal to believe in my own imaging.
The pride my mother had told me to shed, I should now have
mobilized again.

Imaging became immediately the central issue, including
that question of 'who sees what?' in my amendment of
Genette's theory. This became especially significant in the
sense of uncertain and thereby, creative, when I made the step
from documentary to fiction. I now see that as bound to that
high school experience of being unable or unwilling to see what
I had made. My later fiction films are all based on storytelling
texts. And this compelled imaging—how else can we turn words
into images? Lest we fall for the seduction, encouraged by the
infelicitous word 'adaptation', to translate and attempt to stay
close to the letter of the text, in this process it is necessary to
turn not words but the most central issues, aesthetic and intellectual, in the imaginative (pre-)text into an equivalent, but a
different one, in its new medium. I recently (in 2022) published
a book about this, and here I can only give one short example.
An obvious case where imaging turned out crucial was in the
film on Descartes.[19]

As I briefly mentioned in vignette A, I never could bear
the disparaging comments on Descartes. Why? He was not
someone I had studied closely. The dismissal upset me for its
arrogant 'post-'thinking, and also because the world at this
time is mad enough to strongly need some more rationality.
But there is more to it. In my second year of French studies,
my teacher Françoise Guyon had given us a homework assignment that I now see as an acknowledgement of the imaging
involved even in the thinking of this most rational-seeming
philosopher. She read with us the description of a tree, taken
from Descartes' writings. It was simply that: a description, of
something as common as a tree. I don't remember why she read
it or what she considered special about it. I saw it as practicing
French, both reading and writing. The assignment was: to make
a description 'just like that' of something else. I don't remember
at all what object I chose, nor how I pulled it off to describe it.

19 In that 2022 book, *Image-Thinking*, which I consider at this point my most
important one, I theorize and analyze the relationship between textual and
visual works as explored in my films.

It was simply an exercise to write concretely in French. But just as the art teacher's lesson, this little exercise stayed with me in my imagination of Descartes as a thinker, not that hyper-rational one people have made him out to be, but as someone I was able to *image*. How else could he have described a tree? He made an image of it, with the help of his imagination that gave him words producing an image.

Decades later, after not having thought about him especially, I felt the urge to make a film, hence, an (audio)visual narrative, less about the man than about how his thinking happened. Imaging became central in it. When Descartes, played by Thomas Germaine, visits a museum with a friend, he tries to understand the connections between facial expressions and inner emotions. But his friend fails to see it, and Descartes accepts the ambiguities that caused that inability to understand. In thinking, doubt is more reasonable than certainty. That is the case because it incorporates the imaged ambiguities. In the staging of the figure, the mixture of influences on the life of the great thinker becomes visible. From his sister who teaches the orphaned little boy and wakes him with her tentative harp music to an adolescent musician and singer who feed his interest in music; botany with his caring valet in his garden; lonely walks in the dunes where he images what the inside of stones look like; a butcher shop where he examines the eye from behind: the motor is curiosity, which leads to imagining and then imaging. The film also contains an imaging of the two dreams Descartes had in his early days when searching for a direction, and which he has described, or word-imaged— although our dream expert Sigmund Freud thought Descartes had made them up. No matter; the point is that nowhere in his life's search for knowledge can the imagination remain absent. And the imagination contains, or compels, imaging.

I

Justice
... but also Jeopardy and Jealousy

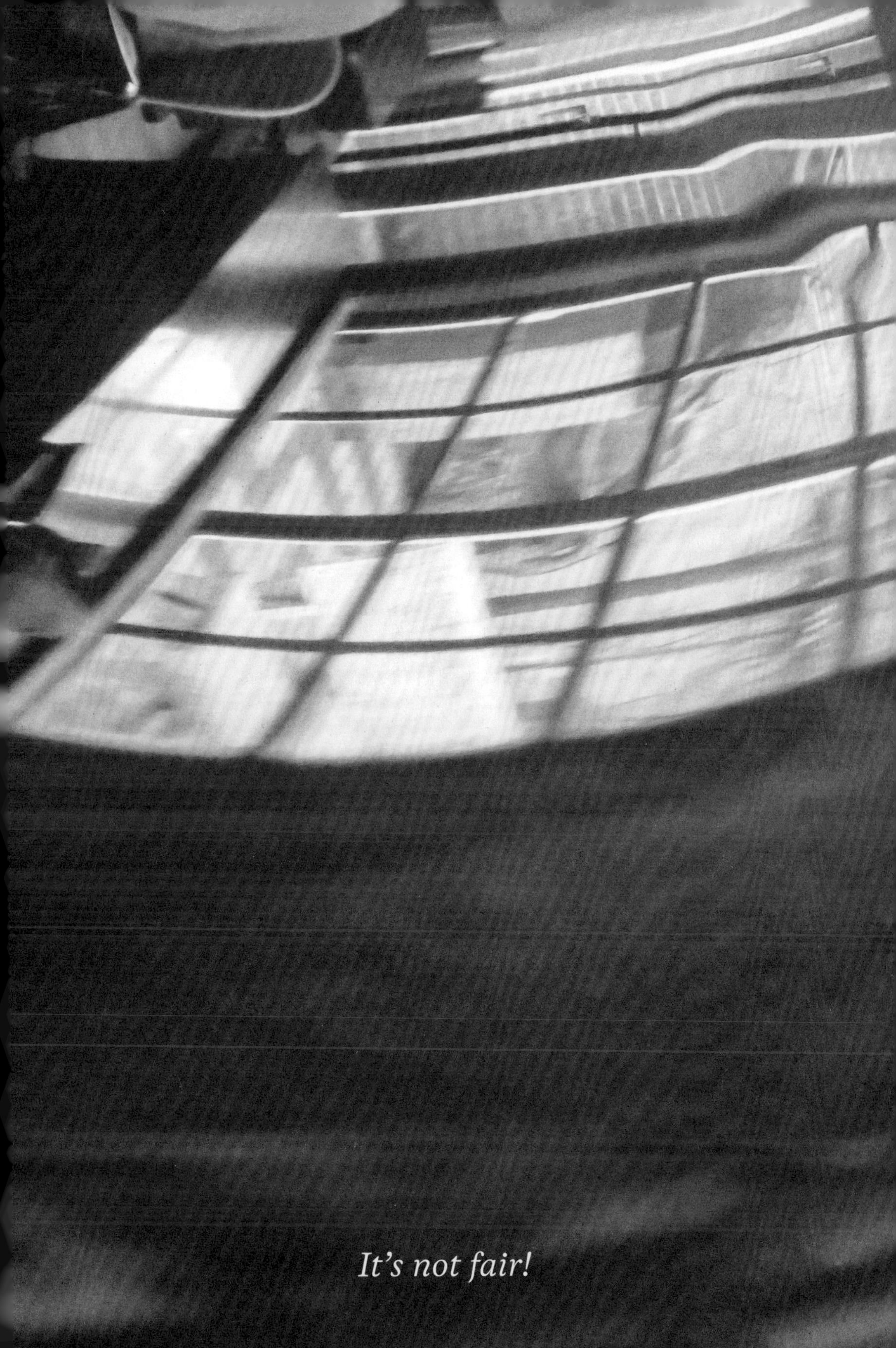

It's not fair!

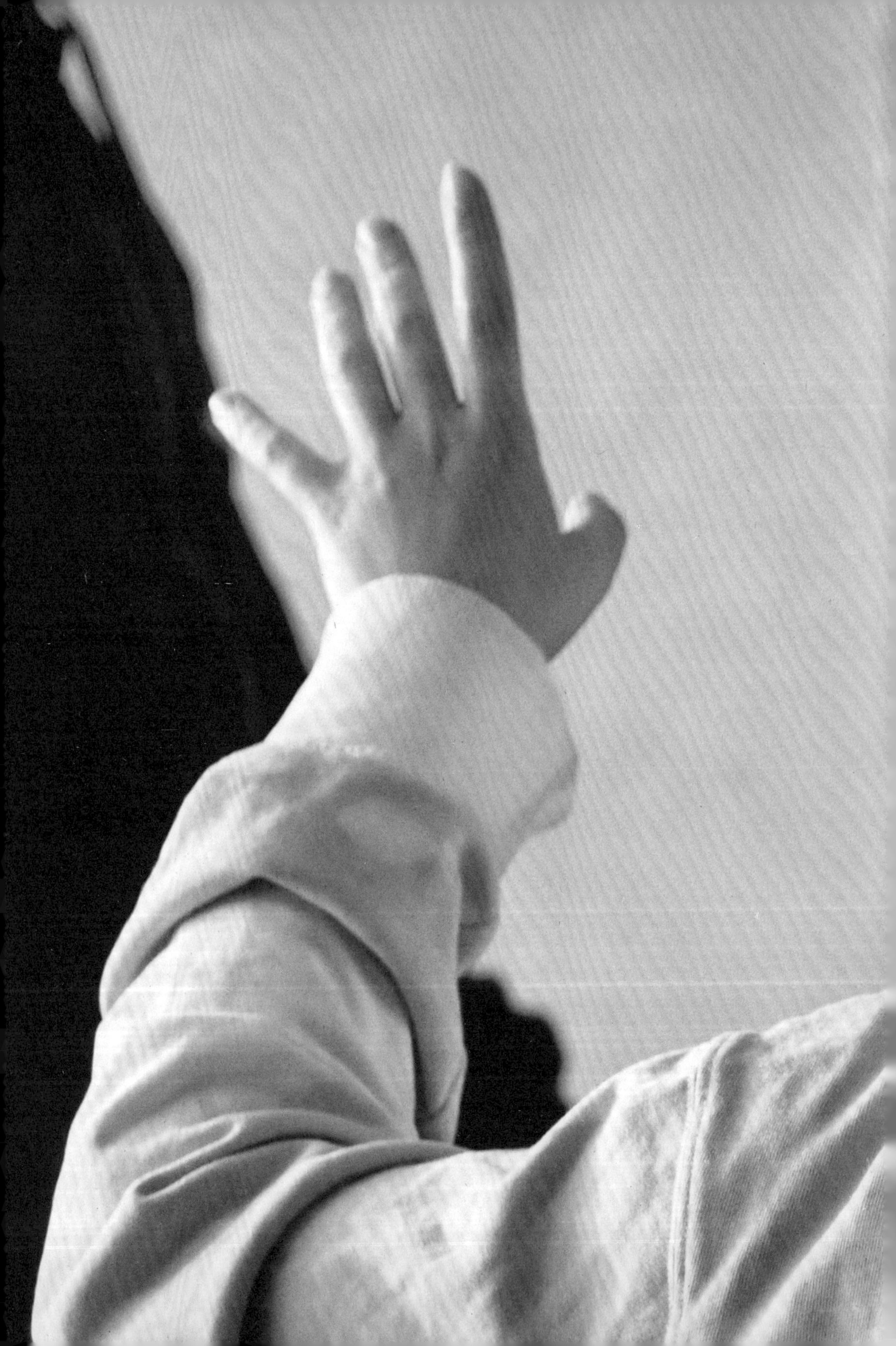

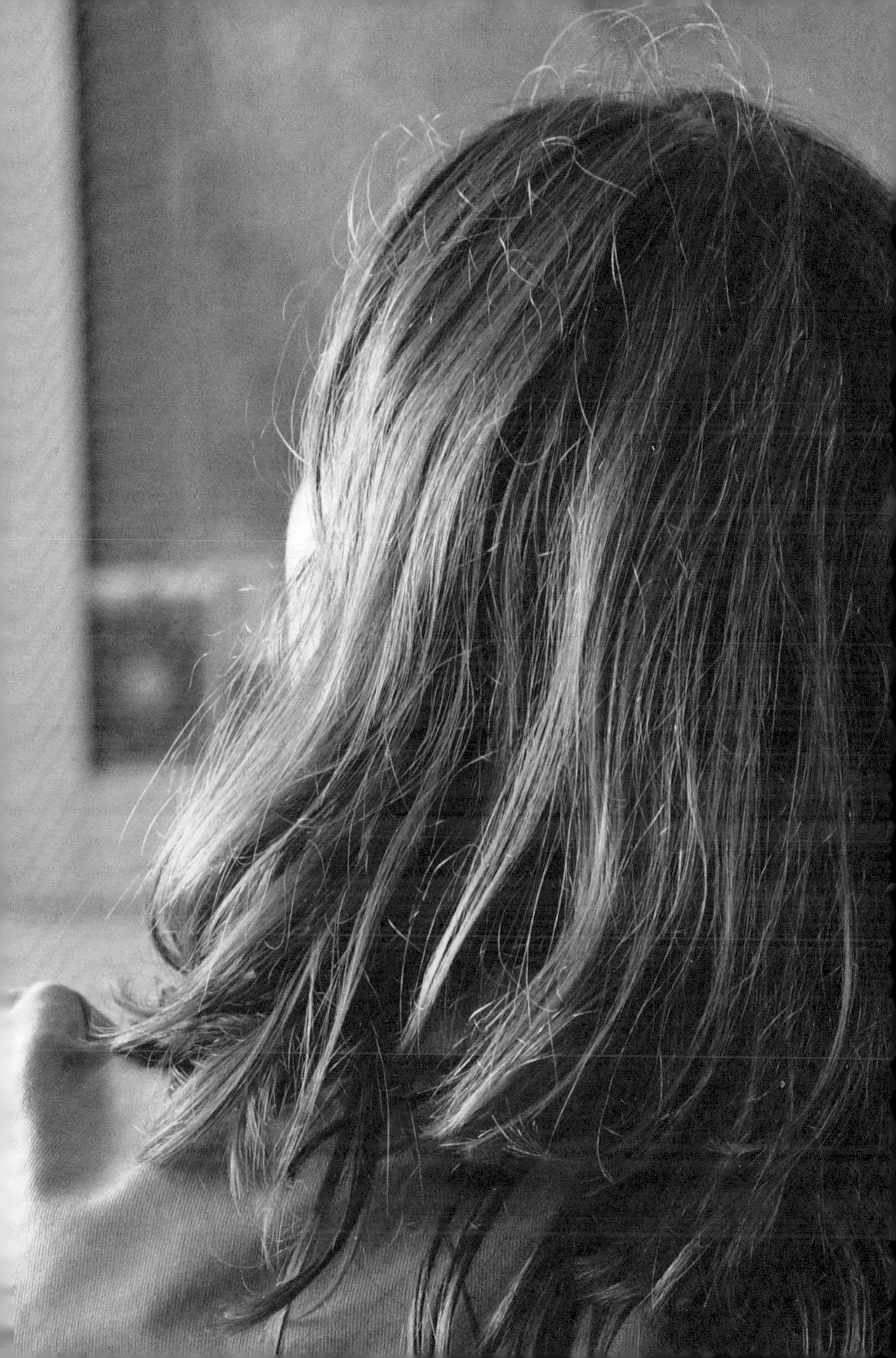

THOUGHTS IN THE PRESENT BRING IN THE PAST

An ordinary weekday in spring 2022. I just watched the news, and open my laptop, according to my morning routine. I begin to write this entry. But I am unable to get the news I just watched out of my head. They announced a strong increase in the number of *executions* for the year 2021. When I heard the anchor pronounce this in a flat voice, my first thought went to my early childhood, to the time when, at a stage in life when I knew so little, the death penalty had always repulsed, revolted me. How strong can the certainties of the Justice System be, I often thought, that the penalty for crimes is so definitive, irreversible? As if errors never occur! And if they do, is it just bad luck for the innocent person who is murdered by the Justice System? Yes, that would be *murder*. I called it that early on, having always been strongly committed to the proper words to use, from as far back as my memories go.

I remember my sense of justice has always been very strong, but where did that come from? I grew up with stories of the Nazi occupation of the Netherlands, in which my parents had suffered. I was born after the liberation, as a baby boomer. Nevertheless, those stories, told passionately by my parents who had lived through those atrocious times, may have sawn the seed for a sense of outrage in the face of injustice. But I think it was discussing the death penalty with my parents that set me more explicitly on that course of thinking. I must have been around four years old when I first heard about executions outside of the situation of war. It confused me totally. So far, I vaguely knew about murder, killing, massacre: I heard people talk about it, but I was too young to be allowed to seriously participate in such discussions. These horrible events were either individual criminal acts, or simply logical, normal when they were part of wars: this is how the adults tried to reassure me.

I revolted especially against the idea that killing could, under any circumstance, be considered normal, let alone 'just'. This seemed to me an exercise in 'an eye for an eye' kind of retaliation or revenge, which went against the idea of forgiveness that, I thought, probably under the influence of my Roman Catholic upbringing, should be involved in justice. The criminal killed, so we kill him. Doesn't that make us similar to the monster who murdered? So, never one to be easily shut up, I began to intrude in the adult conversations. This was not appreciated at all; I was meddling, disturbing their lofty discussions. It was in one of those moments, mentioned under B, that my parents called me, with irony or contempt, a 'Miss know-it-all': the one who always intervened in what didn't concern her. One of those moments, as a consequence, occurred when I felt utterly lonely, even in that very busy household of eleven, plus guests. This loneliness has remained part of who I am. Once I objected to that slurring title, saying that I did not know it all, so, the slur made no sense. But yes, I did have an opinion about a lot of things that I heard of or that happened. May I say it, or are you shutting me up? Knowing and having an opinion was not the same thing, was it? They just shrugged it off. What's the difference between knowing and considering, thinking?

For me, that difference was important, and began to matter more and more. Until this day. I am sharply aware of the many things I do not know. When I feel overwhelmed by a request for a lecture or an article on a subject I don't know enough about, I become insecure. The self-doubt that this elicits can in fact be helpful. The lack of knowledge makes me consider declining, although I find that very difficult, especially when I know the person inviting me, feel I owe them, or when the topic, the place or the other speakers appear so exciting. This, in addition to feeling flattered by the invitation. What to do with not-knowing? That lack of knowledge can be filled up at least partially, of course, by studying the topic in more depth. This is my usual course of action, and always gives me secret joy; I realized that am addicted to learning.

But of course, knowledge is never good or full enough. Yet, even with very partial knowledge, I do have opinions, and the desire to convince others of them. On the way between expressing opinions in a persuasive mood and gathering knowledge helped by my innate curiosity, in the discussions that ensue the knowledge can only increase. But this can only happen as long as *listening* is an important element in the process, which must be truly dialogic. This has always been crucial to me: to be listened to, which was what was not happening when I objected to the death penalty. But of course, also, listening gained importance. Later, in my teaching, this conviction of the importance of listening has served me well. It has induced me to implement a justice of dialogue in teaching, and replace the idea that I am the one who knows more by respect for what people who know less, simply because of less experience and learning time, can therefore, instead, imagine, think through, and come up with.

I am writing these thoughts now, but they have been with me for as long as I can remember. They compelled me to contradict even the teacher when I was convinced she was wrong. This happened quite frequently. And then there was that memorable time when the parish priest who once a week came to the all-girls school to teach religion, explained the virgin Mary and the birth of Christ. Of course, the recommendation of the virtue of chastity—not that I knew anything about sex at the time—was the moral lesson that ended the lecture. I raised my hand and asked: how can something that is physically impossible, be a rule, and the miracle woman who did the impossible, be a role model for girls? This is not fair! The priest looked at me intensely, the other girls in the classroom held their breath, you could hear a pin drop... Then, after a while of that ominous silence he said, in a furious voice: 'Get out!' Being sent out of the classroom into the hallway was the worst punishment in school. And I knew he would probably tell my parents about my transgression. He visited our house regularly, and spoke Latin with my classicist father to keep their conversation confidential. See under Q. The beating by Father, the family form of punishment, loomed. Yet I felt so sure I was right that it didn't bother me.

JUSTICE IN JEOPARDY

'Justice in jeopardy' was a phrase that started to sing through my head when I learned a bit of English in my first year in high school. 'Jeopardy' was such a strange word, sounding so nice and then meaning something that is clearly bad. A strange word, different from most of the English words I was beginning to learn, without any recognizable connection to any of the words I already knew or that resembled Dutch words. The alliteration must have emphasized the sing-song quality of the phrase. It was one of the early moments that the discrepancies between sound and meaning began to dawn on me as a helpful tool for understanding meaning as multiple, wavering, and imperative. Justice is in jeopardy when the punishment for the transgression, or crime, is either out of proportion, or cannot be rectified in case of error. This is by definition at stake with the death penalty. Or, in minor instances, if there is no punishable transgression committed at all.

This was frequently the case during my childhood when my mother complained to my father about us failing to do the household chores to her satisfaction, or accused us of any tiny transgression. For example, not putting on the clothes she had in mind for us for that day, coming home from school a bit late, or not getting the brilliant grades in school they expected from us. I always felt revolt at the decisions of what was wrong in what we did. The ritual was fixed: Father would take the sinner to his study, put her or him over his knees, and gave them a solid beating; this was in store for me when the priest sent me out. If the accusation was serious enough, we would even be forced to take off our pants, so that he could beat us on the bare buttocks. That would hurt more. And although there was never an improper (abusive) gesture involved, I always felt that such physical penalties could not be 'just'. Not that I had an argument about it. It simply didn't feel right.

I didn't have the same strong feeling of justice in jeopardy when, later on, when we became too big for such punishments, grounding or withholding pocket money became the penalty. Something about the physical attack implied in the beatings made it seem wrong, and uncharacteristic for my father, who was never violent otherwise. In a sense it seemed to hurt him, or at least, it hurt my affection and respect for him. It was mostly Mother who accused us, and thus caused the beatings. I resented her for it, but then, I did vaguely know why my mother complained so much about us. She was, to put it simply, almost permanently unhappy. Part of that unhappiness came from her being condemned to give up working, and thus not having a social and intellectual life, satisfaction and respect, and instead being imprisoned in housewife-dom. I mentioned earlier, under B, that the man who came to hang wallpaper was chatting with my mother, and thinking he was complimenting her, he said something about all of us children doing so well in school, and ending his compliment by saying, with a smile: 'They must have the brains of their father.' I don't remember if my mother's facial expression changed, but later she retold the story with indignation. Rightly so; she was as intelligent as Father was. For me this was one of those moments that meaning emerged out of my increasing feminist passion, already mentioned: a merging of indignation and injustice. It was such an insult; I thought she should send him packing! How dare he...

Nothing happened, but in my mind, something did: a moment of meaning-making. I suddenly understood, I saw that issue of justice move into the domestic sphere, beyond being beaten by Father or the grand issue of the Justice System and the injustices it perpetrated. How unfair life was to my mother, and that injustice, beyond her unhappy married life, included her relationship with others. Her social status was damaged by it. This awareness joined the incipient feminism already inside me. But in that earlier anecdote mentioned under B, it was about my own life. This time it was Mother's. Time became unstable. Now I can see how that earlier rejection of Father's ideas about my future life had already been influenced by the constant albeit unreflected witnessing of injustice done to my mother, supposedly my role model. 'It's not fair!' became a phrase that more and more frequently sang through my head. That was the everyday phrase for the more poetic 'justice in jeopardy'.

Another event of injustice happened recently. A colleague was passed over for an appointment as full professor, in favour of someone who had been accused earlier of a lack of academic integrity (plagiarism). It felt like we went back to square one, back to my early days on the job: a woman passed over for no transgression other than being a woman, a man pardoned instead of punished for his demonstrable transgression; being born male, hence, superior. In vignette E I already mentioned the colleague who dared to say out loud, in a staff meeting, that as a woman I should be at home cooking instead of insulting the colleagues by publishing more than they did. But now, my sense of justice merged with my sense of time. I felt pushed back into the past. The fact that the gender issue was obviously not mentioned didn't make it invisible. Comparing the publication lists of both candidates to the professorship, and knowing her teaching skills, made it only too clear: we were back in the time from before the second feminist wave. It made me desperate. The jeopardy justice was in felt like a syrupy substance out of which I could not escape, and which I could not wash off. Like being stuck in hot, melting asphalt. The recurring need of resistance to injustice made me aware that such struggles would never be sufficient, and would remain a burning necessity. And then, when I was pondering this gloomy absence of improvement, this recent, haunting other injustice, known world-wide, came back to haunt me.

It had come to me on the news again. 'Oh no!' This was my response when, totally unexpectedly, I was made a witness to the murder of George Floyd in real time. This unforgettable horror was suddenly there in my living room, when the full video of eight minutes and forty-six seconds was broadcast on 25 May 2020. It was made and shown, watched and protested against all over the world, in a wave of 'here we go again!' In the terse words of the prominent American visual analyst W.J.T. Mitchell, who published a pivotal, mercilessly critical article with the illuminating title 'Present Tense: An Iconology of the Epoch', the video was made 'by a seventeen-year-old girl, Darnella Frazier, who had the courage not to look away.' (2021) This, I learned, and now feel, is what matters in cultural life: not looking away. And looking happens by definition in the 'present tense'. While the world was barely adjusting to the Covid-19 pandemic, the endemic police brutality and racism was thrown into our faces. Indeed, justice was, and is, in jeopardy.

And thus, the #BlackLivesMatter resistance movement of 2013, then already a much belated repetition, had to be re-activated—again. Racial injustice, at its worst, racist violence, let's call it by its name: murder, doesn't seem to go away. Nor does gender injustice. Visual imaging, including the video made by a teenager, reports on it, shows it, in an act of witnessing. Thus, it brings it up for discussion and encourages protest: the kind of action we call resistance. And this visualization is necessary. Words alone would not suffice. That would fail to convey in all its horror what Mitchell describes as 'the unbearably slow strangulation'. For we need to experience that slowness, endure the full eight minutes and forty-six seconds, during which we see, witness, while the victim said several times 'I can't breathe'; to no avail. He was put to death: murdered. Time and tense, and also movement, all matter in witnessing, seeing, understanding horror, and activating us to resist. Clearly, #BlackLivesMatter and #MeToo are the two most powerful activist movements of the past decades, when they were so strongly needed, as they are now, in our present, again. The recurrence, the refusal to go away, makes time so problematic that I feel constantly compelled to argue for its knotty, complex nature. In the case of the murder of George Floyd, the slowness of the crime is key to its torturousness. This is worse than murder alone. *Slow* strangulation: Floyd had not done anything, but even if he had, nothing can ever justify a 'slow strangulation'. The murderer was a police officer: someone empowered to enforce, and representing official justice; hence all of us.

JUSTICE, JEOPARDY, JEALOUSY

Among the many possible grounds leading to jeopardizing justice, something as banal as jealousy is a frequent trigger. I am talking about small instances of a negative feeling towards others that most people would not even notice, and surely not cast in terms of justice. Yet, those are the mini-events that determine the quality of the fabric of social life; so, they do matter. I remember moments when jealousy ruined potentially wonderful experiences. 'It's not fair' is the phrase that calls out that justice is in jeopardy. But that phrase can be uttered rightly or wrongly. I was as jealous a person as most. In our household, there were many moments that one child got preferential treatment, making the others, at least me, jealous.

As mentioned before, when my parents inherited a piano from an aunt, my older brother and sister got piano lessons. I thought that was fair enough. They were older than me, my turn would come. I was not yet jealous, much as I would have loved to get the same opportunity. But then, a few months later, the brother who came after me in age, was also enrolled in piano lessons. That was one of those 'It's not fair' moments. I protested: why he, and not me? Instead of understanding, they accused me of jealousy. Rightly so; I was jealous indeed. Not in the sense of destructive envy (under E) but of wanting to have what the other, here my younger brother, got and I didn't. But the jealousy was triggered more by the lack of justice than by the desire to have what he had. Jealousy can be a form of righteous anger when it is a subjective manifestation of or reasonable response to relative deprivation, as a function of structural inequality. This lack in turn caused a lack of understanding, kept me angry, and produced jealousy. Only some time later my parents explained to me why he had been put in the piano lesson privilege. It was because he was a difficult child, inclined to mischief. The discipline of having to practice the piano would keep him away from the temptations of the outside world. Then I understood. But perhaps, being typecast as the 'good girl' who needed no special care, was not helpful for my sense of self. Moreover, the jealousy was already implanted in me, and remained.

This leads to a confession I cannot avoid. I tried to understand what my brother did wrong that justified the unfair privileging. It turned out that he came home late, got in trouble at school, roamed around the village, fought with other kids, arbitrarily scolded people, and, when the first supermarkets appeared, he did some shoplifting. That became the limit. At one time the police came to our house, sent by the complaining owner of the shop. Of course, brother got the bare-buttocks beating, had to return the stolen items, and, I suppose, must have felt humiliated. He and I didn't talk about it. For me, with the jealousy festering inside, it became an incentive to do what he had done, hoping to get what he got: those wished-for piano lessons. So, I too began to steal small items from the shop. Proud I was, also, that I had not been caught, whereas he had been. So, a sense of superiority over him developed, which compensated for the failure to get what I wanted. Small moments of meaning-making; nothing consequential, but it does add up.

Later on, in my academic life, jealousy turned out to be so common that even trying to evoke memories of it seems a bit futile. I felt jealousy when a colleague got a promotion that in my view was not deserved, or for which I qualified better. Or when an article I did not approve of, or was written by someone I disliked, got published in a prestigious journal. But at that point I had already learned the difference between jealousy and envy. The former I recognized and to a certain extent, accepted as part of 'me'; from the latter I firmly stayed away. For I knew its destructiveness, even before experiencing it. This semantic distinction, thus, became a very useful guideline for my behaviour and my emotional life. I learned to distinguish and recognize, including the risks involved in failing to make that difference matter.

But despite the difference that makes jealousy more acceptable, or liveable than envy, justice remains involved in both. As most readers will know, jealousy is also an issue in love relationships. That makes it a polysemic, 'multi-meaning' word, as so many words are. What is officially called 'adultery', having sex with someone else than your 'official' partner, is a source of jealousy. It works that way because it inspires anxiety: the fear of losing the loved one, the love relationship, the mode of life that came with it. This can be seen as the counterpart of the desire to have what another person has. I have felt pangs of jealousy when the person I loved would have sex with someone else. In Dutch, this is expressed by the phrase 'going strange' (*vreemdgaan*). This Dutch phrase acquired a very interesting and relevant background for me, due to my research. For, as I discovered later, when studying stories from the Hebrew Bible and being already adamant about 'close reading', the word usually translated as 'prostitute' (*zonah*) also has a masculine form. This intrigued me. It took some research to find out that this male form meant not male prostitution but 'stranger' or 'foreigner'. Not only does that cast doubt on the translation of *zonah* as prostitute, in some stories clearly bizarre, as when the 'son of a prostitute' knows who his father is. This was the case of Jephtah, in Judges 11; the man who sacrificed his own daughter. He was, the text says, the son of Giliad. Unlikely. But it also sheds new light on the stubborn tendency to xenophobia—then and now. This is yet another example of how justice in jeopardy spreads its tentacles. If foreignness is fused with sexual promiscuity, and prejudices are based on that con-fusion, the phrase 'it's not fair!' gains new and important relevance.[20]

This leads me back to love relationships. The next issue of meaning, then, becomes the behaviour that jealousy inspires. I read in novels about 'crimes of passion', violence and murder committed by husbands whose wives were caught in adultery. Flabbergasted, I discovered that in France, where the phrase was perhaps invented, such crimes of passion were considered mitigating circumstances, reducing the responsibility of the perpetrator of the violence for what he had done, even if that was murder. The jealousy is then considered to come in a fit, as if physically, and the violence is therefore not premeditated; hence—the causality of 'hence' to be taken with a grain of salt—less criminal. Clearly, this is most frequently the doing of men, and the fit of jealousy stimulated and aggravated by a misplaced sense of ownership over the woman. This brings in another enduring injustice; this discriminatory practice belongs in the category of my refrain *justice in jeopardy*. Currently feminists are attempting to use different words and their meanings to redress some of it. The more appropriate term is, then, *femicide*. Justice in jeopardy indeed. Words do matter.

---

20 Adding a hyphen between 'con' and 'fusion' was a creative invention of Kyoo Lee in a personal communication. It separates the togetherness (con-) from the merging that can, indeed, produce confusion.

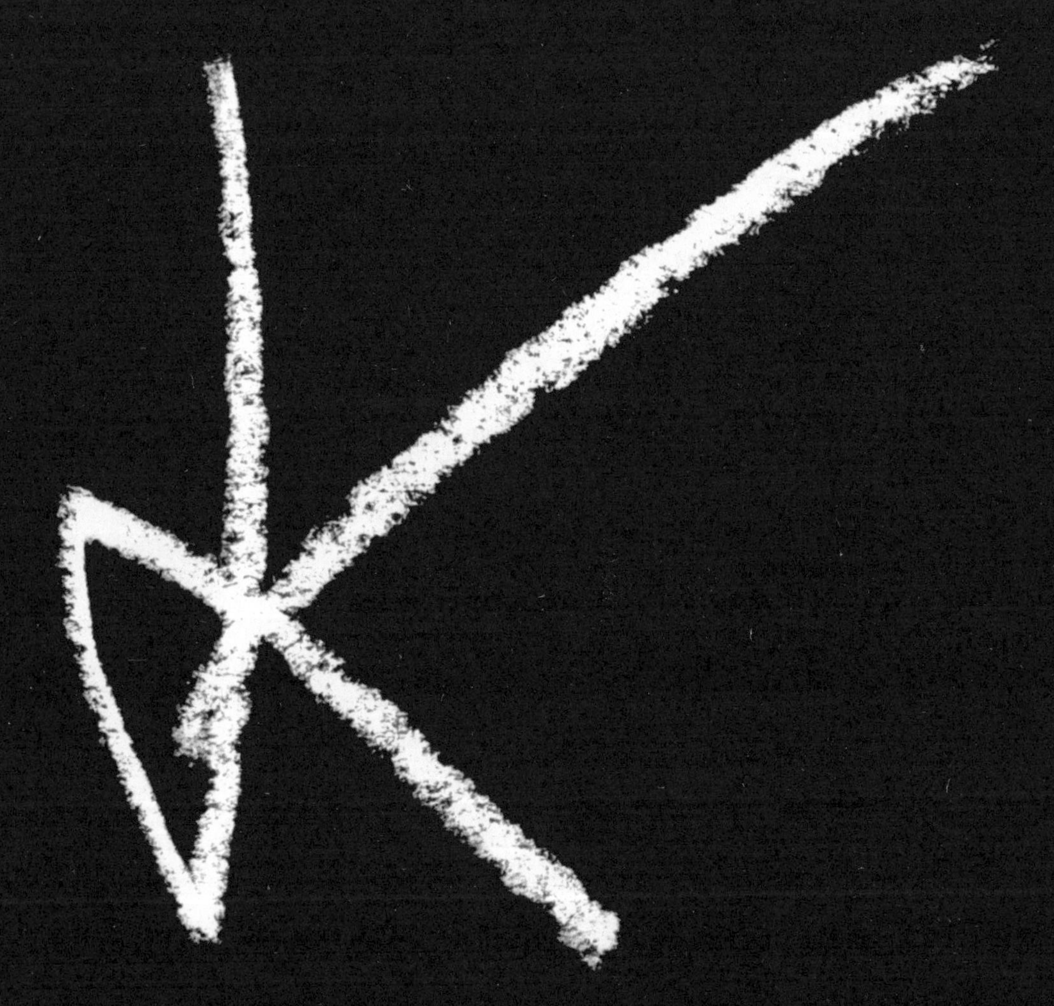

Knowing

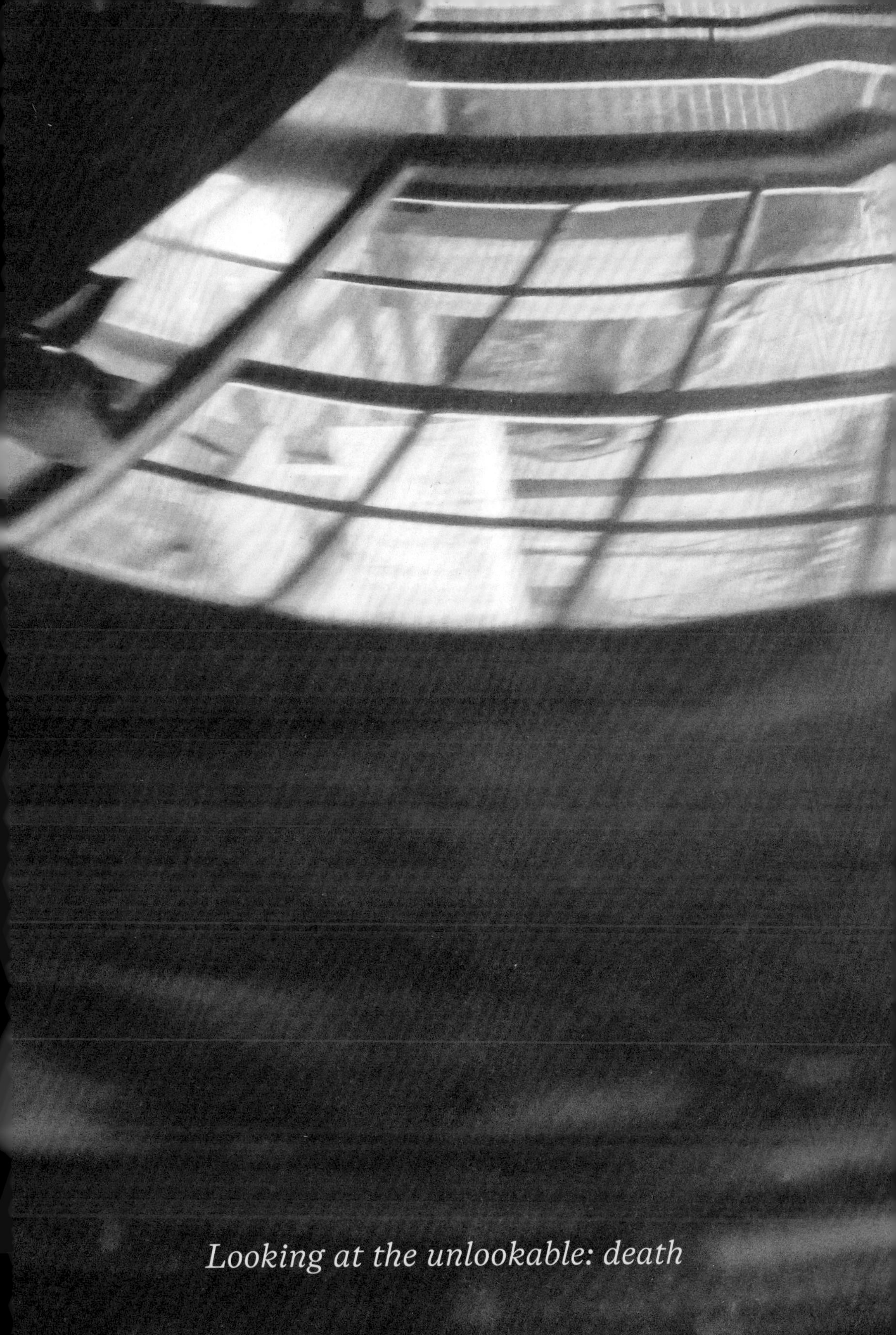

Looking at the unlookable: death

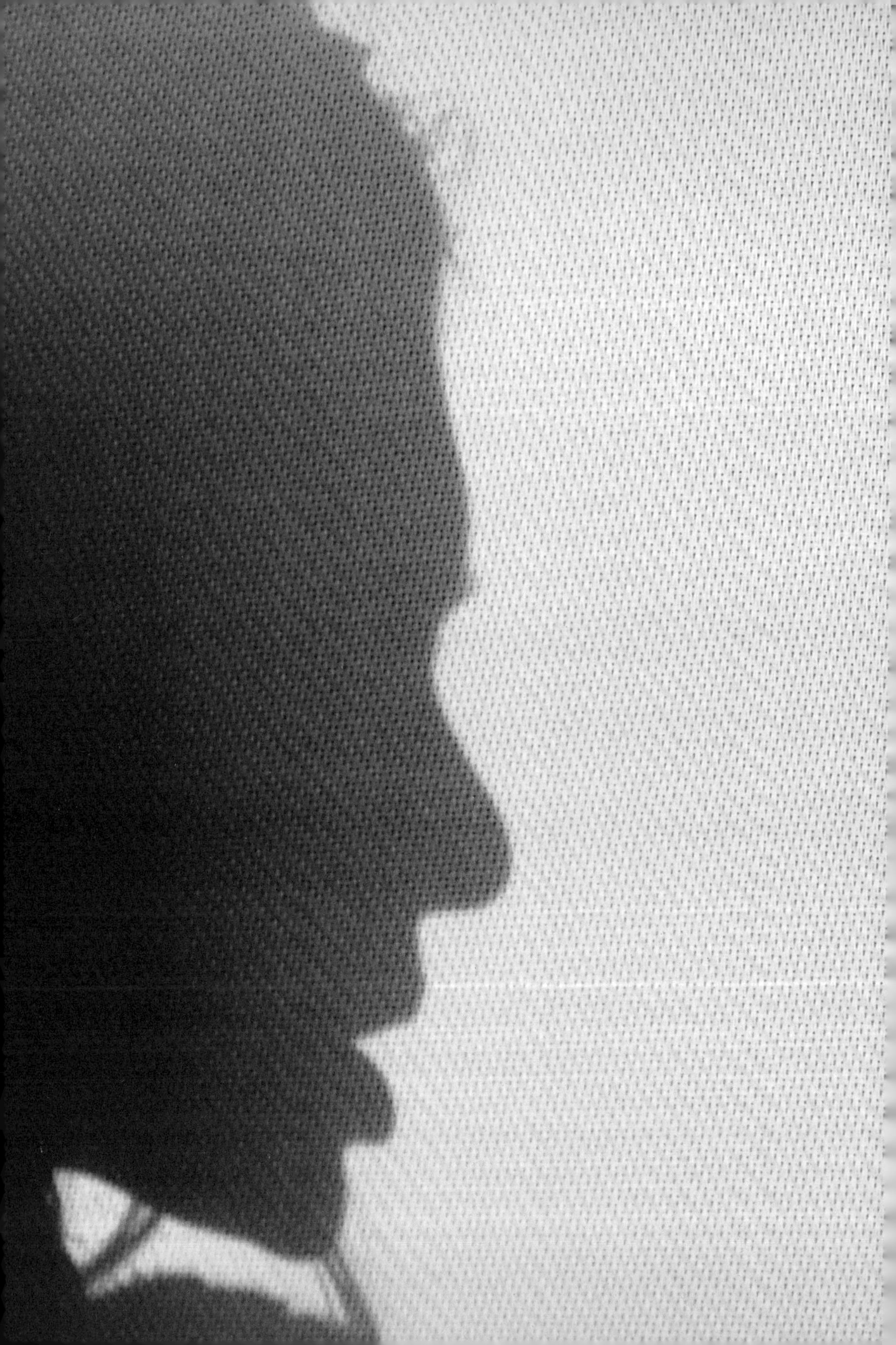

At first, I had planned to call this vignette 'Knowledge'. That would be the most widespread word beginning with a K, even if, to my dismay, the letter K is not pronounced in this English word. But worse, it is, in itself, a wrong word. As a noun it suggests an accomplished, finished possession: to *have* knowledge of something, and as such it matters to me to undermine it. The noun intimates a certain stability, possession, and completion. In contrast to that idea, I only know knowledge as a process. It is something which I can and do strive towards; a goal, an aim. That endeavour is what makes it exciting. It is an activity that is never finished. Hence the insecurity that befalls me when I feel that an invitation is beyond my knowledge, as mentioned in J. Instead of feeling discouraged, that failure to know encourages me to learn more.[21]

I have crystal-clear memories of moments when I understood, knew, or sensorially grasped something that, until then, had escaped me. Those were moments when meaning-in-the-making suddenly appeared as a revelation, a liberation from an ignorance that, I realized only then, had bothered me. To learn, for example, how my parents had been able to survive the war, led to knowing many things at once. One thing they did was, for my father, to hide under the floor, between the floor and the cellar, in a shallow space I had not known existed until I heard that story. Then, when the doorbell rang and they expected it to be German soldiers coming to catch and abduct my father for forced labour, Mother grabbed the baby, and opened the door with a friendly smile and the adorable baby on her arm. She *knew* Germans were sentimental about mothers-and-babies. I learned this only then, through the story.

So, the soldiers left without coming in and checking the entire house. But at the last moment they did turn around and grabbed the woollen man's coat from the coat hanger, so that my father was freezing cold for the rest of that winter. But they did not deduct from the presence of that coat that he must have been in the house. Mother had not counted on that lack of deduction, nor that brazen thieving. She was devastated because of the loss of that rare and indispensable piece of warm clothing. So, she did know something, which was utterly useful,

---

21 This chapter owes much to a very important book by Françoise Davoine, the second chapter of which (in the second edition) is devoted to knowing in the sense I address it here. See Davoine, *Mother Folly* (2014).

saved my father's life, and might have put the baby at risk if she had been wrong. But she did not know everything; such as the occupying soldiers' belief they had the right to steal. Knowledge is incomplete by definition. Never complete: I now appreciate and treasure that incompletion, as something that keeps me on my toes, always alert to learn something new. But still, the knowledge-in-becoming acquired special meaning: as something that, to put it literally, *de-fused* a *con-fusion*, or helped me escape from an ignorance.

Just an early, much less dramatic example. In kindergarten, I must have been four or five, we got a lesson in tying shoelaces. You may wonder how that relates to knowledge. But for me, a bit sloppy as a child, I frequently stumbled because a shoelace had become undone. So, that lesson was utterly helpful, almost life-saving, at least knee-saving. And that usefulness has stayed with me. Today, when I see someone on the street with an undone shoelace, I alert them to it, *knowing* how easily you can fall because of it. Knowing, in terms of learning practical skills: I remember the feeling of joy when that happened; as, in this case, when I knew how to keep my knees from being injured. But the limitation of learning to practicalities was soon overruled by a more general sense of getting close to knowable things, with the subsequent pleasure in learning; learning things I didn't know I didn't know. Not only the skills, but also the desire to know in itself: letters, words, reading; numbers, operations, results. The map of my country; after that, the map of Europe, then the map of the world. Recent history, but also history of long ago, going back from the Middle Ages to antiquity to what is called 'pre-history'. Stop: this was a term I already objected to the first time I heard it. I wanted to know why that term would be meaningful.

I raised my hand and asked. When the teacher then explained that the preposition 'pre-', in this case as always, meant 'before' and hence, that the period label meant the (non-) history from before writing was invented, even as the avid reader I was becoming, I protested against the implications of that notion. I knew it meant that writing was the beginning of everything, and that cultures based on oral transmission would somehow be 'pre-', insufficiently cultural. As a consequence, my desire to learn also bred the critical mindset that has always stayed with me; as has my obsession with the need to be precise with words. I realized that 'pre-' is as problematic as the 'post-' I now frequently critique, with 'postcolonial' as the worst lie. Meaning 'after', the preposition ignores, or denies, that what came before was not only indispensable to get 'beyond' it (another of those deceptive words) but that going through whatever came before always left traces, bits of it, without which the alleged but deceptive 'post-' is impossible.

And a bit later, I acquired skills in knitting, sewing, cooking, dusting, dish-washing, and all those proficiencies we girls were doomed to learn: confining as it was gender-wise, it was also empowering to know those 'how-to' skills. It gave me the authority even to order the boys to shine shoes or peel potatoes—the two things I knew how to do, but that were the only ones they as boys also knew how to do and, as the family ideology had it, where strong enough to do. I discovered quite early that the girl-knowledge was not a display of skills or strength, but rather a tool for the adults to exploit us, forcing us to 'help out' in a household too large for one mother to handle. Doomed by my curiosity, which compelled me to learn dexterities by undertaking the learning myself, I ended up being saddled with 'services' to others, such as the local priests who frequently took my charming mother out for a motor scooter trip. Coming in briefly to fetch her, they would dump a bag of clothes that needed repairing in front of me, saying 'please' (if they thought of being polite). And there went my free Wednesday afternoon. Instead of reading, I had to spend it mending socks, reattaching buttons, repairing tears or holes, and more. Sometimes the frustration and anger overruled my pride in being the handy girl at home, a status that had been instilled in me from early on. That ambivalence has stayed with me forever.

To be able to do, notice, understand something that had so far been outside of my grasp has always felt like an enrichment. Knowing made me feel less that child my parents scolded for always meddling with adult matters, as mentioned under B and J, and more a person standing on my own feet. That progress made me feel less doomed to girlhood; with a future of becoming the unhappy woman of which my mother was the sad example. Somehow, every stage in learning was a progress in knowing, and supported my autonomy as a person. Later, after I had decided, for rather arbitrary, anecdotal reasons, to take on the study of French at university, I tried acquiring the knowledge of that language, while bringing my baby (born when I was 19) in a basket as well as a piece of knitting to class, learning multitasking right away. But here, in my apprenticeship of that foreign language I had come to like for its sounds, my childhood habit of addictive reading came in good stead. I soon learned that to acquire the language, knowing grammar, vocabulary, and especially style, there was no better method than reading. The difference between the paradigms, lists, and rules, versus fluency and feeling for a language, became clear to me through attempting to read books written in that language.

This acquisition of knowledge through the practice of reading became a guideline I also used in teaching, in raising and educating my children, and later, in assisting them in rearing their own. Although one never becomes a 'native speaker' in an acquired foreign language, the internship of being inside a linguistic culture, and conversing with those who had been raised in it, helped me not only to become better at the language but also to understand how learning a language happens through the self-evident fluency of the encounter with the other language that reading it is. Thus, it became a double learning, of the matter and of the method. As a result, I have become a committed teacher, first in language (French) then in theoretical fields, such as literary theory and, later still, visual art, 'exhibition-ism', as I titled a small book about 'temporal togetherness' (2020) and more broadly, cultural analysis. The selection of the field is not what matters; it is how one approaches the cultural objects that, together, constitute that field, which is the reward of knowing. That is what knowing affords.[22]

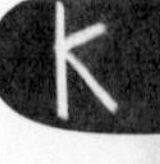

---

22 The book *Narratology in Practice*, about temporal togetherness, was requested as a reflection on contemporaneity, which I decided to devote to exhibition as a mode of being together in time.

ADVANTAGES OF NOT-KNOWING

Not only knowing, but also noticing and understanding the limits of knowing is helpful on the way to insight. Having to speak and write in a foreign language, such as of course, in addition to French, English, which is also the Esperanto of today, and later, Spanish, in order to make ourselves understood by people from other countries, is a requirement that students sometimes complain about. Helping them appreciate the limitation of their knowledge as a plus, as the way it facilitated their 'estranged' look at words or phrases, was a useful teaching activity for which I could mine my own earlier experiences. I had myself been both annoyed and amused when I told a feminist Spanish friend that the word for 'pregnant', which is, believe it or not, 'embarazada', is embarrassing, she laughed out loud and said it had never occurred to her to question that word, even when she was pregnant herself. This is how being a 'native speaker', allegedly an expert in the language, can also hinder knowing. In contrast, it helps the bilingual person to wonder if a word used to denote women also exists in the masculine. And yes, 'embarazado' is used, but with the meaning you would expect: to feel ashamed. This meaning must therefore also underlie that allegedly normal Spanish word for pregnant.

Hence, the gender ideology is at work again in the language. It is a case comparable to the Hebrew word for prostitute, *zonah*, mentioned in J. When that turned out to also exist in the masculine form, my Hebrew studies colleagues—who had never questioned this—told me it meant 'stranger' or 'foreigner', and shrugged it off; just a different word. For me, that explained a lot. Most revealing, it qualifies the negative view of foreigners, still rampant. This is one of those cases where the limit of knowing helps to make the next step. There is so much I do not know... which is why I object to the idea that the noun suggesting knowledge can ever imply completeness.

In the preceding bit I mentioned some cases where not-knowing was due to the automatic assumptions implied in the alleged knowledge of 'aboriginal' or 'native' people. Much of what they assume is right, or almost, or approximately, albeit it never entirely certain. But they can also overlook the obvious, simply because they think they already know, as I have argued for the dubious implications of some words in languages that for me are foreign. The lack of knowledge I have felt so often tends to entice me to learn more, to acquire more knowledge. But there is also, sometimes, the desire for not-knowing, as when I am convinced the knowledge would be abhorrent. I go to museums and read books and articles when I wish to know things. But then, the display may comprehend scenes of torture, murder, rape, and other forms of violence that I must know about but do not wish to contemplate. This is a limit to the knowing-drive. It is also a drawback in visual culture. This may also lead to censorship, however.

As many of us know, because it is so frequently discussed in 'holocaust studies', since Adorno's famous 1949 indictment of making and enjoying poetry 'after Auschwitz', what I call *modesty* is a crucial issue in our relationship to (re)presentation. In order to clear a path to a different knowing, allow me to present the Adorno quote from his philosophical prose in the form of poetry.[23]

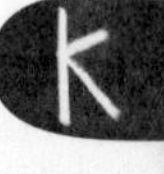

> Cultural criticism finds itself faced with
> the final stage of the dialectic of
> culture and barbarism.
> To write poetry after Auschwitz is barbaric.
> And this corrodes even the knowledge of
> why it has become impossible to
> write poetry today.

Instead of the usual over-citing without engaging, the status of this fragment as poetry helps to de-naturalize its usual exploitation as a simplistic if meaningful ethical guideline. This formal intervention demonstrates my mode of engaging with an object. The 'verses' are bound by *enjambment*, the artful breaking up of words that normally belong together; here prepositions and their complements—with, of, of, to. Poetry is a form of discourse one can learn by heart as well as complicate, and read aloud in musical cadence and tone. Reading poetry is

---

23 I cite this quote from 1974 from the most widely distributed version, since there are many different publications of it. See Adorno, *Can One Live After Auschwitz?* (2003).

usually slower and more detailed, with equal attention to every word.

Here, such poetic reading also entails the need to consider its sequel, where the philosopher gives the reason for this severe indictment: he refuses to make sense of what doesn't make sense. Such sense-making is wrong because it would be honouring violence with semiotic access; and to take pleasure, in other words, in making a potentially pornographic use of the suffering of others. Adorno explains that his refusal to condone such renderings is its potential pornographic use indeed: 'The so-called artistic rendering of the naked physical pain of those who were beaten down with rifle butts contains, however distantly, the possibility that pleasure can be *squeezed* out from it.' It is this pleasure, the sheer possibility of it, that Adorno calls 'barbaric'. I take the verb 'to squeeze' as exemplary; it entails force and violence.[24]

The flip side of Adorno's compelling call for modesty is a forbidding taboo that makes the violence invisible, however. My turning it into poetry deprives the statement of its naturalized self-evidence; of its simple logic that is also a form of censorship. It is against this taboo that French art historian Georges Didi-Huberman spoke out in his short but influential treatise, which is a plea for attention to even the vaguest Auschwitz photographs, proposing how their lack of clarity makes knowing difficult, but not impossible: 'In order to know, you must imagine', as his opening sentence has it. And in order to relate to others we do need to know, and when full knowledge is impossible, we still must try to approximate, encircle, or *feel* it. This is a different kind of knowing, against which the objectivists would revolt, but that is so necessary that I now think it has been the unreflected inspiration for my turn to literary theory, then to visual art, to exhibition practices, and later still, to making films myself. The imagination is indispensable.

Under vignette I, my partiality in favour of the imagination as a vital element of thinking, learning, and knowing was put forward. I am convinced that any attempt to discard the imagination from knowledge under the banner of objectivity

---

24 Adorno, *Can One Live After Auschwitz?* (2003), 252; emphasis added.

is a mistaken desire to limit knowledge to the object of it,
rather than to what matters more: the dialogue, or interaction,
between the (re-)searching subject and the object that, such
objectivists wrongly assume, is dead, silent, unmoving, just
waiting for the grid of theory to be put on it, as an 'application'
that would automatically yield the truth about the object.
Instead, knowing that there is something I don't know but
should know is an effective lure. But it can also yield to curiosity, and with the help of the imagination and the skill of imaging, it can make the subject more open to the kind of knowing
that is richer, denser, and more useful than what before was
taken as the utterly worthwhile knowledge: the objective truth.
For, there is so much more to know that than bare-bone and
illusory knowledge of 'the facts'.[25]

PAINFUL KNOWING

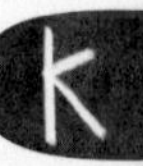

When I was six or seven, the two-year-old little son of friends
of my parents, Robbie, had died of leukaemia. I had not known
he was fatally ill. Shock, horror, weeping all over the house. It
was so unfair that a child had to die so young. That a little boy
I had cuddled and taken for walks in the stroller, suddenly was
dead: I could not imagine what that meant. The child's parents
invited us, the entire family, to come for a goodbye moment,
to see the dead body in the coffin. I was very reluctant to go,
but my parents said it would be impolite to not go. So, dragging
my feet, I went along, fearful of what I was about to have to
see. But then, when we came into the room, where the small
coffin was surrounded by flowers, and the atmosphere smelling
of incense as if it was a church, it seemed like an altar. After a
while I dared glance at the dead child. Two things struck me,
in that important moment of meaning-making. First of all, he
looked angelic, beautiful. Not at all devastated, but quiet, as
if sleeping. Second, I hardly recognized him. This was not the
Robbie I had known. He was a different person. Not a person,
really.

 This was the first time I saw a dead person. But what I

---

25 For more on curiosity, see under N.

knew without knowing I knew it, in that child's room, was that death eliminates the person we have known alive. They look so different, it almost seems convincing, that story of the soul flying away to heaven (if the person had deserved that), which the church tried to make us believe. Although I never really bought that story, the confrontation with the dead little boy put me on the path of knowing that death does, indeed, cancel, eliminate the life that was the only way I had known that person before. The discrepancy between a person in life and what is for good reasons called their 'remains' after death was what I did not know and learned then and there. This knowing included the irreversibility of death, the certainty, also for those who loved the person, that what we call 'moving on' is the only possible course of action. For, as the phrase has it, that person is gone.

The confrontation with death, its radical differentiation, inevitable as it is, also is a useful way of knowing. The suddenness, the shock, but also the acceptance of the reality of the unacceptable: they all contribute to the courage of the survivors to go on with life, and to knowing how to support the most bleakly bereaved. This is why violent death is so unacceptable, including attempts to know it. Adorno warned against the pornographic effect of seeing, contemplating, the results of violence: murder. This makes the death penalty so 'barbaric', to borrow Adorno's qualifier once more. Let alone war. I never understood the term 'war crimes'—aren't all acts of warfare crimes? The verb Mother used to describe the act of the German soldier who took Father's coat was 'theft', 'thieving', 'stealing'—all crimes for which the perpetrators must be taken to court and punished. Knowing the distinction between 'just war' and 'war crimes' is painful. I have refused to know it. War is never 'just'.

Indeed, the endorsement of the imagination as part of the way towards knowing is not only a sensible position, but also one that gives art a vocation. Art can contribute to facilitating such exercise of the imagination in a way that binds the intellect to the affect, so that understanding implies both, and the two domains can no longer be separated. Adorno, in fact, had already written as much, in the same essay where he retracted his earlier prohibition:

> Perennial suffering has as much right to expression
> as a tortured man has to scream; hence *it may have*
> *been wrong* to say that after Auschwitz you could no
> longer write poems.

Still today, the question of political art sits right in the middle of these two positions; not between, but immersed and mired in both. Knowing is more than gathering facts and understanding what is objectively true. It is imagining how to be, and act, and support.

KALEIDOSCOPIC

I want to end this vignette on a more cheerful thought. Although some experiences, such as the one described here of understanding death, are deeply sad, they also help our existence and acting in the multitude that is the social world. Knowing, provisional as it is, also fills the mind with possibilities, and with the constant movement through time that defines life. Another way of considering knowing, I can now say, is a constantly changing pattern of forms, colours, moods, and insights. The most fitting metaphor for this unpredictability and changing movement of knowing is the kaleidoscope; that little gadget that refuses to stay still. When I got my first plastic toy kaleidoscope, I was delighted. Part of the pleasure was to not understand how it worked. Of course, this only compelled me to try it out. And then, slowly becoming aware of the working of the bits and pieces that moved as soon as I turned the end piece of the tube, increased my pleasure, instead of ruining the toy's enigmatic quality. The forms were always beautiful: symmetrical, but moving in all directions, like a multiplied star. This compensated for my lack of drawing skills. Here were forms I did not have to make.

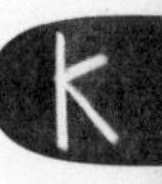

Henri Bergson, the French philosopher who had such a profound impact on film studies and the practice of making films, but more generally on our understanding of how perception works, brought that metaphor up in a passage from his book *Matter and Memory*. Reflecting on the relationship between the universe, the world, and the small element in it that is his own body, he considered his own body as that tiny turn of the perception that changes everything. The first chapter of that important book has a subtitle: 'What Our Body Means and Does', in relation to the way we select images for presentation, consideration: for knowing: 'at each of its movements everything changes, as though by a turn of a kaleidoscope.'[26]

It was many years later that I understood that indeed, a kaleidoscope was a kind of imitation of a body. A slight movement that makes everything change. But not only the physical, bodily movements have that enormous effect. The movements of the mind do the same. Each tiny bit of knowing that I performed, as a child and later as a professional 'knower', made the entire storage of knowledge I was accumulating, change profoundly. This is what makes knowing provisional; this is why I could not title this vignette 'Knowledge'.

26 Bergson, *Matter and Memory* (1991), 12.

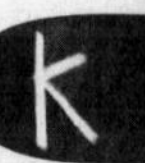

Loneliness

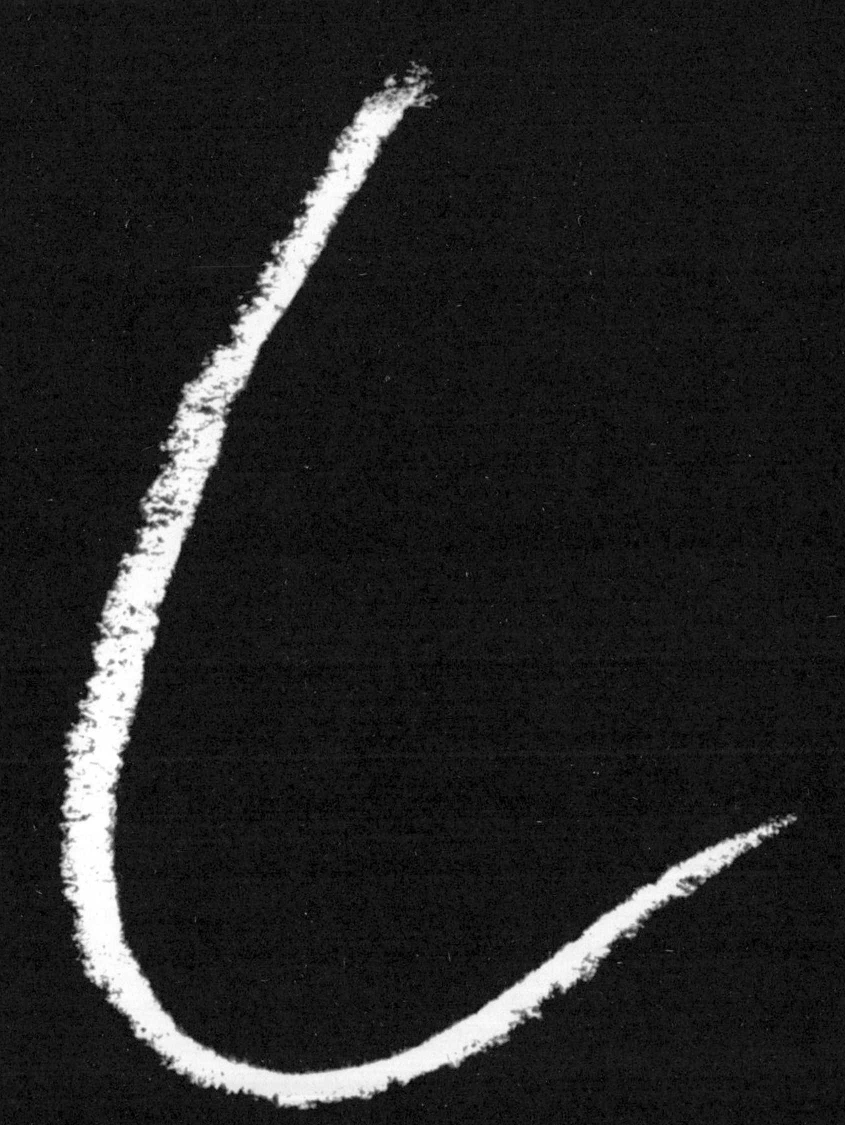

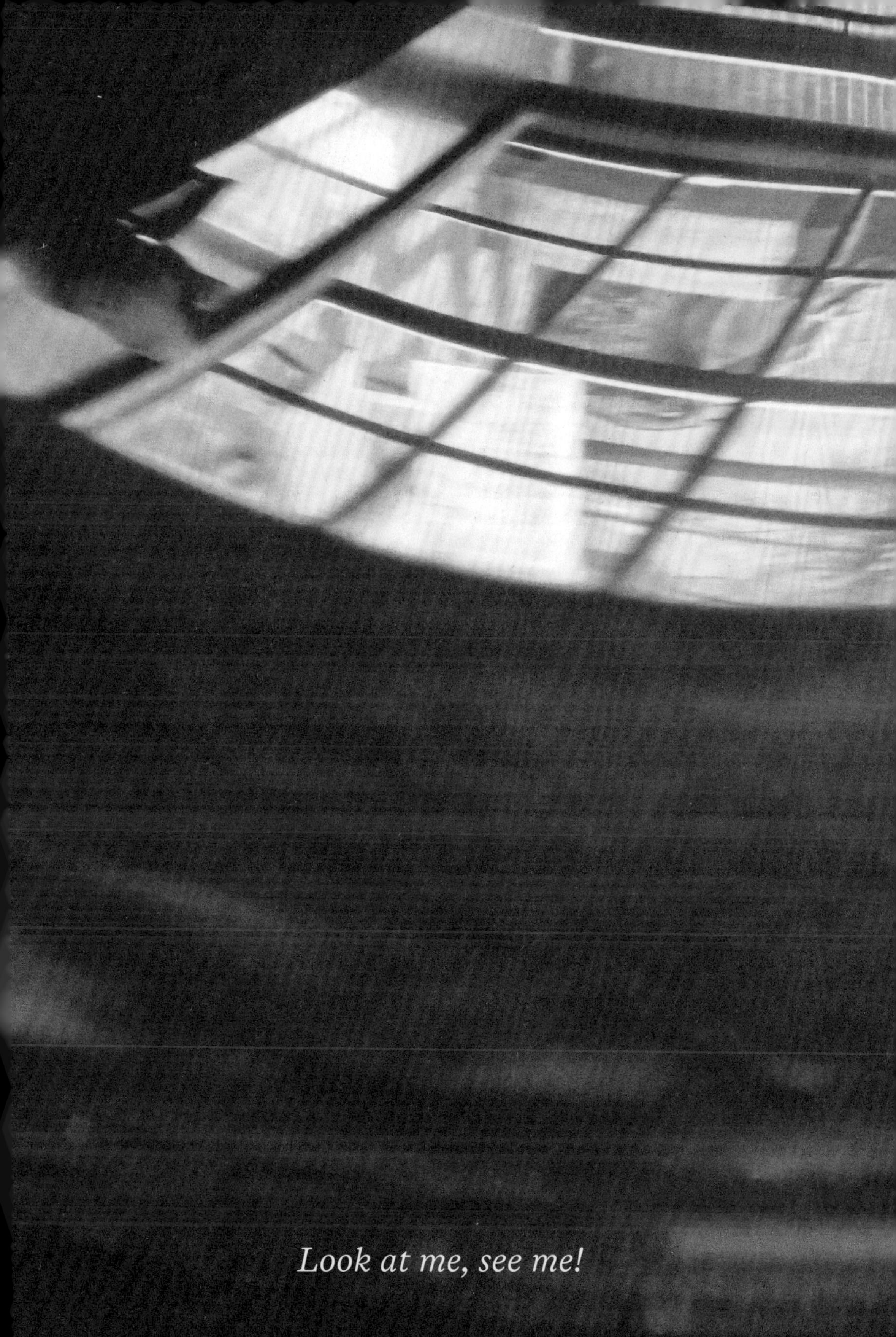

Look at me, see me!

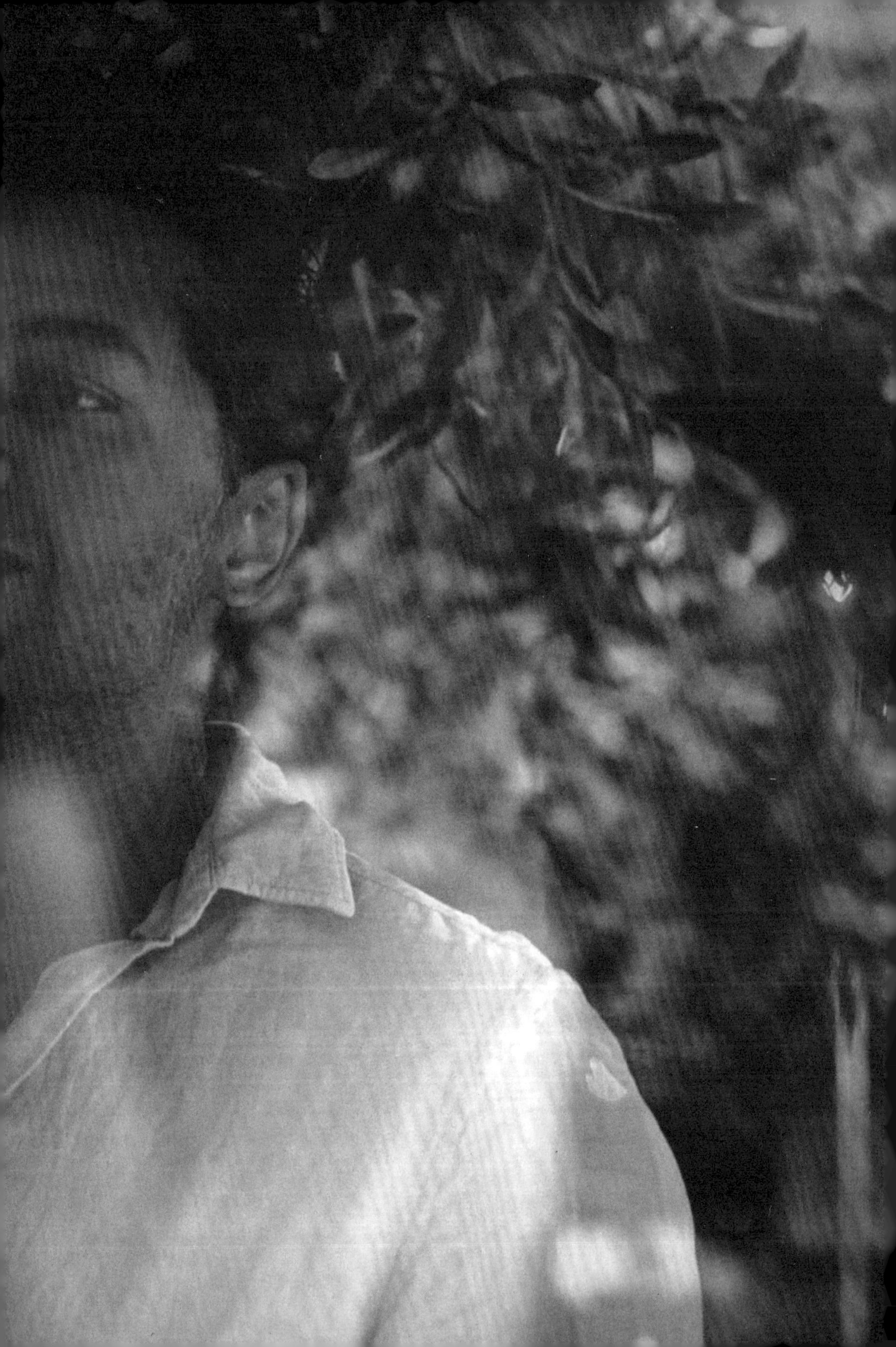

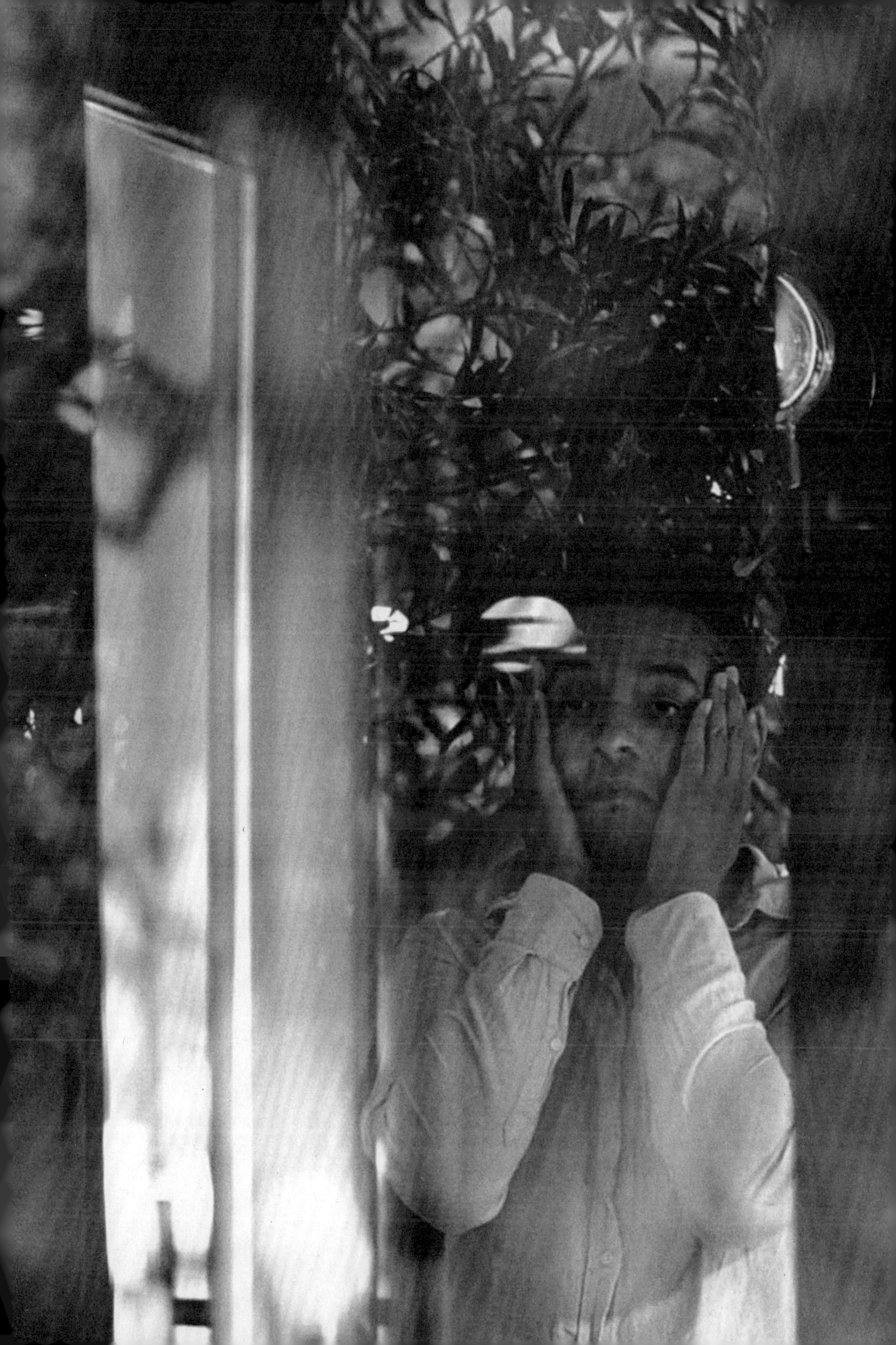

OTHER L-WORDS
ARE LABOUR, AND LOSS

Many of my childhood memories are associated with the contradictory situation of growing up in a family so large that it was almost impossible for my parents to cope. There was not enough money to hire effective household help. Father had to teach full time during the days, then again in the evenings, to earn more money for that mass of kids, the large house needed to house them, the amounts of food to feed them, and the coals to keep them warm, the clothes, the toys—all of it. When and how, between the day and the evening jobs, he found the time to prepare his classes, let alone write his PhD, which he did, even twice, I have no idea; timewise, the pressure was enormous, for both of them. Mother had to try to cook for them all, bring in meals never tasty enough due to the limited budget—a task I would soon take over from her—but also to clothe them all, keep the house tidy and clean, educate us to be 'good', in other words, instilling morality, and more, while she was practically constantly pregnant. No wonder she called on her children to help out. But there is a paradoxical aspect to this. For me, and I suppose for my siblings as well, the large and loud domestic life also produced loneliness. Although we could talk to each other, there was never enough time to discuss a topic in some depth. Alone, drowning in the mass of others.

MEANING-MAKING OUT OF A
STATE OF BEING

I didn't realize this until about the age of ten. A sense of dull unhappiness was all I felt. Until one day I read a slogan in a newspaper item about the royal family. In fact, it was the title of a review of a book from 1959 on the life of Queen Wilhelmina, of which the phrase was the subtitle. So far thinking the royals had a good, because wealthy life, I learned another aspect of that luxury. The statement about the former queen read: 'lonely but not alone'. I saw it, but didn't really think about its meaning. Until my mother drew my attention to it. The queen mother, she explained, who had grown up as an only child, was, like any royalty, always surrounded by many people. The next queen had the same limitation. Not just her children, who were more numerous than her mother's, but much fewer than in our household—the next queen only had four daughters—but also her staff, such as cleaners, dressers and hairdressers, ladies of court, her councillors, informants, the members of the cabinet, charities, all those people who were constantly calling on her, fussing with her, asking for her help and advice. But because of that constant buzz, she never had time for personal relationships. Let alone for being and feeling alone.

Now, I think my mother wanted me to understand this paradoxical, poignant situation as a way to understand and accept her own, much less dramatic but somehow comparable life. I connected it to my own life-in-becoming. The slogan spoke to me on many levels, for many reasons. Lonely: it is a sad state, or feeling. But being lonely without having the opportunity to appreciate being alone, as in quiet, unbothered, relaxing, seemed even more gloomy. I understood that at that pre-adolescent age. It was a meaningful insight, which I stored along with many others. But in that mental storage space called 'memory', things keep moving. As a result, when I was recently invited to make a film on refugees—which I made together with artist Lena Verhoeff, who also created the photos that accompany my vignettes in the present publication—the saying about the queen mother popped into my mind. This seemed surprising. A sharper contrast is hard to imagine. Yet, the phrase applied as perfectly to the suspended state of refugees as to the dignified old lady. As the systemic opposite of a queen's life in many aspects, the life of a refugee is characterized in many ways by a similar tension. This became the aesthetic of our film.[27]

Refugees, I considered, are never alone, always fearful of the others who might turn against them, such as armed border guards, who are hostile to the newcomers and in charge of keeping them out; or just people on the street who may otherwise complicate life for them, by scolding or bullying, or addressing them in a language that is foreign to them. Only the recent refugees from Ukraine are treated more positively; those who for years, decades, have been fleeing war and hunger,

27 The film we made can be watched through this link: vimeo.com/836809823, and in 2024, I edited a small book related to the issue. See Bal, *The Architecture of Loneliness* (2024). Probably there will be a larger volume with more of the lectures from the colloquium I organized at the Collège de France on 1 June 2023.

have consistently been met with resistance. And they are also lonely: not speaking the local language, not having their families with them, homeless and jobless, they have no social embedding.

The awareness of this state of 'refugeedom' made a comparison between the queen and the refugee meaningful. This insight also helped me to realize, when we were conceiving the film, the need to present such meaning-making itself as something to make publicly accessible. The film we made is not narrative and has no dialogue. It only has a voice-over quotation at the beginning, from the Hebrew Bible, and the same story at the end, from the Koran. We thought to make it abstract, to avoid the immodest, voyeuristic tendencies of representation, but primarily to design what 'lonely but not alone' looks like, visually. Once the association with that moment from so long ago became activated, we conceived the film as showing the state of a single recently arrived refugee, on the basis of that paradoxical, tragic situation. And then, as is often the case with meaning, other instances came up, turning the one-to-one association into a denser, multi-valent one.[28]

Just one example of such a productive spreading out of the meaning must suffice. The brilliant Indian multi-media artist Nalini Malani recently brought an underlying paradox home (so to speak), in a very powerful artwork on paper she had made on 22 April 2021. The work is a combination of drawing and text. In the collection of works on paper she made during the 2020–2021 corona lockdown, she abundantly quotes from poetry, philosophy, newspapers, and other sources, as well as her own statements. The figures in her works are thus, also, never alone. The newspaper-derived lettering in this particular work says: 'You only leave home when home won't let you stay'—a quotation from Somali-British poet Warsan Shire. (see fig. 6)

On Malani's sheet, the letters are set in two lines, hence, as a poem, albeit in the semi-official font of newspaper print. They follow the drawn figure, at his back, as if the composition in itself signified the way the

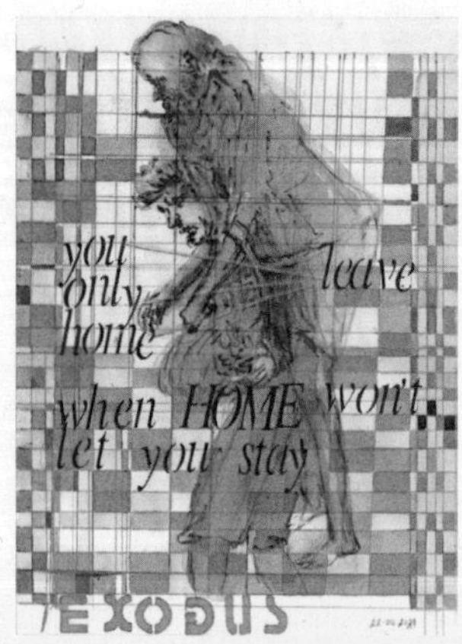

28 The quotes concern the same story of Joseph and the wife of Potiphar, which is quite problematic in the Bible, but represents feminist solidarity among women in the Koran.

fleeing figure turns his back to 'home'. That figure clearly is, or is turned into (by the letters) a refugee. This is emphasized by the direction of his walking: he is going from right to left, a.k.a. from East to West, from 'developing' to 'developed' countries, to use those very problematic qualifiers with irony. The figure is carrying an old man on his back. The composition crops the feet of the younger refugee off, whereas the entire body of the older man is hanging on him, as a heavy burden. The scene immediately built the bridge between the statement about royalty and the state of refugeedom.

But it also built another bridge, a temporal one. For anecdotal reasons, I could not help seeing in this artwork an allusion to the millennia-old story of Aeneas with his father Anchises, leaving, fleeing from, the burning city of Troy. That thought must have come from the presence of Aeneas in my recent experiences, of which I mention two. One of these was the making of a film, also associated with the corona lockdown (made in the first week of March in Poland, in 2020), in which the young man Aeneas interacts with Cassandra, who is his beloved. Towards the end of that film Aeneas and Cassandra split up, on her initiative. She cannot bear Aeneas' obedience to the political power-brokers.[29]

The other compelling association, which was more recent, came from a conference on emotions in classical literature in which I participated just around the same time as receiving the commission for the refugee film. But both were anchored in older memories, most obviously the one of having had to read the difficult Latin text by Virgil in high school. This was quite hard, but through it I learned to distinguish grammar and syntax from bare words, which became a crucial element in my literary education. I lost all the Latin, but retained the insights about language it helped me to understand. When I asked her, it turned out that for the artist, however, Malani's work on paper was meant as an allusion to the fate of the Uyghurs, currently being chased out of Xinjiang, a north-west 'autonomous region' of China. This is one of many situations where people are chased away from home because of their belonging to a Muslim community. The 'home', the autonomous region, won't 'let them

---

29 The break-up is the end of the novel *Cassandra* (1983) by Christa Wolf, not quite of the film. The film can be watched with this link: youtu.be/DK-5lbK4t5M.

stay'. I had not thought of that, and Malani had not thought of Aeneas. But together, something clicked that made us both aware of another tragic aspect. Home as lodging, longing for home, (un-)belonging ...

What would seem a misreading on my part, if I compare my interpretation to the artist's intention—something I don't like to do, for reasons I have frequently explained—the disturbing fact of the simultaneous applicability of the two discrepant interpretations, between a single figure and an entire population, thousands of years apart, is the work's deep truth, which neither the artist nor the reader/viewer alone could have known: refugeedom (as I call it) is of all times, and of all places; east-west, then-now: those fixations cannot be held up. And whatever we know about it, or deplore, try to help, or reject: the sour combination of loneliness and suffocating busy-ness remains. The artist agreed. So, it wasn't a misreading, not really. Instead, it was an interaction between the artwork as a social agent, and my act of reading, as on the way to knowing, as I explained under K, and on which more will come up under W. The conversation about the meaning of that artwork was another moment that brought back earlier experiences, little as they seemed to have to do with it.

As a family, we did not have a car, nor a television, when I was growing up. So, if once every summer we went to the beach for a day, my father had a tough job of transporting all the children on bicycle. The distance was considerable. But even worse, seeing my father's burden through my child's eyes reminded me of his obligation at Christmas to cut that one broiled chicken, which was the once-a-year treat, into eleven pieces. By the time he was done, his own piece, the tiniest left over, was cold. And the lack of a television compelled me, once I knew what such a machine was and what it was for, to sneak out of the house and watch through the window of a family a few streets away, who did have one. I never knew what I was watching. But I did feel I was lonely. And if, then, the owner of that other house came out to chase me away, I knew I was not alone; not ever.

A second tension of refugeedom, I imagine, lies in the combination of physical strenuousness of labour and the relentless loss of family, friends, the social anchors of life. The combination of loss and longing pertains to refugeedom most strongly. Refugees must suffer from exhausting fatigue, either due to the endlessly long travel, usually done at least in part on foot. Or, if and when finally successfully having acquired residency in the new, supposedly safe country, to the hard labour required to earn a living, and to send some of the earnings to that home that did not let him stay, but which is still where their relatives live. That ex-home that kicked the person out, condemning them to refugeedom, is the irredeemably lost place of comfort, of domestic life. The loss of feeling at home.

There is no analogy possible between this refugeedom and my own childhood memories of vague unhappiness. Comparing is not making things equal, however. On the contrary. Comparison can be done only if there is a ground of partial, even minimal similarity that enables the comparer to see the differences. In that sense, precisely because of the resulting insight into the differences, the situation of the other becomes more prominently noticeable, more poignantly understandable, without the banalization that would flatten both sides of the comparison. Protests against comparisons of profoundly horrible situations and events with others—such as the Holocaust being incomparable with any other historical disaster—do not help the realization of the atrociousness of the former, but instead, threaten to erase the latter.

My memories of loneliness without being alone do not imply that I was as badly off as the refugee; far from it. In one sense, on the contrary: they make me also realize how privileged I was. In another sense, this helps me understand refugeedom on a more affective level. This can compel a more empathic attitude than the ones indicated above, of racist bullying, and make empathy replace the fixation on victimhood with the possibility to help. Helping is the task of the government. Ordinary citizens cannot do much, other than giving handouts and sometimes temporary hosting, and voting for the more refugee-friendly political parties. But the one crucially important gesture they can make is that of empathy instead of shying away.

And here another crucial L word comes in, of which I have written already several bits: language. I know people who teach foreigners the local language, volunteering. And one friend who does this had the brilliantly empathetic idea to not only teach, but also ask the 'pupils' to teach her in return, his or her own language. The curiosity about that other, foreign language, which initially was just that: curiosity, was also the beginning of a new relationship. Between the two cultures, the two languages, and the possibility of comparison. But it was also the beginning of a relationship of equality between the foreigner and the resident usually feeling so superior.

Teacher and student swopping places: I have had that experience in my early academic life, when one of my students, who was also studying to become an artist, proposed to show me his artwork, which he had exhibited in the university's gallery. The sensation of turning from teacher to student was amazingly gratifying. The student, who later became a prominent artist, also became a friend. That friendship is what we need in the social texture where everyone can be lonely without being alone. Friendship: I have presented my reflections on it under F. What matters in the context of the present vignette is the substitution of a relationship, however tenuous and limited, for the irredeemable loneliness to which the refugee seemed condemned. It cannot compensate for the loss, nor alleviate the heavy labour, but it changes the meaning of 'not alone' in that statement about the queen. 'Not alone' does not have to mean being drowned in masses. It can become a socially helpful tool for empathy, understanding, and potentially, the fondness that leads to friendship. It makes the teacher-become-student modest, while also enriching her. I cannot imagine a more productive encounter with a refugee.

When I was about eight, I was moved to another school, which was not single-gendered as the previous school had been, but co-ed. I thought I would enjoy that change from the girls-only school I had attended so far. I did enjoy the more boyish games I could participate in, during the breaks. I was never much of a doll-cherishing girly child. But the boys didn't let me be part of their group. Somehow, it turned out, most

of the boys didn't like me, or so I assumed. For, although they
barred me from their footballing, after school, on the way
home, they frequently ganged up on me, bullying me and trying
to take away the book I was reading during the walk home (see
under D). The gang was the mass, the too-many, that I already
suffered from at home. So, initially, I was upset. They also
prevented me from continuing to read. Yet, something about
their behaviour also excited me, as if the attention they paid
me was something positive. Or rather, it inspired me. One day,
I had an idea of something I could do. While they were running
after me and shouting, I turned around, facing them, and I said
something that must have struck them as outrageous: 'Yes,
please, continue to bully me, I enjoy it.'

At first, they didn't get it. One of them said: 'Sorry, we
won't torment you anymore', and gestured to the others to stay
away from me. I said: 'Oh no, it's fine. It's a game that at least I
can participate in.' Somehow, the confrontation didn't change
much. I was still not invited to their schoolyard games, but the
after-school bulling diminished. What it did change, though,
was my own incipient awareness of the lonely-but-not-alone
syndrome. Much later I understood that this event had taught
me to see loneliness in others, in addition to seeing the aggression and even danger of masses. But without having yet that
tacit understanding, I now remember acting upon it wherever I
could. So, on the basis of that experience and others like it, the
empathy I mentioned above bonded with the desire to relieve
the loneliness of others. This became a point of attention in my
social relationships, including when I noticed loneliness and
felt inspired to make that swap of which later, the teacher-student exchange of my friend with the refugee became such a
wonderful demonstration.

For this vignette, I suppose some readers had expected
'Love' as the key word. If I refrained from including that too
obvious word from this reflection, it was because of, precisely,
its obviousness. But to be honest, my resistance to bring
love into it had more to do with a more general reluctance to
delve into sentimental issues that have such near-inescapable
tendency to become cliché, indiscrete, self-centred, and banal.

That disinclination has withheld me for a long time to do what people kept encouraging me to do: to write my autobiography, with the inevitable navel-gazing that comes with it. Moreover, the sadness the words foregrounded in this vignette entails seemed more appropriate to bring the social into the personal, and the small windows of opportunity to stretch out a hand to those most in need of support. Perhaps it was my growing up in a household of too many, the 'never-alone' situations that resulted, that made the reflections presented here more autobiographical than a theme-based, explicit autobiography would have been.

Mother, Misery, and Memory

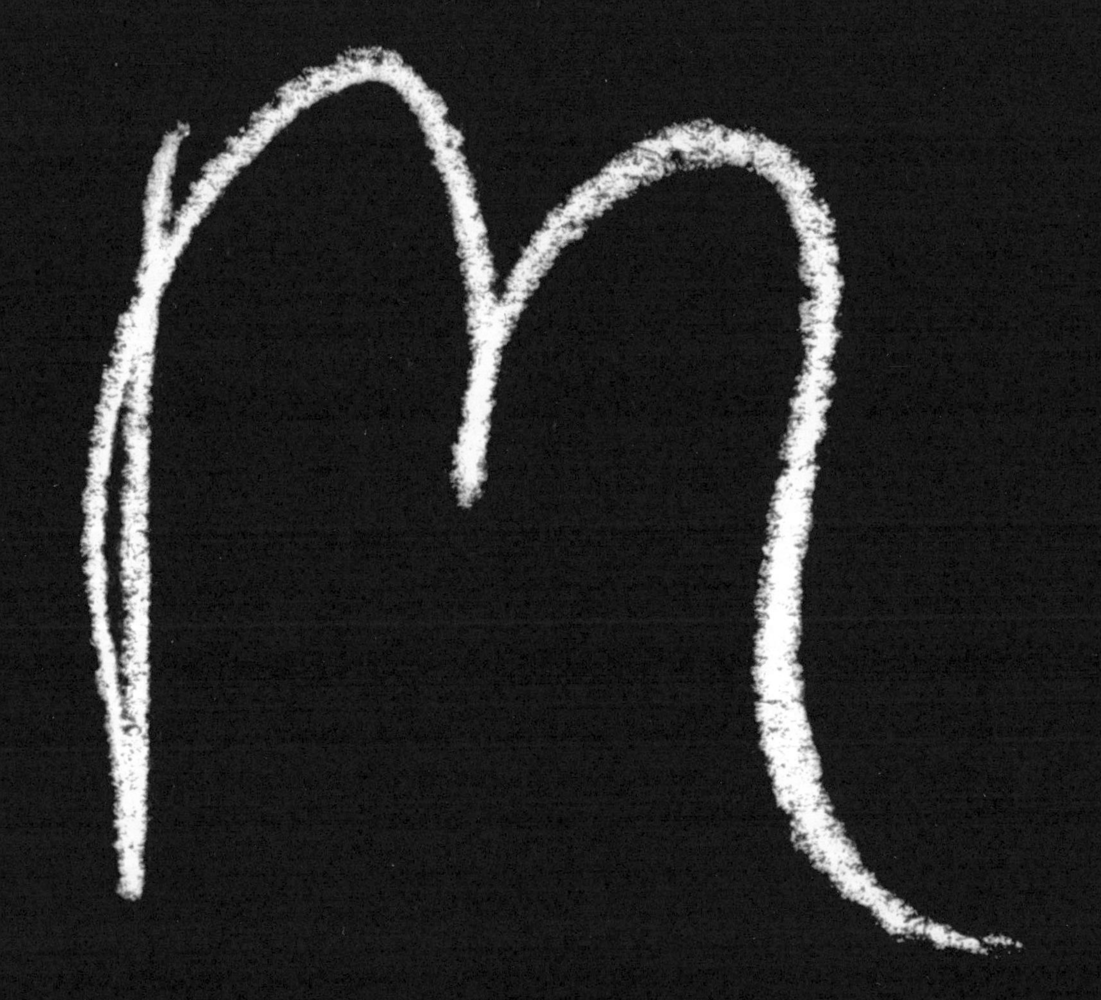

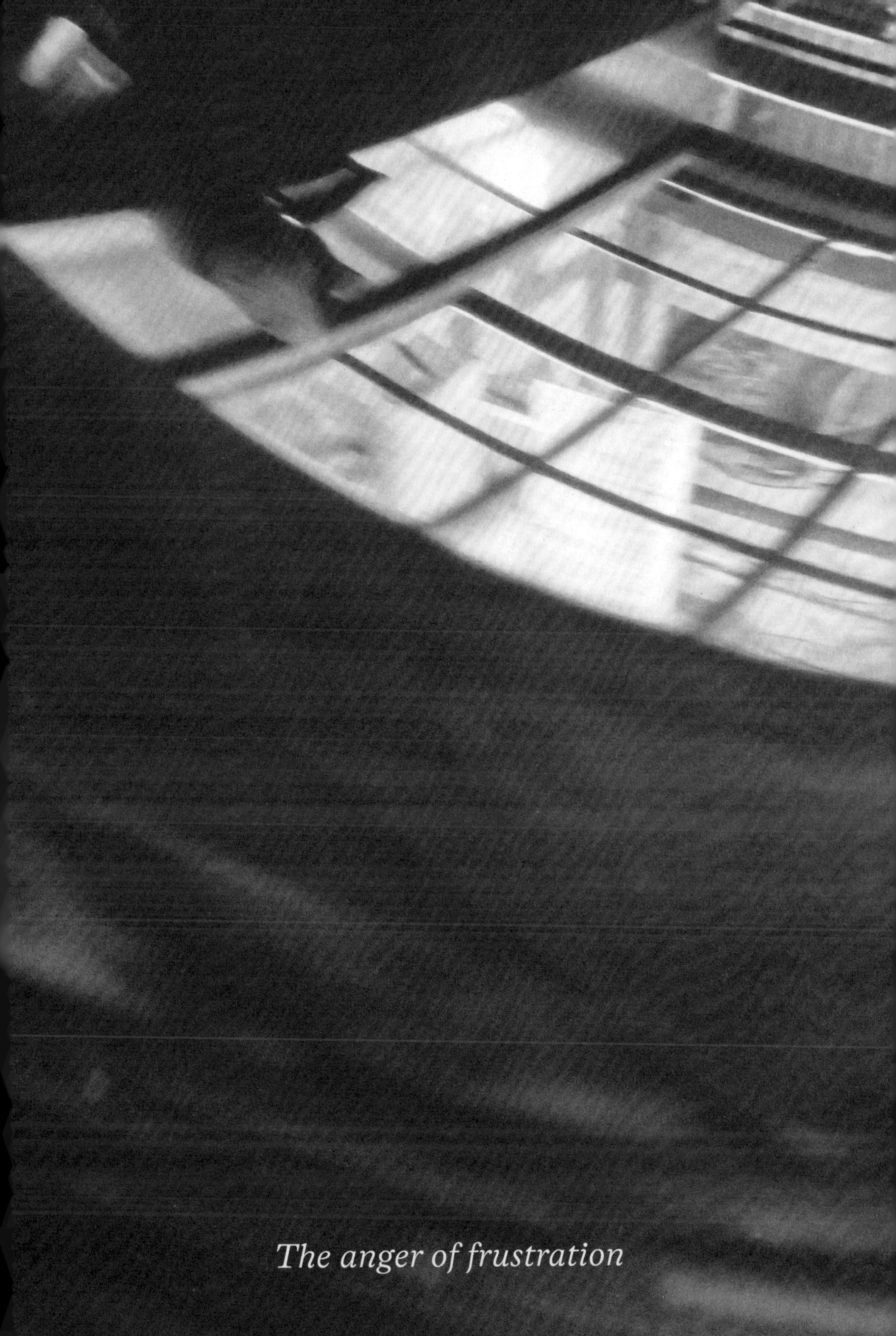

The anger of frustration

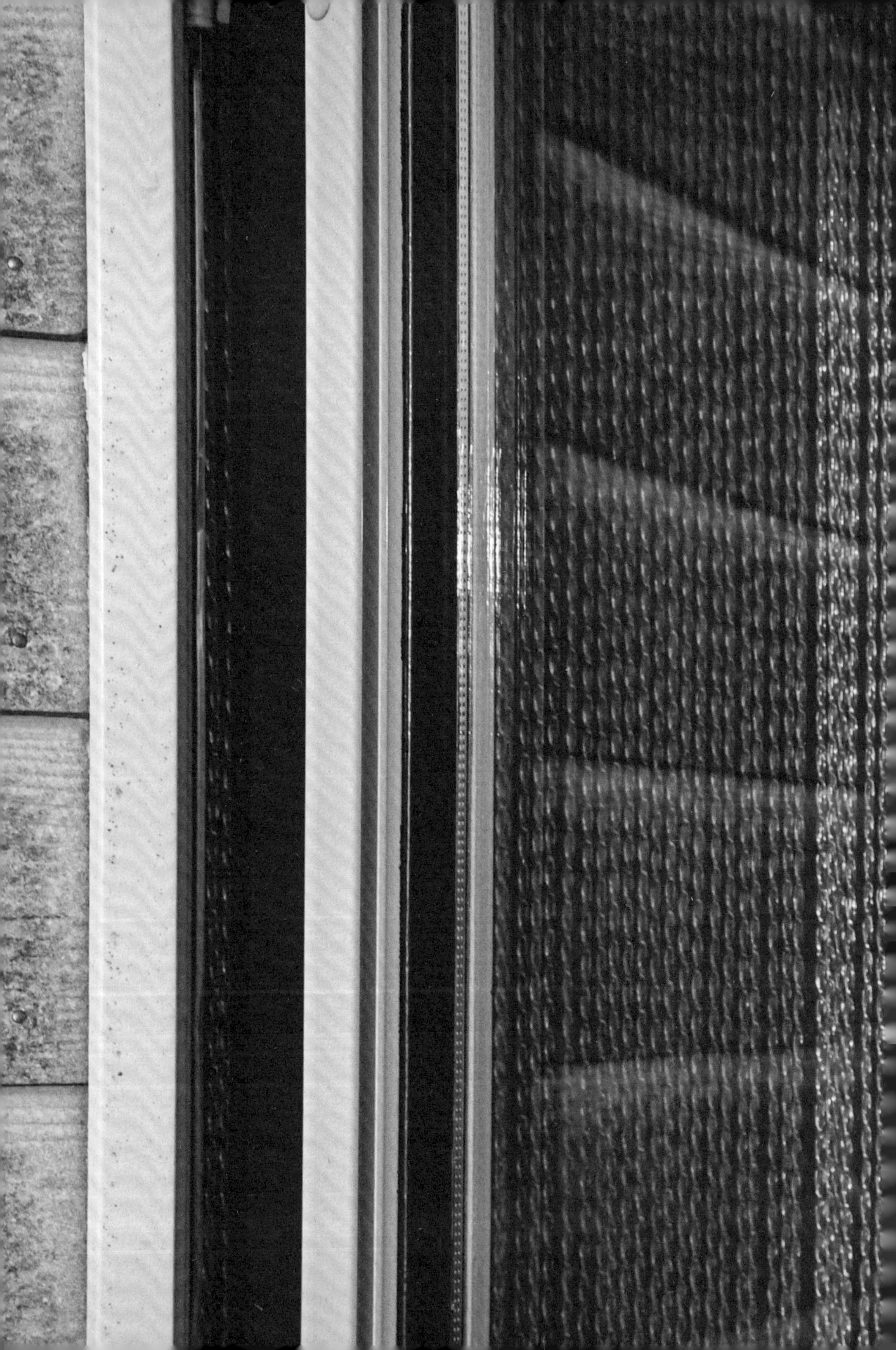

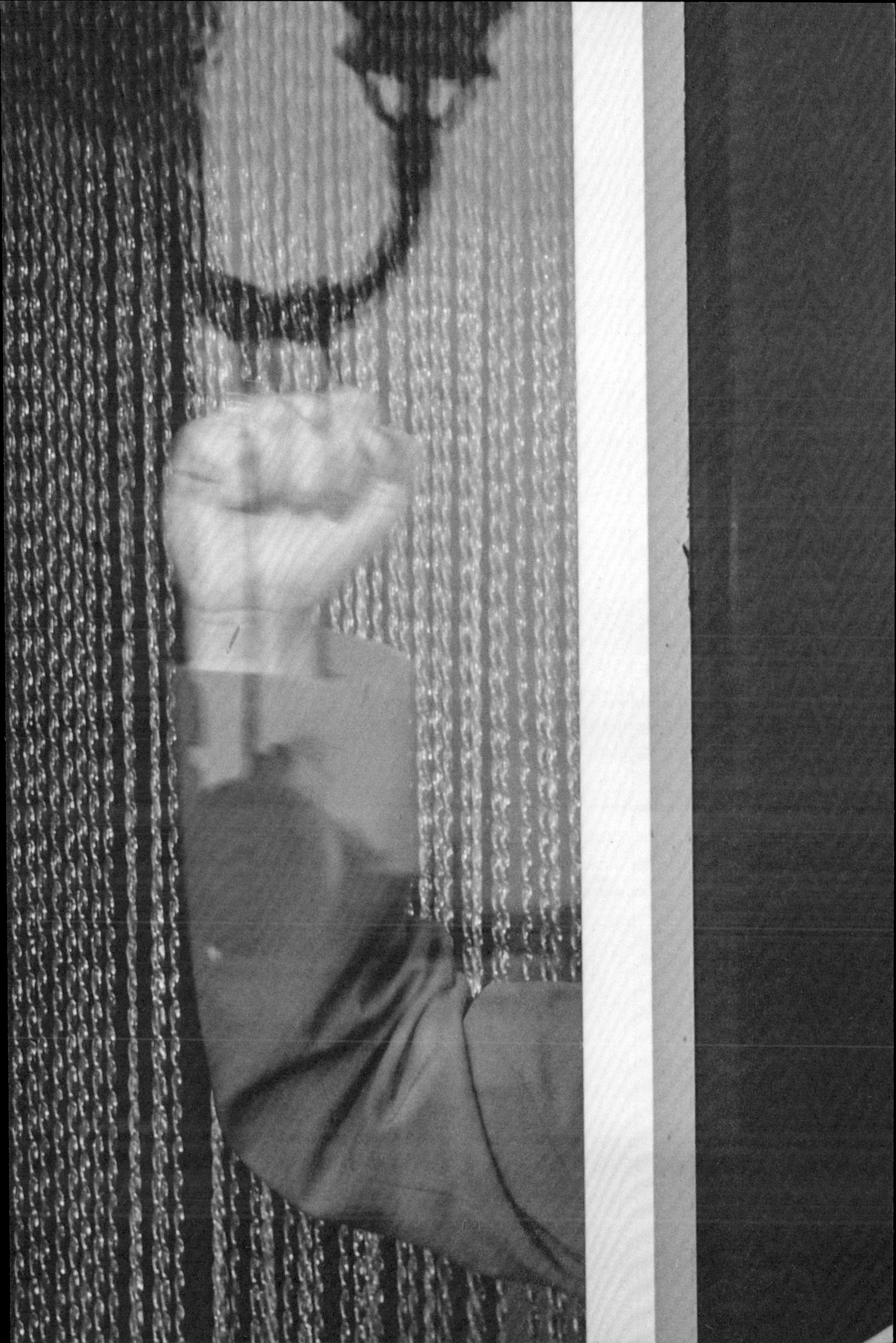

MOTHER'S MEMORIES

As far as I know, my mother had a quite miserable life. Beginning with her (non)-relationship to her mother. As far as my own memories go back, she never saw her own mother again after her marriage, although they lived very close to one another, in Heemstede, the village near Haarlem where I grew up. I never met that grandmother, not ever. All I know is the stories my mother told us; my memories of her memories. Nothing cheerful there. Until her tenth year, the family lived in Indonesia, where Mother's father was a teacher. She had two younger brothers, one of whom later also lived in that long street that led from Heemstede to the beach town of Zandvoort. There, as I have mentioned above, instead of going on vacation trips, we went on bicycles during the long summer holidays to enjoy a day now and then when the weather was good. They all lived in walking distance from each other. That uncle I have known until he died, and we and his daughters were (and still are) close.

The reasons for the clear hatred my mother felt for her mother and which precluded any contact with her, also for us, the grandchildren she would never know, have slowly dawned on me, over my childhood years. When Mother's father died in Indonesia (of the flu) her mother said she had been happily awaiting his last breath. And she denied her daughter the possibility to see her dead father. For the little girl who adored her father, this must have hit hard. He was her only emotional tie of any value to her. Right after that unknown grandfather's passing, the remaining family was uprooted and travelled by boat, first to New York and then to the Netherlands. Months at sea with a non-grieving mother. Don't ask me why. Mother just gave us the facts: her mother hated her husband. And when my mother, who was the oldest child, grew older, she did get the opportunity to study to become a primary school teacher. This facilitated some breadwinning for the family. She was the girl, and thus, had to care for, or 'mother', her two younger brothers, while also bringing in a bit of money. I have already written that when she married my father, she was fired from her job, in the middle of the school year, during a shortage of teachers and in war times.

I don't have clear memories of the stories about the details of Mother's life during her adolescence, but it seems obvious that her mother hated her as much as the other way around. Jealousy between mother and daughter was a common social trait at that time. Later, Mother would take on the same contempt for her own oldest daughter. The puberty time of Mother cannot have been enjoyable. No dancing lessons, no sports, no going out, of course. Let alone hanging out with boys. The only environment where boys could be seen—at a distance—was in church. Which is, obviously, where she and my father met. All she did during her adolescence, in addition to homework for school, was carrying the heavy burden of house-holding on her too-young shoulders. No wonder she had no more imaginative capacities, so that later we, her children, and I especially, got that burden tumbled onto us without questioning. For, once she married and was punished for it by being fired, she got one child after another. When there were nine of us, she was totally exhausted. No wonder.

As I have mentioned, Father had to work hard, with a full-time job as a high school teacher in classics and an additional job teaching evening classes. Because there was never enough money to feed all those mouths, however minimally, he had to. So, unable to help at home—if the thought had occurred to him at all, which I doubt—we barely got to see him. For he too was constantly exhausted. In addition to his two jobs, he was also writing a PhD dissertation, doubtlessly because he was ambitious. As I mentioned under B, once he finished it, another person had written one on the same topic—Roman coins—so that he had to start all over. How he was able to do it I cannot imagine, but a few years later he obtained his PhD with a thesis about Plato. This must have been an ordeal, but he just did it. Mother constantly complained that she only got to see his back, since he was spending all his free time, little as it was, to work on the doctorate.

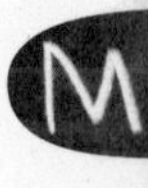

The oldest child Mother bore was a boy. Good for him; boys had a good deal. They were supposed to study and become professionals, and therefore were spared the housekeeping. After him, a sister was born. When she became clever enough to see how the exploitation of us at home would never stop, she found a way—never talked about openly, of course—to save herself a bit by pretending to be somewhat retarded. She did that in the easiest way possible. She was slow in everything she did. Stupidly, I chose another, opposite path. As I have mentioned, I tried, as is customary for a third child, to resolve the tensions by helping out as much as possible. I was constantly trying to relieve Mother's burden by doing chores, including ones not asked of me, especially during Mother's badly-needed afternoon naps. This way I turned myself into a Cinderella type, although without the denouement of the prince on the white horse and the crystal slipper. On the contrary. Something else made a change, not for the better.

We lived close to a seminary, where priests without erotic lives where teaching young boys to become priests in their turn. What happened between the teaching priests and the student boys only became apparent many decades later. For those boys, the seminary was a good opportunity to get to study, whether or not their religious calling was genuine. Some of those teacher-priests started to come to our house. My family was part of the local catholic circle, and so, those visits were totally proper. Except that one of them, the best-looking one, had purchased a scooter, and began to invite Mother for rides. I have mentioned this, and its consequences, already under K. Of course, this was such a relief for her from the constant household burden that I cannot blame her for accepting, dressing up nicely, and leaving us, mainly me, to continue the cleaning and the cooking. I always wondered if they were having an affair, even if sex was forbidden both to priests and to married women.

But happy, Mother was not. In my memories, not ever. That became clear as I grew up and was able to understand the tensions and shouting matches between my parents. Now I can see how this marriage turned sour, became a 'bad marriage', with separate bedrooms and frequent arguments, which was fatally pre-ordained by the miserable lives they both had. I remember one morning when, much later, Father driving to the secondary school where he had become the director after earning his doctorate, with my sister and I in the car, I suddenly saw Mother behind the window beating on the glass with a stick. It didn't shatter, fortunately, but Mother's totally frustrated face will stay with me as an enduring memory of her misery. I don't remember what, in her view, Father had done wrong; probably nothing specific. Just going away to work, leaving her behind, alone. Not that he had a choice, did he? But neither did she. Another memory, a bit later, is that she filled the bath tub and sent the youngest of my little sisters to the local grocery store to buy a packet of razors. Only in retrospect did I realize what she wanted those razors for. What prevented that disaster from happening I have never known. Probably, Father or someone else with enough authority came home in time.

MEMORIES OF MISERY

It feels a bit strange, almost out of place, to come up with the entry 'misery' in the chapter on 'mother'. The combination of grief and sorrow, sadness, and enduring melancholy, with that other meaning, poverty, resources too limited, food too scarce and meagre, clothing so ugly that I became the laughing stock of the classmates: it all seems to overrule my memorial capac-ity. Of course, there were better moments. Usually, these were less caused by play than by listening to stories. For Mother was a great story-teller, a gift probably promoted by her training and experience as a primary school teacher. Sometimes, she would carry on from one story to the next, and I was listening, riveted, to what had happened to her and to the family. Many stories, however, were very sad, so the pleasure of hearing Mother telling them was mitigated by their content. My birth and hence, my childhood years came soon after the end of the Second World War. And clearly, both my parents had suffered from hunger and cold, as well as helped Jews and other people in danger of deportation, to hide under the floor of the house.

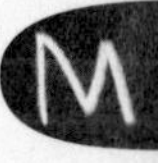

All this is miserable enough. What I did not, could not realize was that the poor meals that always left me a bit hungry, were the miserable consequence of the sparse income. Eleven people to feed and clothe on a teacher's salary: it seems impos-sible. My parents cared for health, so, we did get whole-wheat bread, but no or hardly any sandwich filling on it. The hot meals were always the same: potatoes with vegetables. Only once a week a small sliver of meat, and exceptionally on Fridays, a bit of fish. I don't know where my innate optimism has come from. My eagerness to cook, learning it while doing it, was my hopeful attempt to improve the tastiness of the meals. But to no avail; the ingredients were simply not there. I did what I could, and this has made me quite handy in the kitchen later, when the situation had improved. But during the first decade after the war, there was nothing to gain. Misery, as I now call it, was the rule. It must have been very hard on my always-exhausted parents. For, exhaustion is the worst physical misery. And they were permanently in that state.

The point of this entry on misery is to integrate the three items at stake: misery, mother/motherhood, and memory. The rather vague contents of my childhood memories must have come from the scarcity of events. Rarely were there birthday parties, and very few celebrations. We did have friends, and were allowed to bring them home, albeit with moderation. But they should not expect tea, candy, or cookies. There were never any refreshments available. But on the rare occasions that Mother was in a good mood, her story-telling and singing made up for that lack. Little did I know, then, that later, once a mother myself, I was going to be able to integrate emotional misery with consumptive abundance. During the childhood of my two children, I was either unhappy, having bound myself to the wrong men, or over-stressed with work, since I had decided my mother's fate as a fired teacher was not going to be mine. My somewhat obsessive work drive, ongoing to this day, may have something to do with that, as I will unfold under O.

Memories are not simply fragments of the past floating around, to be retrieved whenever one wishes. Nor are they just coming to us unexpectedly. Unless traumatic events assault us undesired and unplanned, memories are, in my view, acts we perform, in the present. I have written about this in the introduction to the collective volume *Acts of Memory: Cultural Recall in the Present*, from 1999. In that text, and in other bits and pieces, I have theorized memory in terms that fit my double sense of misery: as an act we perform, but also, as a bodily event. In this sense, memory has a political side to it. One of my favourites from film history can help make this crystal clear.

MEMORY, MISERY, AND THE BODY

The moment when in his masterpiece of silent cinema, *Modern Times*, from 1936, Charlie Chaplin's character is physically affected by the high-speed, mechanical work he is (under-)paid to perform in a factory during the depression,
is engraved in Western cultural memory. This monument to the harsh industrial era of the Depression now reads a bit like a political 'ruin', including the risk of nostalgia. We love it, and many a comic artist has imitated aspects of it. But we must realize that the stricture of the labour is so intense that, when relieved for a short break, the character of the worker cannot help but continue the jerky movements with hands and their extension, a pair of tongs/pliers, automatically going towards any small object that has the shape of the bolts he is tightening during work hours.

He is perceived as a threat to his environment because he cannot stop his body to do the work; he becomes certifiably mad, and is locked up in an institution. He exits the madhouse after a few months, cured but told to keep away from stress—an injunction impossible to obey in the exceedingly busy city streets and the hunger pangs of the unemployed; their misery. All this is superbly put into images, superimposed, faded, and scary. More adventures follow, all equally poignant. Like the episode when these adventures are turned into good laughs only through the comical genius of their author. Watching this film for the umpteenth time with my then seven years old grandson, the little fellow came up with an amazingly articulate remark: 'His body continues without him.' I'll never forget that. How much I learned from this little boy! No wonder that now, as an adult, he just achieved his diploma as a journalist—the socially committed one I know now, he was then already at heart.[30]

---

30 This boy, called August Voskuil, is now an adult, socially committed journalist, whose writing must be a strong comfort to his readers.

This scene turns *Modern Times* into a keenly political film—confirming Svetlana Boym's discussion of reflective nostalgia. While the figure acts upon the world that holds him in pliers, so to speak, the viewer, in a parallel movement, laughs at what at the same time is revolting, and absorbs a hauntingly beautiful image of a grim social situation. Misery is always lurking. But importantly, the little man is too much of a strong character to allow for commiserating, condescending pity. Instead, he solicits, not identification at all, but a strong solidarity and empathy instead. The viewer cannot help being on his side, *moved*—to use a phrase—to stay with him by means of the laughter mixed with horror that strongly affects her. I invoke this scene to draw attention to two issues concerning cultural memory that for me have an impact on the integration of memory and misery.

One is the *bodily* character of memory, aggrandized by the lens of comedy and its stock exaggeration. The other is the 'madness'—hyperbolically standing for the unreflective, sub-conscious, un-intellectual nature of the memory; the way it splits or suspends the individual's subjectivity. Chaplin's character is not aware that he is re-enacting what he had first been forced to do (even if the artist Chaplin is, of course). He just does it—pretty much like a Pavlov reflex. The buttons in the shape of bolts he sees everywhere, require his pliers; even the noses of his co-workers and bosses are irresistible little protrusions around which to stick his tools. Not to speak of the nipples of women passing by. These protrusions are, in a complex sense I would like to spell out, *traces*. But traces in the double sense of the word: leftovers or ruins of the past, but like ruins, taking place—spatially and evenementially—in the present, and thus, in the second, Derridean sense of the word, pointing to action, hence, future-oriented. In the ruin, history appears spatialized and built space temporalized; and this can be generalized to all kinds of traces. Another way of seeing traces is as images based on indexicality—pointing both back and forward in time, and visible.

Thus, like ruins, traces cater to that different, modern temporality with its radical asymmetries of past, present and future. Architectural ruins are such sites where time and space conspire together to trigger memories, in particular nostalgic ones—replete with affect, in this case, longing. The subjectivity involved in memory obliges us to reflect on the affective load that 'colours', 'inflects', or focalizes memories. Some of the consequences of this—of the subjectivity-based nature of memory, and of the 'colouring' that follows—make my memories of Mother and her misery, ambivalent. This 'colouring' is a factor of memory's status as *narrative* as well as *image*.

When we talk about memory in terms of contemporary culture, it is important to remember that memory is not a passive occurrence that overcomes people, but an activity, and act; something we *do*. Both responding to ruins and establishing a link between image and past reality is, indeed, an act. Even if it remains to be seen what the medium of the telling is—and who its listener—it is, I think, crucial, because conceptually fruitful, to consider this provisional definition of memory as narrative. This has major consequences for the structure of subjectivity in memory.

First, there is the question that accompanies any diagnosis of something as narrative, namely that of the *narrator*. While the specifically narrative nature of memory may be questionable, because a large part of the content of memories consists of images, the fact that a subject calls them up and thus acts as a 'voice' or 'director' of what the memories are is easily absorbed into the standard idea of narrative, where a voice or narrator 'utters' the story. Second, although narrative is not inherently set in the past tense, it very frequently takes that form. Narratives in a present tense that does not function as a *praesens historicus* are perceived as experimental. Third, stories also contain a certain type of content, or subject matter. Events, strung together in chains usually causally linked, tends to be the standard content of narratives.

In relation to these three basic features of narrative, at first sight memories do not smoothly fit into this definition of narrative. First, the narrator of memories is not unified. This clearly shows in the merging of my memories of my mother and her memories of hers. Second, the past tense is intensely

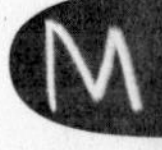

central, yet also subverted, turned into a kind of presentness. These two issues are bound together. If the subject exists primarily in the present—if presentness defines subjectivity—then memory is an act of refusing that confinement, of a schizophrenia that incorporates other, previous selves—and why not, others—into the self. Third, in terms of narrative content, too, memories may refocus our standard views of narrative and suggest less causal coherence, but more incongruous juxtapositions and shifts in focalization than we expect. And—relevant for my pondering about my own memories and those of my mother—I contend that this is so because memories are usually replete with visual images. But, instead of taking this uneasy fit as evidence that memories are not narrative, we can also use it to modify the concept of narrative itself.

Let me point out that, not in spite of but because of these possible challenges that memory puts to narrative, the idea that memories are narrative serves analytical purposes, the primary one of which is distinctive; to show how certain recollections do *not* fit the definition. But this may be the case not so much because they are not exactly narrative, but, precisely for that reason, not exactly memories either. I am alluding, of course, to *trauma*, wrongly called sometimes 'traumatic memories'. Like Chaplin's jerkiness, these have a persistent presence in the subject's mind and body alike. This is relevant for the discussions on trauma itself. One discussion has emerged around the question whether trauma causes either repression or dissociation. The differences are important from a narratological as well as a psychological perspective. Far from being repressed—a term that suggests some form of agency—traumatogenic events cause dissociation—the doubling of the string of narrated events by splitting off a sideline, thus creating what in rhetorical theory is called a *paralepsis*. This feature of trauma makes it not so much unsuitable but rather, fruitful for a more complex narrative definition of memory.

The other feature is the uncontrollable, repeated occurrence of traumatic recall. This suspends the assumed subjectivity of the narrative 'voice' of the memory. In terms of literary genres this would turn such recall into theatre, rather than narrative, but a theatre of which the subject is not the director, although he or she is at the centre of it, like an involuntary actor or manipulated puppet. The repetitiveness of the occurrence also makes such recall timeless, relentlessly incessant, hence, durative without specific duration.

I am not suggesting that Chaplin presents an *instance* of trauma; rather, that this scene offers an imaginative *pre-sentation* of a feature of trauma—its bodiliness—that is more generally inherent in memory, although there we don't often realize it. Chaplin's incapacity to de-cathect his body from the movements of work seems to imaginatively hover over the abyss that separates memory from trauma. Thus, the scene also proposes another distinction relevant for memory. With one foot he stands in routine memory, with the other in trauma. Routine memory is a form of memory characterized by a lack of reflection, yet possible to recuperate retrospectively. This is a kind of memory that is distinct from narrative memory. It is ubiquitous in everyday life, and becomes noticeable only when it is interrupted. I have always wondered whether my mother's story about her mother's relief at the death of Mother's father was an instance of 'normal', routine memory, or a case of trauma. Given her miserable life, I suppose the latter was the case.

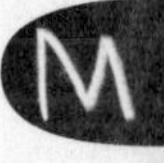

Nosiness

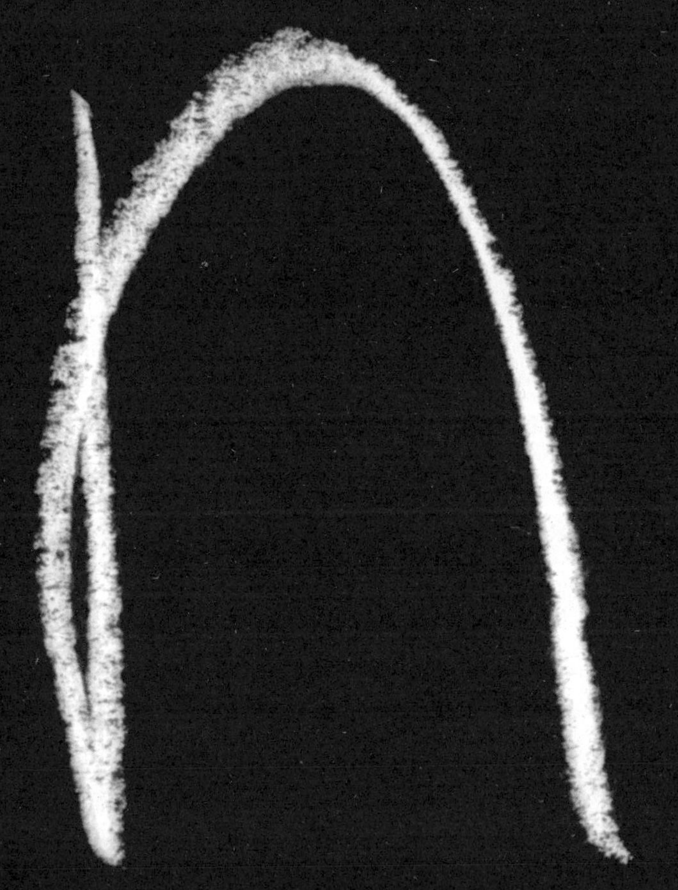

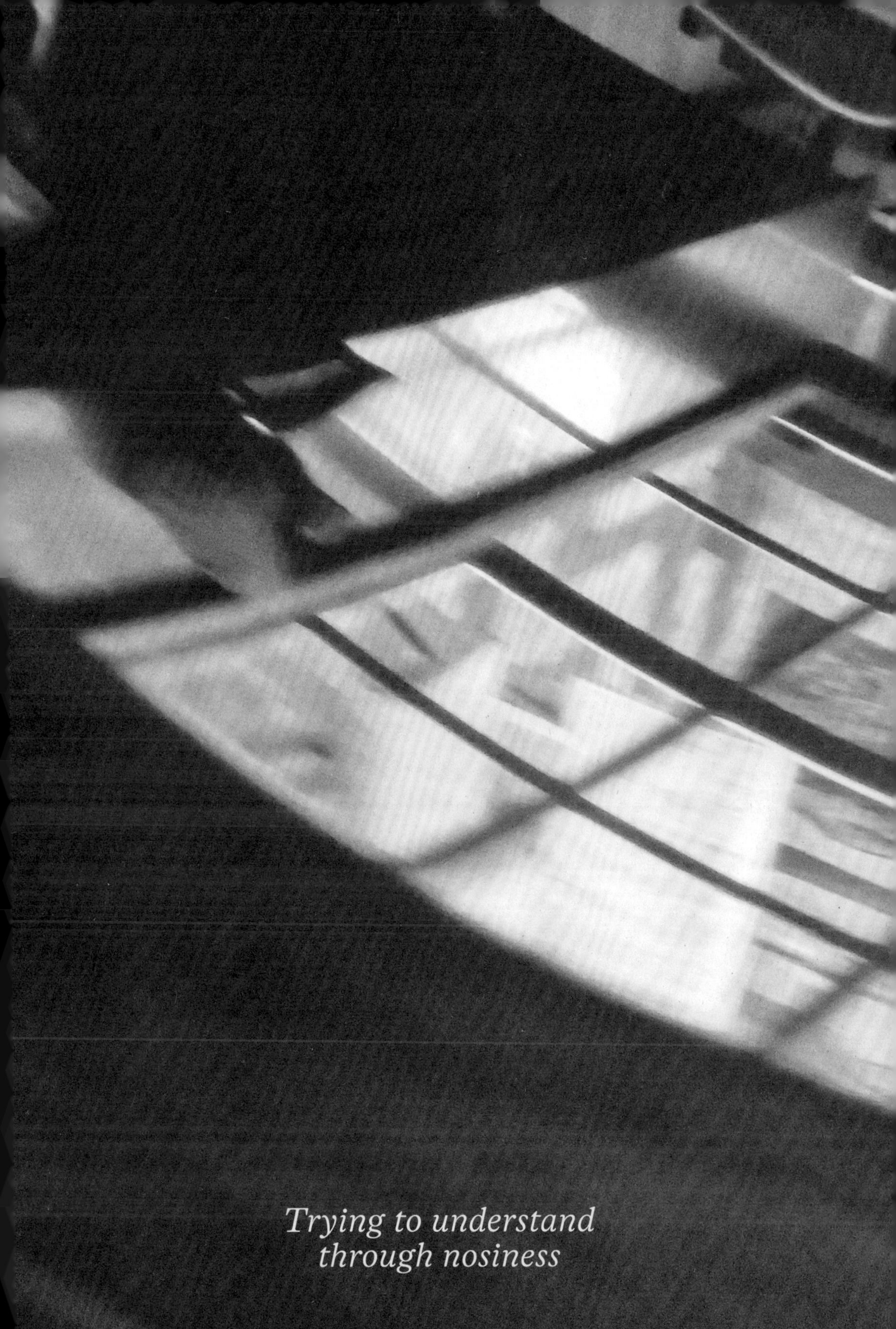
Trying to understand
through nosiness

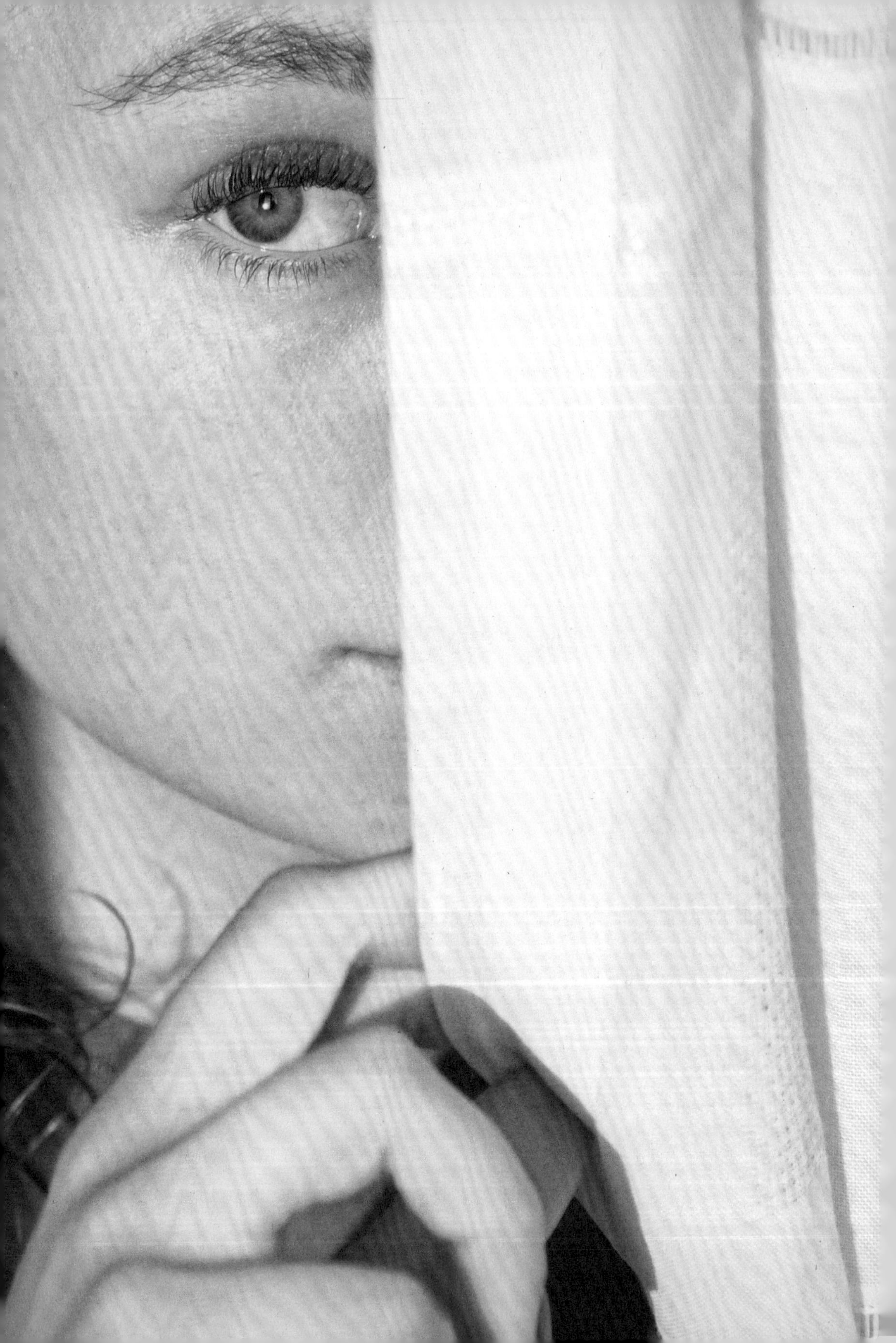

As far as I remember I have always been curious. Again, it is one of those ambivalent qualifications. My parents found it bothersome that I was so 'inquisitive', as they called it. Never could I leave something alone that I didn't understand or fully grasp. 'Don't meddle' was their irritated response. I protested that I didn't mean to meddle, just to understand or know. I was convinced myself that being curious was not just 'normal' but necessary if I wanted to understand the world, what happened there, my environment, and other people. Later, once I began to become a student with slowly developing scholarly ambitions, I felt that curiosity was requirement number one for a successful excursion into the process of acquiring knowledge, discussed under K. Yes, I also see how irritating it can be.

Snooping and prying was what my parents called me with my roving eyes. Those are somewhat negatively coloured verbs-turned-qualifiers for curiosity, which made it a little painful sometimes. It also made me hesitate how far I would go in my nosiness. This always made me stop for a bit before carrying on, sometimes even giving up. But that was always difficult and hard to sustain. And to my shame I must admit that I did overstep boundaries I knew to be prohibitive. One obvious one was reading letters addressed to someone else. I tried to avoid that. It is a taboo I fully understand and endorse. But sometimes it is almost inevitable, when a small sign, like an index, triggers the curiosity. But I know that it is a serious transgression.

One day, however, my older sister and I were cleaning our parents' bedroom. Among the bits and pieces of trash was a letter. Quickly glancing at the name of the sender, I saw it was a friend of my mother who was living in a Carmelite convent, as a nun in a monastery bound to silence. I had never understood how my mother, with her extremely noisy large family and her chatty personality, and this tight-lipped woman hidden behind a veil, could be friends. My curiosity got the better of me. What? I wondered. What could a nun who never speaks, have to say to my mother? And halfway the first page of the letter something seemed to explode. 'I pray for you and the baby who will be coming this summer.' That was big news! Another baby!

The current one, number eight, was barely a year old. It seemed very exciting news. But knowing I couldn't talk about it with Mother made it uncomfortable. Yet, this news was too big to keep quiet about it. Exciting and unsettling. For, I also thought: more work!

My problem at that moment was: now that I knew this 'secret', how to deal with it towards the others? My parents, my siblings, my friends... This became an emotional turmoil that lasted for days. Until I decided to tell Mother of my transgression, and what it had revealed to me. I felt too guilty to keep silent about it. At first, she was furious that I had read the letter. But then, she started to see it was also useful. I would now be more willing (as if I wasn't willing enough) to help with the housekeeping. And so, she calmed down and began to ask if I was prepared to do more of the ironing, for example, because standing on her feet is painful for a pregnant woman. And the load of washed items was of course enormous. The tension between housekeeping and homework, if I may play on these two near-synonyms with opposed consequences, could only become stronger, with another baby on the way.

NOSINESS HELPS (SOMETIMES)

As I have written under H, I learned by self-teaching how to use the ironing machine my parents had purchased. And although this increased the burden of having-to-iron, it felt totally natural to me. A new machine? Then just learn to use it. I saw something that looked complex, so I had to uncover its secrets. This tendency has often come in good stead, helping out in difficult situations. In order to learn to ice-skate, to which the canal beyond our garden invited as soon as the ice was solid enough, the first thing I had to know was how to bind the ribbons of the skates around my feet. And once I knew how to ride a bicycle, with Father's help, the first time I saw someone repairing a flat tire I stopped to see how they did it, asking questions that might have somewhat annoyed them, about how to find the hole in the inner tire, for example. I now think that this nosiness was just a way of learning life; the tendency to curiosity never really left me. Only the things about which

I wanted to learn did change, which brought them to life. The remainder of this vignette goes through a few of these.

How, for one, could the wooden floor, which was dull and uneven when I left for school in the morning, be bright and shiny when I came back for lunch? It turned out, Mother explained, that there was a machine that would rub the floor, and when someone put a liquid on it in small puddles, the machine would spread out the liquid until it was everywhere on the wood, and then, after waiting for it to dry, in a second round the dullness would disappear, like snow in the sun. Of course, I had to try doing this, but at first the machine was too heavy for me. Mother had to call either on the boys, or, in the short periods she was lucky enough to have a house-cleaner come in once a week, that lady would do it. Mother herself could not, with her practically-permanent pregnancy. Something of the same order was at stake with the windows and mirrors, which tended to get stained so frequently. But then, what was the fundamental difference between the thick white liquid for the floor and the thin, blueish, badly smelling one for the windows and mirrors? Go figure...

Of course, I had to ask, and when Mother just shook her shoulders, probably because she didn't know the answer, I had to find out by myself. That is when I began to read the directions on bottles. This was a new habit of nosiness. It didn't take long to find out that the liquid for the floor was a kind of wax, bringing a greasy substance to the wood, whereas the thin one was doing the opposite: it dissolved and absorbed the grease on the glass. I got it, the difference, and the need to use these different materials for cleaning. The one brought greasy material to the wooden floor; the other took the grease off the glass. Two opposite forms of cleaning. The insight that this opposition actually wasn't one, that it only was a material difference, was crucial for me. In the same move, I discovered that both were to be kept away from children, and that the thin one was more poisonous that the thick one. This experience of not-yet-knowing not only helped me to get the drift of these two forms of cleaning, but more importantly, to keep the little ones safe.

As a result of that learning, I decided, strong-headed as I was, to re-arrange the cabinets with the cleaning materials. When Mother found out, she was quite upset. She couldn't find anything anymore. So, I had to explain my 'system' and the reasons behind it. Reasons that included the safety-for-children issue, the breakability of the glass bottles and the flexibility of the plastic ones, but especially, the combination of particular cleaning products with particular materials in the house. I learned, and taught her, about materiality, without knowing that concept. At such occasions, she seemed to appreciate my inquisitiveness. From being furious she moved to smiling.

Much later, after graduating from high school, my nosiness became 'professional'. Once I had spent four weeks in France training and then working as a 'monitrice de vacances'—a group leader for the children in the 'colony'—and got a certain fluency in the language, I began to wonder with the key-question 'why?' always at the forefront, about details in the foreign language that seemed odd, like the particularity of 'amour' of which I described under D the inconsistency of the gender and number of that noun and its ideological implications. Then came the typically French issues of which I had no inkling, such as the two different past tenses, the *imparfait* and the *passé défini*. This fired up my curiosity. Why? Why that difference? Once I understood it had to do with differences of duration, the one ongoing, the other instantaneous, I had learned something that I later used in my literary analyses, and even later, in film-making. A life-long lesson. My interest in temporality, already clear from the example of 'pre-posterous history' discussed under A, became more and more encompassing. Not only the tripartite presentation of time as order, duration, frequency, which I learned from my first excursions into narratology, but many more nuances, among which rhythm is, of course, crucial for filmmaking and also for fiction, but also geological time as distinct from evenemential time. And much more. Every time I learned something more about time I was excited. This topical curiosity that didn't stop multiplying made me also understand curiosity itself better.

But some things somehow did not make me curious. The

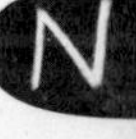

naked truth about the naked body, for example, did not invoke my nosiness at all, until I was way past the 'normal' age of the awakening of sexual interest. Probably it made me a bit fearsome. A certain prudishness seemed part of me. I never saw my parents naked, for example. Until one day... On a Sunday morning, I walked into their bedroom, thinking they were long gone downstairs for breakfast. To my utmost horror, I saw my father stark naked. But worst of all, his penis was larger than I could have imagined. And it was a bit upright, not quite hanging down as I expected. Now, I realize, it seems obvious that he was having or had just had an erection. But since I did not know anything about sex, I could not make sense of that odd-shaped body part. It frightened me, as if there was something wrong with him.

The vision of Father naked and with a distortion of his penis made a deep impression on me. However, rather than making me curious, it shocked me as 'not normal'. I was too shy to ask my brothers, and felt too guilty about storming into their bedroom to ask any other family member. But the strange sight stayed with me. Somehow it changed my image of Father. He seemed an altogether different person. Bizarrely vulnerable. Only much later, when I began to get closer to sexual experience, did it begin to dawn on me what I had seen. The naked truth of nudity slowly crept into my consciousness. It wasn't a state, such as the state of undress, but an activity, just finished or about to begin. The all-pervasive sense of movement came to me due to that visual experience of not-understanding.

When, again, much later, I got curious about the frequent appearance of nudity in visual art, that other aspect of it, the look it solicits, clarified the point I missed that Sunday morning. I began to understand that nudity was meant to be appealing, not expressing vulnerability. Instead of feeling anxiety, I could, I should have enjoyed the sight. That is what lookers at nakedness are supposed to do: enjoy, admire, and long for the next stage: the transition from seeing to touching. But is that the 'naked truth' of seeing and looking at nudity? The question that soon after came to me was the one of consent. Do people being seen naked, really enjoy their exposure, and is the follow-up touching what they want? Perhaps, sometimes; perhaps not. The crucial distinction between erotic enjoyment and suffering abuse was the next step in the learning process I needed to figure out. In this, my early-acquired feminist inclination, explained under B, helped enormously in learning to distinguish looking and seeing from voyeuristic abuse.

QUESTIONING 'ART'

That distinction became crucial when my curiosity brought up new questions related to specific research projects I was involved in. In the early 2000s, I began to make videos in order to either be a witness to social problems, such as the injustices perpetrated by the police, or to get a better, that is, more profound and more direct insight into the issues I was studying. One such issue was migration. By chance of an event that happened to my then-neighbour in Paris, I made a video meant as a witness statement. I was upset about the unfair way the police treated him, and I felt the world needed to know about what was done in our names. The resulting film, *A Thousand and One Days*, from 2002, revised in 2004, had a weird consequence. It got nearly accepted for television, but because we refused to add a voice-over, which would disempower the migrants' voices, they ended up turning it down. However, soon after that failure, by chance, the film got invited for an art exhibition in Berlin about 'masculinities'. The moment that invitation came, in 2005, I had to endorse a new self-image: I was considered something I never expected to be, namely an artist. Taking that title with a grain of salt, it did make me wonder what it could possibly entail, or contain. Curiosity roared its head again.[31]

Slowly, I began to endorse the idea that I could and should make 'art', if only to understand what that word means, which I will explain under W. It became clearer and clearer that, rather than simply providing the means to get more profound insights into my research topics, the act of showing, making public and thereby inviting other people to view the images and act upon them, was more than just increasing my own understanding.

31 I published several articles about the documentary (which for modesty reasons is not online). See for example: Bal, *Mektoub* (2011).

But while still vaguely questioning this new 'identity', I did feel other questions coming up that might not have done so before. Questions that had to do with the public nature of art. And one question that kept going through my head was the state and fate of the mothers of migrants, who were left behind in their routine lives when their children decided to leave. The incredible loss that befalls them must hurt them deeply. I became more and more curious. However, I also began to feel the limits of what is proper in that curiosity. How to avoid immodest nosiness?

This concerned my partiality for interdisciplinarity, which I had been developing early on. The most obvious case seems also the most problematic one: the place of psychoanalysis, the darling of some and a changeling for others. Of course, for many of us the conjunction of art history and psychoanalysis is both accepted and constantly challenged. In the context of what I later called 'migratory aesthetics', I allege two reasons for a privileging of the latter option, albeit provisionally; the need to be cautious. First, I contest the often-heard complaint that psychoanalysis is thoroughly Western—following this line of reasoning deprives others of a tool we consider appropriate for ourselves. Just think of Frantz Fanon, the African-Caribbean psychoanalyst whose last book, *Les Damnés de la terre* (The Wretched of the Earth) from 1961 is probably the best-known, most powerful psychoanalytical treatise against colonialism and its dehumanizing effects.

But that this approach is Western because, and to the extent that it is thoroughly albeit ambivalently individualistic, seems nevertheless obvious. I do wish to suspend, if not erase, psychoanalysis as a conceptual tool for the articulation of migratory aesthetics. However, although psychoanalysis is a thoroughly Western discourse, the British feminist literary psychoanalytic critic Mary Jacobus, whose work I admire enormously, never tires of pointing out how, *qua* theory, psychoanalysis displays characteristics of a migratory aesthetics. And although it remains somewhat stuck in individualism, it grounds the individual subject firmly in a social environment. I also find it a bit dubious to dismiss the theory due to the notion that, since non-Western cultures did not invent this theory, the non-Western subject would not be traversed by the unconscious that, psychoanalysis claims, is inherent in the human being. The Western-only limitation did not fit the all-humanity generalization.

The caution against emotional exploitation became more and more forceful, precisely because of my natural curiosity. One of the mothers involved in the project *Nothing is Missing*, called Massaouda, was the first one we interviewed. Being the mother of the main character of the film *A Thousand and One Days*, and having been forced to be absent at her son's wedding, she triggered the project *Nothing is Missing*. My curiosity about how she had lived down the departure of her youngest and favourite son was the direct motivation for the project. The video of her provides a striking instance of a culturally specific reluctance that cautions against psychologizing or psychoanalyzing her. Not coincidentally, this is at the most strongly performative moment of the video. It is also a moment where performativity and performance in the theatrical sense of role-playing merge quite strikingly. This is the situation: Massaouda and her new daughter-in-law, Ilhem Ben-Ali Mehdi, get along famously. But in their relationship remains the stubborn gap dug by immigration policy. This is partly due to Ilhem's French nationality—she was born in France—and upbringing, so that her Arabic cultural and linguistic identification is choice- and training-based.[32]

But also, and this is the point here, when Ilhem married Massaouda's youngest son Tarek, the mother was not allowed to attend the wedding: the authorities had denied her a visa. Hence, not only had Massaouda not been in a position to witness who Ilhem was, while she must have been deeply curious about her, but even more obviously, she had not been able to fulfil her motherly role as her culture prescribes, which is to help her son choose his bride. At some point, Ilhem rather bluntly brings this enforced failure into the conversation. She ends up asking with some insistence what Massaouda had thought of her when she first saw her, after the fact, hence, in a kind of powerlessness.

---

32 For more information on this project, see miekebal.org/nothing-is-missing.

First, Massaouda doesn't answer, which makes Ilhem anxious enough to insist, and to ask in a variety of versions: did you find me ugly, plain? The older woman looks away at this point. The young woman insists. We will never know what Massaouda 'really' felt, but the power that the filming bestowed on her, as if in compensation for her earlier dis-empowerment, was to either withhold or give her approval. She does the latter, but only after some teasing. When I saw the tape and understood the speech, I was convinced Ilhem would, outside of the filming situation, never have felt authorized to ask this question, insist on it, and thus vent her anxiety. As for the mother, she was given, and performed, the power she had been denied, and she used it to first mark the gap, then to be kind, to help her somewhat insecure daughter-in-law.

How and why is this art? This interaction is thoroughly social, performative, and bound to the medium of video—to the making of the film. But it does not allow psychoanalytic interpretation. Neither did I as maker have any influence on this occurrence—it was not my 'intention', to mention my increasing critique of the invocation of intention in art criticism. Nor can we construe it as a realistic, documentary moment where an 'occasion' was recorded—it would never have happened outside of the situation of video-making. There would never have been an external reality the film could have documented. It is a moment, in other words, that was staged, yet real, thus challenging that habitual distinction between fiction and reality. Nor can we pinpoint a psyche offering symptoms for interpretation. For this to happen there was, instead, a need for a culturally-specific relationship between two women related by marriage and separated by the gaps of migration; and for a relationship to the medium that allowed the women to transgress cultural boundaries.

Thus, my wilful abandon of mastery—leaving the room after setting the shot, and returning at the end, declining to edit, and leaving the installing to the local hosts where the project was shown—extends from the filming to the reflection on what I have learned from this experimental filmmaking. The filmmaking, performed by the women in their inter-face, with their relative behind the camera first of all, indicates—but does not dictate, since I remain responsible to be responsive—what approach it is appropriate to take to the resulting installation. The art-making, in other words, is not an example to illustrate an academic point, nor an elevated form of cultural expression—'art'—to which no criticism can do justice. Instead of these two things, equally problematic for a productive interaction between art and cultural analysis, the performance, including the moment of slight tension between Massaouda and Ilhem, is a genuine form of research the results of which impinge on what I was groping towards articulating as an academically fruitful concept.

The performative moment is the product of an act of filmmaking that required the absence of the filmmaker. That is where my curiosity and the need for modesty joined forces. But more than that; it also required the surrender of the two women to the apparatus standing between them. This surrender occasioned a cultural transgression—to ask, and insist on, a question that in the culture of origin would be unspeakable. This, more than her linguistic pronunciation of Arabic as a second language, is Ilhem's 'accent', which emblematizes the productive, innovative and enriching potential of intercultural life. Ilhem engaged in a more-than-usual intimate conversation with the woman she venerated, as she had been taught to do, but had never before been so close to, in a language, a body-language, and a novel mode of demeanour. And I learned about and from this event after the fact, during the translation process, with Ilhem's new husband who did the translating, and who was as astonished as I was. This interdisciplinarity—between the people performing and the critic reflecting on how to understand what they did—would be stifled if a too-well-known psychoanalytic apparatus were let loose on this event. This is not to say that academic critics ought to enslave themselves to artists. In fact, in this instance, it is not the artist but the performers who framed what we can theorize about the work.

There is an especially significant issue of interdisciplinarity here, of 'migratory aesthetics'. The interdisciplinarity of the project emerges from the linguistic situation as intermedial. The spoken word is central to the installation in many ways and on many different levels, all of which converge in the attempt to turn a condescending act of 'giving voice' into an affirmation of our need to be given the mothers' voices, to be accepted in my nosiness. And once on that path, I kept wondering and probing, and thus became more and more an 'artist', but one who kept asking questions, about how to pursue this project without immodesty and with hospitality to the public. Video, like film, binds the image we see to the sound we hear. That sound is, in this case, primarily and almost exclusively the human voice and the words it utters.

The centrality of the spoken word impinges on the visual form, the close-up. For, it is also in order to foreground the privileging of the voice of the mothers that the films consist of single shots of their faces as they speak and listen, and that remain unedited. This presentation enhances the key idea that the women who were all but forgotten, hidden away in their modest situation 'back home', are yielded the floor, for once, to say what they wish to say, without interruptive editorial manipulation. The effect of the camera, mitigated as it is by the intimate interlocutors and the absence of the filmmaker, since I left the room once the camera had been set, is that they strike a tone of awareness of the public nature of their account.

The intermediality has been foregrounded also graphically. The translations presented as supra-titles also embody the close bond between linguistic and visual aspects of the images—the bond between face and speech. The viewer is confronted with different languages, foreign to most, audible in their foreignness and visible in an emphatically visualized translation. The decision to place the translations above the image rather than underneath it, came to me when I reflected on possibilities to foreground the acts of speaking of the women who said they had never spoken about this issue. I also felt the need to de-naturalize reading (subtitles) to hint at the fact that most of the women cannot read or write. Placed, visually, above their faces, the language is both made important and presented as somewhat of a burden. English as the sole

entrance is de-naturalized, both by this visual foregrounding
and by the translations themselves.

The translations are as literal as possible, bringing out
the poetry and the music in the original languages instead of
prioritizing clarity. In many of the cases, the relative who is the
interlocutor in the film is also, at least in part, the translator.
None of the translators are native speakers of English. Their
assignment was to help me stay as close as possible to the
phrasings the women used, even if that meant sacrificing
clarity or fluency. This method results in an 'accented' English
that maintains the bi-cultural status of the communication.
The most acute intermediality occurs in the faces, which
visibly produce the sound of the voices, the language we do
not understand, and the need to translate, all in one. It is really
difficult to separate sound from vision, as the mouths articulate
with the rhythm of the sounds. Video, that easy-to-transport
engine to make home images and home speech, is the medium
of this intermediality. The moving quality becomes a poetic, a
self-reflective statement about the medium that re-integrates
what the predominance of English and the home-boundedness
resulting from a lack of education, aggravated by misogyny and
colonialism, have severed. The face and its acts, thus, opens up
a dimension of the person that no translation, no high-fidelity
recording, and no perfectly filmed movie can open. It makes
the viewers curious. About the lives of those mothers and their
losses, and about what viewers are entitled to get to know,
without probing and meddling.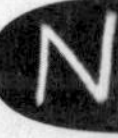

Overdrive

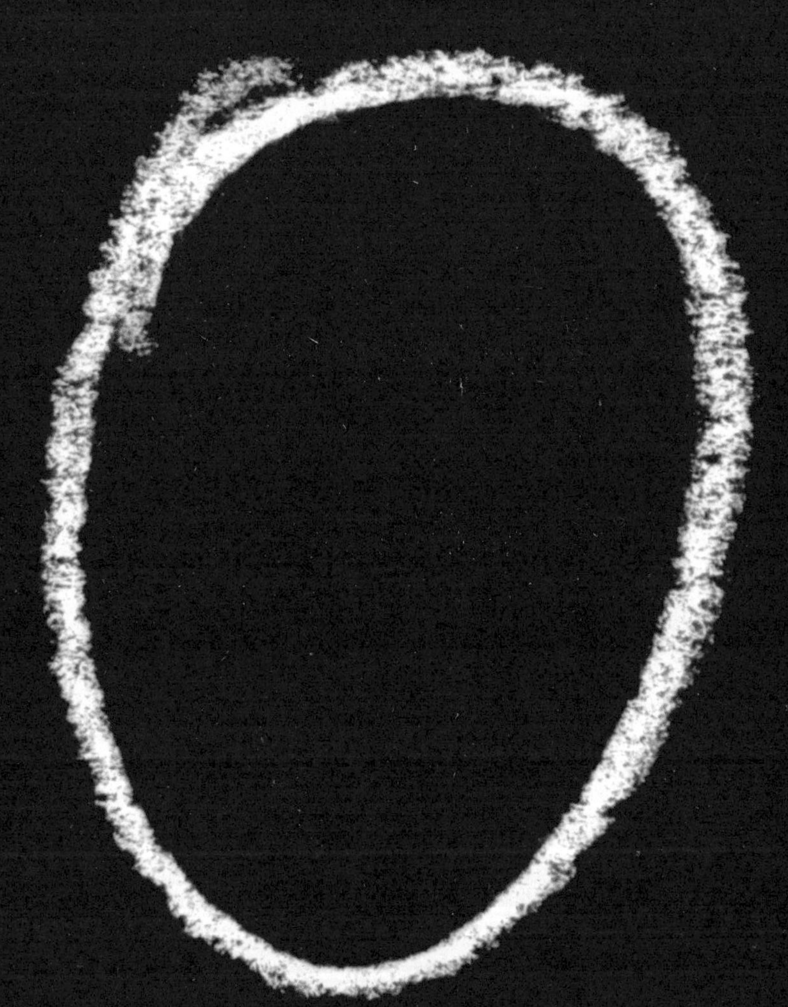

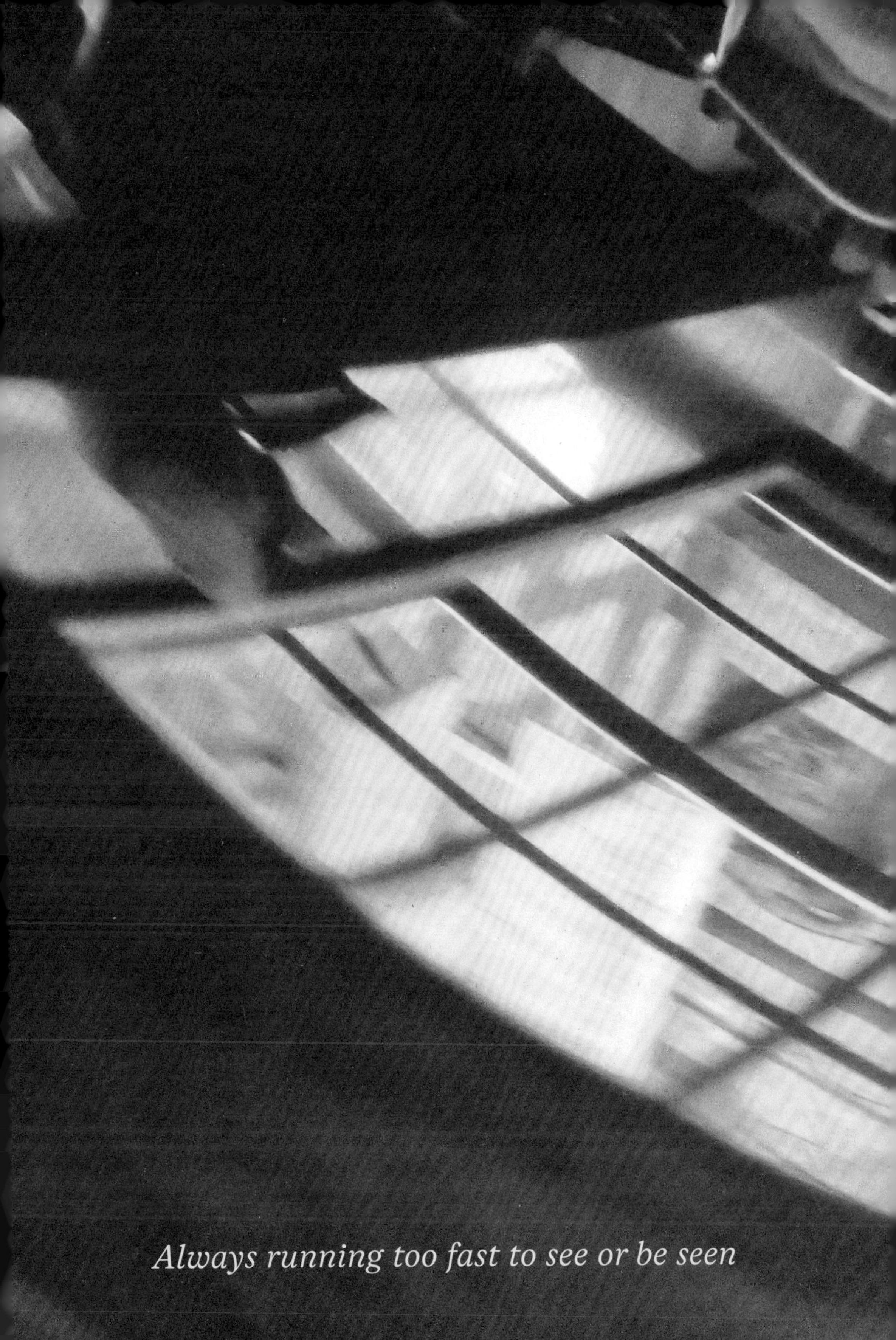

Always running too fast to see or be seen

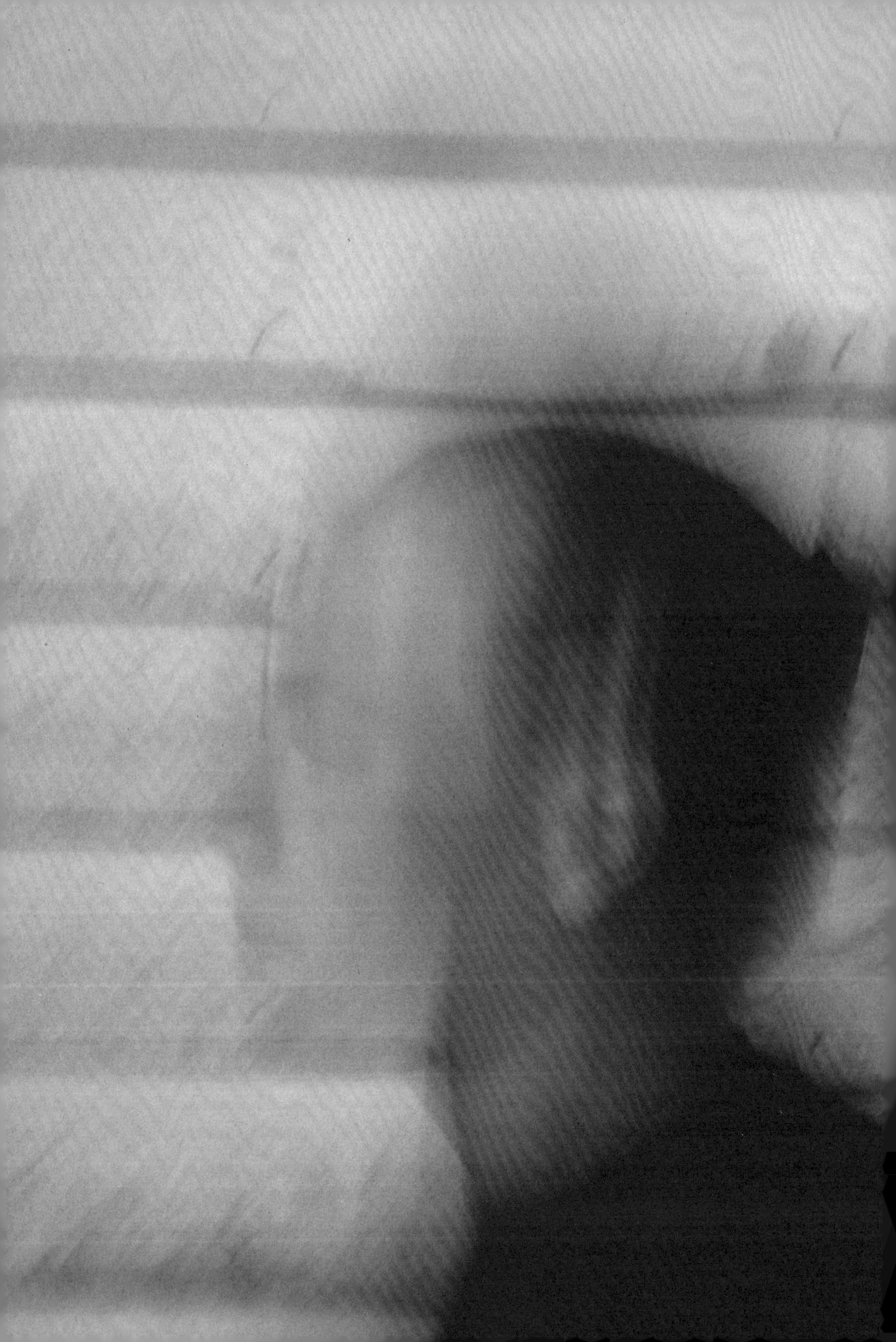

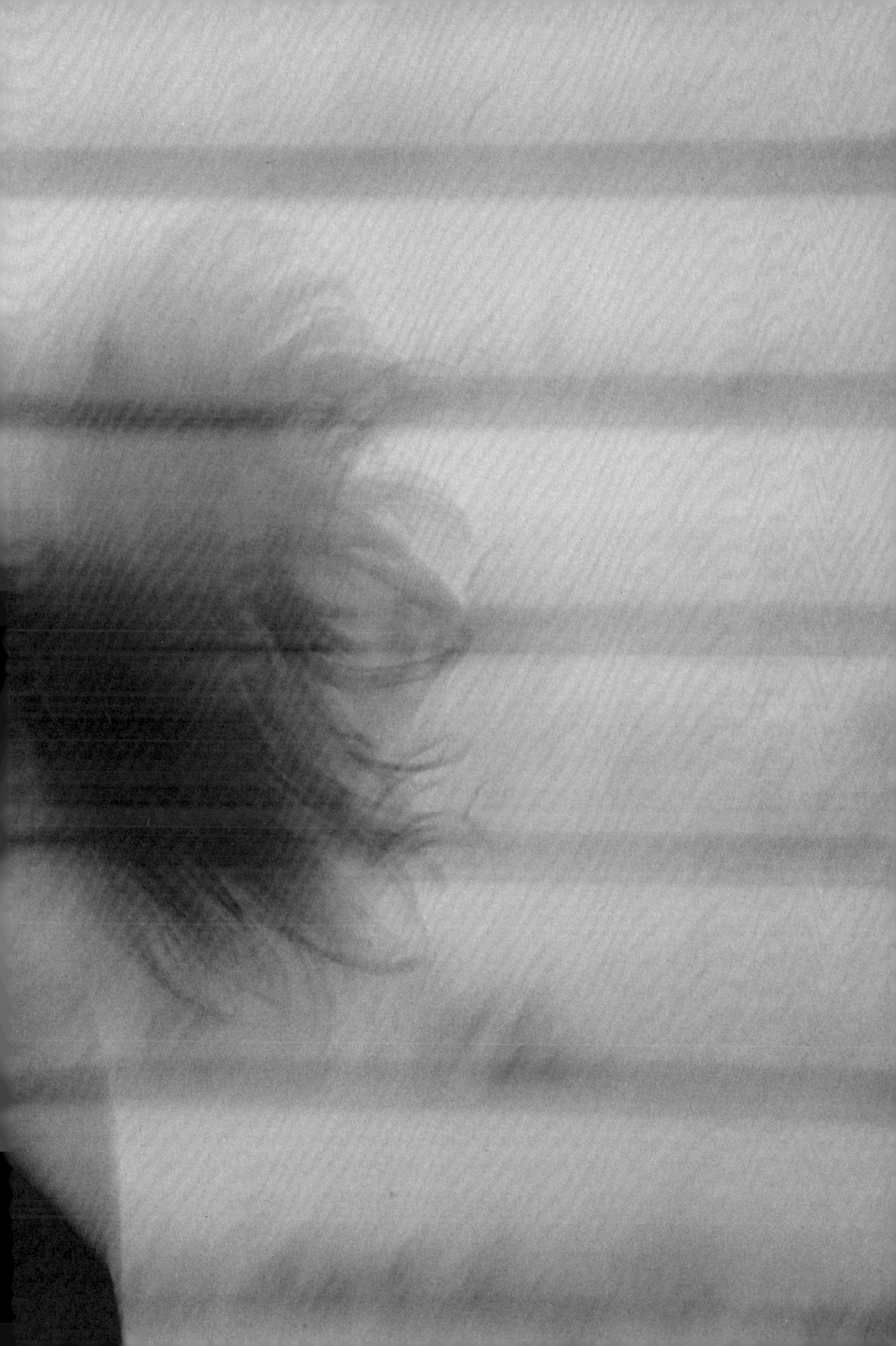

With all the pressure in my early years, I developed another feature, apart from, or rather, in addition to that relentless curiosity just mentioned. The only way I could cope with it all was speeding. I developed a way of doing everything fast. That, also, stayed with me throughout the years. Up to today. Fastness felt like a necessary trait; a required performance. Now that I function so frequently in English, it has become a way of translating *doing* into *rushing*. This makes sense in a funny way if I consider that the English word 'overdrive' is more than what dictionaries make of it within the frame of driving a car, namely: a gear in a motor vehicle providing a gear ratio higher than that of direct drive (the usual top gear), so that the engine speed can be reduced at high road speeds to lessen fuel consumption or to allow further acceleration.

By a comical coincidence, it sounds very close to the Dutch verb *overdrijven*, although the meanings of the two words are quite different. The Dutch word means 'exaggerating'. And that, I must admit, comes close to my sense of pressure, which I also tend to exaggerate. I feel pressured even when, in retrospect, I must admit it was not necessary at all to do what I felt pressured to do. But the state of feeling great pressure to involve myself in excessive activity is, according to many around me, 'typically me'.

In the early days of becoming a professional scholar and teacher, which I really wanted to develop into a career, the pressure grew through the need to 'network', to go to conferences and speak in discussions. Declining invitations to give lectures, write articles, coach MA and PhD students, or other things that take time and effort, is the hardest thing to do. It always feels wrong, like a missed opportunity, for both sides of the collaboration. And it seemed unfair towards colleagues, students, and the programmed objects of discussion. Practically all invitations come with their reasons for acceptance. Either the inviting colleague is a friend, or someone very important in my field of study, or the place where the event is held is appealing, if I have never been there, or it is a particularly beautiful place. It can also be an important, famous research centre. Or the topic fascinates me. Or, another possibility: I am curious about them, or it. This is where those two traits, curiosity and haste, join forces. And once I accept, which I clearly do too frequently and too quickly, cancelling is out of the question. That is something you cannot do to the organizers, who have already scheduled you into their programme. Hence my overfull agenda, that kept and still keeps me in overdrive. For, every commitment I accept involves work: reading, thinking, writing, making PowerPoint presentations, booking travel arrangements... And that newly acquired work comes, of course, on top of what is already there, which fills my calendar densely enough as it is. So, speeding up is the only solution.

I am often told by friends, relatives, dear ones, to calm down that over-the-top rushing. I see their point. I really do. But what I lack is the knowledge, the insight, the skill, of how to do that. Part of the rushing comes from the way my double tasking of housekeeping and homework has early on become a habit, almost an addiction. I could never find a way to diminish either one. And that inheritance from my childhood was not easy to shed. It had become a pattern. At home so much was expected of me that all I could do was do it all, and as fast as possible. School was the side of my life that suffered; I got sloppy with the homework. Not so much by laziness, although that also sneaked in, as a companion of the inevitable fatigue. But rather, because there was simply not enough time for it. Sometimes I had to stay home, couldn't even go to school, because I was needed to assist Mother for some reason. I resented that not going to school most of all. But also, studying after such long and exhausting days was not so pleasant.

Exhaustion: another meaning, or result, of 'overdrive'. The word joins extreme fatigue with enervation, even the danger of collapse. One of the meanings of 'overdrive' is 'to drive or work someone to exhaustion'. I cannot deny that this is what frequently happened to me, that I was the 'someone', although I was too proud to admit it. And, I must acknowledge, part of it, especially later, was my own doing. Somehow, I unlearned to stop, even to slow down. Overdrive had become my way of living, and stayed with me, even long after I had liberated myself from the pressure coming from the outside. Working fast always seemed the most effective way of getting things done. And that is always the goal. Getting it done: but if I hoped that would mean sitting down afterwards, it rarely came to that, because the next commitment was always already lurking.

OVER-ZEALOUS

My tendency to work more and faster than necessary most surely has its roots in the tumultuous household in which I grew up. But why that background, those roots, persisted for so long, is beyond me. One factor is the integration with the curiosity described under N. That seems obvious. Also, there was a lot of fear. I was an anxious child. I was always afraid my parents would divorce, which they eventually did, but only long after I had left home. Fear for the safety of the little siblings, who were always a bit at risk, given the canal beyond the garden, the cars in the street, and the nearby park where they could get lost, be abducted, or drown in the river that streamed through it. Those fears drove me to the over-the-top zealousness that I invested in saving the family. It never felt like a simple obligation. I just felt better myself if things went well. I later learned that this was typical of a third child: the first one rebelled, the second one slipped away, and the third one tried to resolve it all, as I explained under H.

And I was also quite insecure, mostly about my looks, for example. I didn't consider myself pretty, not at all. I thought I looked rather dull, mousy. And at some point, when my father, after I had a haircut, thought he was making me a compliment by saying: 'You look quite Christian', I felt, instead, deeply hurt. What does it mean to look 'Christian' and how should that make me better-looking? Of course, Father wasn't interested in seeing me as pretty. My clothes were rather boring, always second-hand coming down from my older sister, and there was no question of putting on make-up. And although I knew I was intelligent enough to get good grades at school, that did nothing to mitigate the insecurity about the rest of me. Perhaps, but this is just a guess, I was afraid I was going to be too much like Mother, with the latent hysteria and potential cruelty always lurking, even though she, unlike me, was beautiful. In a sense,

my 'overdrive' (*overdrijven*) must have been a desire to be ready
to flee. Running, fast, running away: a dream. Running, a sport I
was never very good at, seemed the most pleasurable thing one
could do.

This fantasy about running away was also, I realized
later, influenced by Mother's tendencies. During years of
my early adolescence, she had a small suitcase stored under
her side of the bed. In it were the necessities for an escape:
toiletries, a change of clothes, her diploma as a teacher, and her
jewellery. She called it her little 'despair-suitcase', as one day
she explained it to me, when I complained about that obstacle
to my cleaning under the bed. When she felt she couldn't
cope with her life anymore, she would pick it up and quietly
leave the house. And yes, she did. Usually, she went to walk
on the nearby moorland, sometimes going so far that Father
had to call the police to find her. Sometimes she took the car
and drove to a friend who lived in another town, asking her
permission to stay there overnight. Without reassuring Father
by telling him where she was. Of course, this despair-suitcase
act did nothing to cheer me up. Nor did I have anything of the
order of diplomas or jewellery to imitate her. The only thing I
had in common with her was the desire to escape. And, according to my tendency, to do it fast: to run as fast as possible.

It never happened, in spite of my dream-fantasy about
it. I simply could not do it. One reason was that I felt too
responsible; another one was fear. That burden of responsibility
always won over. I could only get somewhat rid of that when
the little ones grew older and became able to do their own share
in the housekeeping. Only somewhat, though; for ingrained
habits never go away. But still, it got a little lighter as time
went on. I remained over-zealous, but slowly it began to feel
more like a choice than a semi-slavery, as it had felt for so
long. No more Cinderella-without-prince. So, life got better as
I grew older, away from the permanency of duties and closer
to actually working for my own career. This change, although
slow to develop, brought with it a happiness about being free to
choose what I could do with my life. But doing everything fast
remained an innate trait. And then came, of course, the next

stage of overdrive: barely having begun studying, in the first semester, I fell pregnant. The story of how that happened will come later perhaps; it had nothing to do with love or desire. That story will make clear why I use the verb 'fell', which is more usual in French than in English.

Having been raised with an absolute taboo on abortion, it felt simply 'natural' to carry the pregnancy to term. So, I kept the baby. My parents were quite shocked, even furious, when they learned of the pregnancy. They barred me from the house, so that I wouldn't 'infect' the siblings with my wicked lifestyle. I had to stay in the too-small room I rented during semesters. The word 'sex' was not pronounced at home. But it was obvious that I had done something very bad. My younger brother, quite a bad boy himself, came to threaten me: if I didn't abort, he would do it himself. Fortunately, he never got around to doing it. It took months before my parents allowed me to visit the home again, and see the no-longer-little ones, who were very warm and welcoming. For them, getting a little nephew or niece was pure joy. Neither they nor my parents had any idea of how miserable the situation of my life was, living with a guy who never liked me and only stayed because of the child, and the meals I was expected to serve every evening. But fortunately, within a few years I was able to pack up and leave him. The unforgettable story of Bram under G explains how that was possible.

Life got better, although even more hectic; having a baby to care for was more than just another chore. I went to classes with a basket containing the baby, bottles for feeding and diapers, and a knitwork. During the classes I knitted, while listening to the teacher. Mercifully the little fellow was very well behaved, and slept through the thundering voices of the professors. Once the professor of Renaissance Literature said: 'Ne tricotez pas!' (don't knit). I just explained I had to, so that the little sweaters I was making in automatic gear would keep my son warm during the upcoming cold season. He understood, but wondered how I could follow his lectures in that way. He didn't know about my frantic over-zealous way of living, and the attention-schizophrenia it nurtured. I reassured him by saying: 'Just wait until you read my term essay.' He relented and gave me the highest possible grade for the paper.

OVER-ACTIVE

Somehow, I managed to meet the requirements of the study programme. This was not so easy, but I did, in spite of the difficulties of having to work on the side for a living. My parents had withdrawn the meagre allowance I had received so far—for two or three months. From now on, I had to save up for the next tuition fee, the next month's rent, the everyday food. Not to speak of clothes. I was determined to dress better than the hand-downs of my adolescence, so I roamed the city centre when sales were on. As if I had nothing else to do! To earn the necessary money, I worked in restaurant kitchens, washing dishes, but my preferred job was speaking in a microphone as a guide on a tour boat that sailed through the city centre. There, my task was to describe the important buildings along the canals, those seventeenth-century jewels of architecture, in four languages: French, German, English, Dutch. Due to my resistance to that language caused by my parents' after-war stories, my German was very bad. In high school, where German was on the mandatory curriculum, I stubbornly refused to learn it. So, I bargained with the director of the boating company to stay with just Dutch, English, and French, pretexting that it would also be less of a burden on the passengers. He took one of my tours to check me out. He was satisfied by the quality of my three languages, and he even liked my comments on the buildings. So, I was allowed to stay on. Just another activity for the day, to squeeze into the schedule. One I quite liked, actually.

Luckily, I had begun the study programme with already sufficient fluency in French, thanks to the summer job I had done before starting, between graduating from high school and starting at university. That was a great help. And much of the homework consisted of reading: literary texts and essays about them, in addition to books on history and French culture. Reading was, had always been, my favourite occupation. But of course, between the tour boat guiding and the cooking, even when later my little son was old enough to go to nursery for full days, the activities were over-the-top many and my days, hectic. This didn't bother me as much as I would now expect it would have done. The overdrive *worked*, in the sense of 'functioned'. Of course, there were times when it really got too hectic, and I had several bouts of near-collapsing. Exhaustion was one of my many habits.

But the reason why I could stand it was simply that I enjoyed the activities. Reading had always been my passion, as I have mentioned under B and D. Childcare was in my blood, thanks to the task of caring for the little ones at home in my childhood. And the tour boat guiding helped to improve my fluency in speaking foreign languages. Moreover, I enjoyed learning about those interesting historical buildings. And with my overdrive tendency, I made sure to find out things about them that would engage the tourists. These guided tours were my first tasks of speaking in public, and in foreign languages. It helped me overcome the shyness that had always bothered me. Later, when I began a career of conferences and lectures, having overcome those inhibitions was a great asset.

So, it will by now be clear that my activities were over-the-top, but also helped me to get on with life in a better way than during my childhood and adolescence. More autonomy, the possibility to make choices, and assess what needed doing, then doing it. This remained the mode in which I did 'it'. The French studies programme was not too hard, the teachers, at least most of them, quite engaging, and the obligatory readings were gripping. Who has not shed hot tears reading *Madame Bovary*? The teachers did more than the books alone would have done. Some were so spellbinding that they made me overcome a reluctance, or an indifference, for certain fields. I was hanging on their every word, whatever their specializations were. The professor of Medieval Literature, the well-known Swiss Paul Zumthor, was so 'enthusiasmatic' that I got up earlier than usual to attend his early-morning class, even without the obligation to take it, and without any intention to continue with the Middle Ages. It was just him: hearing his voice, seeing him scribble, and above all, his constant movements. I would never have learned anything beyond the boring facts without him.

He almost jumped around the front of the classroom when jotting down things, names, concepts, on the blackboard. No, I had no personal interest in the Middle Ages, and such an interest never really accrued. Yet, thanks to him, I got more and more fascinated; so much so that later I even wrote something on an artwork situated in that time period, with a gratefulness to him. So, thanks to that professor, the Middle Ages did creep in, just a bit. Now, decades later, I realize that my fondness of his moving personality must have had something to do with recognizing myself in him. Enthralled by movement where no logic prepares me for it, I felt an excitement that was like a contamination. Later, when working in the US and Canada, I reconnected with him. He was getting old. But the first thing he proudly showed me in his house when he and his wife had invited me for dinner, was his home trainer. Clearly, moving was not something he would ever give up.

OVER-DOING IT

The element 'over-' in the headings of this entry all point to an aspect of my life in which I exaggerate, over-act, over-do. This is a bit my 'nature', my personality. Where it comes from has hopefully become clear enough. Where it goes is a different question. Will I ever been able to 'cure' myself from this over-the-top tendency to do too much, too fast, and too constantly? Although I have my doubt about this, I know, and as my dearest ones never tire of saying, I put myself in danger if I don't. Just now, writing this vignette, I do it once again. I should be working towards the upcoming commitments for the weeks ahead. Or better still, take a walk. But no, the deadline of the journal is coming up. Yes, I know, and have written about it in vignette A. The English word 'deadline' must be taken seriously, literally: dead-line. The hyphen helps remembering that.

But before going into the valuable meanings of the hyphen, which I hope to do in a different vignette, I must mention a

stream of over-doings that has been an unforgettable experience involving *movement*. Inspired by a personal coincidence,
I began to make films, at fist documentaries about issues of
migration and 'refugeedom', and then 'theoretical fictions'. I
mention this activity, to which I will return, here only as a case
of my tendency of over-doing and my fondness of movement.
For if anything is heavy-duty work, it is filmmaking. Not only
are there so many jobs involved, from conceiving, script-writ-
ing, casting, rehearsing with actors, and then shooting, editing...
but also, there are so many different people involved that my
childhood skill of dealing with the 'little ones' in a positive
spirit, came in handy. As did my teaching experience, and my
convictions about how to be a good teacher. My slogan 'if you
don't learn from your students, you are a bad teacher' compelled me, in the filmmaking, to solicit and heed the opinions of
every participant. This worked wonders. The actors, the camera
operator, but also the assistants, the catering crew, the make-up
artists: every participant had something valuable to contribute.
Yes, this meant more work, over-doing it again. But it was so
productive and fruitful that I never regretted any of it; on the
contrary. I began to realize that I took pleasure in it.[33]

The only way I could make that filmmaking work was by
letting every actor speak their own language. That way I was
able to cast people I already knew, from different countries.
Most of the actors have become enduring friends. This helped
the process, without making it easier, but I have always
believed in the value of this 'method', and the results go to
show it. The different sounds of the languages make a kind
of music. A Finnish actress, speaking a language where the
accent falls systematically on the first syllable, paired up with
a French actor who, true to his language, puts the accent on
the last syllable of each word, unwittingly producing a musical
dialogue. This was the case in the film *Madame B*, which I made
in response to Flaubert's novel, together with British artist
Michelle Williams Gamaker, in 2012–2014. There, in a flash we
decided to cast one actor to play the three men in Emma's life,
which he did brilliantly (Thomas Germaine), partnering up with
Finnish Emma (Marja Skaffari).

---

[33] On my views on teaching, see Lutters, *The Trade of the Teacher* (2018).

The hectic nature of filmmaking once we are on set is easily absorbed by the joy of the doing, albeit it over-doing. The collective effort helps overcome my resentment about the over-tasking to which I had so often been subjected. The collectivity is a social hyphen; a binding among people. And the different languages spoken contribute to that hyphenation. This is why I prefer the preposition 'inter-' to its more frequently used alternative 'trans-' that gives no meaning to the connection—there is no connection, only a traversal. So, knowing that I was—again—overdoing it, adding a heavy activity to my already over-flowing calendar, did not bother me. Not at all.

Precarity

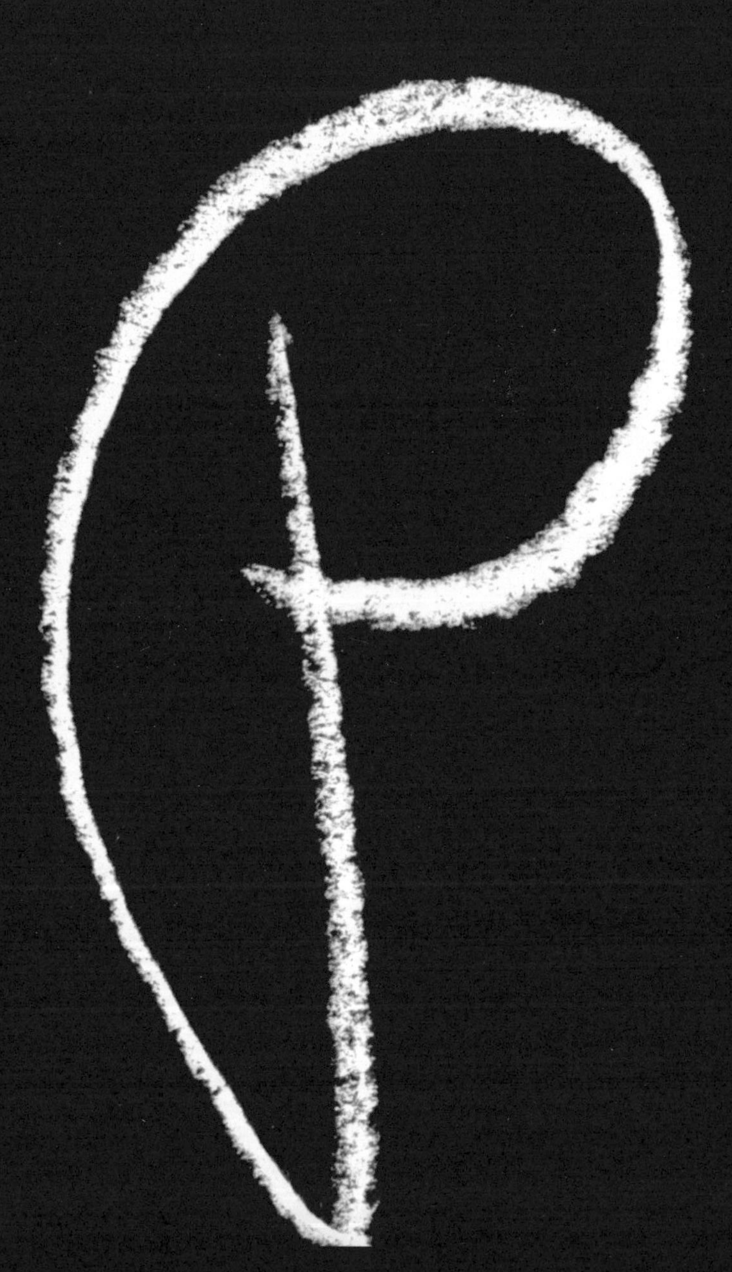

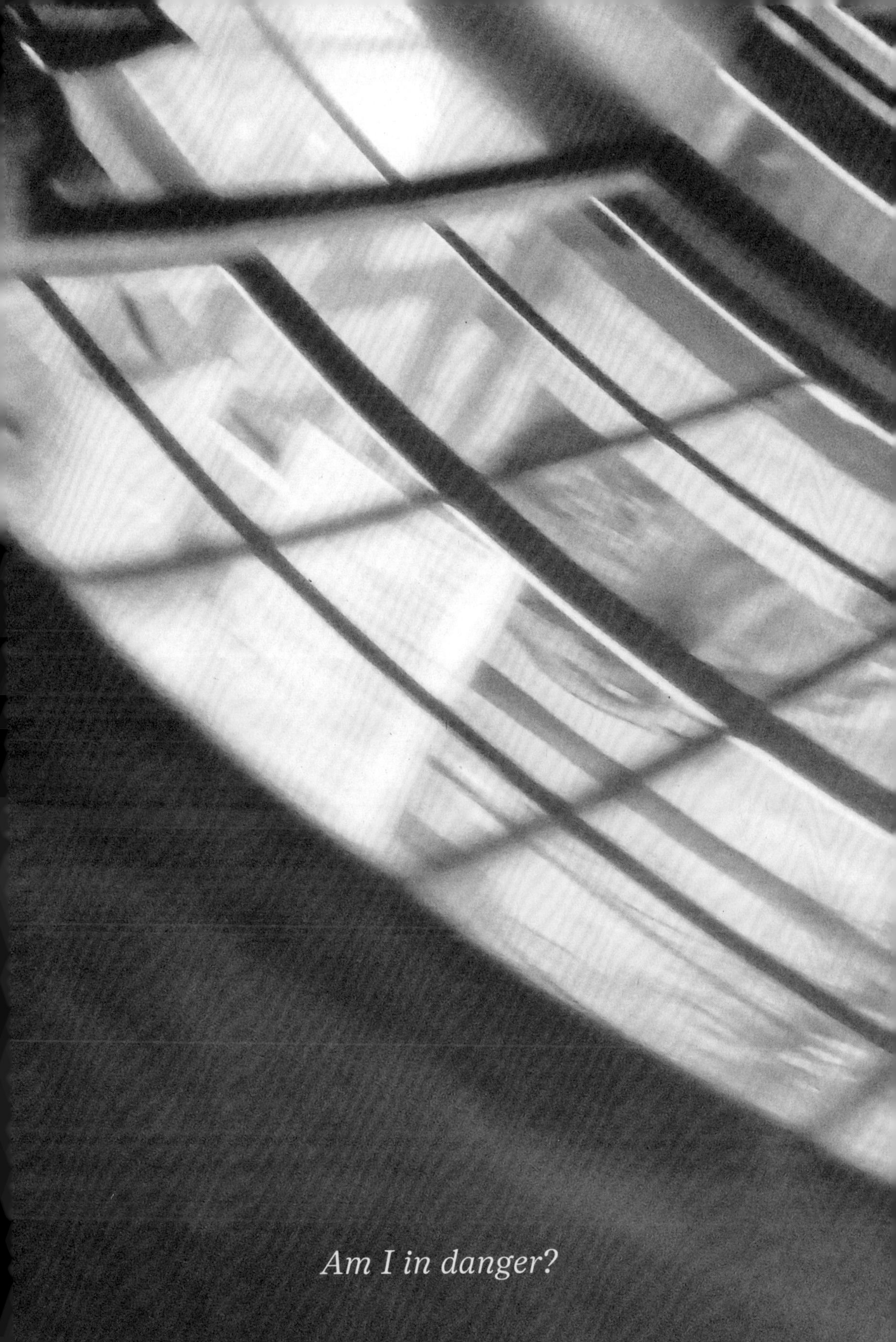

Am I in danger?

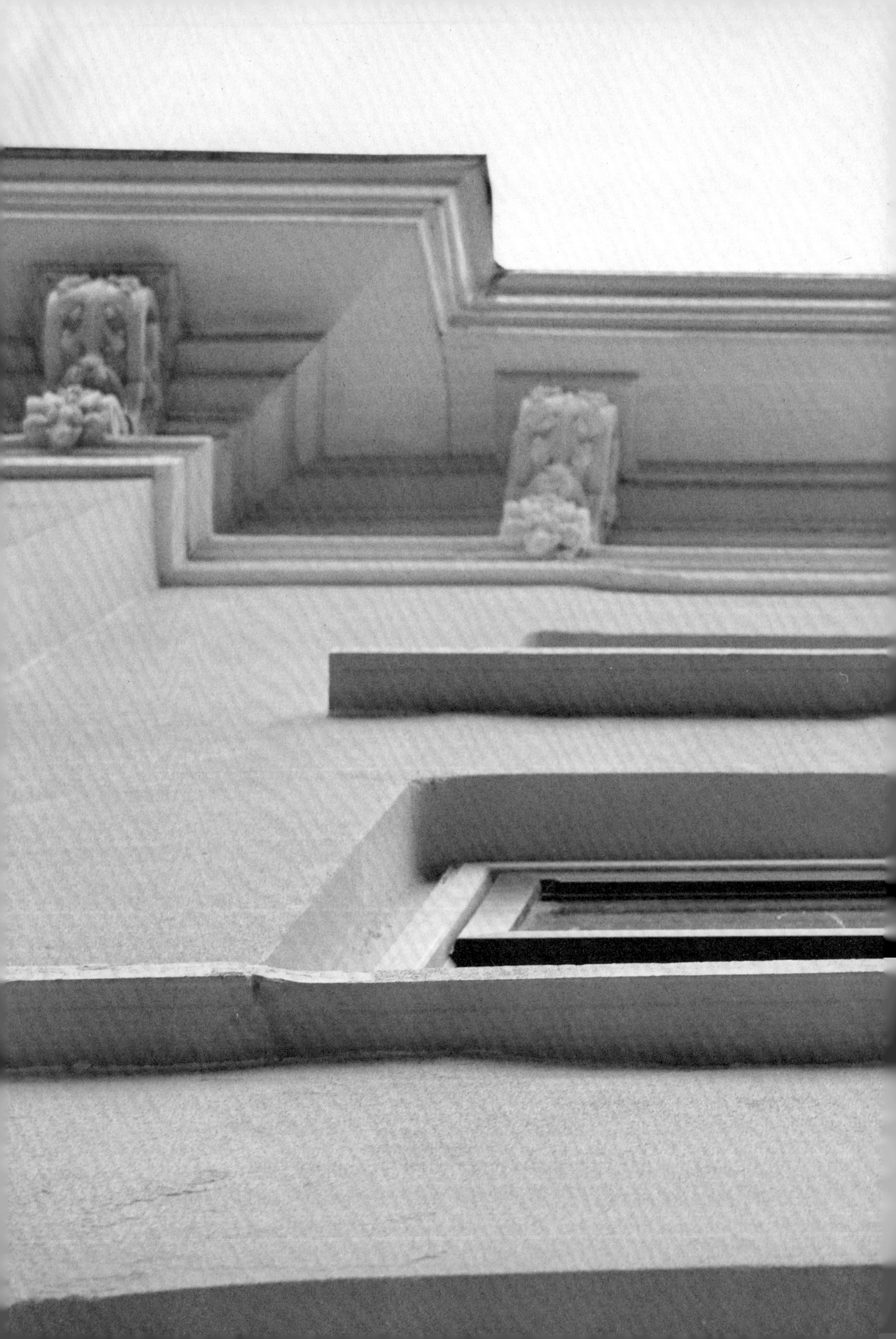

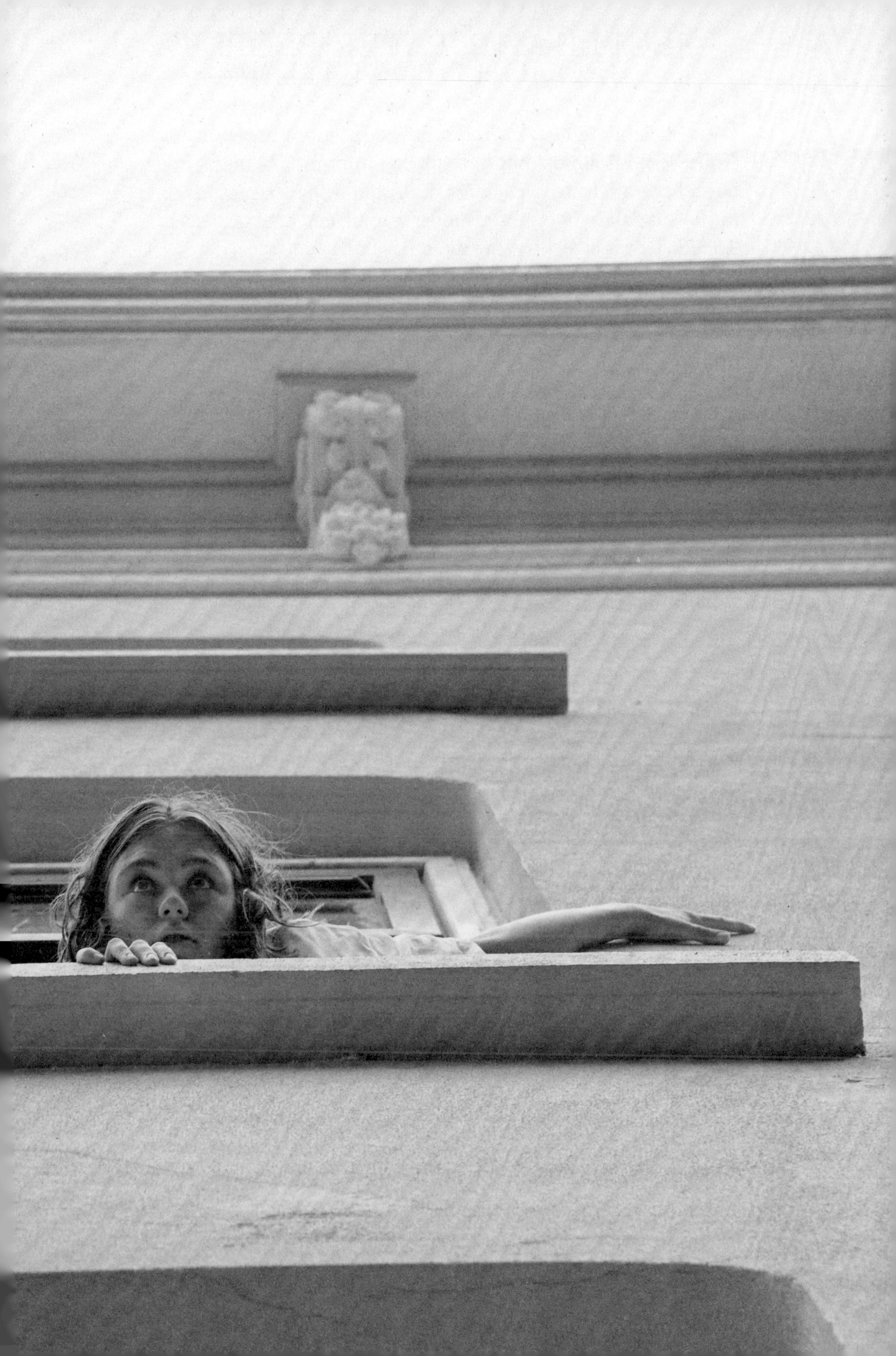

PEOPLE AND 'PAPER-PEOPLE' BROUGHT TOGETHER

I was once invited to write about the concept of the threshold. A threshold is almost but not quite a limit; not a boundary or border but an 'in-between'; not a line but a space. And this, in the spatial, temporal, sensuous, medial, and artistic sense. The idea, or image, of a threshold has been widely used in discussions of *liminality*, proposed long ago by anthropologist Arnold van Gennep (1873–1957) in his theory of the transitional rituals—*rites de passage*—from 1909. With that concept he described rituals in which adolescents were sent out of the inhabited world into the wilderness to fend for themselves, in order to get ready for adulthood. In that sense of threshold, the in-between can be seen as an indicator of precarity, specifically in the temporal sense of a life phase when all certainties tumble and new certainties take a long time to emerge. That theory made me retrospectively aware of my own sense, in adolescence, of not knowing what my life was going to be. I knew what I did *not* want to end up being; nothing like the miserable life my mother had lived, for example—which I have described a bit, with some hesitation, under M. But what I did want instead was not so clear; according to logic, the negative is undefined, vague, unclear. Of the experience of adolescence, I remember that uncertainty and the trembling fear it sometimes made me feel, especially when I compared myself, my life, with other people's lives. Those were moments that I realized the precarity of life, and the need to develop and choose a special interest, in order to stabilize my sense of self.

Precarity is an uncertainty about the possibilities of life. The state between states; a threshold between a liveable and an unliveable life; the 'precariat', to coin a word analogous to Marx's proletariat: the millions of people who stand balancing on that threshold. This is not a transition or a learning experience but for many a permanent state. Keeping this in mind, attempting to survive the fundamental precarity of that period through learning from people I didn't know and would never meet, I began to seek to bring in the uncertainty, the threshold, the in-betweenness as an important area of intellectual work: between thinking and doing; the intellect and the imagination, the past and the present, and literature and visual art. I think this need to escape, to run away from the precarity, has become my focus in life, and my source of inspiration. This, then, became my ongoing search, a kind of vocation, which, as soon as my intellectual pathway became a bit clearer, I realized that in-betweenness, or threshold, is also relevant for what later became my interest in the narratological concepts that denote specific agents of those agents that make up narrative, such as narrator, focalizer, and actor. Of these, the middle one is what lays in between the medium—text, film, game, painting—and the story (better termed fabula) which together forge the narrative. It has become key in all my work. This has become an attempt to bring my memories of adolescence and my later professional searches in contact with each other. Therefore, in this entry I focus on precarity, with focalization as a narratological tool for analysis, and the state of the world—or more limited, of the people's world—as the fabula.

This is how I began to turn my life-long passion for reading-as-escape into something a bit more consistent; a permanent preoccupation. I began to realize that this passion was, at least in part, an attempt to concentrate and not fall off the threshold, or out of the window, or into the abyss; in other words, to combat that sense of precarity through looking around me and thereby standing more solidly. The people I read about came closer to myself. Of the 'paper-people' or personages (as I called them soon, when French became a special interest) I got to meet and know through reading I began to develop a special interest in those with whose precarity I empathized most strongly. Not necessarily through identification, since their precarity was the last thing I wished for, but through getting to know them better, according to my sense of the desire for knowing (see under K). And that knowing included a strong wish to connect understanding to imagining, brought together in the making of images that facilitate understanding on a deeper level, what I have termed *imaging* once I began to make films.

Combining an aversion against the simplifications that the logic of binary opposition entails with an interest in the discovery of the subtlety that defines literature, from the beginning my work has been based on the in-between; in other words, the threshold of precarity. In this vein, in narrative theory I developed the concept of focalization as between the medium of text and the imagination of fabula to enable an analysis of narratives that could be truly literary: to grasp the surplus value of literature as distinct from common narrative, without privileging either form or content, which cannot be separated. This allows for comparison between media as well, as I will bring up under Q. I strongly advocate a close analysis of focalization in its capacity to manipulate, persuade and, thus, have political power. That power can be understood, and thereby either undermined when damaging, or enlisted when supportive in view of a wider cultural-political interest. I briefly refer to Flaubert's novel and, with a view of intermediality, the video project responding to it, to explain how focalization and its close reading can do this. True to the idea of close analysis of both works and the relationship between them, I will do this through a few cases visible in the installation *Precarity*. The installation is a selection from the film *Madame B* that in 2012–2014 I made with Michelle Williams Gamaker, a long-term co-maker who became a close friend.

Precarity is at the heart of human existence. Life is precarious, always under threat. This precarity is subject to historical change. But in spite of the ideology of progress under which we live and in which we tend to (but should not) believe, change does not equal progress at all. Today, everything, from health care to relationships to labour rights, human rights, and world peace, as well as economic survival, is precarious. As a consequence, many people stand on the threshold in a precarious balancing act, always in danger of falling down. All those things I just mentioned should be accepted as human rights, but they are *de facto* abducted and held hostage by power brokers and financial predators. Today, this includes the so- but wrongly called neo-liberal university, for which the five-minutes-to-midnight bell should be tolling right now. I worked there, and hence, I could not avoid being complicit in it. But I could resist it from within. One way to do that is to be precise about language, form, and art. For language is precarious, too. Even words. For example, the word 'radical' doesn't mean 'terrorist', as it has come to mean lately, but 'going the whole way in resistance, by promoting thinking'. French philosopher and art thinker Marie José Mondzain has set a brilliant example with her book on the word 'radical'; a merciless analysis and indictment of what we do with words. More on this under R.

I discovered the importance of art that is due to the precarity of language, retrospectively, when I made it my professional subject. Art matters, because it is both self-re-flexive and constantly reconsidering the world. It cannot be instrumentalized, not even for good political causes. As Derek Attridge famously wrote in 2004, in *The Singularity of Literature*: 'There is no way it [literature] can serve as an instrument without at the same time challenging the basis of instrumentality itself.' (13) But importantly, this justified resistance to instrumentalization does not preclude a profound, enduring, and complicating engagement with the world and its ills. On the contrary; Attridge's caution opens up a different, more dialogic mode of such an engagement.

The work British artist Michelle Williams Gamaker and I have done in interaction with Flaubert's *Madame Bovary*, attempted to explore those possibilities. We sought to release aspects of the novel that have been either under-illuminated or ignored. With its wide readership and the even wider knowledge of its story of a precarious life, so similar to many novels that followed—unhappily married women, presented as hysterical; transgressions, ruin, and suicide: how nine-teenth-century!—I reckon I am allowed to be brief about it. The project we did consists of a feature film and video installations of a varying numbers of screens, re-edited for every exhibition occasion with different inflections. The 19-channel one is the fullest, extended version of the film, with the title *Madame B: Explorations in Emotional Capitalism*. In a 13-channel installa-tion, titled *Cause & Effect*, we focused on the main character's confinement to the domestic, and her desperate attempts to escape from it, foregrounding the political causality involved. And the shorter, 5-channel work, made especially for group shows and smaller venues, is titled *Precarity*.[34]

Showing is sharing. In this entry I 'expose' precarity,

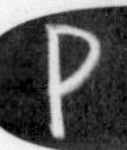

<u>34</u> On this novel and the subsequent project, I have published several articles. I mention only two here: 'Breaking the Narrative' (2016) and 'From "Madame Bovary c'est moi"' (2022). It all started with the article 'Théorie de la description' (1982).

standing on those grounds or thresholds. This means I will bring together the audio-visual exhibiting of the story in the 5-channel installation and the precarious life of the main character, Emma; for now, my central paper-person. With the verb 'exposing' I am alluding to the French equivalent *exposition*, and the act of exposing, unpacking, analyzing, laying bare. I mean to con-fuse 'exhibiting', as in the installation, with 'exposing' Emma in her plight, and her vulnerability to the seduction of emotional capitalism, con-fusing the French and the English meanings of the word.[35]

COMPARISON AGAINST EMMA'S PRECARITY

The precarity of Emma's life is embedded in her tenuous and shaky relationship to the world. In making this the centre of his novel, Flaubert the literary artist and formal perfectionist, 'pre-posterously' answers our time's anxieties about the political in art. In school, Emma in her precarious existence of longing and frustration, dreams away during classes about reality, but she is the best student in the singing class. She takes extra-curricular lessons in art and deportment, for elegance. Well-groomed for the marriage market, she is talented, but lacks commitment to the present, the world, and social reality. As a result, she is ostracized from every environment she enters. She is radically alone. Having been raised to expect constant thrills and excitement, Emma is exposed in the precariousness of a beginning adult life. She faces a world that seduces her into risking what she has and craving for what she doesn't have; and grasping at last straws, she takes more and more dangerous decisions. How can I compare this literary masterpiece with our humble video installation? The latter serves here to foreground aspects of the former, by staging similarities and differences together. The common ground is the intermedial nature of art. That ground is a ground to stand on against the precarity to which she is doomed. Her goal to survive does not work out. She dies of it.

35 The different versions can be watched with these links: the link to the 19 screens that together form the installations: vimeo.com/album/2782150, password: MadameB Cinema Suitcase; the link to the 8 installations,

For the concept and method of comparison I refer to the work of a French colleague with an English first name and a German family name, William Marx. His extensive output is a jewel of readerly scholarship that preserves the complexity of thought. For a comparison between the artworks, a ground is needed. The first specific ground, the threshold between literary art and audiovisual installation, is immersion: the condition of immersive viewing both similar and different to reading a captivating novel. In neither work the point is to lure us into passive consumption; instead, 'lure', an instrumentalization of the 'second person', is itself the primary target of critique in both works. This common aspect is the *ground* of comparison. Lure means an interaction, a seduction, but as per Attridge's statement, the works also reflect on, critique, and challenge the perpetrator-victim opposition that a simple view of 'lure' might encourage. Emma's 'mistakes'—damaging her own life, transgressing standard morality by doing evil things, such as adultery, irresponsible over-spending, and neglecting her child, things that only men are condoned to do—accumulate to ruin her; together, they constitute the precarity of her life. This is not an individual ill but something towards which she has been pushed all along by her surroundings. The second installation piece, *Probing and Meddling*, foregrounds this collective responsibility. The fellow townsfolk we condensed in the character of the meddling pharmacist Homais, represent the probing of the curious and their chilling rejoicing in Emma's misfortune and downfall. In the novel, this callousness of Emma's environment is narrated in bits and pieces and attributed to different characters. In our installation piece, Homais stands in for these characters, in a metaphor or condensation. I use metaphor here quite casually—with 'tenor' as the initial object that is obliterated or transformed by the 'vehicle', the thing with which it is compared. 'Condensation' alludes to Freud's theory of dreams.

But the precarity of Emma's life also has a source in what we can call 'content'. The central theme, running through most of the novel, is the one that has lost nothing of its contemporary relevance: *seduction*. Seduction demonstrates

the combinations of the screens: vimeo.com/album/2823521, password: MadameB Cinema Suitcase; *Precarity* (5 screens): vimeo.com/album/3170262/sort:alphabetical/format:thumbnail, password: MadameB Cinema Suitcase the most important ground appealing to the character to stand on, seemingly against her precarity, but which it also reinforces. In its turn, seduction is also an ambiguity of subject-position; a precarity of the wobbly ground of guilt and innocence. Is she doing it, or is that other person doing it? The inextricable conflation of capitalist and erotic seduction, constantly making the one to stand in for the other because they are so intimately comparable, makes up the precarity. It is what Flaubert saw in his environment, as a symptom of the ills of his time. In our time, it is what sociologist Eva Illouz has aptly conceptualized as *emotional capitalism* in her 2007 book *Cold Intimacies*. I have mentioned this concept before, but here I reiterate and specify its relevance. To be taken literally.

Flaubert was such an obsessive stickler for literary perfection that he 'tasted' every word for sound as much as for adequacy; yet, he was engaged in a profound critique of his time. This places a particular burden on art works that come in the novel's wake. It also cautions us against a misreading of this deeply feminist novel as a feminist manifesto. Flaubert, an overt, well-known misogynist, would turn in his grave. I take the phrase 'to release the potential' from the 1921 essay 'The Task of the Translator', where Walter Benjamin wrote about translation: 'While content and language form a certain unity in the original, like a fruit and its skin, the language of the translation envelops its content like a royal robe with ample folds.'

This unorthodox, *fruit*ful view of translation seems to me an excellent starting point for a retrospective comparison; its multi-sensuousness brings it into the present. Comparison is the release of the potential of 'the original', the other work. In contemporaneity, this potential includes the idea of standing on the threshold of time. This makes not only Emma, the paper-person, but also time itself, precarious. The comparison, here, is meant as an analysis of a nineteenth-century novel translated, remediated into a twenty-first-century video work. The differences and challenges of the cinematic help understand, better than even the very extensive critical literature has done, what makes Flaubert's novel uniquely innovative in its time, and deeply relevant in ours, for its staging of precarity as the threshold between a liveable and an unliveable existence; ultimately, between life and death. In the current academic climate shamelessly identified with a term that lies, 'neo-liberal', as if the term meant new and free, what is being destroyed is the imagination. And yet, the imagination is what we need most, to imagine a way out of the precarity, for it is our primary task as people, persons, or personages, in this world of regulated exclusion, violence, and misery, to think 'out of the box', and deny the legitimacy of the box's existence, presence, and power to confine. We need, instead, what anthropologist Arjun Appadurai has termed 'the research imagination'. (1999)

I have learned from Deleuzian thought to appreciate relationality between domains rather than those boundaries that produce precarity. With a neologism that associates itself with the learning through practice implied in the more common word 'internship', I call that mobile relationality, *inter-ship*, and try to bring it to bear on my work as an intellectual-artist. And I don't just mean interdisciplinary, but also intertextual, international, intermedial, intercultural and interdiscursive relations. Here, I want to add another 'inter-ship': that between analyzing and making, as a form of inter-medial analysis, as a way of liberating, expanding, and deepening our insights. This goes back to an encounter, in drawing class in high school, when the teacher highly praised an abstract drawing I had made somewhat automatically, without much thinking. The endeavour to write this book in which my own memories merge with the ideas and associations of others, and with my own later intellectual and artistic developments, is one attempt to try this.

A book I published in 2022, *Image-Thinking*, was another one. Making, in my case, is filmmaking, but of course, there are many other ways of making that are merged with, or nourished by, thinking. Film making shares three activities with analysis: sharp and imaginative looking, including framing and visualizing, or to propose another word, 'imaging', before and during the making; reading and writing; and most creatively productive, collaborating with others who all bring their own expertise and focus to the process. In filmmaking these three activities are more intense than in (academic) analysis alone. I call this 'thinking in film'. First, I made experimental documentaries on migration, with the small collective of young artists called Cinema Suitcase. From this we learned enormously for an understanding of the contemporary world. Michelle Williams and I took the next step, and examined if and how fiction-making could even increase that intellectual yield. We created a genre, which we called, after Freud, *Theoretical Fiction*. We then proceeded to make installation pieces, with the hope of understanding better the different combinations of images and affect in visual interaction.

For the *Madame B* project, the increasing importance of *affect* in the economic, and of the economic in culture was key; the bond between visuality, romantic love, and capitalism was and is the ultimate source of precarity. We must understand how we all participate in causing the economic crisis—in order to resist it while acknowledging our complicity. And no one imagines it more adequately than Flaubert did: 'Then the desires of the flesh, the longing for money, and the melancholy of passion all blended into one suffering, and instead of putting it out of her mind, she made her thoughts cling to it, urging herself to pain and seeking everywhere the opportunity to revive it.' (II, 5) This perspective places affect at the centre of attention and focuses analysis on the resulting interactivity of artworks. Instead of taking what is there to be seen on the surface, for example, affective analysis will establish a relationship between that sight and what it does to the people looking at it, and, precisely, being *affected* by it.[36]

The opening sequence of *Madame B* with the wobbly images that imply the invisible other people, posits ruin. Broken financially and emotionally, Emma balances precariously on the threshold of a broken house. This ruin is the present state; what follows gets us back there, in a circular movement that turns out a vicious circle. This circularity proposes the power of habit, Flaubert's primary opponent. Rather than deploying narrativity for suspense, the idea was to immerse viewers in affect from the beginning. This affect helps viewers watch

---

36 I quote from an English translation of *Madame Bovary* and, because of the many circulating versions, I mention the parts (in Roman numerals) and the chapters instead of page numbers.

with a delicate balance of empathy, understanding, and critical distance, all at the same time. We aimed to make the destructive power of habit affectively tangible. Habit runs along with its opposite, surprise, of which it constitutes the backdrop. Narrative, and especially Flaubert's novel, offers an affectively experientable alternation between the one and the other. Flaubert's originality is the preponderance of habit in his prose, rather than the events that produce surprise.

FOCALIZATION FOR FILM

There are more ways in which Flaubert has challenged traditional ways of storytelling, specifically by keeping the threshold between telling and showing ambiguous; by deploying the narrativity of looking itself as precarious. In the case of a novel and a video installation we cannot avoid narrative. But nor do we need to bow down for the traditional view of narrative. To explore intermediality through performativity, in our full nineteen-channel installation we staged particular kinds of looks as carriers of narrativity. This converges with Flaubert's emphatic deployment of looking as consequential. I had often been struck by a cinematic quality in Flaubert's writing. This may seem strange, since his writing predates the invention of cinema. One of the passages that triggered the intermedial reflection is the prelude to Charles' first encounter with Emma, early in the second chapter: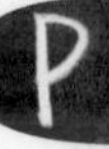

> About four o'clock in the morning Charles set out
> for Les Bertaux, wrapped in a heavy coat. He was
> still drowsy from his warm sleep, and the peaceful
> trot of his mare lulled him like the rocking of a
> cradle. Whenever she stopped of her own accord in
> front of one of those spike-edged holes that farmers
> dig along the roadside to protect their crops, he
> would wake up with a start, quickly remember the
> broken leg, and try to recall all the fractures he had
> ever seen. The rain had stopped; day was breaking,

> and on the leafless branches of the apple trees
> birds were perched motionless, ruffling their little
> feathers in the cold morning wind. The countryside
> stretched flat as far as the eye could see; and the
> tufts of trees clustered around the farmhouses were
> widely spaced dark purple stains on the vast grey
> surface that merged at the horizon into the dull tone
> of the sky. (I, 2)

This passage is practically a script for an opening scene. One sees the colours (or lack of them at the nightly hour), hears the trot of the horse, then in close-up Charles' sleepy face, followed by his attempt to remember his knowledge. A hard cut to another close-up, of the birds on the tree branches, foregrounds Charles' loneliness, and makes the transition to the long shot of the country road more dramatic. This shot will be durational, lasting long enough for the hunger for human encounter to intensify in affect. In the last sentence we see an elongated perspective most clearly, with the compositional device of patches of dull colours to turn a line into a landscape. Flaubert did so 'from within'. He was able to imagine, with empathy, what it would be like to live as a woman in a world ruled by men and money. Staging the money-men as her seducers and enemies, it is more than proto-feminist: prophetic, radical, of a progressive vision that is rare even today. The arrival of Charles at the farm demonstrates both the cinematic quality and the erotic beginnings of the encounter with Emma, presented in an image that, seen in the present tense, could be a perfect filmic close-up.

In the work on this film and its installations, narrative looks became key: we staged looks to which social behaviours are bound and judgments frequently attached—voyeurism and flirting. This combination insures the power structure of social life, in which we all participate. We made a visual form of encounter where the kind of looks determines both the beginning of a relationship and the inequality at the heart of it. This is when I once more realized the central importance of concepts. Like images and memories, concepts have the power to *act* because they make alternative states of affairs thinkable and thus promote their *becoming*. Furthermore, a concept is not discursive, for it does not link up propositions. This is why concepts maintain the flexibility and multiplicity of meaning that fully-fledged theories, discursively elaborated, inevitably lose.

Concepts are moving, just like images. They act, they perform. To understand, then, what the 'actions' are that concepts consist of, I end this entry on Deleuze and Guattari's statement that concepts are *centres of vibrations*, each in itself and every one in relation to all the others: they resound rather than cohere. This resonates intensively with the busy and noisy family life in which I grew up; where vibration overruled understanding. Resonating may well be the best result of comparison, its ground, attuning us to the liveness of the art and literature, ancient or modern, contemporary of historical, that we study. If resonance stops, the world becomes mute, and we all, deaf. This is how precarious as well as necessary comparison as an activity is. Precarity is precious as well as risky.

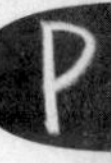

Quoting

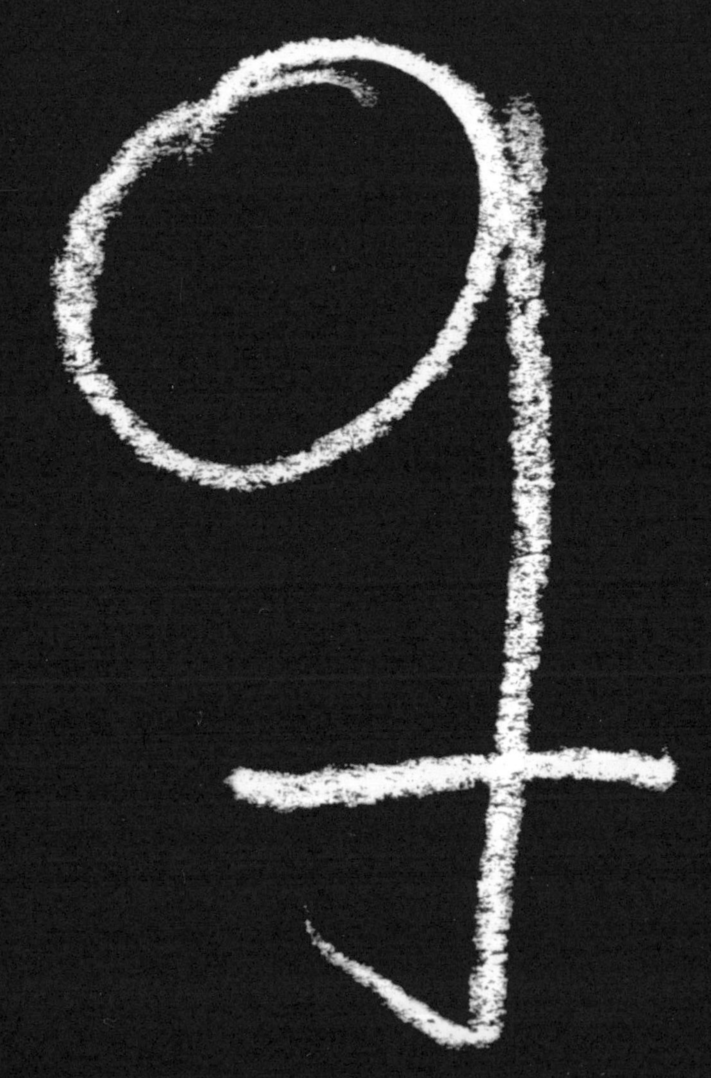

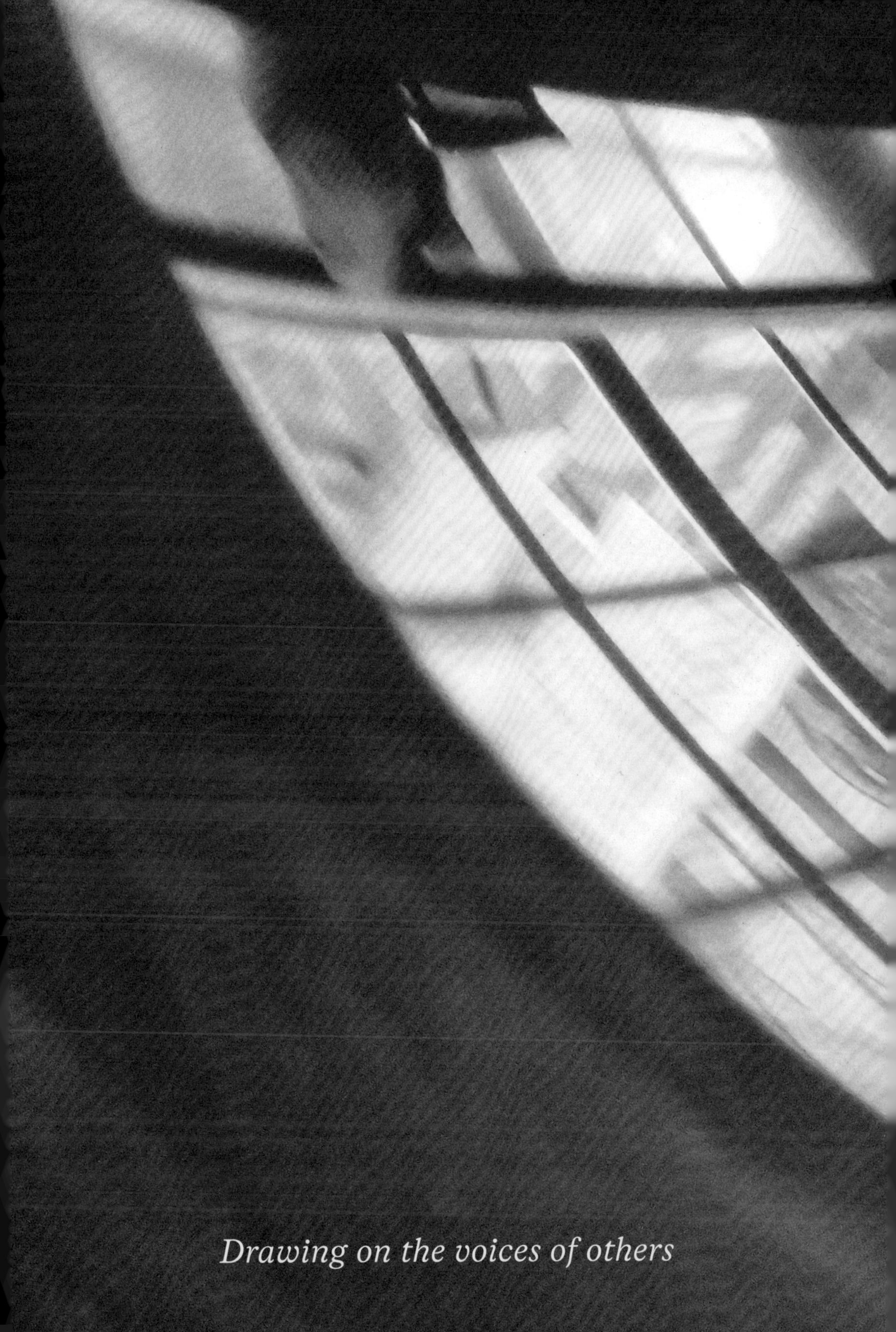

Drawing on the voices of others

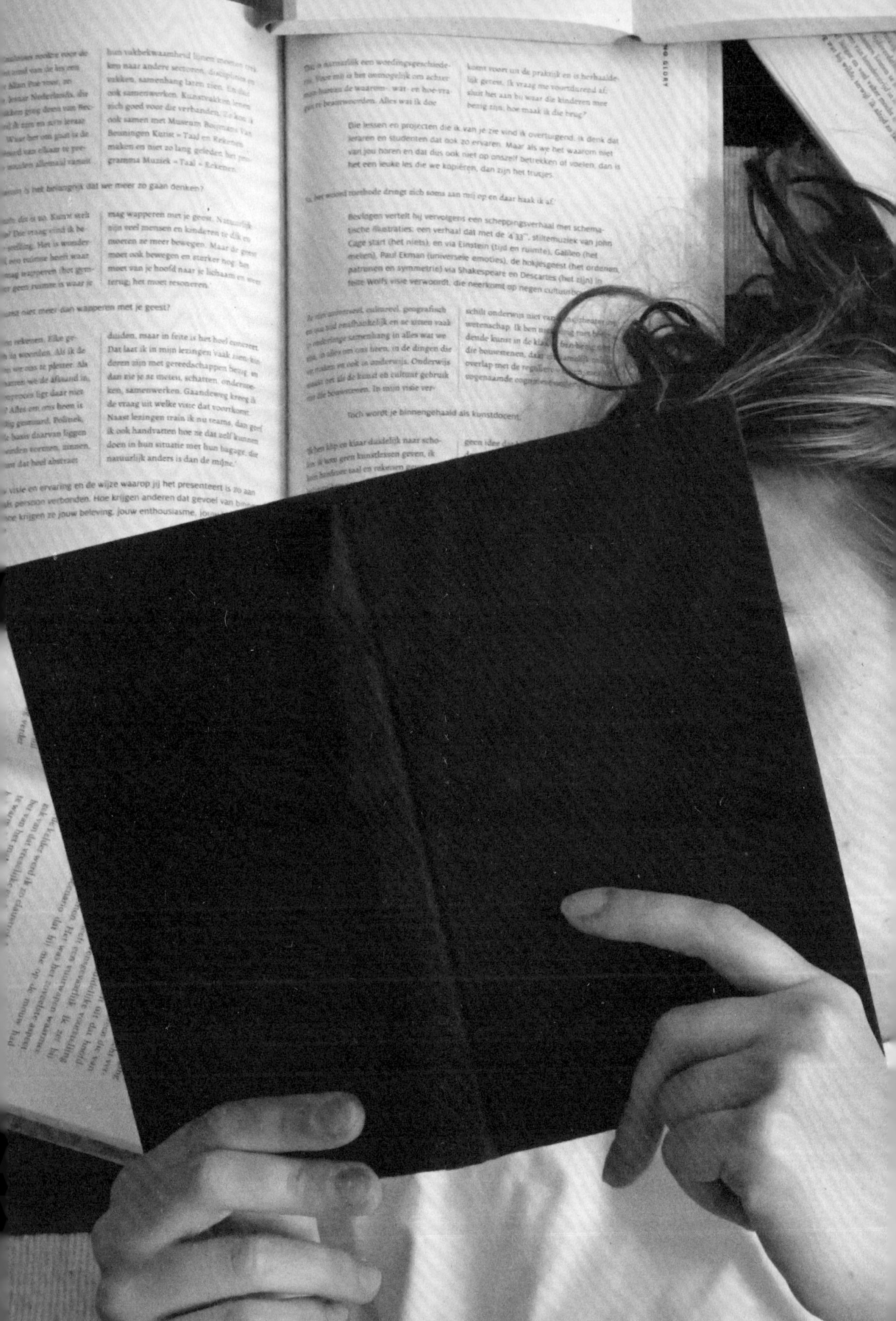

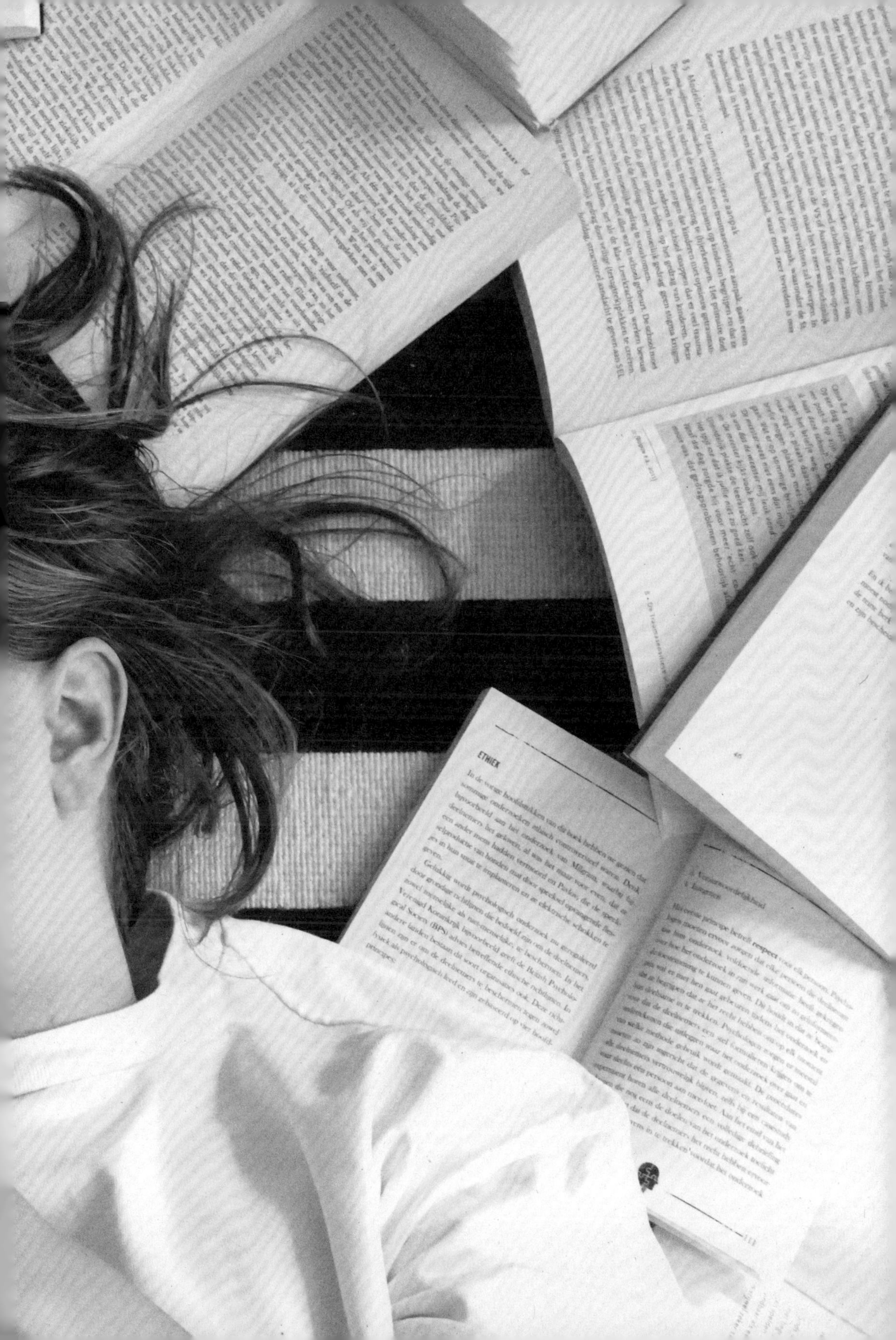

QUIETLY QUOTING

As a child, I was always fascinated by that strange sound of my father talking with the parish priest. To prevent us kids, and probably also Mother, from understanding what they talked about, they spoke in Latin. With my somewhat pathological curiosity (see under N) I memorized some of their sounds and looked the words up in a dictionary. Those were moments of meaning-making. That memorizing took the form of repeating; a kind of quoting. But to avoid being caught in my 'spying', an annoying transgression of the ban on knowing what they were talking about, I did that quoting silently; quietly. The habit of doing that made me aware of the role sound plays in speech, and how the combination of sound and meaning constituted the language. Later we would call that repeating of the words of others a form of plagiarism. Only when, much later, I learned the syntactics of narrative, with the colons introducing direct speech, quotation marks on both ends, and the attribution of the speech to particular characters, I understood the specific status of direct discourse as a form of quoting.

Quoting can be seen as a recasting or reframing of past words and images, sounds, or even styles in new, later, or contemporary media products. Each case of quotation shows specific ways in which this relationship between media products is vital to the new artwork as well as to the source from which it is derived, and for which, due to the mutuality of time (as opposed to chronological linearity: pre-posterously) it thereby becomes, in turn, a source. Such quoting media products thus present issues as they are implied in the representational practice of the past, yet can only be perceived through the detour of the present, which transforms both the issues and the preceding works. In short, quotation is indispensable to understand this particular type of intermedial practice and the media products such a practice produces. In filmmaking, the inevitable integration of words and images, colour, sound, narrativity, technological effects and more, clearly demonstrates that no single disciplinary framework will do to understand, analyze and teach the significant and pervasive participation of intermediality in culture.

Quoting happens across media borders, hence, disciplinary

fields in that domain that is best characterized as one that doesn't fit any of the traditional disciplinary concepts, yet is probably the largest, most frequently practiced mode of communication among humans, indispensable for human life: intermediality. Little did I know, secretly and somewhat naughtily listening in on those conversations of Father and the priest, that such borders existed, and that they delimited fields. On the contrary, for me it was just one activity: talking, or what we now call 'communication'. I was not aware of different media; and only much later, when I began to make films, it became clear to me that there are no fundamentally different media, but that they all required specific knowledge and understanding. I was never good at drawing or painting. But I did create a very simple, one-line figure if I needed a human being for a story. The idea, or practice of meaning-making, after which I titled this series of reflections, is central in all human interaction. And quotation is recurrent; useful because recognition is part of its processing and interpreting.

Listening in and then imitating those adult conversations enabled me to learn a lot about language but also other forms of communicating. And whereas it sometimes solicited angry reproaches from the adults who felt caught or exposed, it also made it impossible to un-learn the implicit, improper knowledge I acquired. It also facilitated my increasing interest in what I later called interdisciplinarity; the skill of translating from one medium, or field, to another. And in that package, I also learned to seek out the mutuality among fields, and even, among temporal moments. By adopting forms from the work of an earlier artist, according to textual and visual antecedent studies, the later artists seem to be under the spell of their predecessors' influence; they implicitly or explicitly declare their allegiance and debt to them.

I learned much later how the British art historian Michael Baxandall convincingly proposed reversing the passivity implied in that perspective, a move that gave me a push for a revision of chronology into 'inter-temporality', which I then later termed 'pre-posterousness'. He proposed to consider instead the work of the later artists as active interventions in the material handed down to them. This reversal, which also affects the relation between cause and effect and even the meaning of these two concepts, complicates the idea of precedent as origin, and thereby makes the claim of historical reconstruction very tricky. This is why I like to use the term 'pre-text', to merge the temporal sequence with the intellectual posture that so easily becomes dogmatic, as well as implying an ironic wink, with the meaning of 'pretext' as deceptive pretention or excuse lurking around the corner.[37]

Instead of classifying and closing meaning as if to triumphantly solve an enigma, an intertextual, quotational study of after-effects or what Freud would call *Nachträglichkeit* would attempt to trace the process of meaning production over time in both directions: present/past and past/present, as an open, dynamic process, rather than map the results of that process. I emphasize here what I have learned over time: the active participation of visual images in cultural dialogue. And that implies more than most people consider when looking at visual images. In the dynamic between the works as objects, their perceivers, and the time in which these come together, accompanied by the social buzz that surrounds both, a compelling collective, dialogic thought process emerges. This is what constitutes culture. The artwork has the capacity to motivate, entice, and even compel thought. This insight grew out of my quotational misbehaviour in childhood.

By recycling elements, motifs, or forms taken from earlier works, a quoting person, whether they are artists or not, takes along, as a framing, the media product from which the borrowed element has been broken away, while constructing a new work with the debris. The new image-as-text is 'contaminated' by the discourse of the precedent, and thereby fractured so to speak, ready to fall apart again at any time. The fragility of the objectifying, distancing device of mythography and history, as well as contemporary reality, is displayed by the taint of 'first-person' subjectivity in, for example, Rembrandt's painting *The Night Watch* from 1642 (Amsterdam, Rijksmuseum), where the artist subtly inserted the visual discourse of self-portraiture in the middle in the far background. Seeing this, again, quietly, and thus noticing the transformation of an epic military scene into a subjective one, later enticed me to undertake a more

---

37 See Baxandall's influential book *Patterns of Intention* (1985).

substantial study of this artist's work. I was rewarded with insights into his multiple ambiguities, which constitute the brilliance of his work. My 1991 book *Reading Rembrandt* says it all.

In visual art, the embedding structures that are common in fictional literature, are less conspicuous and rarely studied, despite the frequent use of quotation. In artforms that are in and of themselves intermedial, such as most clearly, cinema, unpacking the dense mixture of source or pre-text and quotation is even more complicated. Direct discourse, or the 'literal' quotation of the words of characters, is a form that reinforces mimesis, the classical term for realism. As fragments of 'real speech' they authenticate the fiction. In narrative, the quotation of character speech is embedded in the primary discourse of the narrator. In their new (quoting) framework, these fragments of things having been said or shown before, are the product of a manipulation by the later producers and their context.

Thus, the quotes function like shifters, allowing the presence of multiple realities within a single image. This conception of quotation recurs throughout film and (its) history. One instance where this happens perhaps most emphatically is the way one of the most deceptively illusionistic works from the past, such as Caravaggio's *Head of Medusa*, from 1598 (Uffizi Gallery, Florence) resurfaced in Belgian sculptor Ann Veronica Janssens' abstract sculpture *Corps noir*. Caravaggio's *Medusa*, painted on a convex shield, is a prominent instance of ambiguity between two- and three-dimensionality. Janssens takes this up in her sculpture, and includes the first-second person discourse as well. Her sculpture is, however, concave, although there is a way of seeing (it) that includes the quotation of convexity. Quotations stand for the utter fragmentation of language itself. They point in the directions from which the words have come, thus thickening, rather than undermining, the work of mimesis. (see figs. 7 and 8)

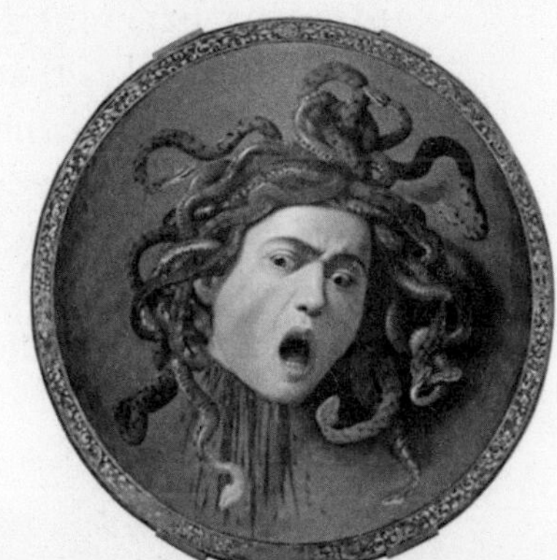

FIG. 7 Carravagio, *Head of Medusa*, 1598

This conception of quotation turns the precise quotation of utterances into the borrowing of discursive habits. And this accounts for pluralized meanings, typically ambiguities, and stipulates that meaning cannot be reduced to the artist's intention. It is possible to see that deconstructionism paradoxically

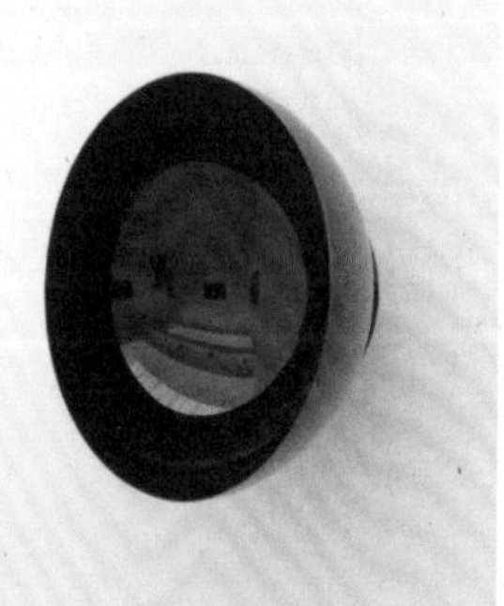

harks back to what this same view might repress when it presents the polyphony of discursive mixtures a little too jubilantly. Stipulating the impossibility of reaching the alleged, underlying earlier speech, the 'pre-text', this view emphasizes what the quoting subject does to its object. Whereas for Bakhtin the word never forgets where it has been before it was quoted, for Derrida it never returns there without the burden of the excursion through the quotation.[38]

QUOTATION LESS QUIET: AS A CRITIQUE OF INDIVIDUALISTIC VIEWS OF AGENCY

So far, my discussion of quotation suggests that it leads from the image to the outside world in which it operates; from the close environment of the work's own frames to the world outside those frames. In contrast, other meanings and deployments of the concept focus on meaning coming from the outside in. Hence, their simultaneous mobilization also entails a questioning of the very limit that separates outside from inside; a limit, or border, beyond which we must move if we are to grasp what cultural interaction not only is, but what it *does*. Quotation makes that border clearly visible. This questioning in turn challenges the notion of intention that is so pervasively predominant in the cultural disciplines. My parents' censoring of what they called my 'meddling' ('mind your own business') is, in fact, an appeal to their privileging of their intentions. In more recent media art, this question has faded into the

38 Bakhtin, *The Dialogic Imagination* (1981); Derrida, *Speech and Phenomena* (1973).

background. One reason for this is the collective nature of the making. This compels the realization of the equally collective nature of looking.

The predominance of intentionalism has a forceful ideological import. Briefly, the more there is known about an artist's life, the more seductive the trap of intentionalism becomes, and the less we understand the art; because the 'intention' can only be, contradictorily, fantasized as unconscious. By opposing precisely, the unrestrained projection that takes place in the kind of psychoanalytic criticism that turns effect into intention, what gets lost is the media products' persistent appeal, or their address, which I call their 'second-personhood'; the meaning and importance of their intermedial travel through quotations. What do these older media products contribute and mean to today's culture, including its political domain? Is understanding this, the same as getting 'what they have to say' or 'what they do', and how does this emerge from quotation? The subject's agency, which matters in the sense that his or her intention or psychic makeup does not consist of *inventing* but of *intervening*, of a 'supplementation' that does not replace the media product it explains, but adds to it. It is in this sense that I have proposed the specific, verifiable, and, I submit, socially relevant idea of quotation in contemporary media practice as a valid ground for an interpretation that accounts for a different sense of 'understanding', without recourse to the fantasy of intention.

Quotation does not construct a fictitious intention or unconscious psychic makeup, nor is it a totally relativistic subjectivism in which anything goes. Instead, it supposes that the media products are rigorously contemporary in their *effect*; there lies their agency. Therefore, it makes the historical art more important because it keeps it alive and does not isolate it in a remote past, buried under concerns that we do not share. All of the different meanings attached to the idea of quotation carry with them an epistemological view, a concept of (re-) presentation, and an aesthetic; all these aspects are inseparable. Engaging the art of the past in its theoretical potential is a way of quoting it. When I imitated, quoted, the Latin words the two men exchanged, I was doing just that, without being aware of

it. And just like words, images can be quoted. In the practice
of iconographic quotation, the Old Master art is endorsed
as the historical 'real', including the iconographic precedent,
which determines the belatedness inherent in being situated in
history. In making films based on cultural heritage literature,
I did this in shifting from words to images, relativizing that
distinction.

Contemporary artists, acting as narrators who quote and
thus appropriate the cultural inheritance, embed the appropriated Old Master art in their own work, thus endowing it with
the glamour of historical reference, the historicizing 'reality
effect'. Moreover, such visual quotations fragment and pluralize
visual (re)presentation into a 'polyphonic multitude', whose
aspects are neither arbitrarily collated nor 'democratically'
distributed. Instead, they demonstrate the difference between
the illusion of wholeness and mastery pertaining to the artist
caught in art history and the somewhat messy, yet much richer,
visual culture of live images. Thus, the images of today present
us with Old Master art that is entirely ours; one of which the
old master could have had no knowledge, nor agency upon,
what we see 'him' to be now; an irreversibly *New*-Old Master,
who changes the one we thought we knew as well as the historical illusion that we knew him. And let me not overlook the
fact that the use of the qualifier 'historical' inserts a temporal
reflection into the sense of quotation as critique.

HAND-HOLDING:
QUOTATION AS A SEMIOTIC TOOL

In the course of my studies not only language, then imagery,
but also semiotics has become crucial—the theory of the
emergence and use of signs and the meaning-making they
entail. From a semiotic point of view, to take the presence in
the present of what historically precedes into account through
focusing on quotation as an active element, makes the analysis
more, rather than less, historically responsible. It also makes
the works from the past as well as their ongoing presence,

continue to matter. This is where quotation 'intermediates'
on behalf of contemporary social relevance. This reflection
on the implications of the production of meaning through
time, by means of quotation and intertextuality, can be pushed
further in the direction of self-reflection, as I am attempting
to do in this collection of vignettes, in which live thinking and
memories merge. Self-reflection is important because art historians or literary scholars, like any perceiver, be they viewers
of images or readers of texts, cannot help but bring their own
legacy of discursive precedents to the media products. This
attention to self-reflection matters for the emancipation of
the perceivers from the passivity wrongly attributed to them.
The formerly called 'recipient' is not a passive mailbox, but
participates as a perceiver in the construction of meaning. This
is why I insist on staging readers and viewers as participants.
This input from the present is emphatically not to be taken as
a flaw in our historical awareness, nor as a failure to distance
ourselves from our own time as is the case in naive 'presentism'.
On the contrary. It demonstrates an awareness of the ongoing
presence of the past. For, it is to be taken as an absolutely
inevitable proof of the presence of the cultural position of the
perceiver as a participant.

Hence, this involves, affects, also the analysts and their
students, and their 'cultural community' or what semiotician
Juri Lotman (1922–1993) called 'semiosphere' within the
analysis. The latter term brings quotation into the realm where
it meets semiotics. In the course of my work as a teacher and
researcher, always returning to the childhood memories of
those conversations in Latin, I became more and more attached
to the practice of detailed analysis, to the point of co-founding
the Amsterdam School for Cultural Analysis (ASCA)at the
University of Amsterdam in 1995. This matches Lotman's
commitment to what used to be called 'close reading'. This
requires an attitude that challenges the traditional boundaries
between disciplines. Those boundaries have never satisfied me,
and always hindered both the breadth and depth of thinking
and analysis, as well as the communicative nature of teaching.
Lotman, and Charles Sanders Peirce (1839–1914) have been my

semiotic sources of inspiration. With that detailed attention, I have also developed a view of concepts as the tools for analysis.[39]

The fact that concepts, and conceptual thinking, are never stable and cannot be fixated in definitions, but instead, 'travel', adapting to and transforming through disciplinary, geographical and historical shifts in different semiospheres, was particularly relevant for Lotman in his Russian-European (space) and politically transforming (time) context. And although he remained primarily focused on literature, that art form was never isolated from the wider environment in which he worked. Nor is it mono-medial. My interest in semiotics concerns the integration of philosophy (thinking) and (close) analysis (doing), and from 2002 on, making. It also feeds the resistance against media-essentialism and disciplinary constraints, with their methodological dogmas and the resulting blindness to the dynamism of artworks as well as the concepts we use to analyze them. This can thus be summed up as an eagerness for movement. Quotation as a practice is part of that mobility. This entails ambiguity.

Ambiguity, with the subsequent instability of meaning, which necessitates recognition of the participatory work of the perceiver, provides a great contribution to our interaction with art and literature. I put ambiguity at the heart of the concept of *semiosphere*, which denotes the larger socio-cultural environment within which art functions. This is what makes it, as well as semiotic practices more generally, both stable in the sense of theoretically (but not practically) delimited, and unstable, since no meaning functions alone. Ambiguity is crucial to meaning-making, since the pre-text always resonates along. This is due to the omnipresence of quotation, which precludes the isolation of artworks. An alertness to ambiguity as productive is of great importance. The contribution of quotation to nourish this fruitfulness turns it into an indispensable practice. Far from the association with plagiarism, quotation is where semiotic elements, such as words, images, sounds and others, hold hands.

39 For understanding Lotman's work, the best resource is the book *The Companion to Juri Lotman* by Tamm and Torop already mentioned; for Peirce, see 'Logic as Semiotic' (1984).

The memory of my quietly listening in on those conversations in Latin, as the pathway to my understanding of what language is and does, further leading to my interest in, even attachment to narrative, has nourished my understanding of and empathy with the precarity of those paper-people's lives I read about. My experience as a child who knew nothing yet, my quietly quoting those adults who knew enough to talk in Latin as a tool for secrecy, has continuously resonated with my unlimited, somewhat indiscreet curiosity: What are they talking about? What is happening to them? How can they survive the precarity to which they are doomed? It is on the basis of that resonance that my later studies, and my intellectual life as a whole, has developed into an intellectual and artistic ability to understand, explain, analyze, and make those cultural objects that enrich social life.

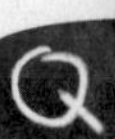

Radicality

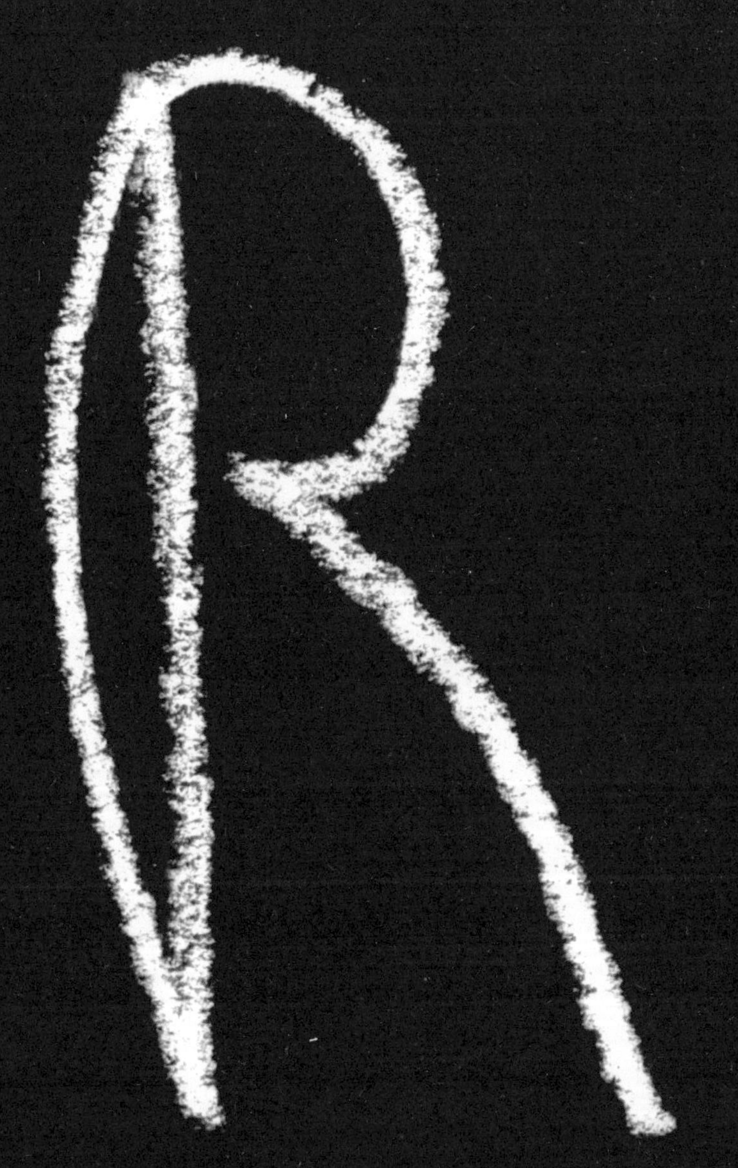

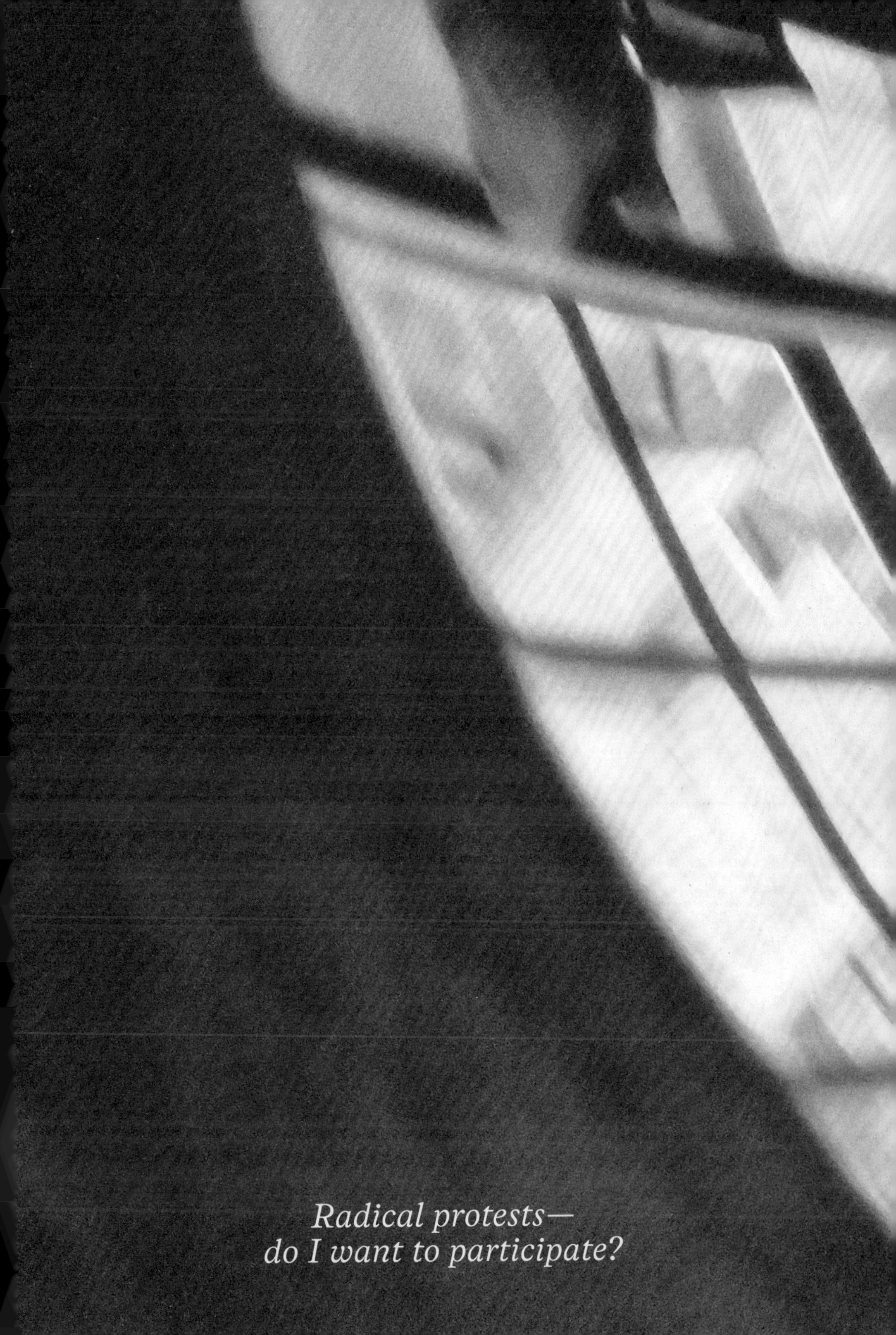

*Radical protests—
do I want to participate?*

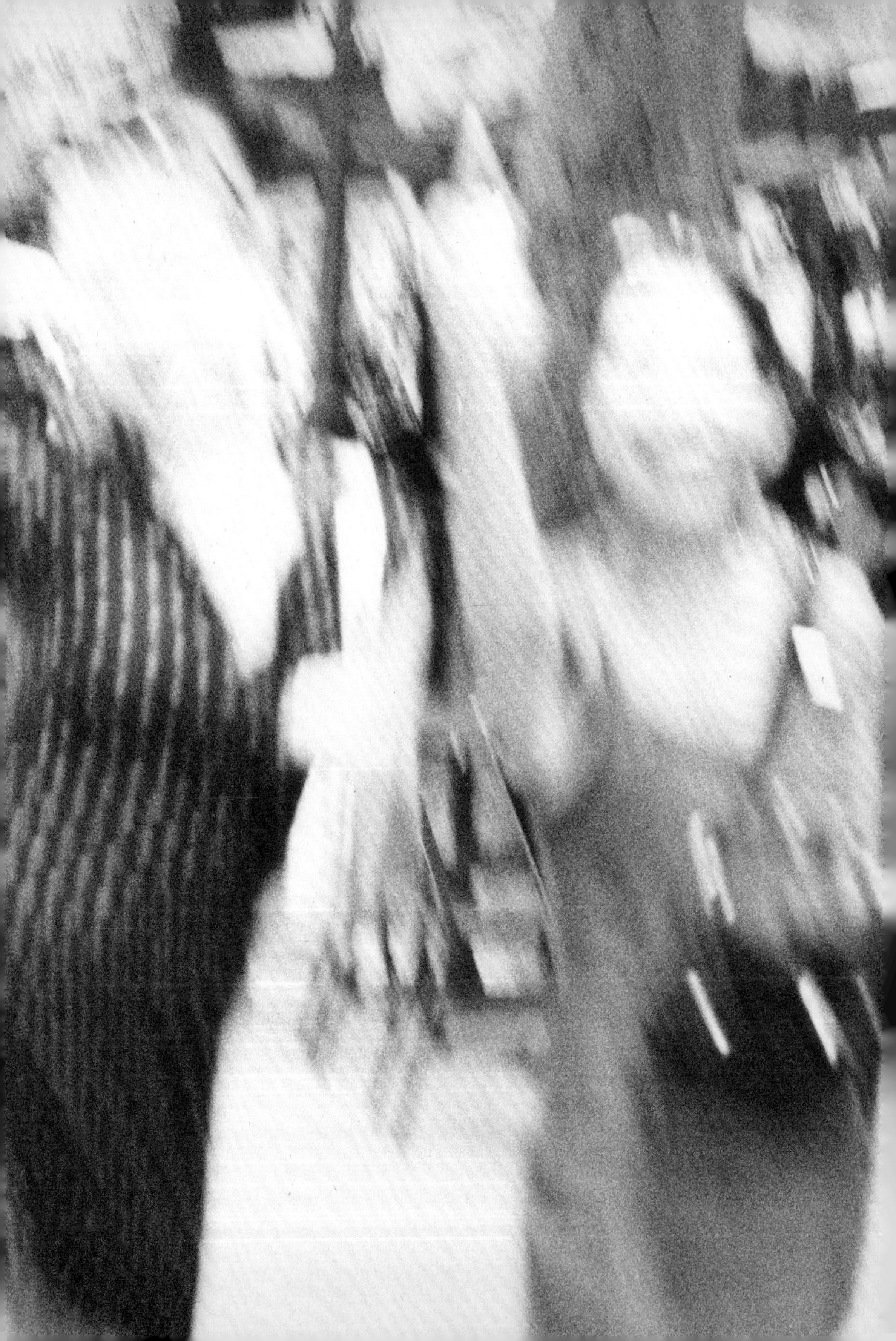

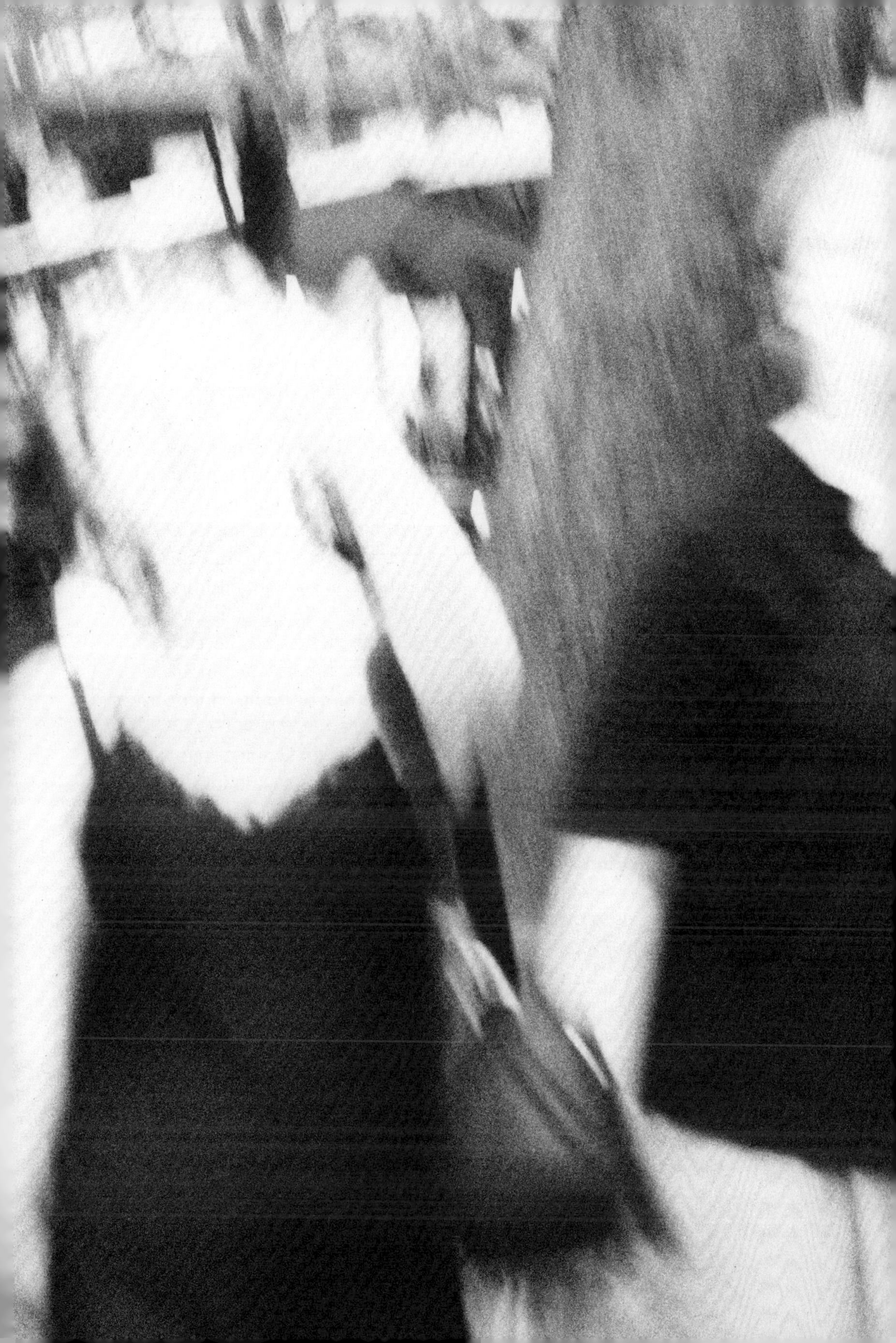

ROOTS, ROADS, REFUGEEDOM: RADICALITY UNDER SCRUTINY

A bit different from most of the other vignettes, I invoke in this one a few colleagues whose work has had a defining impact on my thinking. In my high school years I earned a reputation for radicality; or rather, for being 'too radical'. In religion class I tended to contradict the teacher-priest, in literature class, my favourite subject, I found the teachers often too tame, too literal, and raised my hand to say so. I was regularly sent out of the classroom to report to the principal, who happened to be my father and who scolded me severely and punished me at home for good measure by withholding that week's pocket money and sometimes more. And frequently, at home I protested against the nuclear threat of the Cold War. Once I had moved out of the house and had my first baby, I tended to participate in powerful protest marches against the Vietnam War. I marched along, even when police officers on horseback persecuted the protesters, and with my baby in a pram, I ran ahead of them, sometimes taking refuge in a school building that had left its doors open. I didn't quite realize how risky this running could be. It was the nuclear threat and the killing sprees that frightened me, more than the immediate danger of falling, having the baby fall out of the pram, or being caught by those I considered the people's enemies.

Decades later, the word 'radical' had been sequestered to mean something quite different. Ambiguity this is no longer; it is the *abduction* of a useful, positive word and its meaning. This was the result of the hostility to and from Muslims. Adherents of that other monotheism, who were considered threatening and planning assaults, were adorned with the swearword 'radical'. Suddenly, that old word I had always taken in a positive sense, had become the worst: violent, dangerous, but also, primarily and simply, of a different ethnic background, which for me didn't count at all. This made me alert when I came across an in-depth reflection on it.

I'm referring here to one of the sharpest, most creative critical thinkers of our time, the philosopher and image-thinker

Marie José Mondzain, of Polish Jewish background, born in Algeria and living in Paris. She never ignores a problematic social tendency but every time one emerges, comes up with a detailed study to undermine it. In 2019, she published a book in which she indicts what she calls 'confiscation': the tendency of our time to abduct positive words and turn them nasty; from praise to curse. Radicality was the most important one of those. I translate the title of her 2017 book (which, unfortunately, so far has only been published in French) as *Confiscation: of words, of images, of time: for a different radicality*. The book came out with a publisher with the beautiful, telling name: 'Les Liens qui Libèrent', the connections that liberate. On the back cover the author wrote the following:

> Shouldn't we give back to the term 'radicality' its virulent beauty and its political energy? Because today, every effort is being made to identify radicality with the most murderous gestures and the most enslaved opinions. Thus, it is reduced to only designate doctrinal convictions and strategies of indoctrination. Radicality, instead, appeals to the courage of constructive ruptures and to the most creative imagination. (my translation)

She combines in this short presentation words that may seem contradictory, such as 'virulent' and 'beauty', a contradiction compensated by the obviously relevant combination of an issue, or state of the world, with a live power, 'political energy'. Retrospectively, I understood, when reading her book, that running to escape from the police officers on horseback was, at the time of the Vietnam protests, my personal political energy. Entering a school building that should probably have been locked, since those demonstrations usually occurred on Saturday afternoons, was on the verge of an illegal action. And doing this with a baby was frankly irresponsible. But I had no choice; the baby's father didn't care, didn't stay home to babysit, and I had too much radicalism in my blood to skip the demonstration. My political energy required my participation; never mind the risks.[40]

40 I consider Marie José Mondzain the most brilliant historian, philosopher, and critic of visuality. I refer here to *Confiscation* (2019). Her earlier book, *Image, Icon, Economy* (2005) on the political power of images in Byzantine culture has been published in English. See also *Le Commerce des regards* (2003), on the activity of looking, which fits my reflection under W. The choice of the noun 'commerce' for the title of that book is significant, given her leftish political views.

In her analysis of the words that were confiscated and that she wanted to return to their positive meanings, Mondzain mentions at her beginning the plant saxifrage; a plant that is so forceful it can break stone by simply pushing with its roots. And 'roots' is another R word that deserves some closer attention. In addition to designating the elements of plants that make it possible for them to grow and survive, the word is also used to indicate where people come from. Source, origin, cause, or beginning, starting point, foundation: 'root' is yet another word that has both a positive and a critical meaning. The idea of roots is no stranger to radicalism. But for Mondzain, the primary association with radicalism is more important than the question where people, ideas, or things originate. For her, it matters to defend radicalism as a figure of the dignity of thought and the freedom to act at the heart of political life, as she writes.[41]

Earlier, in a discussion of ideas on knowledge as developed by a philosopher who also happens to be one of my favourites, Baruch Spinoza, Mondzain distinguishes three kinds of knowledge as presented in the seventeenth-century philosopher's *Ethics*, coming from the experience we have of the world, of reality. The first is an experience of shock; reality shakes us up, pushes us, wounds us, it is something we undergo, so that we become passive playthings of forces that we don't understand. The second kind of knowledge stands at the crossroad and is positively undecidable. And the third mode of knowing (here I switch from knowledge to the verb knowing, as discussed under K) implies the access to the immanence of nature within us. For Spinoza, these three modes of knowing come with our bodies' reactions to the world, and our growing or diminishing capacity to act.

If radiality is an attitude that should be returned to its positive meanings, it is the road, more than its roots, the trip towards it, that we need to know, to find. The primary tool we have to do this, to find the road to its productivity, is the imagination. With the noun 'road' we declare to be on the way, in process. This idea contradicts any static meaning, and in particular the one so frequently implied by the noun 'roots'.

41 Mondzain, *Confiscation* (2019), 137.

The road towards a restauration of radicalism as a positive force is not dictated by the map or any other 'direction for use' coming from a bossiness 'above'. It is an unclear trajectory, through which each person can 'walk', imagining what the best road for them will be. For me, that unclarity or not-yet-clarity is the evidence that knowing cannot happen without the imagination. No political life, nor even a life of thought, is possible without the imagination. And that noun implies the active participation of each of us in the thinking process. But beyond thinking as solely an intellectual activity, indispensable as it is, the noun 'imagination' introduces another element, included in this one word: it implies the idea of image, that other specialty of Mondzain.

REFLECTION: THE ROAD TO RADICAL INTERDISCIPLINARITY

In another, earlier book mentioned in footnote 40, from 1996, *Image, Icon, Economy: The Byzantine Origins of the Contemporary Imaginary* (translated into English in 2005) Mondzain integrates beautifully the history, theory, and *ongoingness* of the participation of those objects we call visual, in the imagination of the road to a renovated radicalism, and the politics that have been part of it from the earliest times on. The words join forces; imagination, image, *imaging*, and the verb that French philosopher Jean-François Lyotard has coined on that crossroad: *figuring*. For he came up with a term, a noun, that integrates the two pathways: the *figural*. I have already quite frequently quoted (as per Q) in various frameworks the succinct, effective formulation of that live verb 'imaging' that philosopher and film scholar David N. Rodowick had presented in relation to Lyotard's struggle against the word-image opposition as fought out radically through 'the figural'. I cannot help doing it once more, here in a different kind of reflection.

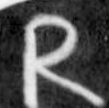

The *figural* is where the intellectual argumentation and its narrative concretization in the character or figure, seamlessly merge. The key word is 'force'. Lyotard's concept of the figural argues for language as more dynamic, turning it into a force, a movement, closer to the Freudian unconscious as laid out in *The Interpretation of Dreams* from 1899 than to any structuralist conception of it. Including, especially, *force* in his concept of language, Lyotard describes meaning as sense, in terms that include affect, sensation and intuition, and also spatiality. Force, for Lyotard, is inherent in language, and it is 'nothing other than the energy that folds and wrinkles the text and makes of it an aesthetic work, a difference, that is, a form... And if it expresses, it is because movement resides within it as a force that overturns the table of significations with a seism that makes sense...' Rodowick's indispensable book *Reading the Figural* from 2001 is my source here.

The formulation I am quoting from Rodowick's paraphrasis of Lyotard's concept is especially striking due to some words that shake up any form of knowledge that fixates. 'Seism' cuts it. These words affiliate language with, specifically, cinematic language, based on the etymological sense of 'movement' rather than any technical specificity. Words like 'affect', 'energy', 'folds and wrinkles', and especially, 'a force that overturns the table of significations' join forces with Mondzain's severe critique of 'confiscation' and her endeavour to correct it. But here, it is not to restore radicality alone, as such, but to bring the linguistic and visual domains into each other's orbit, in order to do justice to the multiple contributions of the imagination to our attempts to effectively think, in order to be able to act politically. In my work, this has become the royal road to interdisciplinarity, at the end of which we can encounter a new, renewed, radicality. For this is only possible when we move our efforts to think beyond that stark opposition between words and images, the linguistic and the visual, that has ruled over the standard academic distinctions called 'disciplines'. No wonder that this noun that defines the fields we study contains that regulation, even includes punishment, through which the bosses of the world try to organize the wish for knowing as a mode of experiencing our connection to the world as 'natural'.

STAYING ON THE RIGHT ROAD: TOWARDS REFUGEES

Refugees are roaming around, in search for a safe place to live; a social problem for the world of today. What is their state, existence, life? With its anchoring in poetics, fictionality, imagination and above all, *imaging*, art can contribute more usefully than ever to the social world by (re-)connecting disconnected people (living in 'refugeedom') with a culture where they are being noticed ('visibilization'), and through reciprocity and contact ('inter-ship'). These three nouns are non-existing words I have coined. Now I seek to connect the road towards a positive radicalism to a group of people who are doomed by the power-brokers to stay on the road: those people who have been chased from their homes by violence. This is another issue Mondzain is keenly committed to, and so am I. In the remainder of this vignette, I cannot do more that invoke a few aspects of the lives of people who are constantly threatened in their existence; made invisible; denied access; without housing; under-nourished and exhausted. It matters to Mondzain and to me to counter—radically—the tendency to simply preclude access to Europe to people who have no place else to go—a road to follow, or even to imagine one.

How can refugees and the imagination be brought together in a reflection and analysis that won't betray one side of this duality? I prefer to avoid that other R-noun 'representation', so frequently used. Representation is a problem when it comes to the disempowered people who have had to leave their homes in order to survive, without having a clear and welcoming place to go. At the same time, 'representation' is an ambiguous word. It means not only speaking about, but also speaking for, as in political situations. This form of representation remains acutely necessary. That is a problem that we cannot wish away. Representing—in artworks, documentation, literature—people and their situations, imports both the lack of modesty and the distortions caused by the inevitable fictionality that participates. Because the makers of artworks, but also of academic studies, are bound to appeal to the imagination alongside their account of the social reality they seek to make visible for others. This produces a tension as well as a fruitful domain of communication.

How to better understand in the moment, in the *now*, the contemporary culture in which I live, in ways that challenged me to divert from, or expand, the classical academic disciplines? This is difficult; it produces a tension between the single voice of the academic doing the research and the plurality of the interlocutors—whom I decline to call 'subjects' in the traditional, subordinating sense common in ethnography and sociology. This is why the genre of the essay, with its ongoing *attempting* as the genre's name suggests, seems more appropriate than the monologic, polished scholarly analysis or overview. So, to quote Donna Haraway's title *Staying with the Trouble* (2016), instead of overcoming or surpassing it to end with firm conclusions, I want to *stay with the attempt*. The essay as form, as Adorno famously phrased it (published in English in 1991), precludes propositional conclusions. And so does the discrepancy between what I know and what other people experience. This brings Spinoza's tripartite typology of knowledge/knowing back. The essay, taken at its word, is therefore the only possible genre of writing that has the slimmest chance to at least soften the opposition between the impossibility and the necessity to write about—inevitably (re?)presenting—refugees.

But I have tried other means as well, in addition to broadcast conversations and journalistic articles. The most different and difficult, for an inveterate academic, of these attempts that I tried, was video-making—without formal training as a filmmaker. This just happened, when in my social environment I witnessed an injustice done to someone that I felt compelled to address, analyze, and make known. Since this was done in the name of European law, I could not disentangle myself from what happened to my neighbour, an immigrant from an Arabic country who was trying to evade the poverty and the lack of education to which he was doomed. This became the first of a series of documentaries and installations on issues of migration, identity, and the need to escape. I chose this genre, or medium, mainly because the feature of video- and filmmaking

that is the collectivity, interactivity, contact-based mode, is
what has glued me to that ongoing attempt. In this respect it is
opposed to the monologic tendency in academic writing. This
has brought me not only a precious new experience, but most
importantly into close contact, friendships, and contemporaneity with people I would probably never have met otherwise,
and to whom the events presented in the films were happening
then-and-there. That experience has taught me more than anything I had read about refugees, immigrants, or other 'others'.

The concerns I cannot shed—to which I am radically
committed—are all anchored in tensions. First, the news on
television works *against* any (audiovisual) engagement with
the fate and plight of people in hard times, such as refugees.
It is too repetitive and each item is too short. German artist
Monika Huber made a beautiful, powerful visual analysis of
this issue in a book titled *Archive OneThirty*, with the number
standing for the time, in seconds, devoted to each item in the
television news (Deutscher Kunstverlag 2023). Second, refugees
live in long duration, without having the perspective of an end
in sight. This enduringness, as well as having to leave behind
their entire life and relations because where they were they are
no longer safe, must be a traumatic experience. However, third,
trauma cannot, indeed, must not, be represented. It *can*not for
reasons of psychic foreclosure, which is the defining aspect of
trauma; it *must* not because trying to do so would entail being
trapped in voyeurism; the lack of modesty. But neither can it
be ignored. My political view is obviously radical in Mondzain's
renovated sense: refugees have the same 'human rights' as
everyone on the planet has, or ought to have these. This all
converges in the impossibility of what is necessary, and that
is my fourth concern; a fundamental contradiction. The life
and experiences of refugees must, even if they cannot, become
known to us, if we are to be of any help whatsoever to these
people who are our fellow humans.

It seems preposterous (the first of my made-up words:
pre-posterous) to just come up with non-existing, new
words. To phrase this in more acceptable terms: the problem
of the conjunction 'and' is vital in the examination of art,

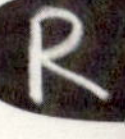

representation, and social reality, in particular of the life of refugees as members of our social world. My reflection concerns an issue that is both strongly socio-political, and raises artistic, educational, and intellectual questions; an issue that invokes some serious concerns about social life, art, and the helping hand they can give each other in the attempt to make both visual art and the social world 'better': more relevant, meaningful, mutual, and compassionate. This has assisted me in making the case for learning through/from/with art. I wish to consider such learning as, necessarily, an educational *internship* in looking. Then, that better-known term that indicates 'learning through practice', connects this learning with the interconnectivity, reciprocity, and mutuality I call *inter-ship*. I seek to understand the skill of looking we take for granted too easily. Looking-seeing is not obvious. In view of this in 2023 I (co-)made with the young artist Lena Verhoeff, who also makes the photographs accompanying my vignettes, a short film *Refugeedom: Lonely but not Alone*. We considered the subtitle 'A Lesson in Looking', but discarded it for its over-the-top educational meaning. Instead, if we want to see, looking requires learning/teaching. How can refugees and art be brought together in reflections and analyses without betraying one side of this duality? The tensions in the conceptualization must be addressed clearly and frontally. The concerns they raise are vital for the potential of visual art to contribute to current cultures.

But I also seek to attempt seeing refugeedom from the inside with empathy and without voyeurism. This double requirement is not so easily satisfied. The lines in a poem by Somali-British poet Warsan Shire, mentioned before under L: 'you only leave home when home won't let you stay', are of vital importance, constituting a key to understanding 'refugeedom'. This became a 2020 artwork on paper by Indian artist Nalini Malani, exhibited in 2021 in the Kunstmuseum in The Hague. The poetry and the artwork together invoke both the generalization and, thanks to Malani's 'imaging' or 'figuring' of Aeneas carrying his father Anchises in his flight from burning Troy to what would become Europe, also the historical ('pre-posterous') enduring need for an understanding of refugeedom.

As my quotation above from Rodowick's paraphrasis of Lyotard's vision indicates, a key issue is intermediality. This is why I always wished to examine how photography, film, painting, and literature speak to one another as forms. As the great image-thinker W.J.T. Mitchell famously said: there is no pure visuality. This is important as a view of visual art without visual essentialism, yet bound, in 'inter-ship', to other media or forms of imaging. Intermediality is not simply a merging of different media. Each 'cultural object', as the late Lars Elleström called it, in order to avoid medium-specific terms such as 'text' or 'image' and the vagueness they carry, performs in-between different medial utterances of semiosis. Which is the reason he avoided such medium-bound terms. To make a long story short: from early on I have been committed to radicality, in the positive Mondzainian sense. And our co-existence with refugees makes the case for the urgent need for such radicalism, all over the world. This is the only way Spinoza's vision of knowledge can work, as a process; a knowing how to be as strong as saxifrages.

This entails a radical rejection of dogmatic disciplinary boundaries, policed by those academics who are convinced they know best how to deal with, analyze, understand cultural objects such as literary or visual artworks, and feel justified in trashing colleagues who hold different views. I have experienced enough of that attitude, which is not simply unpleasant, disloyal behaviour, but utterly damaging for the students eager to learn. Interdisciplinarity, therefore, is a most useful, educationally fruitful approach. 'Inter-', there, does not mean rejection of disciplinary knowledge, but what I have termed 'inter-ship': a relationality that supports both sides of the encounter.

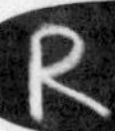

Silencing
and
Speech
and
Seeing

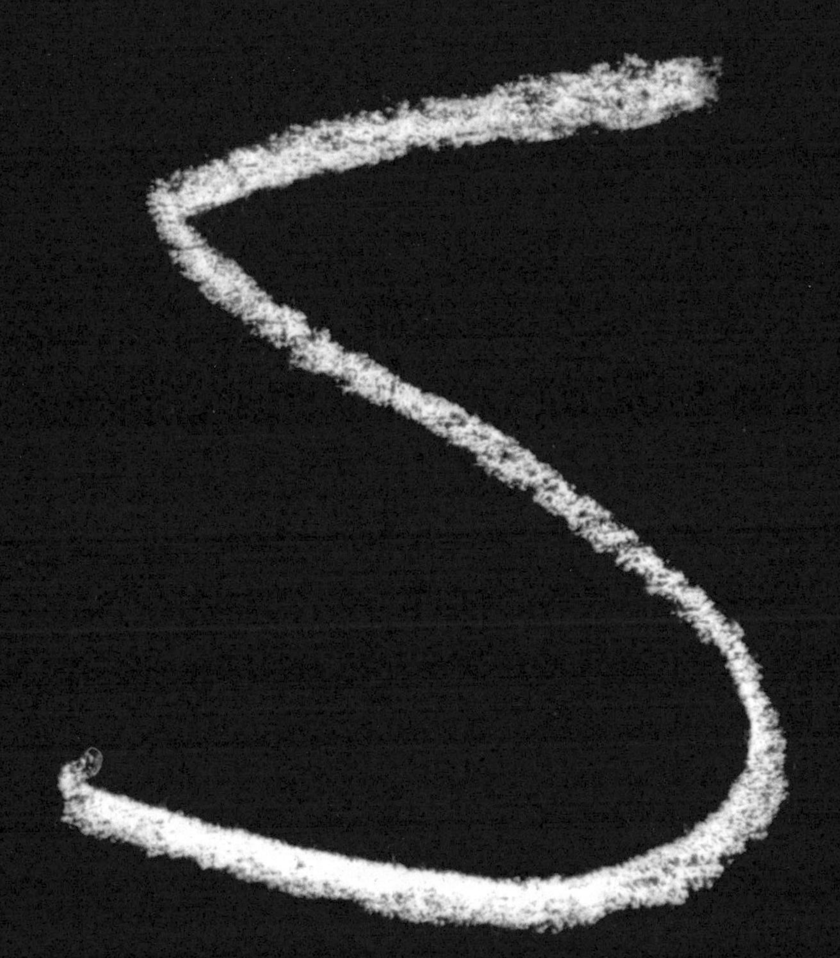

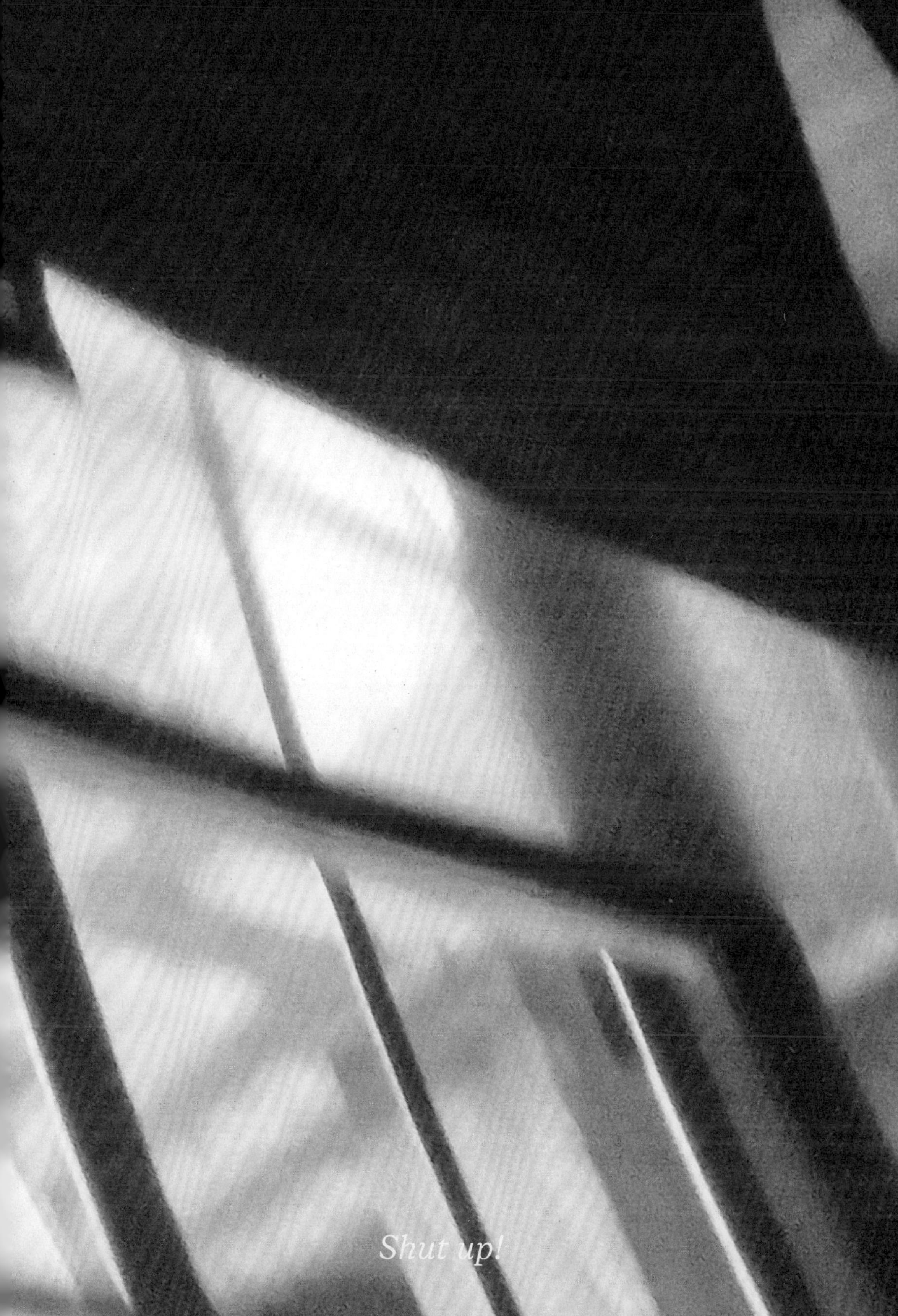

Shut up!

I have written already more than enough about the noisy family life I grew up in and the effect this had on my development; on the kind of person, including the kind of professional I became. Today, I am still over-sensitive to noise. When I enter a restaurant where loud, and mostly (in my view) bad music is being played, I run away. And today, with the dictatorship of mobile phones, I am totally allergic to the socio-autistic half-conversations I am forced to hear. This current noise-development has made me understand much better what characterized my parents' sturdiness, severity, and as I saw it, constantly correcting speeches. Retrospectively, I grasp well why my parents were always trying to make the house quieter than it could ever be. Having nine children must be a maddening situation, with the constant noises, screaming as well as laughing out loud, arguing, and fighting.

But the word 'noise' doesn't cover it. What I can now see as very demanding on the parents, is that, in addition to constantly being surrounded by loud voices, they were also very conscientious about our education. They were Roman Catholic; they had met in church, and for a long time, every day we went to the 7 a.m. mass. The parish priest was a habitual presence in our house, as we saw under Q. But there were also many lessons in the correct behaviour we were being told to learn to practice: politeness to adults; helpfulness with the little ones; honesty and sincerity; housekeeping chores, and praying before and after the meals, thanking God for it, whatever those meals had on offer. And school performances were also high on the agenda. The grades we earned were never good enough. Father's intellectual passion made him wish to see his kids as sources of pride, and he felt disappointed if we were not up to it.

I lost many classes when Mother needed help at home and I was forced to miss schooldays. I was fast and smart enough to catch up quickly what I had missed. In primary school this happened often, a little less in high school. Father was a high school teacher and later director of the girls' school we attended, so he knew that missing classes was dangerous, near-fatal; accepting that would make his own work redundant.

So, at the end of such days, often Father tried to catch up what I had missed, on the days he did not have to rush to teach evening classes. This had a big impact on me. I tried to be a good girl, but I also liked to argue when I did not agree with the home lessons and their morality. So, as already mentioned under J, from quite early on, I 'spoke back', as my parents called it with some contempt. My tendency to talk back, to express my opinions even if they did not agree with theirs, was considered a bad habit. 'Mind your own business', their habitual response to whenever I spoke up, was their attempt to counter what they saw as my meddling in adult stuff that I shouldn't be involved in. So, they silenced me.

This was a regular act on their part. The other siblings were not less noisy, but they cared less about being right or wrong. They would scream, fight, and protest, but they did not argue as much as I did. Because I was always alert, anxious to participate, and considered the opinions the adults expressed important enough to contradict them, I suppose I presented to them somewhat of a danger in the smoothness of our education. I now think their attempts to silence me were a kind of censorship. But then, in school, silence was crucial for teaching to be possible at all. We were not supposed to talk in class. Hence, the silencing I had experienced as oppressive at home, became 'normal' in school. And later, when I became a teacher myself, I understood, although without approving of it, why we needed to be silent. Just so that we would listen to the teacher. Raising your hand to ask permission to speak was the means to obtain access to speech. But that was meant not so much to express opinions and contradict what the teacher had said, but to ask for clarification if what the teacher had said wasn't quite clear enough.

When I say 'without approving of it' I refer to my conception of teaching as I have laid it out in interviews; most explicitly in the 2018 book of interviews published by Jeroen Lutters, *The Trade of the Teacher*. There, I argue that teaching must be dialogic, based on equality. I don't mean that the students must have the same knowledge as the teacher; that would make the entire endeavour of teaching redundant. But they must have the same access to speech, to express opinions, and disagree with interpretations if they have a different one to propose.

The quality of the communication between teacher and students concerns their right to speak, to differ, and thereby, to learn from participating in a discussion. But the students are not the only ones who must learn. In such a context, the teacher can and must learn from the differences of opinion and interpretation the students, if only due to their large numbers, can bring up for reflection. As I have said many times with my other slogan: 'If you don't learn from your students, you are a bad teacher.'

Speech is performative; it is an action, not a flat laying out of what is already known, and fixated. And because it is an action, it changes things. Performativity makes differences possible. I am not saying that knowledge is redundant; it is not; not at all. But it is not as fixed and permanent as we often take it to be. And silencing propositions of different views, hence, contradiction and argumentation, assuming the monologic position of the one who knows it all, not only reduces the cultural potential that a dialogic school situation can produce. It also disempowers, and thus, deprives not only the students, but also the teacher, of what they must most importantly learn: the possibility to think, the encouragement to propose their thoughts to others, and thereby develop their thoughts from an inner vagueness to an explicitly articulated idea. This is the sense in which speech is performative. And so, then, is speech's opposite; silencing. In its negativity, shutting up dialogic partners is, to put it simply but truly, censorship; a politics of suppressing thinking. And that suppression of the possibility to not only articulate one's thoughts, but also convey them to others and listen to their responses is a socio-politically oppressive act.

This was, of course, not what my parents aimed to do. I don't think they even realized that they were shutting me up. They just aimed to improve the sonic environment at home, as well as my education; to better shape my personality, and to make me understand that I was not always right; that I didn't know everything; that I should listen to those adults who had more experience, hence, knowledge, than I could have at my age. But their slur when they called me 'Miss know-it-all' had a devastatingly silencing effect on a child over-eager to learn and get to know more and understand better. They meant well; they wanted to educate me well; but the way they used silencing as a tool to do that, had the opposite effect. Later, when I became a researching teacher and was constantly attempting to improve my work, I became sensitive to the effect of time in the process of cultural production (on which more later, under T). This, together with my passion for the dialogic situation instead of the silencing of students, drove me to make videos *with*, rather than *about* people whose culture, different from my own, I wanted to understand better, but in the only effective mode: the dialogic one. This new endeavour also expanded speech with the visual; seeing as an indispensable part of communication.[42]

SEEING WITHOUT SILENCING AS A CONDITION OF THINKING

This opening up of speech without silencing, and connecting it with seeing, has profound implications for thinking. I have become keenly aware that thinking is not a solitary, individual act we perform alone in our armchair, at our desk, in our study. Nor is it mono-medial. Instead, it is a social process, embedded in what I have called quoting, and what the brilliant Colombian artist Doris Salcedo called 'the social buzz'. This makes the act of thinking collective, even when done in aloneness.[43]

Three aspects can be derived from that collective nature of thought. These are the aspects that, in my view, are most central in that activity. They are, respectively and bound in implication: performative, theorizing, and 'anachronizing'. I have often argued that thinking is neither individual nor particular. Nor is it bound to the time of articulating the ideas. The life of thoughts is like that of images: both enduring, even if also constantly changing, and collectively sustained. They are subject to debate, which is why silencing is so destructive; and

42 On this, see the film *A Thousand and One Days*, which I made with the collective Cinema Suitcase in 2002–2004.

43 On Salcedo's work, and the way she used this phrase, see my book *Of What One Cannot Speak* (2010), also published in Spanish.

thus, it entices people to do the thinking *with*, *through*, more than *about* the world, with the indispensable help of its visual manifestations, as well as the other senses. We do not 'read' the content of thoughts in an image but make, construct it, in interaction with it. Seeing is performative, too. This un-censoring merges thinking, as collective, with seeing. And as much as seeing seems to be an individual act, it cannot be done alone either. This connects it to speech.

As a result, at any given time, what each of us sees when considering an idea, is a new idea, fresh from the thought-act the viewer and their baggage of thoughts brings to bear on it. This is not, not ever, our own thinking power only, but primarily the idea, or word, metaphor, or image we encounter, which persuades us in the interaction. Seeing, thus, is a form of speech. This is why monologic, silencing teaching is bad teaching, whatever the brilliance of its contents may be. This is how ideas themselves can be said to think: in interaction (performatively), in theoretically relevant ways (as theoretical objects), and across time (anachronistically; or phrased in that other made-up word: pre-posterously). This thinking power of ideas makes thinking *with*, rather than *about* the ideas of others, an indispensable contribution to the understanding of the social world. That is, for me, the process, the activity of what is generally called 'philosophy'. And thinking-with requires speech and forbids silencing. In these respects, it is quite like art. I find it useful to keep thought and art in each other's company, both in their mutuality and collectivity. Creativity is essential to both. And the act of *seeing* helps to better grasp the multiple sensuality involved in thinking. This also required a sense of space, where being together constantly happens.

According to French philosopher Henri Bergson (1859–1941), space is not geometrical, as in Renaissance perspective; consequently, it is neither measurable nor identical for everyone who perceives it. Instead, we have a *sense* of space. Our sense of space develops according to what Bergson calls a 'natural feeling'. This natural feeling is heterogeneous, and different for everyone, depending on wherever they are. This comes to the fore in the images of Descartes in the 2016 film,

Reasonable Doubt, which, as I have mentioned, I made on this seeing-thinker. I filmed him when he, armed with a magnifying glass, is roaming around the world, whether the small portion of it that is his garden, the tiny world of the butcher shop where he studied anatomy, or the larger one of the dune landscapes, where he walked around to facilitate his thinking by *placing* it. The multiple screens of video installation exemplify heterogeneity with their non-synchronously moving images. In video installations, space is precisely that: heterogeneous, multiple, both fictional and real, both subjective and 'extensive', or deictic. The story may be fictional; the contact with it is real. *Deixis* does that.

Bergson considered the body to be a material entity, and he consequently saw perception as a material practice. This makes Bergson's conception of the image indistinguishable from the moving image. It is a deeper level on which images move; it comes closer to affect. The image itself—not its support—is both moving and material. This implies that it is plural and functional—it *does* something. It does that while never happening in isolation, hence, it cannot be silenced, even when the thinker is a bit of a recluse. For, thinking is also subjected to the dialogic relation within the self, of which a good teacher must have given the example. In the second scene of my film on Descartes, the mood is the difficult-to-live combination of pride and fear. What might seem a weakness of Descartes for those who wish to bind him to stern rationality, turns out to be his primary strength: he dares to doubt, fear, and panic. This may indeed surprise those who have fixated him to the cliché of being the 'father' of rationality. But then, do read Kyoo Lee's crucially important book, *Reading Descartes Otherwise: Blind, Mad, Dreamy, and Bad*, from 2012, already mentioned, which, to my regret I only found after making the film on Descartes.

One scene of my film begins with a (fictional) meeting with Spinoza. The passionate plea of the young man converges with the mature thinker's conception. It is as if they repeat one another's ideas. Throughout the scene, Descartes acquires the status of the famous master of thought he had become in his lifetime, and simultaneously runs into his personality problems.

The philosophical doubt of his somewhat sceptical leanings joins his paranoid tendency and his suspicion of others. In a series of short episodes, I merge the many friends and correspondents of his historical social buzz into one, called, after the loyal and longstanding one, Hector-Pierre Chanut, French ambassador to the court of Queen Kristina of Sweden. This friend regularly appears.

The meeting with Spinoza shows that Descartes' attempt to consider the ideas and lives of others—his democratic statement at the beginning of the *Dioptrique*—shipwrecks on his sense of superiority. When he pontificates to the younger man about the interaction of light and colour, the future master of ethics interrupts him with challenges. He puts forward the need of the imagination, and of the togetherness of people in the present. This insistence has turned Spinoza into an anachronistic master of contemporary social thought. Spinoza, here, articulates the elements of thought that sustain the need for the Humanities, and the study of images, as serious 'theoretical objects' generating thought of their own. Slightly flabbergasted, Descartes' understanding dawns. Who is this young craftsman? He sounds like a philosopher! Yes, he is; because he sees, and he doesn't let the older man silence him.

After challenging Descartes' class prejudice, Spinoza disappears. A symbolic figuration of a lonely Descartes' ambition is enacted when he (fictionally) visits the Royal Academy of Arts and Sciences in a professorial robe. There, he encounters a portrait of Christian Huygens, the son of his good friend Constantijn, and prophetically, or anachronistically, recognizes the successful scientific career of the young man. Then he recalls the death of the young scientist's mother. In the film, these moments are my (Bergsonian) ways of showing how we merge personal memories of childhood with what we notice about others and what we strive to achieve. Descartes' father was not proud of him the way Huygens was of his brilliant son.

In Descartes' biography there is a crucial scene of silencing. He gave an early writing, a treatise on music, to his new friend Beeckman, but prohibited him from sharing it with others. Beeckman disobeyed. The issue is that the mathematician appears to have spoken about the music treatise to others. The anecdote is historical, and scholars agree that the philosopher's angry reaction is excessive; we can call it hysterical. Chanut suggests René should see a 'soul doctor'—the theoretical fiction kicks in again. If it doesn't help, it will at least teach him something about the body-soul relationship; instruct him about the 'passions of the soul', says Chanut—anachronistically citing the subject and title of Descartes' last and, for me, most important book. So, to figure how Descartes came to become the de facto (albeit unaware) inventor of psychoanalysis, which is how I see him. Instead of making him talk about it I stage him as going into analysis. To the 'soul doctor' he reveals his childhood traumas, which had made him an angry child—see Kyoo Lee's book—but we only hear it from the doctor, not from Descartes himself. For the patient is silenced by the trauma. Yet, the attempt to get professional help with his anger fits comes to naught when the doctor picks up on a metaphor Descartes' father had used to malign his son: he was ashamed to have produced a son who 'let himself be bound between two layers of leather'. A historical anecdote, which can be updated for what it would mean today, not then. The analyst asks if the metaphor might have other connotations. The allusion silences him; it disturbs the patient, who runs off in fury. End of story.

The scene is meant to hint both at Descartes' possible interest in men and to the idea that his conception of the subject made psychoanalysis possible; to his childhood and his present troubles. His view of subjectivity, especially as articulated in 'the passions of the soul', will become the foundation of psychoanalysis. In these scenes, anger is the mode of thinking; because he is 'beside himself' and directs his emotions to the people who challenge his mastery, he closes off his thought process, self-silencing. The relationship between the two scenes of anger fits is based on a sense of futurality. Not only does this excitable man have a great impact on the world through his inauguration of modern thought. Also, his own life is filled with hints to the future, including future difficulties anchored in his complex personality. This master of rationalism did his thinking often in the turmoil of extreme emotions.

Descartes also shone as an expert in what we would now call 'mental illness'. Where did that skill come from? My guess is, to quote Eve Kosofsky Sedgwick about homosexuality, it takes one to know one. This is why I credit him with the 'invention' of psychoanalysis—his conception of the subject making its later explicit invention possible. I imagine he suffered from the symptoms of what we now call neurosis, specifically an *abandonment complex*—a tendency to reject affective bonds while constantly seeking them. Out of fear to be abandoned again, he preferred to be the first to do the abandoning. This is what underpinned his passionate attachments to, then rejections of, other people. Always craving, but feigning indifference out of fear the parental abandonment would repeat itself. Making Descartes' thinking seeable, and rejecting the silencing that would lock it up in an over-the-top rationality, was my way of getting back to my childhood rejection of being shut up, and instead, start all over, in a process where silence is not an ideal.

It is probably due to my childhood experience of being silenced that so much later, my cinematic work has so frequently focused on this issue of silencing. Not only *Reasonable Doubt*, as I have commented on just now, combats Descartes' reputation, formerly a compliment, today with contempt, as Mister Rationality, a reputation that silences the other aspects of his thinking, acting, performing, living. It is thanks to the other, 'bad' (Lee) aspects of his personality that he regains relevance for today's world; that this thinker from the past remains with us, in the present tense. This paradoxical personality has affiliations with other figures of whom I have made cinematic figurations, such as *Don Quijote*, an installation work of which the subtitle, 'Sad Countenances', resonates with the sad undertones in *Reasonable Doubt*. It is particularly relevant in connection to the first 'theoretical fiction' we made, *A Long History of Madness*, from 2011, entirely devoted to the silencing effect of trauma. This film and installation work were based on Françoise Davoine's crucial book *Mère Folle*, from 1998 (English: *Mother Folly*, 2014). And, as a counter-action to silencing, the documentary *Hubert Damisch: Thinking Aloud* I made in 2011 focuses on the way this thinker speaks, articulates his thoughts, out loud.

Time

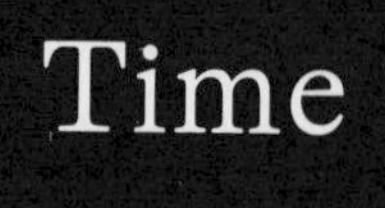

*And its tyranny,
and its many tentacles*

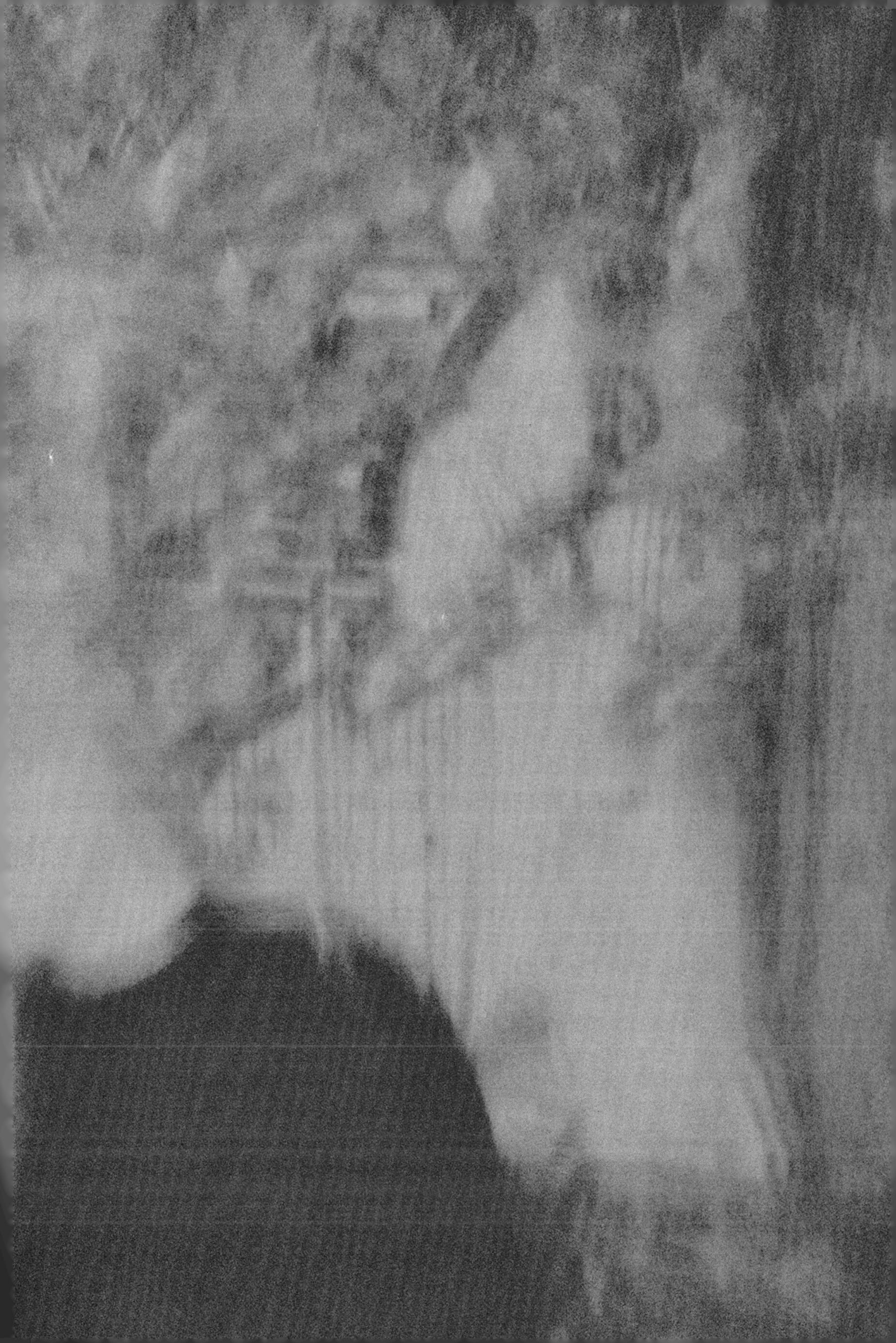

In my early days, time was tyrannical. We had to get up early, so that we could wash, dress, make up the beds, prepare breakfast, eat, and go to school on time. As the third child in the large family, from early on I was in charge of making everyone get up on time. When my parents gave me an alarm clock as a birthday present, they probably assumed I felt good about the responsibility. I did not; I felt burdened. But since I had no choice, I just shouldered the burden. And from that day on until I left the house at age eighteen, I had to wake up everyone, including the boys who refused and pretended to be asleep. I had to shake them physically. The task compelled me to get up even earlier than all the others. Time, thus, became my primary boss. Later in life, I began to reflect on what time is, means, and does.

Let me begin by mentioning an important article by an intellectual friend, W.J.T. Mitchell, a great specialist in visual thinking, the title of which is 'present tense'. Just think about that title and its multiple tentacles! In the wake of my chapter on time in my 2022 book *Image-Thinking*, I consider Mitchell's title an *octopus* for its triple wordplay: on the *present* as an era or moment; on verb tenses and the implication that looking, thinking, and existing happen in the present *tense*; and the added meaning of 'tense' as stressful, fitting with Mitchell's acutely relevant political vision. The occasion for writing that article is relevant here; it was the violent death of George Floyd, murdered by police brutality in 2020. This murder is a profoundly disturbing piece of evidence that the present time is *tense*. And Mitchell's essay is as rich and complex, full of sharp visual analyses, as we are accustomed to in his work. For my reflection in this entry, I propose to continue to 'complexify' *time*. We all know, or think we know, live in, are subjected to, the self-evident dimension of life we call 'time'. 'All the time' is a very current phrase.

But what is it? In spite of George Kubler's brave attempt from 1962 to argue for the contrary with his widely-known book *The Shape of Time: Remarks on the History of Things*, time has no form, no shape; it is not a *thing*. It can *leave* shapes, in the sense of weather-induced wear and tear, as I had the unfortunate experience some years ago and again more recently, in

2024, when travelling by train through a flooding disaster area in Germany. And it can leave historically specific styles, which is more in line with Kubler's essay. It can also be 'imaged', of which Mitchell's essay 'Present Tense' gives the most convincing visual iconology possible. But *time itself is formless*. Here are some words indicating in what way the formlessness of time is nevertheless very significant:

Time-image
Contemporaneity
Art as event
Co-existence
Heterochrony

This makes time multi-tentacled.

TIME AND ITS TENTACLES

The sculptural quality of the octopus is clearly visible in photographs; there are also sculptures of the octopus, such as the one by the Dutch artist duo Heringa/Van Kalsbeek shown in my 2022 book (on page 134). Time can be used in rhythm, which can sometimes create the impression or feeling of form, something we take from music and rhythmic poetry. However, the one-directional arrow that usually symbolizes chronology is a big lie. It is not time that has that form; it is the music, verse, or even the rhythmic breathing that espouses time, that has a form, although not necessarily, mostly not, that arrow-form. Or, as in the case I want to present in this entry, the actions, words, and attitudes of the figures.

This matters, because formlessness does not entail invisibility. The choice is not to either see fully shaped forms or to see nothing, but, as the brilliant cultural analyst Kaja Silverman puts it, to learn to practice a 'visual habitus' that enables us to see what, by lack of recognizable form, seems invisible, but profoundly informs, *in-forms*, what we see. She argued for this in the introduction to her wonderful book from 1996, *The Threshold of the Visible World*. In general, as the time passing in the everyday, 'all the time', time is so self-evident that one would not wonder about its potential form. It only accedes to awareness when its apparent flow is interrupted. This can be due to nature- or man-made disasters, traumatogenic events, which change the course of time, in one way or another, or to an exceptionally intense experience, called 'in-tense' for a good reason. The short film *It's About Time! Reflections on Urgency*, which I made in 2020 and can be watched at youtu.be/ DK-5lbK4t5M, thematizes a form of such formlessness of that important visual—or, to broaden the concept, sensorial— habitus. If I am here connecting visuality with time, this is a statement about the need to take, or give time, to visual images, including still ones, where that time-giving is not as automatic as it would be with literature. I advocate a visual habitus that makes time a self-evident aspect of engaging, absorbing, dialoguing with visuality and its products. I have made a point of this in the exhibition I curated in the Munch Museum in Oslo in 2017, and explained the need to give visual art time, in the book published with it, *Emma & Edvard Looking Sideways: Loneliness and the Cinematic*.

But visuality is not mono-sensorial. There is one crucial cultural element, aspect, or skill that is bound to time and in which vision participates. The first skill necessary for understanding and acting within culture, is *listening*. Although she speaks and figures in enigmatic differences from today, Cassandra, the young woman who emerged in antiquity and is still with us, needs to be heard, listened to. For, she sees the future, and wants to warn us, but the gift of prophecy the god Apollo gave her as a means of seduction, was cursed when she refused to sleep with him: she would know the future, but no one would listen. It reminds me of Harvey Weinstein & Co, a typical case of #MeToo. A feminist, contemporary issue: to be safe in the workplace, and not forced to swap jobs for sex. Barring her from being listened to was a cruel way of isolating her from her cultural environment.[44]

Listening is crucially important indeed. In 2019 and 2020 the Indian artist Nalini Malani has been arguing visually in several exhibitions: listen! It's about time we listen. Her insistence on listening was connected to that antique figure so

---

[44] The most important actualizing source is Christa Wolf's novel *Cassandra* (1983).

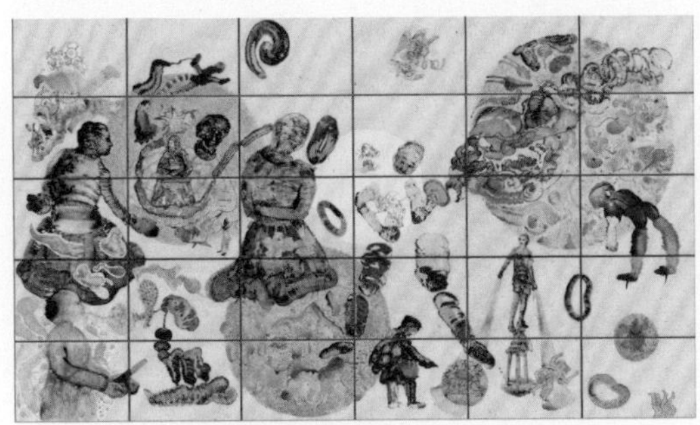

cruelly banned from being listened to. Malani made a thirty-panel painting on Cassandra in 2009. The multi-panel form of her painting intimates an affiliation with a cinematic quality. Malani is an intermedial, and also a 'quoting' artist; she engages both Eastern and Western myths and literary texts, and brings them to the present world, in surprising, original forms. Her art, I contend, is a form of cultural analysis. I have written about her work several times, most extensively in a 2016 book titled *In Medias Res: Inside Nalini Malani's Shadow Plays*. (see fig. 9)

In March 2020, one week before the corona lockdown, I was invited by the Polish National Film School in Łódź to participate in an experimental programme for which the school had received a grant, to explore what an 'essay film' is, can be, or can do. Dr Jakub Mikurda (we call him Kuba), the project's leader, asked me if I was interested in coming to Łódź for a week to make an *essay film*. Even regardless of the question of whether I considered myself capable of making a film of any length or genre in one week, which is *trying* in more than one sense, I had never thought about this essay-film question. So, I was slightly flabbergasted; even more so when, upon receiving his invitation, I said so, and Kuba's quick answer was: 'But all your films are essay films!' The truth of that answer stunned me. Why did he know something about my work that I didn't realize? Upon reflection I had to agree, and was grateful, both for the invitation and for the way it compelled me to think again about my own films in the light of this concept.

The mini-dialogue between Kuba and myself I would qualify as an instance of 'intellectual friendship', an affiliation that makes discussion possible and productive as, in itself, a form of cultural analysis. Is the essay film a genre, an approach, a characterization of a specific content? If the latter, how could

I briefly describe the content of each of my films? With my innate curiosity, the topic of the essay film began to haunt me. Might the term 'essay' simply be the equivalent of 'trying'—an attempt? The tentative character the term suggests is quite appealing. It does not suggest a finished state but an ongoing process, as is the search for knowing described under K. Hence, it involves time; the time of duration. Instead of considering the essay a 'thing', genre, or product, reflecting on what the essay, as genre, approach or, as Adorno would have it, *form*, is or does, helps understand some nuances which, for me, have always been very important in cultural production and analysis.

The essay film I was to make, I had decided, had to be, this time, more explicitly an essay in the multiple senses of the word, and to affiliate it with the practice of cultural analysis, it was to contain theoretical issues. These included temporal issues, such as the connection between present and past as reciprocal. It also required a socio-political weight. Today, the connections between those requirements are more urgent than ever. I was to come up with the concept, the script, and make the film, with cast and crew Kuba selected and the school provided. I brought in Adorno's essay, to recall the philosopher who cared about and for the fate of all those who were and are victimized by war and other horrors. I was surprised that the two volumes of Adorno's writings on *literature* in the English edition open with an essay on... the essay, titled: 'The essay as *form*'. The essay as literature, as that title and its framing in the opening of the volume suggest? Yes. The following sentence contains a profound reflection on the essay:

> The essay allows for the consciousness of nonidentity, without expressing it directly; it is radical in its non-radicalism, in refraining from any reduction to a principle, in its accentuation of the partial against the total, in its fragmentary character.

In this sense, (fictional) novels frequently harbour the two fundamental features of an essay, in Adorno's view of that (non-)genre, the two meanings of partiality: fragmented, not whole;

and subjectively passionate, engaged, committed.[45]

For, of these words of wisdom, 'partial' has a felicitous ambiguity indeed, one that can help us understand better why literature and art matter. And 'fragmentary' in particular seem to bring us closer to what an 'essay' can be or do; it resists wholeness. Both words resist the idea of the total, of the encompassing whole, but also, in its shadow, the totalitarianism that seems to have many places of today's world in its iron grip. Through a reflection on 'thought-images', which I see as the result of 'image-thinking', I argue for the *intellectual* gain to be had from 'essaying' thought *artistically*. In 2022, I published a big book about this issue, titled *Image-Thinking*, and amazingly, the publisher released the paperback edition immediately, offering a 30 per cent discount on an already modest price; so, it is affordable for students.

In addition to the opposite of totality, 'partial' also means 'subjective', in the sense of acknowledging that what the essayist brings forward cannot pretend to be an objective, factual truth; 'passionate' in that what the holder of the view brought forward cares about it; and 'rational', since partiality also encompasses the wish to persuade, which can only be done through rational arguments. As for 'fragmentary', this accords well with the non-total(itarian).

When thinking with Adorno about a subject for my essay film experiment, the figure of Cassandra came to my mind. Through that mythical figure, who could foresee the future but was cursed to never be believed, I tried to 'figure', make a figural shape for the thoughts on the indifference of people towards the imminent ecological disaster of the world. This is an issue that encompasses *time*, in two ways: the climate change predicted to be held back in 2030 is already widely spread and making victims. And the reason that this gets the chance to continue is that no one listens.

As I argued under R, the verb 'to figure' I used above is key to what I aim to contend about the productive merging of intellectual and artistic work in relation to time. This brings language itself already into the realm of the cinematic and its moving quality, which implies time, with dynamism as opposed

---

45 Adorno, 'The Essay as Form' (1991), 9.

to structural stability. This view creates waves that might work for transferring not just meanings but thoughts and their forms, including but not limited to images, from one medium to another. And due to a blindness for intermediality in theoretical writing, the importance of visuality in Freud's theory of interpretation has been often more or less neglected, whereas it is crucial for his thinking.

In East-German writer Christa Wolf's novel *Kassandra*, apart from a short first paragraph that gives Cassandra, literally, a place, the novel is entirely written 'in the first person'. If you read it, you cannot help listening to her. Here is the beginning of the novel: 'It was here. This is where she stood. These stone lions looked at her; now, they no longer have heads.' After a few short sentences, Cassandra slowly recuperates narrative power. 'This fortress—once impregnable, now a pile of stones—was the last thing she *saw*.' Seeing: her final act of perception in this presentation of Cassandra, her focalization, casts her gloomy eye on the destructive passage of time. This is reinforced by the final short sentences of that paragraph, which enlists us all: 'no trace of blood *can be seen* seeping out from beneath. Point the way into the darkness. Into the slaughter-house. And alone.' The passive voice and the negative of 'can be seen' indicates that we readers as co-focalizers are as powerless as Cassandra is. That final clause foregrounds her fate. Death, by violence ('slaughterhouse') and loneliness.

This beginning of the novel sets us up as the *listeners* Cassandra lacked. From the nine lines of this opening paragraph on, we are compelled to listen to the voice of the 'first person', and give her our *time*. This narratological element contends that we must learn, not *about* art but *from* art. About the world, time, urgent matters that need intervention. And looking at its details helps that learning. In this sense, a (fictional) novel has the two fundamental features of an essay, in Adorno's view of partiality: fragmented, not whole; and subjectively passionate.

When we then enter into Cassandra's mind, the first thing we read is a single-sentence paragraph: 'Keeping step with the story, I make my way into death.' Then follows the narrative of Cassandra's thoughts and memories on her final day. For example: 'the closer you come to death, the closer and brighter are the pictures of childhood and youth.' This matches the entire conception of this book, which con-fuses memories from childhood with later intellectual thoughts. And when she says: 'I lived on in order to see' (4), the importance of witnessing, that special, socially relevant form of focalization, comes to the fore. Moreover, witnessing is the indispensable 'second-personhood' that is a precondition of life. Second-personhood has been theorized in linguistics, psychoanalysis, and other fields, but nowhere better, more lucidly and consequentially than by feminist philosopher Lorraine Code. For now, I wish to foreground the temporality involved in it.

What Cassandra sees is the horror-to-come. And in the act of seeing, she is aware of the force as well as the problematic of time as we read later: 'For it was, it is, an experience when I "see, when I 'saw'". Saw the outcome of this hour was our destruction. Time stood still.' This aspect of time, and the urgency to finally listen to Cassandra's prediction of destruction, interwoven with the testimonial focalization—seeing *with* her—is what makes this novel relevant for, and in fact, an essay on, the issues of time it obliquely invokes. Today we see how war and other forms of violence and the wilful neglect of the ticking time-bomb of destruction—of the planet—are rampant. If only we would listen to Cassandra... if we would give her our time.

FROM ACTIVISM TO ACTIVATING

As a literary scholar and cultural analyst specialized in narrative theory, I am interested in considering how literature, fiction, novels, art, those products of the imagination, can support the necessary insistence on these issues, usually considered political. I seek to argue and demonstrate, however, that their presence, as per Mitchell's brilliant multi-tentacled deployment of the qualifier 'present', lies not primarily in the thematic or semantic domain. Two seemingly 'a-political' dogmas in the study of art and literature I have often tried to critique and subvert, have an impact on political issues.

One is the iron-clad idea of *chronology* as the skeleton of history, the only way to be 'historically responsible' and avoid that historians' object of contempt they call anachronism. My resistance against chronology accompanies my memories of the tyranny of the recursive linearity so 'alarmingly' embodied by the alarm clock of my childhood. The other is the appeal to the author's intention. The appeal to biographical information and documents, anchored in the belief that every author knows consciously what they want to convey, and that this intention is what matters. This makes cheap of the artistic process of writing, and ignores historical changes in meaning. In other words, even with a firm belief in chronology, scholars neglect time in this sense.

The second dogma I seek to disempower is the disingenuous invention of the 'implied author'. This is the projection of the critic's interpretation on the text, giving the critic and the teacher an unwarranted authority that unduly silences (as under S) the students or lay readers. In three books I have made these points: *Quoting Caravaggio: Contemporary Art, Preposterous History; Louise Bourgeois' Spider: The Architecture of Art Writing*; and before these, *Reading Rembrandt: Beyond the Word-Image Opposition*, a book that earned me the contempt of the Rembrandt specialists. At the background of my thinking is always the persuasion that forms, precisely because of their apolitical appearance, have political impact, more strongly even than 'official' activist art. Forms, I contend, are *activating*. In that sense they impact on time. They make you think, which takes time and implies consequences in its future.

The painting by David Reed you can see appearing in the short film *It's About Time!* makes the argument that later readers cannot understand the earlier works without the screen of later works hanging between the present and the past. In this sense, the present impacts on the past as much as the more traditional view that it is only the past that influences the present. That more common view implies an ideology of development, an evolution from the 'backward' past to a more progressive future. Recent events of destruction belie such optimism. The political violence, and, in addition to the horrible wars going on as I write this entry, the increasing numbers of rapes and murders of women, including young girls, and the police brutality against 'people of colour' wherever colonialism has cultivated hostility against 'others', show that the movement can rather be seen as backward; the future returns and surpasses the past on its own terms. And, conversely, delving into works from the past counters the contempt for pastness it implies. The two movements of #MeToo and Black Lives Matter are both more actual, more urgent, than ever.

It is because history does not go away and is with us in the present that I argue against the way chronology puts the past at a distance. History is contemporary. This is the reason for the impersonation of Caravaggio's *John the Baptist* in the film on Cassandra, and for the way Walter Benjamin's important quote had to be included. The allusion to Benjamin in the round, thin-framed glasses the actor is wearing in that scene, underlines this:

> [E]very image of the past that is not recognized by the present *as one of its own concerns* threatens to disappear irretrievably. (in the fifth Thesis of the Thesis on the Philosophy of History. italics mine)

My ongoing academic struggle with chronology and the idea of authorial intention is always intertwined with my feminist and other political persuasions. In that struggle I have encountered figures of young women in world-wide famous texts who are trapped in a bad, say, tragic situation. This is the case with Cassandra. Many of these works of world literature were written by men, some of bad repute when it comes to women's issues. These texts demonstrate that both dogmas mentioned—chronology and authorial intention—do not hold, and in fact, hold us back from seeing feminist art and writing when it stares us in the face, even where the author is unaware, 'innocent' of it. An outstanding example is Flaubert, known for his problematic relationship with women, who nevertheless 'invented' what was later conceptualized as *emotional capital-ism*, decades before Marx and Freud each came up with one aspect of this dual syndrome. His masterpiece *Madame Bovary* from 1856 stages, in fictional form, an 'essay', in Adorno's sense, about this devastating social issue that is still with us. In addition to showing that time is not unilinear, these works also demonstrate that the cultural impact of literature and art is not bound to what the author wants to say.

I recommend we think with artworks such as the brilliant installations and sculptures by Colombian artist Doris Salcedo that 'essayistically' entice people to remember past violence as acts of memory in the present. My 2010 book on her work, *Of What One Cannot Speak: Doris Salcedo's Political Art* demonstrates this extensively. Acts of memory happen in the present, even if the remembered violence is perpetrated in the past. Cassandra can be considered the personification of 'pre-posterous history', in the sense that her flimsy presence in the texts from the past does *concern* the present, the warning of imminent mortal danger. In addition to being a victim-heroine of #MeToo, she is also a companion to Greta Thunberg, roaring up from ancient times. Cassandra, the young woman, needs, requires, and has the right to be *heard*, listened to; we must give her *time*. It's about time we listen. Hence the title of my film with its intended pun: it analyses and discusses time in this theoretical sense of pre-posterous, and it warns us that it is time to act, urgently; *now*. An academic intellectual issue bound to a socio-political issue in reality. This is also a lesson on fiction. Art is not opposed to, nor an escape from, but an integral part of reality.

Literature and film, but also painting can develop 'essay' art: living thought that is partial in the two senses of the word: subjective and fragmented. The form of Malani's thirty-panel painting intimates not only a cinematic quality as well as fragmentation, but also compels detailed looking. The panels are both separate, and, due to the figurations, continuous. Cassandra speaks, through Malani's distorted voice, also in her 2012 video-shadow play *In Search of Vanished Blood*.

The essay is literally a 'trying'. And we know that in English, that also means 'difficult', challenging. Trying to do something in trying times, through activating forms. From the short opening paragraph of Wolf's novel on, we are set up, as readers, addressees of the narrative, or 'narratees', to listen to the voice of Cassandra, the 'first person' who speaks the novel in its entirety. This narratological form solicits us to be committed, empathetic witnesses, who *care*. It goes to show that we must learn not *about* art but *from* art. About—no, *for* the world, time, peace, and other urgent matters that need intervention, *now*. The backbone is Cassandra's temporal awareness. Her repeated call for urgency is key. And the most personal, intimate moment in the film, I thought, should be when the near-future infringes on the figures' personal lives. This is when Cassandra breaks up with Aeneas because he remains too close to the powers-that-be, resulting in a near future in which he would become stultified. This concerns the future—one she rejects. At the end of the novel—not quite the end of the film—she abandons him with the poignant words: 'I cannot love a hero. I do not want to see you being transformed into a statue.' She breaks off their relationship, because the call to war deprives Aeneas of his sweet nature, and that is what Cassandra cannot bear.

Time is a timely topic. From the image in time to the temporality of images, especially the moving images of film and video, time is currently being considered in its many aspects and manifestations. Think of sequential ordering, duration, rhythm, memory, uncertainty and undecidability, movement, affect and suspense, and the kinds of time the combinations of these aspects entail, such as deep time, geological time, narrative time, and more. We can also bring these considerations of time to bear on the capitalist time we are submersed in. It is useful to remember that clock time, dating from the colonization period, is fundamentally in the interest of capitalism. The term 'alarm clock' thus gains more meaning. This becomes clear in William Kentridge's 2012 video performance *The Refusal of Time*. This video was alluded to when in the film Aeneas mentions a 'South-African artist' in this connection. It made me reflect a bit more on my brothers' refusal to heed my attempts to wake them up. They, too, refused time, with its devastating impact on society.[46]

---

46 My film *It's About Time!* (2020) can be watched with this link: youtu.be/DK-5lbK4t5M.

Unifying

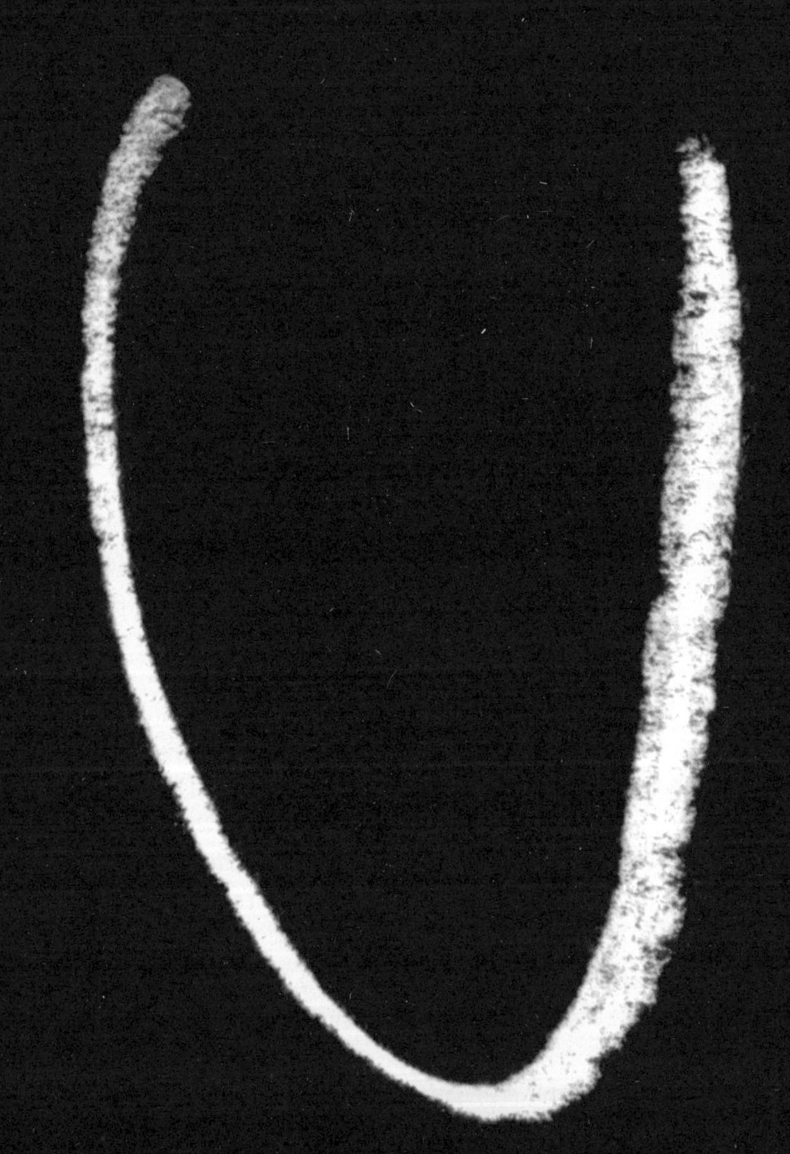

Even arbitrary lines come together

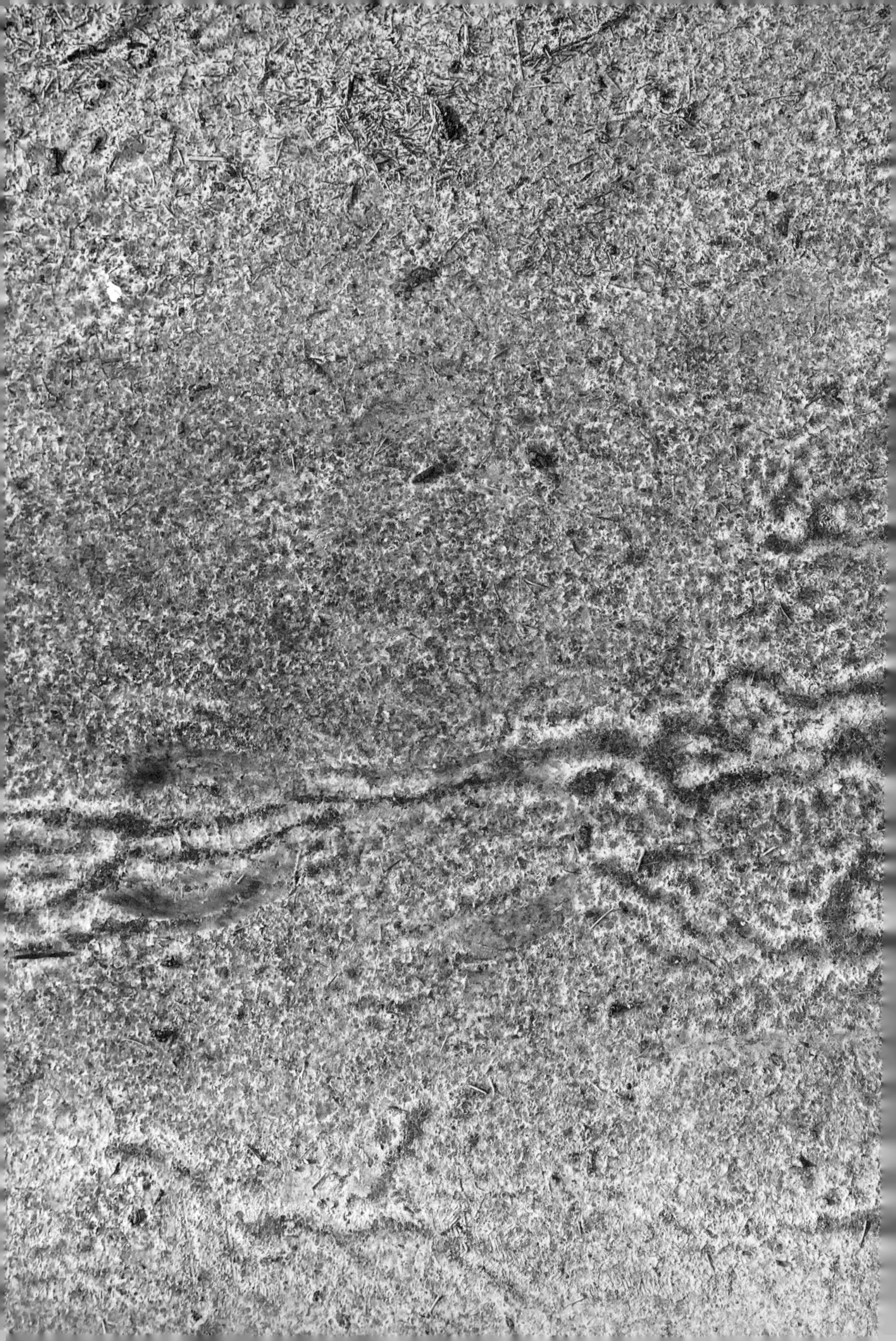

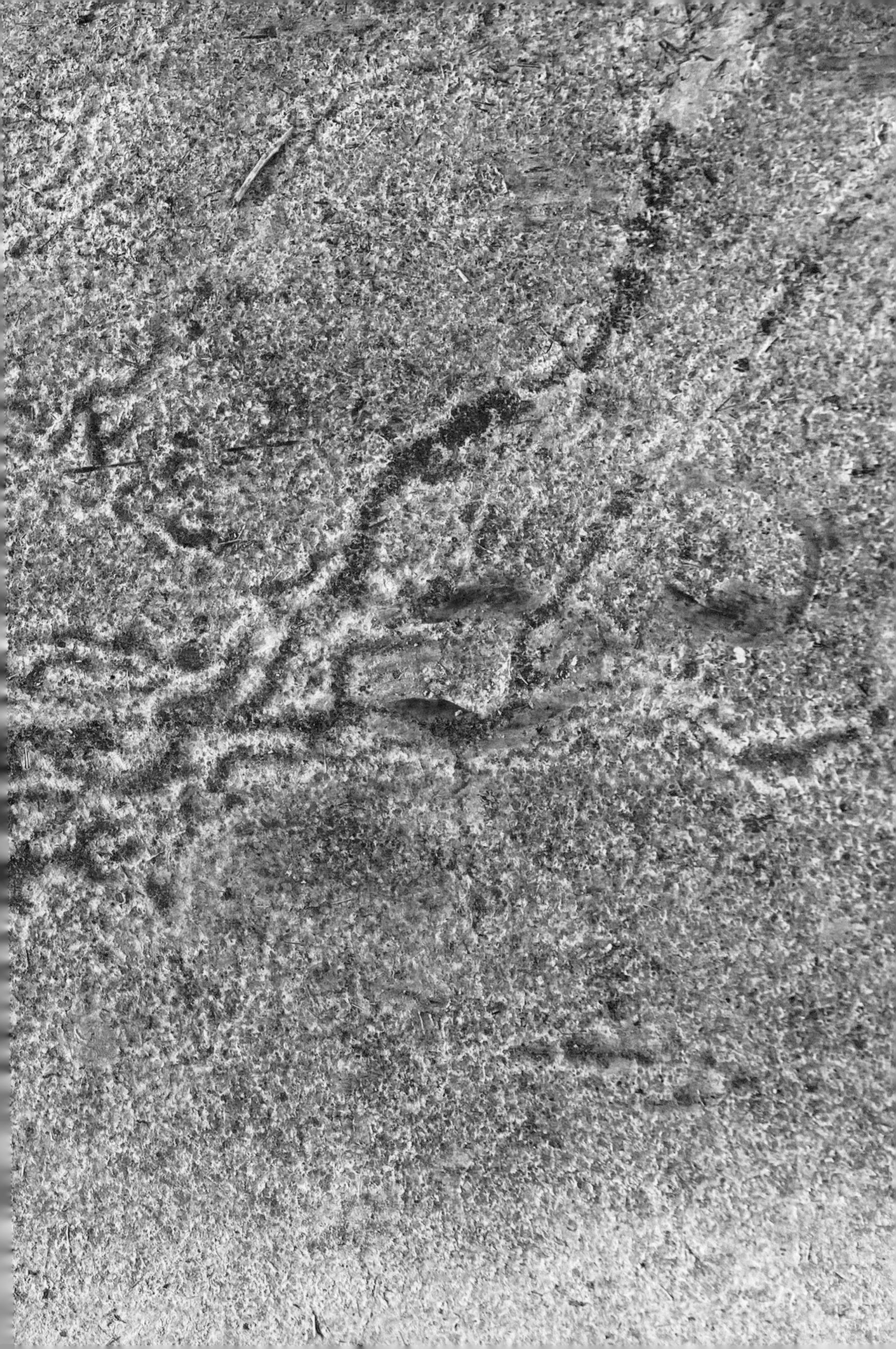

For some time now, people have been adorning the country name United Kingdom with a question mark after the word 'united' or even the U: United(?) Kingdom or U?K. They do this since this is the country that enforced 'Brexit' and thereby made a lot of commercial and political issues more difficult. That was the result of the referendum won by only a very few votes, enticed by anti-immigration propaganda. And some regions of the country are striving for independence. The question mark makes me smile. And with the recent move to the extreme right in many countries of the European 'Union(?)' the entire idea, or ideology, of unionism, unification, unity, seems to have become extremely precarious.

While growing up, I was made aware of the need for unification, which was my parents' reaction to the horrors of WWII, that promoted discriminations and splits among 'kinds of people'. Our family lived as a catholic minority in a predominantly protestant neighbourhood, which is why the compelling idea to get along with the 'others' reigned, was nurtured, in the family. I am still grateful for that aspect of my upbringing. The somewhat rough division between the protestant north and the catholic south of the country did not prevent friendships between the two groups, so that I had friends in both. And of course, another supposed 'unit' was the family itself. My parents did not have a happy marriage, and they argued a lot. And so did we as siblings. But the idea that the family was a unity never left us.

Whatever the many ups and downs, all along I kept the ideal of unity, the effort for unification, in the back of my mind. For me, unifying was the struggle we needed to fight in order to live in peace. When, later, I learned about democracy, a regime where (ideally) all people participate in governing the country, it all made much more sense. Then, the idea of a European Unity began to rear its head. Just when I made my first modest trips abroad, the borders between countries were still in place, but created no severe problems. I became more and more committed to the thought of internationalization, the idea of Europe, and the sense of belonging even across borders. What began as an idea became a 'natural' way of life. And also, the wish to learn to speak foreign languages: English because I had a lovely American aunt, and that language seemed to be close for everyone, and French, which was compulsory in the final two years of primary school and according to the textbook's title, was 'la plus belle langue'. The puny but pleasant, because exciting tension between a self-evident but unanalyzed unity and the encounters with otherness, which stayed with me for the rest of my life, became a constant resource for creative thinking. Unifying is necessary but does not speak for itself. It needs efforts, work. More on the concept and practice of 'work' under W.

Work, effort, struggle, remain key to improving society, for which unification is a primary necessity. In this framework, let me just mention two Dutch artists whose current projects I recently met, photographer Rob Hornstra and filmmaker Arnold van Bruggen. In a long-term project, they are exploring about twenty somewhat marginalized, peripheral regions of Europe. Each trip yields an exhibition and a book publication, of which the first had just appeared when I started my year at the Collège de France (on which more below). The regions are not named, which suggests a general condition of marginalization within Europe. Amidst the current tensions the artists present a vision of Europe with an eye to the future. Here, no nostalgia or idealization whatsoever, but, on the contrary, a pessimistic vision formulated and demonstrated by the victims of the increasing hyper-capitalism.

Their project is loosely inspired by that of Henri Cartier-Bresson (1908–2004), whose famous book *Les Européens* contains photographs by that master photographer, pioneer of street photography, theorist of 'the decisive moment' as the definition of photography in its distinction from painting, although he also wrote that 'you make a painting while you take a photograph'. This multi-talented and productive artist also painted, sketched, made films, and played in films, co-founded the agency Magnum, and created, a year before his death, a foundation to preserve his cultural heritage. In 1955 he published a large book with a spectacular cover designed by Spanish artist Joan Miró (1898–1988), for which the photographer chose the title 'The Europeans'—an ambitiously programmatic title in the ongoing process of analyzing and

reflecting on a further, future-oriented inventing of Europe.
The seventy-years gap that separates the Old Master and
the two contemporary artists clarifies the crucial difference
between a somewhat nostalgic view recalling the past, and a
sharply critical one of the present.

The present is dominated by the regime that is falsely
called 'neoliberal' while it is neither new, dating back to the
eighteenth century, nor liberal, since it imposes more and more
rules. These rules cause people to lose their homes, bought up
by businesses of the Airbnb kind and by Russian oligarchs who
buy up villa after villa. The inhabitants are victims because they
are losing on all fronts, including their language that fewer and
fewer young people speak among themselves. Their livelihood
is constantly limited and threatened, in a situation where capitalism destroys everything, with the added help of European
regulations that falsely suggest, and try to impose, unification.
The vision, here, is rather one of shame, not of pride. Shame, to
see their environment and their way of life fading away.

On the back cover, the artists quote in fat letters an
anonymous farmer who says with sad resignation: 'I am pessimistic. In ten years, we won't be there anymore. Everything
turns around money. And if there is one thing I know: money
always wins.' Inspired quite loosely, as the artists say, by Henri
Cartier-Bresson's photo book from seventy years ago, indeed;
in strong (not loose) contradiction to the latter's nostalgic
vision. The inhabitants of the marginalized regions enact the
prejudice against them, in a self-ironic auto-portrait: 'We are
the Barbarians!' It made me think of that famous, doubtlessly
apocryphal phrase by that author who was personally quite
misogynistic but literarily fiercely feminist: 'Madame Bovary,
c'est moi'—a phrase I have updated to 'Emma, that's us' in the
film mentioned under P. The phenomenon that sociologist Eva
Illouz has so aptly analyzed and named 'emotional capitalism'
acts up, all the time.

While all this made me passionately aware of the need for
and lack of unity, it was a wonderful stroke of luck that in 2022
I was unexpectedly elected to function for a year in what is
the result of probably the oldest truly democratic gesture by a

power-broker. This gesture was made by an 'absolute King'. The French king François Premier founded the Collège de France in 1530, almost seven centuries ago, to replace the then-current Latin in learning and scholarship by the common language (French) in the development of knowledge. And the Collège had as its goal to allow everyone to come and attend the lectures, regardless of previous education and current position. No costs, no diplomas, no registration. Knowledge development for everyone. When, at the beginning of my functioning, a taxi driver asked me what I was doing in Paris and I explained this, he said: 'Oh, that's brilliant! I'll come to attend!' and he did. The temporary Chair I got to occupy was titled 'The invention of Europe through languages and cultures'. Both the idea of 'invention', bringing in creativity, and the plural nouns inspired me. 'Europe' stands for a unity, problematic as that unification may be. At least, the unity is an aspiration; a hope. Unity, unification, counters the nasty differentiations between groups—be they religion-based, racial, sexual, linguistic, or ethnic, or, to say it with a broader term, cultural—that elicit tensions, hostilities, struggles and, in the end, wars. Now. In the present (tense).

My first intuitive reaction upon reading the document in which the content of the European Chair was described, with its plural use of 'languages and cultures' as instruments of that ongoing invention of Europe, and the 'thinkers and artists' as its subjects, was congenial to my ongoing wish to devote my work to, precisely, those plurals. Differences, yes; but 'difference' not as the equivalent of 'separation'. On the contrary. The multiple differences among the European languages and cultures encourage interaction, exchange, sharing; the curiosity and the wish to get to know, rather than turning your back to those 'others' who share with us the space and what I call the 'semiosphere' of the continent: modes and moments of meaning-making, beyond, or through the differences among the languages and media. That term 'semiosphere' integrates in a crucial way the geographical aspect and the meaning-making one. Differences remain, among traditions, age-groups, economic classes, and states of health: the goal is not to erase differences, unify into banality, and make everyone seem alike.

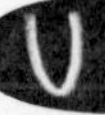

On the contrary; only as long as differences are accepted and respected, is a true, productive unity possible.[47]

What matters for a truly unified and plural Europe today is, in contrast to a fake, banal, and permanent communality, the acknowledgment, curiosity, and appreciation of differences, both among the countries and their sections or provinces, as within each of them, as within each region. In my exciting teaching and discussing during that year, I have brought up a few of the issues that simultaneously distinguish the European countries from one another and thereby encourage debate and mutual curiosity, and the merging that results, which is really what Europe *is*, what defines it, and what it *does*. This is possible thanks to the common ground that is the European 'semiosphere': the shared modes of meaning-making and communicating outside of the linguistic differences. The term implies possibilities for thinking and inventing a Europe that is both plural and unified. Thereby, discussions around those issues are possible, whichever language one speaks as one's 'mother-tongue', and within which the boundaries that separate also connect, in a single performative act.

The variation of European languages and cultures demands a respect for diversity on all levels, without turning differences into prohibitive borders. As I mentioned under Q, the concept of semiosphere was coined by the founding semi-otician of Russian-Jewish heritage teaching in Estonia, literary scholar Juri Lotman. An accessible explication of that concept and Lotman's other theoretical insights has been published by Marek Tamm and Peeter Torop (eds.), *The Companion to Juri Lotman: A semiotic Theory of Culture* (London: Bloomsbury, 2022), mentioned in footnotes 33 and 47. Lotman was very keen on what we used to call 'close reading', a detailed analysis of the literary and other artistic artefacts. Without endorsing the idea that the art is totally independent of society that frequently came along with close reading, I am still a convinced adherent of that practice.

This respect for an acceptance of differences is crucial because it alleviates the concept and the functional reality of borders that is a primordial problem on a continent consisting

47 The term 'semiosphere' is Juri Lotman's and is discussed usefully by Peeter Torop in Tamm, *The Companion to Juri Lotman* (2022), 296–307.

of so many countries—all with their own language or languages. Borders are the enemy of unification. As the cultural analyst Inge E. Boer has demonstrated in an important, posthumously published book: fundamentally ambiguous, borders are both lines and spaces for negotiation, simultaneously connecting and separating. Her book, which appeared in 2006, is extremely rich in insights and analyses.[48]

In the eighteenth century, Jean-Jacques Rousseau, a philosopher and artist-writer, hence, thinker and artist and thus perfectly fitting the assignment for this European Chair, had already well understood the border as a problem. He opened the second part of his *Discourse on the origin and the foundations of inequality among men* of 1755 with the frequently quoted sentence, in which he gives a very pessimistic vision of what we tend to see as so positive, namely 'civil society': 'The first who, having enclosed a piece of land, had the guts to say 'this is mine', and find people simple-minded enough to believe him, was the true founder of civil society.' The devastating critique of 'sociability' this implies, and the injustices it causes fills the pages of the *Discourse* with insights that makes readers recognize them and hang their heads in sadness. It is currently of actualizing importance that the *Discourse* of Rousseau has been republished in 2008 with abundant notes, an introduction, bibliography and chronology by Blaise Bachofen and Bruno Bernardi, and in an English edition: *Discourse on the Origin and Basis of Inequality Among Men*, trans. G.D.H. Cole, London: Penguin Classics, 1985. In addition to Boer's important book, an in-depth philosophical-anthropological reflexion on borders was written by Étienne Balibar in 2001, *Nous, citoyens d'Europe? Frontières, États, peuples* (esp. 15-30).

DO WE NEED BORDERS?

In spite of the reality of borders, as they function primarily bureaucratically and economically, but in practice, also linguistically, the engaging features are what makes interaction and dialogue captivating. This entails a caution against a

---

48 I say more about her work in the article, 'Making and Breaking Borders', in the Polish journal *Artium Quaestiones* (2024).

too-easily-assumed concept of comparison. This concept and its unifying as well as distinguishing features have been brilliantly analyzed and criticized by William Marx, whose work I mentioned under P, in the inaugural lecture at the Collège de France in 2020 by that scholar of *comparative literatures* (note the plural). In the practice of the discipline of comparative literature, the obsession is often to trace the differences, preferably between linguistic domains, easily made equivalent to national ones. Marx takes to task especially the more recent unifying concept of world literature, meant to extend the canon without, however, questioning the particularization and the hierarchy it implies. He resolves the dilemmas he is facing by pluralizing the noun and the qualifier as 'comparative literatures'.[49]

It is in line with this act of pluralizing in order to unify differently, and to express my respect for the creativity of this colleague, that I had pluralized Europe in my title for the publication of my inaugural lecture at the Collège de France, even if the name itself doesn't admit a plural form. The publication, which appeared in 2023 at Fayard, is titled *Un rêve culturel: L'Europe au pluriel*. It appeared in English in the *Journal of Visual Culture*. What matters is a form of integration rather than comparison, without focusing on commonality nor erasing differences. The latter constitute the ground for a cultural dream of a unified Europe in the plural. To avoid confusion with the standard that 'others', newcomers, are one-sidedly imposed the duty to 'integrate'—as an equivalent of 'assimilation'—I proposed the neologism 'inter-ship'.

I used the term 'semiosphere', which is for some people perhaps a bit obscure, a bit too much jargon, in order to avoid two traps in the discourse on the unifying force of Europe. The first trap would be to define, and hence, to fixate a geographical region, whereas the European Union is constantly in transformation, with new nations as members, candidates already accepted, and others that leave. Still other (candidate) states are being destroyed by a jealous imperialist state that refuses to let them enter or even exist. The second trap would be to obey too strictly the rules determined by politicians under the influence

---

49 Marx, *Vivre dans la bibliothèque du monde* (2020).

of powers, especially economic ones; an over-regulation that is, in my view, the most painful point of the unifying process. In my line of work, which was at the beginning the teaching of French as a foreign language, rules are useful. They aim to guide students in how to pronounce and write the languages correctly. Later I have oriented my work in other directions, always also in the plural. But I have constantly avoided the rules when they became dogmatic and limiting, thus hampering the creativity of thought and the pluralizing unification of encounters. Thereby I found myself, a bit to my amazement, becoming an interdisciplinary thinker and an intermedial artist, both at the same time. My experience of that double 'being in-between' is my topic for the present vignette.

Rather than fixating Europe as a region ruled by regulations, we were invited to reflect on the *invention* of Europe. This entails a continuous renewal; and that, by means of the languages and cultures. The ensemble won't accept being fixated. The concept of semiosphere facilitates evaluating and analyzing communication, in a domain necessarily fluid, unfixable, of which the borders are areas of negotiation rather than limit-lines, and the multiplicity of languages simultaneously helps and hampers communication. The semiosphere provides other signs than the words correctly written and pronounced; signs that add to, and thereby constantly transform, the usual discourses. The term 'sign' refers to the combination of something perceptible and an idea, an image, or even a phantasma that such a perception invites us to form mentally and also sensorially. And the perception happens through a perspective, which thereby also tends to be plural, as philosopher Emmanuel Alloa has recently argued.[50]

Invention, or inventiveness, and pluralization constitute a good combination for a productive unification. The mission of the Chair is calling on thinkers and creators, rather than politicians and capitalists. As the document that described the Chair formulated it: thinkers and creators 'live and deepen 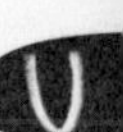 the European experience' with and through that plurality. In that way they are able to work at the inventive intellectual and artistic creation of a Europe of which the plurality is the most

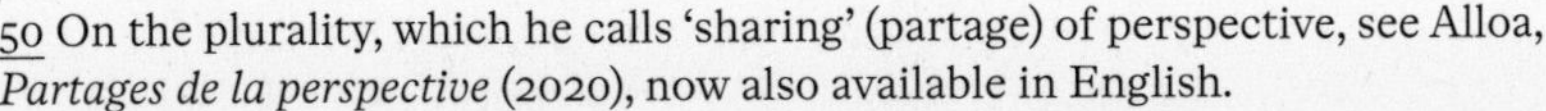

50 On the plurality, which he calls 'sharing' (partage) of perspective, see Alloa, *Partages de la perspective* (2020), now also available in English.

important characteristic and the key condition of unification. This explains my neologism 'inter-ship', a non-existing word that contains the hyphen that in French has such a much more adequate name, 'trait-d'union'. 'Inter-ship' is an attitude. It signifies an existence in movement, never fixated nor rigidly identified; nor ever autonomous, independent, isolated, indifferent.

According to one of the most creative thinkers of the twentieth century, Gilles Deleuze, that moving situation produces and encourages an aesthetic that he has called 'saharienne'—perhaps we can call it in English 'Saharic'. Mireille Buydens explains the concept lucidly in her 2005 book *Sahara: L'esthétique de Gilles Deleuze*. The forms of that aesthetic are like the hills of sand in the Sahara, in constant transformation and movement. Hence, the term itself is a metaphor. This is not to say that Europe looks physically, visually, or morally like a desert. It means, rather, that thanks to the artists and thinkers, the aesthetic and thought move and encounter each other in a universe of plurality, while simultaneously constituting an ensemble. During the beginning of my Chair, the artist Ann Veronica Janssens had set up an installation in the monumental building of the Panthéon in Paris, which was a perfect example of such a plural inter-ship. It consisted of enormous sheets of mirror that reflected the visitors as well as the frescos in the building, on the walls and the ceiling. It seemed relevant to me that the seams of the gigantic sheets of mirroring glass did the triple job of rupturing the unity, pluralizing the mirror images of the visitors looking down into the reversed abyss of the dome of the building, and showing the immensity of the space.

As do most of her works, this one reoriented the look, turning looking-seeing into an active act of engaging the visible into an unstable spectacle in movement. 'Travelling' inside the architecture of the monumental building, visitors were enticed to take the verb 'looking' in an active sense. Janssens is, indeed, an artist-thinker, who addresses in her works natural, physical phenomena, one of which, in the case of the Panthéon installation, was the movement of the earth itself. The inter-ship of thought and art assists us in identifying with the elements of a whole that, while inevitably in movement, moves us to live in unification with the ideas, sensations, landscapes, and people, in a semiosphere where nothing can be pinned down to an identity nor be seen as arbitrary. Because it precludes fixation, movement is the basis of life.

We must invent a Europe where differences are not erased but celebrated for the way they embody Europe's richness and uniqueness. If there is a possibility for a European 'union', this is where it must be positioned. This requires the integration in whatever way possible of the languages, literatures, and cultures in a communication anchored in the pleasure of curiosity and without the phobias that so frequently intervene with destructive results. And also without the assimilation so often required of newcomers, which erases differences and subjects the assimilating ones to the ruling assimilators. The fact that in the 1930s German Jews celebrated Christmas, simply because it was expected of them, has not saved their lives a few years later.

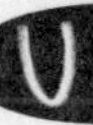

Victory
and Vanity, Virtue, Void, and Video

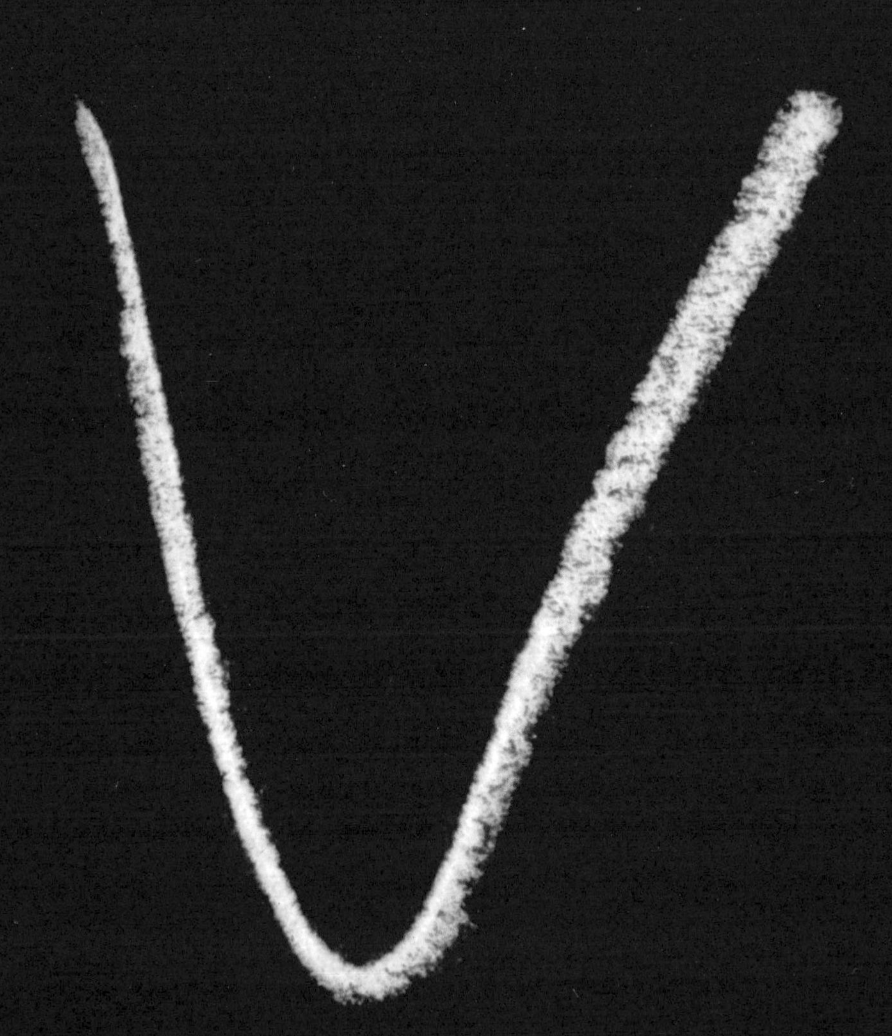

Victorious body movement

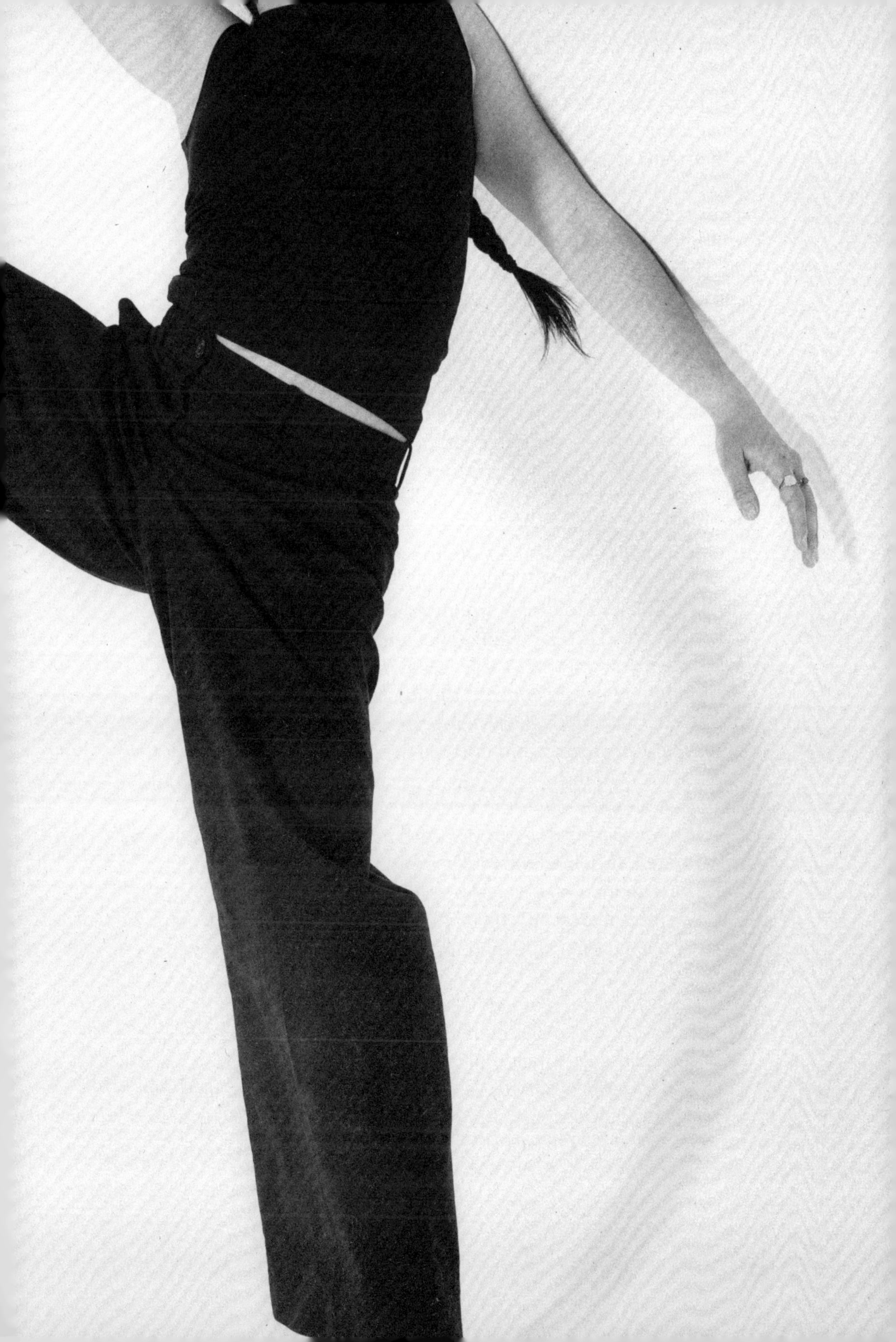

'Victory' resonates very positively, doesn't it? It is an equivalent of winning, success, triumph. But first of all, it suggests a happy feeling, a sense of satisfaction. I remember moments of victory when, as a primary school student who was always being severely judged by my parents, I was able to answer difficult questions that most of my classmates did not even understand, let alone could answer. True, I was a good student. Not because I worked so hard; for I did not. But I was curious. And also, I was alert, attentive, made ambitious by severely critical parents, and, as I have mentioned before, I was an avid reader—which is the best educational tool. Those features constituted the package that led to victory, as a winning, even if relative, only valid in the classroom situation. I can still feel that sense of victory when I think back to my childhood. I can identify with that little girl, at moments when the meaning 'victory' was made.

But that happy feeling would vanish quickly, to use another V word. For then, when I went home with my report card full of the highest grades and proudly showed it to my parents, my mother blamed me for 'vanity', meaning pride, self-importance, arrogance. You are vain! Pride was not accepted in our family. She said it emanated conceit; the idea that I thought too much of myself. Instead, *modesty* came first in the family-ideology. I quickly got the lesson and, instead of waving the report card, I just put it down in front of one of my parents so that they could sign it—a parent's signature was obligatory. But I must admit that the sense of victory stayed with me, if now secretly and interiorized. It helped me to determine later steps in the ongoing learning process. I enacted modesty, while feeling great by knowing that it was a bit false; that I really had done well. My pride of the victory remained inside, invisible. The reigning ideology was that modesty was a virtue, a sign of integrity, whereas pride was a void, non-sensical emotion.

It sounds a bit cruel, to make a young child repress a sense of achievement, of which children have such a need. Later, however, I was glad for that lesson, because I began to see pride and vanity all around me, and began to despise the boasting people for it. And I had to agree; there is no victory in getting a good grade, in doing well in class. For, victory is relative, comparative, and it depends on talent, which is not a personal merit. It comprises a sense of superiority over others, and that is not, not ever, justified. In that regard, the other educational lesson we received at home, that all people are equal, came in good stead. Of all the moral lessons I learned at home, this was the one I truly believed in, as I still do. And equality is incompatible with victory. Being good, skilled, handy at things, does not justify the arrogance of considering oneself superior to others. This turned 'victory' into a bad word. Equality is the basis, the condition of social life. The idea of victory has no place in it. Of course, it is okay to feel happy when something testing, like an exam, goes really well. But there is no need to boast about it, to stick out your tongue at those with lower grades.

This became very clear to me when once, much later when I was already a faculty member, in the departmental annual meeting we all had to submit our publications that had come out during that year. This was a moment of being, secretly, a little proud. As I mentioned under E (for 'envy') it once happened that I had a number of publications that equalled the total of the other members of the small (seven people) department put together. I was never forgiven for this. The envy-driven hostility became so harsh that I decided that, next year, I would withhold some achievements, so that the difference wasn't so glaring. This is where my mother's lesson in modesty came in handy. This was, indeed, what I did. But I knew the modesty was a lie. And the seed of competition, jealousy, with the accompanying anger that would lead to envy had already been sown. Victory entails envy, and social interactions promote it.

That other V word, 'virtue', that came with the educational lessons, was less uplifting. It was supposed to mean 'being good'. But what is 'good', as a behavioural or personality trait? Principally, goodness was bound to restrictive, forbidding rules. In addition to honesty, courtesy, politeness, and charitable behaviour with others, during adolescence the primary virtue was soon to become 'chastity': restraining from physical pleasure in contact with the bodies of others. This always made me uneasy. I have never believed in it. Virtuousness entailed a boring restraint, a sense of quietness, of holding back one's

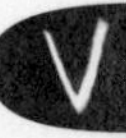

enthusiasm. And with my stubborn tendency to enjoy excitement, and to want to share its pleasure with others, the limiting feature of what they called 'virtue' but was simply chastity, annoyed me greatly. Nevertheless, my awareness of the tricky aspect of 'vanity' as a feeling of superiority has not left me.

VANITY CHANGES SENSE

But then I encountered the concept of vanity with a different meaning. This mainly happened through the history of art. Instead of indicating a sense of pride, vanity became a symbol of death; of the void and futility of life, the restricted time frame of it, and the pointlessness of earthly goods, wealth, possessions. Its symbol, as it turned out, was the skull. I once was asked to write an article about it and in writing it I realized the importance of that symbol. The skull as the symbol of 'vanitas', as it was called, appeared in still-life paintings, significantly called 'nature morte' in French, which literally means 'dead nature'. The tension between death and time turned out to fascinate me. That the relentless passing of time is the meaning of the vanitas of life and the imminence of death, turns the vanity feeling, caused by victory, into a void one. To sum up my conclusion in that article: it is not time that needs killing, as the saying has it, but it is people who kill, and not just then, but *now*.[51]

Time passes, lifecycles end. We all die. Along with the hourglass, the skull reminds us of the ephemerality, the precariousness of life, including its riches, its successes, the food that (temporarily) sustains it, the beauty it offers, e.g. in flowers with their forms and colours, but with a threatening insect on one of the petals; the void. Time passes, life ends, and so, we should make the best of the little bit of time we have. Time is the perpetrator; it is due to time that life is so brief, that decay takes over, and that particularity disappears. Some contemporary artists rebel by rejecting the uniformity, the stillness, and the immobility that the skull denotes, as well as the idea that still,

---

51 The title of that article is quite programmatic: 'Hetero-Chronical Experiments Between Life and Death: Vanitas Revolts Against Time Management' (2022).

immobile images are just that: still. Instead, they argue that time is not more uniform than life; that rhythm is variable; that the experience of time differs for each individual, and that as a consequence still images are not really still.

The concept that helps understand this mobility is what I have termed 'heterochrony': the experience of the variability of time. The issue is to promote intercultural understanding through the awareness that people in situations of migrancy and of living as a refugee, experience time very differently from those who live in the routine of, say, Western capitalist clock time. Social issues pop up in the discussion of heterochrony, even if the century-long tradition of vanitas in painting is less obviously political than the awareness of heterochrony for people in unstable situations, which compels them to feel the hot breath of time in their necks. Nevertheless, that old tradition does have a social-political background, which is obvious in the religious culture of the Renaissance and Baroque countries, where the vanitas motive served primarily as a *memento mori*.

In *Creative Evolution*, a book devoted to the enigma of life, the French philosopher Henri Bergson, the most prominent philosopher of time, wrote, in the chapter on 'The Endurance of Life', in his life-long effort to theorize life, time, and the world in terms of a continuum, about the difference of what he calls the 'real whole': 'The systems we cut out within it [the real whole] would properly speaking, not then be *parts* at all; they would be *partial views* of the whole.' I see here an implicit prefiguration of an intervention in my favourite concept of *focalization*, which harbours a temporal aspect as well. This is hopefully clear in my theoretical work on this concept, best consulted in the last edition of my book *Narratology*.[52]

Bergson's reflection also implies a shift in our conceptions of fragments and details. As I have written in a book on Norwegian artist Jeannette Christensen: 'Fragments are pieces, broken off, and continuing existence alone. They always carry the idea of the whole with them, even if that whole is no longer around; even if we can no longer say what the whole was.' In this, the fragment is different from the detail. When the whole

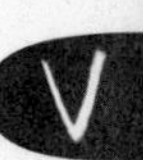

---

52 Bergson, *Creative Evolution* (1983), 31. *My Narratology* (1991) has been revised for new editions every ten years, the last one, from 2017, is complemented by a *Narratology in Practice* in which I develop the examples deleted from the 2017 edition for being too varied, according to colleagues in literary studies.

is available, details of it help us understand it in all its complexity. That is why details are such favourites of critics. Fragments, in contrast, are the melancholy bearers of irretrievable loss, of irreparable destruction; of time's relentlessly stormy passage. Matter is also at the heart of our bodies. We *are* matter. We are bodies that need care and that give care, helping themselves and those of others to endure. Bodies are matter that exists in time and will fade away on its wings. The realization that matter is not durable inspires ideas of something else that lasts longer and is temporarily housed in the body. Hence the invention of the idea of the soul. But mortality is evidence of our materiality, not of its opposite.[53]

This brings me back to the tension between matter, as pseudo-permanent, and time, as rushing us to death. As is well known, Bergson revolutionized the conception of time. He replaced measurable, divisable time—the model of clock time against which the South-African artist William Kentridge so beautifully protested in a performance from 2012, *The Refusal of Time*, as I have mentioned—with the continuous duration that Bergson theorized so brilliantly. Clock time divides our time in pieces; duration accepts its longer or shorter, fast or slow continuity. The tension between fragment and detail can be considered as that between part and partiality in Bergson's passage. Apply this tension to time, as Bergson is wont to do, and the key to Christensen's work emerges. Her most famous series is discussed in my 1999 book: the Jell-O benches that are given duration in exhibition, until they begin to mould, and stains drip out of them. Separating the colours of yellow and red.[54]

The bond between matter and time is a logical consequence of the becoming (social) 'details' rather than remaining 'fragments'. Comfort in the face of fragmentation is only possible when anchored in facing time, not escaping from it by hiding your head in the sand. Comfort becomes possible when fragmentary existence is the starting point, not a gruesome truth to be repressed. For, matter also matters because it is never *only* itself. We invent other things for which matter can be a home: forms, sense experiences, souls, minds, sociality,

---

53 On Christensen's work, see my book *Fragments of Matter* (2009).

54 For a clear visual presentation of this, see my book *Quoting Caravaggio* (1999), 173.

life. This turns fragments (of things) into details (of social life), in line with Spinoza's view that all bodies touch other bodies and therefore can only exist in the company of others.

VANITY AND VIDEO

I recently encountered a book by a French video artist, Richard Skryzak, the title of which, *Vanité et art vidéo*, at first sight made me shiver with annoyance. It seemed a vanity to speak of video as art. I have been making video art since 2002, and although I have always been convinced that the step towards a kind of work called 'art', that I found pretentious, was in my case really a new mode of doing the research I always wanted to pursue, into the lives and cultures of people I didn't know and couldn't understand. But due to my education in modesty and the insecurity it generates, I never felt comfortable with the title of 'artist'. But clearly, Skryzak, in contrast, wanted to endorse that title-of-honour, which was what annoyed me due to its lack of modesty. It seemed a vanity to speak of video as art. When I started to read Skryzak's book, fresh from the press (2024), I soon realized the entire book is devoted to his own video work. So, at first, I thought he was deploying that other, in my childhood forbidden sense of vanity. But reading on, I had to shift my view of vanity once more. For, the author writes about vanity in a beautifully complicating way. First of all, this video artist is just as much a philosopher, which made me consider my own work on 'image-thinking' in connection to his concept of vanity. When discussing Bergson, he pays serious attention to the latter's profound interest in painting.

The point, it turned out, is the contribution of duration to invention. And that, of course, is the key to temporality's crucial role on the creativity that art needs. He quotes a sentence from Bergson's 1941 book *L'évolution créatrice* that says it all: 'Time is invention, or it is nothing at all' (Le temps est invention … ou il n'est rien du tout). I realized thanks to Skryzak's book that in my earlier reading on Bergson I had more or less overlooked how he theorized the intertwinement of art-making

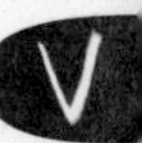

and thinking that has become so important to me, with the help of thought on time. So, Skryzak's total concentration on his own video work is not a deployment of vanity as boasting, but an indispensable reflection on his own need, as an artist and academic, to give time, duration, a serious place in the creativity he needs in his art-making. The shiver of dread became a shiver of admiration. Time, then, is not void; vanity is not an absence of the virtue of modesty, but an indispensable tool for the complexification of time in Bergson's sense of duration.

This made me happy, not as in that childhood sense of victory but as a comradeship, an 'inter-ship' if you like, between myself and someone I just met, only on paper, intellectually. All I could do was re-read his book. And yes, there they were: those moments I had overlooked for reading too quickly the first time. That early passage where he assigns to Roland Barthes the idea of anachronism, again one that is very important to me, as crucial, defining, in the processing of literature. The temporal discrepancy between writing and reading makes literature by definition only processable as anachronistic. This also turns up in the visual domain, and this is where the different areas of interest join forces. Skryzak, again quoting someone whom I have encountered, even adored, but not done justice: the artist Paul Klee. In his early theory of modern art, Klee writes that 'The factor time intervenes as soon as a point begins to move and becomes a line' (Le facteur temps intervient dès qu'un point entre en mouvement et devient ligne). This point, when the point becomes a line and thus not only produces an image but sets that image in movement, lies at the heart of Skryzak's conception of video, of video as an artform, of its visuality and thus its primary distinction from literature, but primarily an artform of movement.[55]

That I have undertaken to make videos that, out of my control, began to be considered art, was something I had not at all given any in-depth philosophical reflection at the time. I just did it, finding myself in a social situation where buying a camera to bear witness, as a durational counter-action, was suddenly necessary. As I mentioned before, I proposed the video to a television station, but they declined when I refused

---

55 Klee, *The Thinking Eye* (2013), 37.

to replace the voices of the people by a voice-over speaking
about, *for* them. Then, totally out of the blue, the video was
invited in an art exhibition in Germany. These were moments
when my professional ambition unfolded a joyful achievement I
had neither foreseen, nor strived for. Later, I would say, anachronistically, those accidental moments did incrust themselves
into my sense of self, of what I was doing. And since then, now
over twenty years ago, video-making has become part of my
sense of self, without victory or vanity, but with a terrific sense
of having 'done' something. Not an achievement, but an act.
John Langshaw Austin's concept of performance, and its 'other',
performativity, have given my doing relevance. And for the
many people who keep asking me this: making videos has not,
not at all, prevented me from continuing my intellectual work.
I like to think: on the contrary. The academic work did not slow
down nor lost its quality.

Just a quick example. While I am writing this entry, in
2024, one of my most recent video works, the sixteen-screen
exhibition of *Don Quijote: Sad Countenances*, made in 2019 with,
and at the initiative of, French actor Mathieu Montanier, is on
show in Poland, in the city of Worcław's Art Center until the
end of July 2024. Although I had read Cervantes' world-famous
novel before, in its entirety, the challenge Montanier posed
was profoundly thought-changing when, in connection to his
strong physical likeness to the figure of Don Quixote as artists,
especially Gustave Doré, have installed the looks of this 'him'
into our culture, he proposed to make a film on the subject. It
revised the reading I had done without much thinking, just for
the fun of it. But now, the idea of filming, of making a sequence
('line') of images based on it, revolted against such a project.
The entire project had to change, because the re-reading
declared the trauma-induced impossibility of the linearity of
time as the literary masterpiece had shaped that impossibility.
So, reading prohibited the video-making I might otherwise
have taken on.

For me, recalling my sense of victory of my childhood
moments of achievement, and the subsequent moral lesson of
modesty, did help me to see the point (the point turned line,

turning image in movement) of making video art as an integral
part of the intellectual work I had always devoted myself
to. I dedicated a book to the complex issue of thinking and
writing, imagining and imaging, which appeared after making
that video exhibition. Its title is *Image-Thinking: Art making
as Cultural analysis* (2022). That book has gained in depth and
quality thanks to the experience of doing something that was
impossible. Should I call it 'void'—a void not to be avoided? I
am not sure. The political issue brought up by the change of my
anachronistic vision made, I think, both my intellectual work
and my artistic work henceforth inseparable, thereby better,
in the sense of more productive and useful for others, and in
connection to other projects.

This reflection does not help me to better understand how
the term, or concept, of 'vanity' connects victory, temporality,
life and death, time and its passage, duration and its creativity.
But this is the lesson I learned from it: it doesn't matter. I have
never cared much for scientifically validated definitions. I
don't like the (classi-)fixation definitions imply. The processes,
the movements, the visions: all this constitutes a pleading for
video as an artform, as a form of thinking, where making is
not separable from, let alone an illustration of, the ideas that
help culture and politics go hand in hand. For video is capable
of making ideas present. This brings me back to Spinoza.
According to him, understanding doesn't happen in isolation,
no more than existence itself. 'The complex interactions of
imagination and affect ... yield this common space of intersub-
jectivity ... and the processes of imitation and identification
between minds, which make the fabric of social life. The awareness of actual bodily modification—the awareness of things as
present—is fundamental to the affects; and this is what makes
the definition of affect overlap with that of imagination. All this
gives special priority to the *present*.' The present: this is where
we must eliminate victory, and replace it with the modesty that
makes peace possible.[56]

---

56 With the dots I indicate that this is a fragmented paraphrasis of passages in
the highly illuminating 1999 book by Gatens and Lloyd, *Collective Imaginings:
Spinoza, Past and Present* (1999), not a continuous quotation.

V

Work
and Waiting, Wondering.
But it Can also Be for Word, War,
Watch, Worst, Writing, Waiting,
Wondering, Wrap, Warp, Woe,
Ward, Wonder, Women,
and Many More

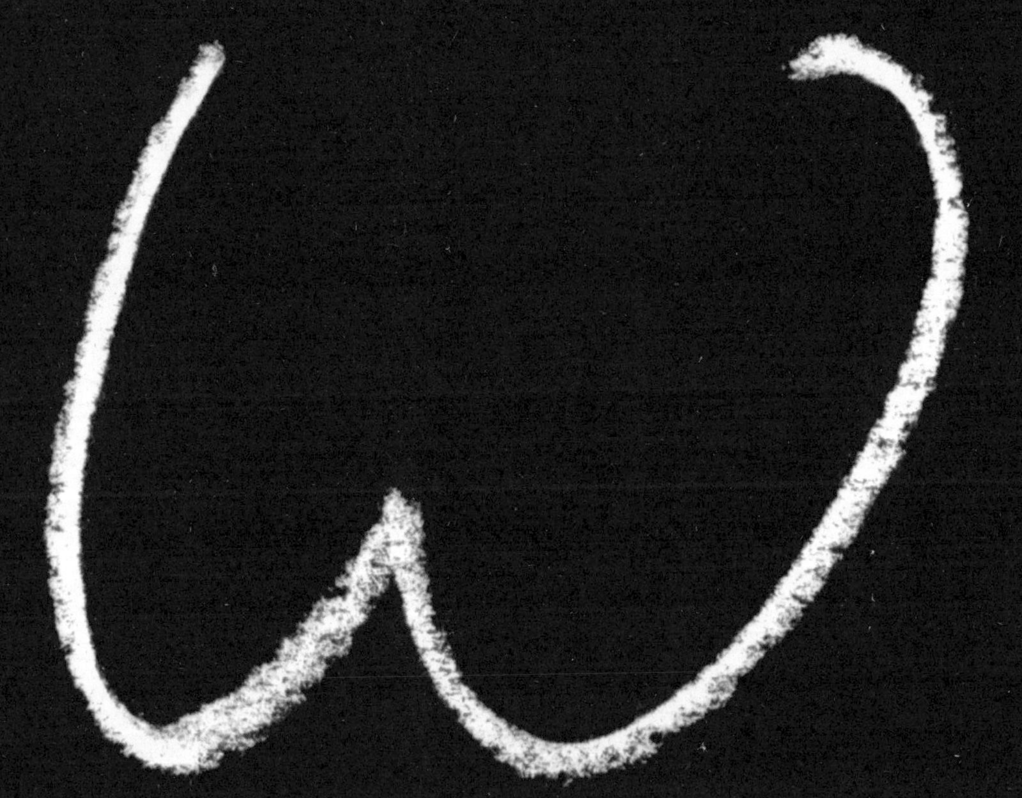

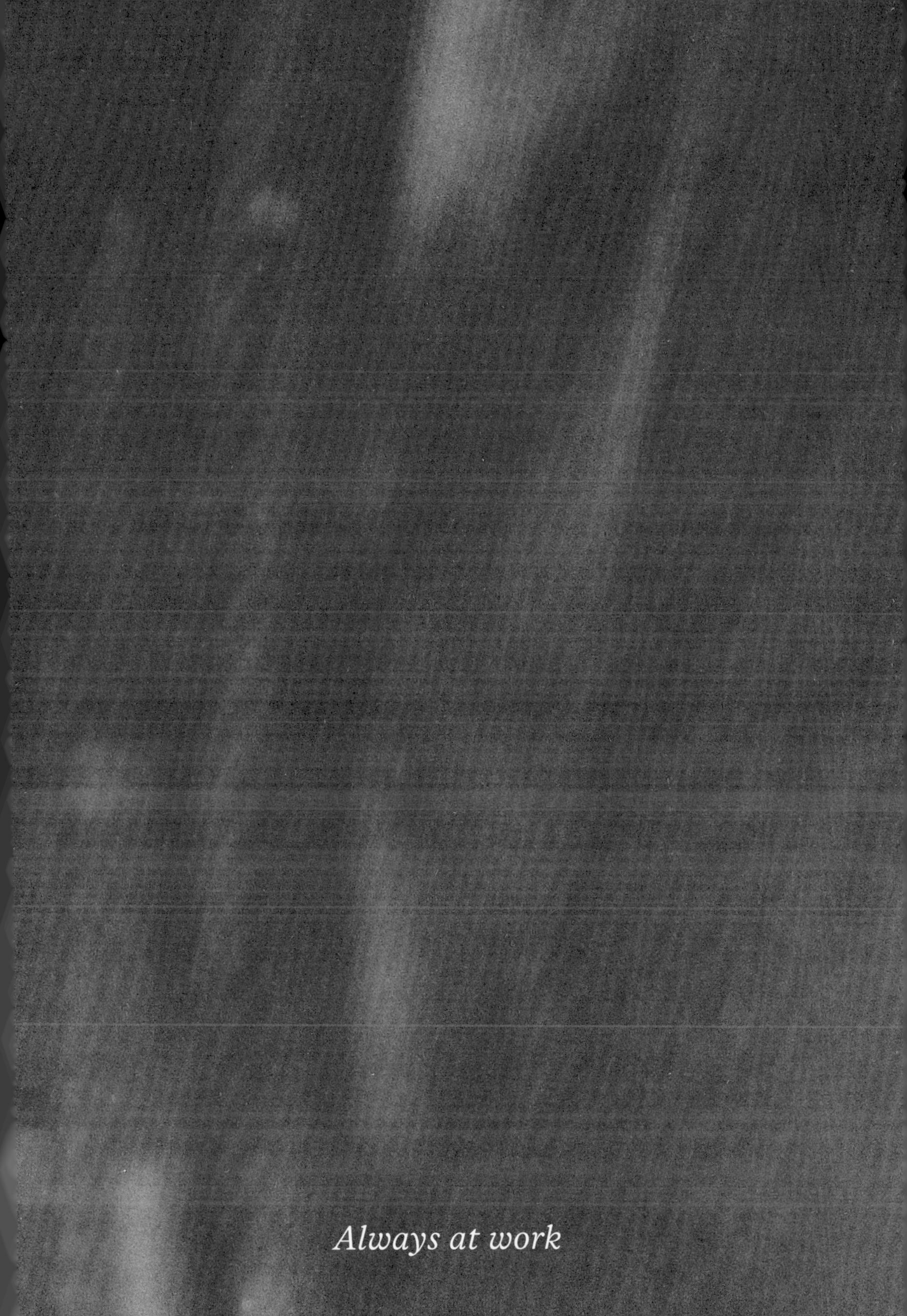

Always at work

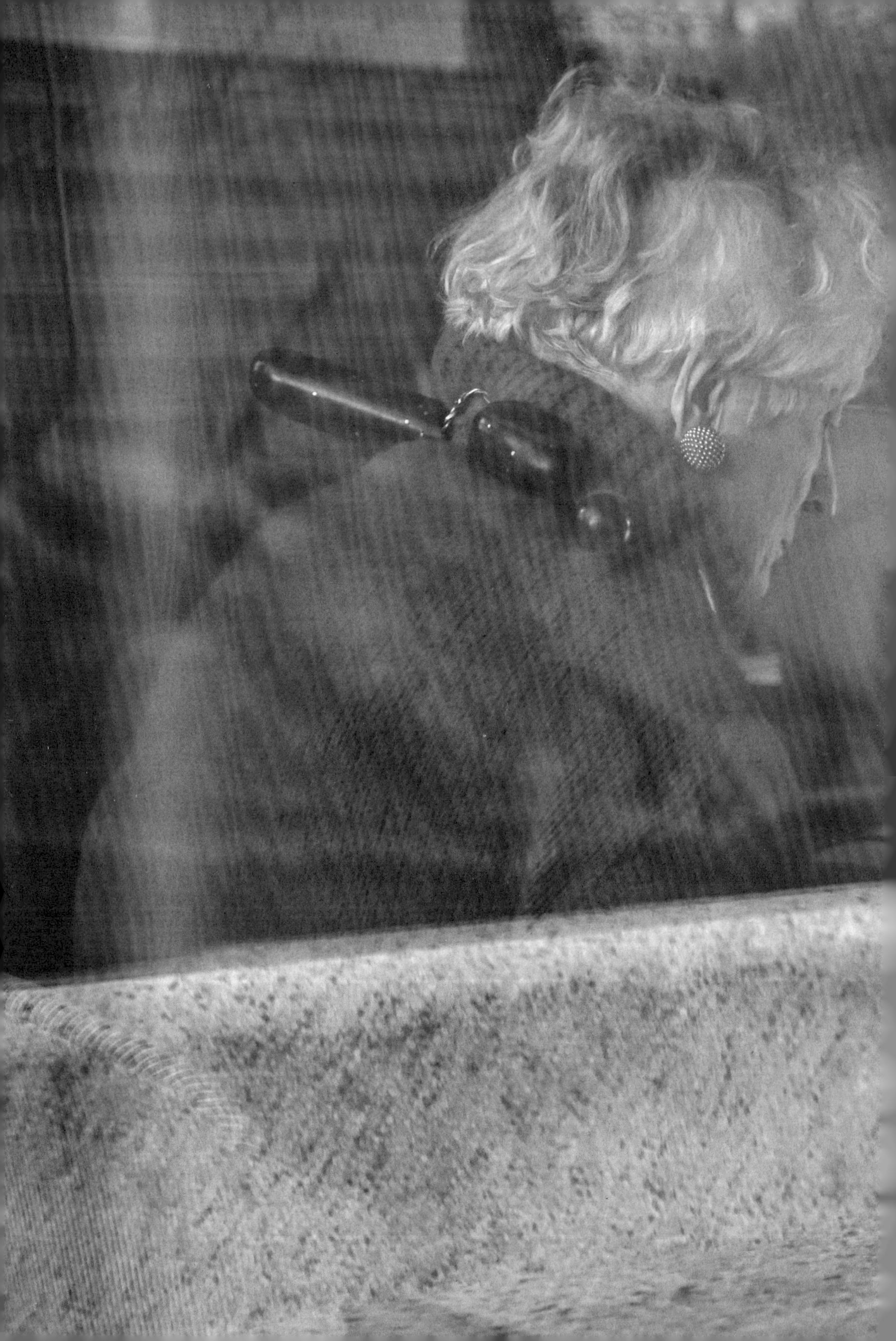

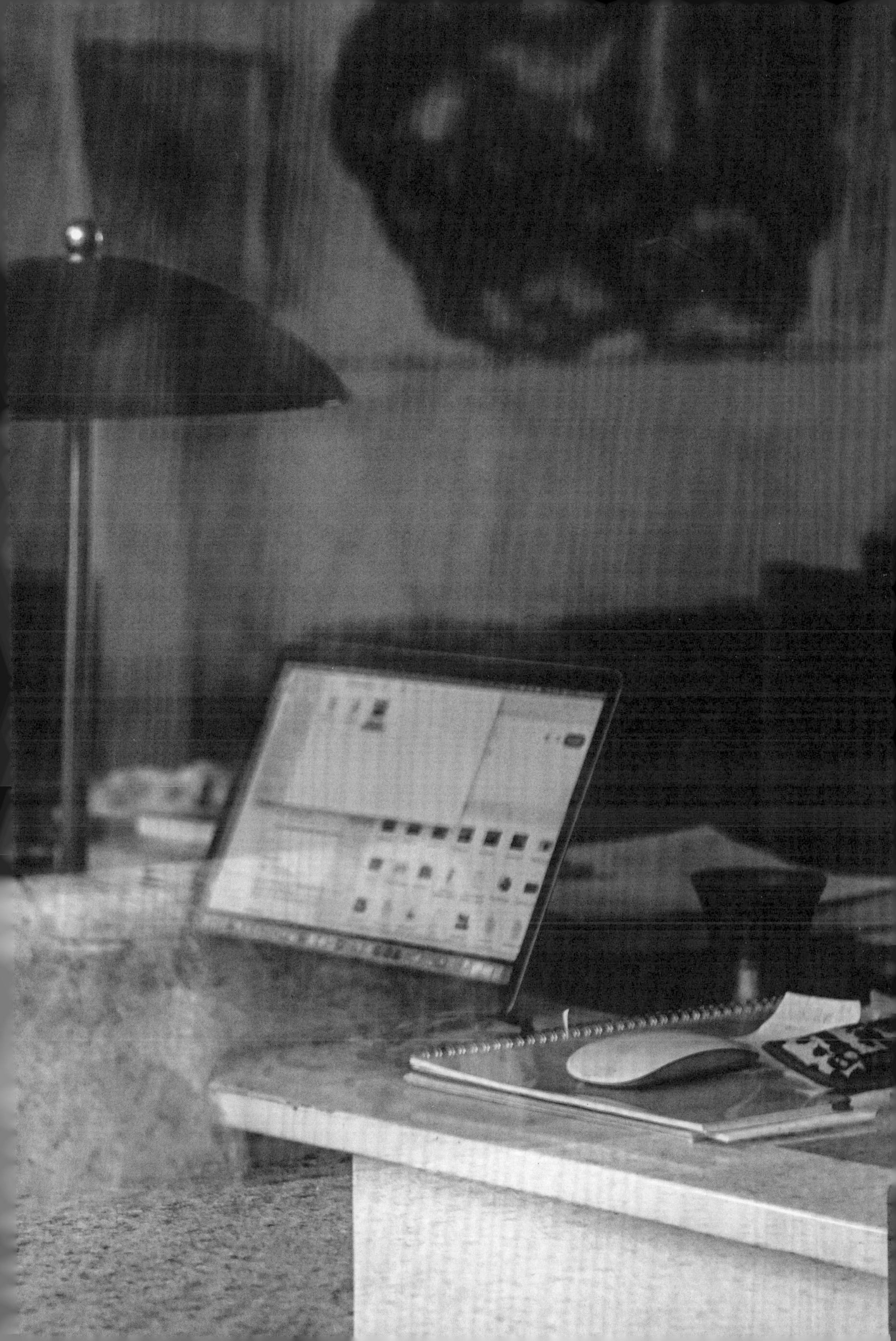

For a long time, I had assumed that for this vignette I would put 'war' as the main word. War is both past and present. Not only is the war of World War II the key memory of the beginning of my education, or my thinking about life, as well as about life-and-death. This was due to the fact that the war was the central topic of storytelling by my parents. This was also when I learned to practice identification. The stories of my parents shaped my earliest memories. These include the stolen coat of my father, briefly mentioned under K; the hunger and the need to eat disgusting tulip bulbs, because there was so little else to eat; the compulsion to hide people from the neighbourhood who were in danger, under the living-room floor; my father risking his life by going out, at night, with friends to gather food wherever possible; and, above all, the constant fear.

I was lucky enough to have been born in the aftermath, not during the war, as were my older brother and sister. But I did grow up with war stories. However, now, next to those earliest memories there is the actuality of today's world, with its two wars (in Ukraine and Gaza) so close by, where on a daily basis thousands of people, mostly civilians, are killed by bombs. Oops! A bomb meant for a military base 'accidentally' hits a children's hospital. War is the world's worst disaster; unliveable. Therefore, it is simply too painful to devote an auto[bio]graphical reflection to it, especially if that entry is meant to yield conceptual possibilities. Instead, I want to forget it. Forgetting, the opposite of memorizing, is a way of erasing memories one doesn't want to live with. But precisely, forgetting is not easy, not automatic. Memories stick like glue, especially if they resonate so painfully with the present time.

Instead, there are so many W words that I have an 'embarrassment of riches', to quote not only a common expression for richness and multitude but especially the title of historian Simon Schama's brilliant book from 1987 about Dutch culture in the seventeenth century. Of this abundance of W words, some of which I cited at the start of this vignette, 'word' is the most obvious one in an alphabetic series of, precisely, words, wherein each entry is named after a word. Using words to reflect on the past-present interaction makes it easier to wish to forget the horrors of war, but also to realize that we cannot really forget them. For the wars are going on, right now, with no end in sight. Both north and south of where I currently live wars are raging. And I personally know people, colleagues and friends, who are deeply involved in these wars. Hence, they will stay in the back of my mind. It is impossible to avoid their constant presence and the horrors these wars cause. Television news, with its too-short accounts of it, will not allow me to forget it. The brevity of those accounts ruins the adequacy of the news, as the German artist Monika Huber has made clear in her powerful book, mentioned under R. But when I think about the purpose of these vignettes, memories invoked for their occasioning of concept-building do not welcome pure horrors.

WAITING FOR MEANING

Another area of W words concerns time; the time of waiting. But what do we wait for? For peace, yes. But more generally, I have an impatient personality and waiting, for me, has always tested my endurance. I often mentally rehearse the rhyme I made up: I hate to wait. I am not the only one who gets impatient and annoyed when waiting is required, but for me, internally, what makes it stand out is that it feels so lonely. Waiting enforces idleness; doing nothing. I find that hard, since I enjoy social and work-related activities, and find time-wasting a terrible loss. And then, what is it that we are waiting for? This question also remains active. It is what come after the preposition 'for' that counts.

This impatience that plagues me reminds me of a work by one of my favourite artists, Marlene Dumas, which I saw just a few days before beginning to write this vignette, in an exhibition at the Amsterdam Rijksmuseum devoted to gender (July 2024). Dumas is not only a brilliant visual artist, but an equally brilliant poet. She even published a book of titles of her works and notes on and about them, serving as poetry, titled *Sweet Nothings: Notes and Texts*. One of her poems is titled 'the fog of war', the hand-written litho version of which comes with a series of heads of people killed by war. The text line on the small work I just saw is 'I Won't Wait (for the Authority of

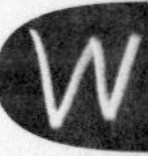

Meaning)', as number seven of a series of eight works on paper of 21 x 26,5 cm each. The ensemble of these eight works is titled *Defining in the Negative*, from 1988. They are, indeed, all titled with negatives. But the element 'meaning' in the number seven and the refusal to wait for the authority—of the art historian, I suppose—to determine what the work means, its meaning, is typical for Dumas' attitude, which she ridicules with a wink. Also in 1988, Dumas painted a much larger work, of oil on canvas of 50 x 70 cm titled *Waiting (for Meaning)*. There, a naked dark body is lying on a bed, perhaps sleeping. Meaningless. That's why she/it is lying there, waiting. (see fig. 10)

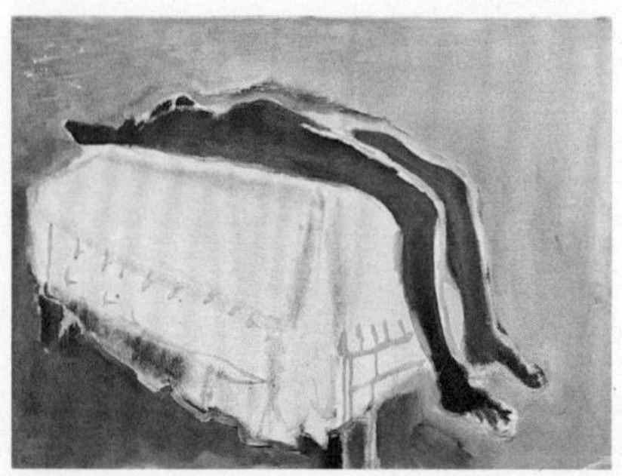

'Meaning' is as ambiguous as most of the words I deploy here. It can be semantic, suggesting an interpretation for a work, or it can be intentional: 'I mean to say this...', I intend this to happen. I think Dumas refuses to 'wait for meaning' in that double sense. She rejects the authoritarian dictation of interpretations in dogmatic disciplinary frameworks, and instead delivers her artworks to a public that she declares to be free to make of it what they wish; to mean what it means. This liberates art from methodological strictures. And thereby she gives art over to freedom of experiences. All of her art emanates that sense of freedom, for the works never have a clear, predictable meaning. The verb 'waiting', thus, is rejected when it concerns attempts to fixate interpretations and instead, as in the larger oil painting from 1988, lets the figures simply wait until they are fed-up with that doing-nothing. Time, in this oeuvre, indicates a relaxation.

WONDERING ABOUT WONDER

Leaving 'waiting' and 'war' behind me, let me make a new start. For, of the many words with which I can write this entry—with that W verb 'writing'—I am craving for a positive, rejoicing one. So, I opt for the beginning of a new book currently in press, by my dear friend, the art historian Michael Ann Holly. The book, soon, hopefully in 2025, to appear at Edinburgh University Press, is titled, quite simply and clearly, *Somewhere Between Art History and Phenomenology: At the Still Point of the Painted World*. She begins with the magically-sounding words 'Wondering about wonder' Not as a title or heading but simply as the first three words, followed by a full stop. As I am myself, Michael is fond of ambiguities. She knows how to enliven them and wants to do so. Wondering means questioning, doubting, reflecting, but also marvelling and admiring; and 'wonder' can be sensational, even miraculous, as well as simply amazing. In her view, art is a strong comforting phenomenon in a world suffering from wars and other negativities. Hence, the book is devoted to questions about the power of beauty, to put it simply. The stillness of artworks is questioned; for she fore-grounds how the artworks, once experienced, begin to move. This is again an ambiguous verb, with movement and emotion intertwined.

To avoid philosophical jargon, Holly calls the kind of looking-seeing she is going to explore, not quite, as Merleau-Ponty had it, 'embodied perception', but 'visual poetry'. The connection, or interaction, perhaps merging or, as Korean-American philosopher Kyoo Lee suggested (on page 18 of her important 2012 book, *Reading Descartes Otherwise*), con-fusing, with the hyphen changing the negative word 'confusion' into a positive one meaning togetherness ('con-') and 'melting into a unification', between the visual and the poetic, hence, words. This is what Holly's approach is seeking to grasp. For this, she brilliantly sums up, quite briefly, the ideas of some of the major phenomenologists of the twentieth century. And while most of these are especially considering literary, poetic cases, Holly's use of the idea of 'poetry' as bound up with 'visual', ends up as a plea for slow (time) and attentive (intense) looking. And following Husserl, one on her list of pheno-heroes, who pleads for the meticulous description of phenomena, she does pre-cisely that. However, her phenomena are not just the artworks,

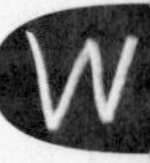

but rather, the way the artworks *work*. From objects, the word 'work' moves on to demonstrating how they work. How the artwork works: this, for me, is the best way of writing what art not only *is*, but *does*. This, then, is the meaning of 'work' here. And this working involves writing. Thanks to her brilliance and commitment, I have read Holly's book as the most productive view for students as well as scholars.

Holly has a fondness for the poetic that is quite remarkable for an art historian. In her second chapter, primarily devoted to the pheno-heroes (heroes of phenomenology), she writes: 'I often find that it is poets who capture phenomenological sentiments most profoundly.' This, for me, entails the kind of interdisciplinary encounter I have attempted to articulate and for which I have argued when, after having worked exclusively in literary theory, I looked around the corner and began to analyze visual art. My book *Reading Rembrandt* from 1991 was the first product of that encounter. Like Holly, whom I met and befriended for life at the university of Rochester, NY when I began working there in 1987, I deeply enjoy encounters as unifying what or who is before that, separate and different. There, she was head of art history and I of comparative litera-ture, that 'stranger', for her as an art historian, who needed the encounter. Our interdisciplinary encounter was powerful and inspiring. Soon, for her, astonishing for an art historian, poetry was her guideline; and for me, as a narratologist, visual art became mine. Together, and with brilliant colleagues such as Kaja Silverman, Norman Bryson, and Constance Penley, among others, we founded a programme then called 'Comparative Arts', later renamed Program in Visual and Cultural Studies, around 1990. As far as I know, this was the first interdisci-plinary programme in the arts in the world. Later it became a much-followed model.

Holly's advocating of phenomenology as an approach to art is also, perhaps primarily, an attempt to liberate art from confining approaches that are blind to the *work* of art; an attempt to be, and make others, less interested in the art as object than in what it *does*. Phenomenology, in Holly's words, is

.... an established semiotic, suggestive, and poetic
process. [...] a phenomenological perspective
legitimates a poetic turn away from the straitjacket
of art historical objectivity. Phenomenology bestows
an intensity of feeling to our studies that liberates
the visual from being cocooned in routine protocols.
Into our everyday labors it injects a dose of magic
and wonder.[57]

The magic and wonder, then, are the results of the work the
artworks do. From objects they turn into subjects. This entails
a profound emotional-perceptual impact. It gives an innovative
meaning to the idea of meaning. And it foregrounds the moving
nature of art, in the two senses I have mentioned above. In her
third chapter, which starts off with a landscapish work by the
sixteenth-century Belgian artist Joachim Patinir, Holly writes
on the poetry of this work of visual art, because of what it does.
She is explicit in her fierce critique of what Dumas would call
'the authority of meaning' when she writes:

.... his palette's poetry so often overlooked in the
effort to decipher an (iconographic) meaning. [...]
From whence comes the compulsion to attempt
verbal mastery over such unconquerable visuality?
The curse of art history.[58]

'Verbal mastery' says it all; less the verbal side of it, than the
striving for mastery. And she binds movement, in the literal
sense, to sound, including yet another sense organ, when she
writes in the fourth chapter, apropos of the work by Dutch
painter Pieter Aertsen, also from the sixteenth century: 'Iron
keys seeming to dangle noisily from its lock.' Where does the
word 'noisily' come from, in a comment on a painting? When
looking at the painting we don't hear that noise. Or do we?
Yes, we do, for we remember having heard it before, and that
is the work: bringing the painting to life, sensuously. My guess
is, while writing about what she is seeing, she does *hear* that
sound. Of course, this is because what she sees con-fuses with

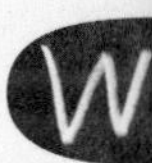

57 Holly, *Past Looking* (1996), 108.

58 Ibid.

her memories of what, in her life, she has heard. The senses work together. That is, precisely, the *work* of such artworks: it brings the viewer back to their own memories and experiences.[59]

THE OBJECT SPEAKS BACK

There is another aspect of this work of the artwork that brings the fourth chapter of Holly's new book, Dumas' paintings and notes, and my own work closer together. This can be summed up as what I have written many times, and resonates with Holly's view: 'the object speaks back.' I wrote this most explicitly in a short article requested by graduate students in cultural analysis, 'Learning Listening'. Holly says precisely that, but then on the visual activity: 'If paintings are meant to be looked at, they also have the capacity to look back.' That capacity brings the work-object to life as working; it is what the 'wonder' mentioned above consists of, or *does*. Looking back implies that simply putting in a figure as an 'illustration' of an intellectual argument is wrong. For me, that word 'illustration' ought to be banned from intellectual work. For it subordinates the image or quotation to serve as evidence that the argument that precedes it, must be right. This degrades the images to a subservient non-function. But no; if you take on the habit of looking back, after putting in the image or the quotation, to see if the two match perfectly, you will almost always see that the object quoted only partially, if at all, matches the preceding statement about it. When thinking of this argument, I suddenly had a strong, sensuous recollection of what picture books meant to me as a child. The story *was*, consisted of, the images. No need for the parents to read me the story, but when they did, I learned to listen.[60]

Instead of feeling frustrated by or denying the part where the two, the argument and the 'illustration'-quotation don't match, accepting and taking on the difference is the moment of learning. That moment of learning is the most precious, because innovative moment of meaning-making. It is when

---

59 See Holly, *Somewhere Between Art History and Phenomenology* (2025). Because the book is still in production, I cannot cite page numbers.

60 Bal, 'Learning Listening' (2019). Holly's quote doesn't have a page number yet.

the 'illustration' is not or not totally adequate, that as a scholar or student, you *learn*; something new appears. And that is the primary educational value of such acts of looking back. This retrospective comparison empowers the object to become, to behave as, a subject. Listening is a practice, as is looking. But, as with all practices, before we can practice it, we must learn to listen, learn to look, slowly and attentively. In the noisy world of today this demands serious commitment. In this acoustic whirlwind, and its visual equivalent, we have to learn to make (acoustic and visual) distinctions between voices, languages, tones, and moods; between colours, shapes, brush strokes and figurations. Only then can listening and looking be a socially useful practice; a critical one, in the constructive sense I have put forward under C. The objects of study of the Humanities have the unique potential to 'teach' us that practice. Through their complexity and subtlety, artworks, but also other cultural practices and even, simply, languages and their uses, can help us move beyond simplistic slogans and cursory readings of their alleged meanings.

To continue the entry on Q, quotations should not be used to confirm what a student says, but to complicate it. If we make a habit of systematically looking back at a quotation and carefully checking to what extent it confirms our point, we will often notice that this is rarely entirely the case. However, instead of panicking, thinking we are wrong, or worse, suppressing the differences, this complication can help us move beyond what we (think we) already know. Listening carefully to the object, treating it as a 'second person', an interlocutor who/that will take up the temporary role of first person, rather than a mute 'third person' *about* which we speak, is the 'apprenticeship' of listening and looking as a critical practice. There is no more concise way to explain how I envision the difference between cultural analysis and other approaches in the Humanities. In this, Holly's sentence just quoted is perfectly adequate to make that difference and its usefulness clear. What she foregrounds as phenomenology merges, con-fuses, with cultural analysis as we have articulated it with the foundation

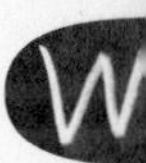

of the Amsterdam School for Cultural Analysis (ASCA) in 1995.[61]

That the object *is* a subject is quite obvious when the artwork is 'about' figurations of people. In my video work, this cannot be overlooked. One example makes this clear. Over the years 2006–2010, I built up a body of video works in which mothers of migrants spoke about what the departure of their child meant to them. I filmed the migrants' mothers in their own houses, where they talked about their motivation to support or their attempts to withhold their children who wished to leave, and about their own grief to see them go. The mothers converse about this crucial experience with a person close to them, often someone whose absence in her life was caused by the child's departure—a grandchild, a daughter-in-law, or the children themselves. I staged the women, asked their interlocutors to take place behind the camera, set the shot, turned the camera on, and left the scene. This method is hyperbolically documentary. To underline this aspect, I refrained from editing these shots.

The resulting slow, unsmooth, and personal monologues are confrontations with the need and difficulty to listen and look. The uninterrupted presence of their faces in the frame, compels viewers to look the women in the face and to listen to what they have to say, in a language that is foreign, using expressions that sometimes seem strange, but in a discourse to which we can affectively relate. The translations were made together with the close relative who did the interviews, and were placed above the faces instead of below as subtitles, so that it was easier to read them without looking away from the speaking face. This example is almost too obvious. Of course, those mothers are subjects! But what if the object is not a filmed person but a depicted one, or even not a figurative person but a landscape, a river, the colour of which does all the 'talking'? This is made explicit in Holly's analysis of Patinir's painting, where the central element is a blue river. The impactful colour is the painting's effect. But the effect is that it entices viewers to feel connected, so that, as she writes, effect leads to affect.

---

61 A collective volume appeared in which the pioneers who started the conceptualization of cultural analysis, theorize the specific approach that distinguishes cultural analysis from the traditional disciplines and from 'cultural studies'. See Aydemir, *The Future of Cultural Analysis* (2025).

And affect is something that *happens*; a moment that moves, so that movement becomes emotional entanglement. As Holly writes in the final chapter of her new book: 'An original work of visual art only becomes the viewer's when it elicits some kind of entangled response.' That idea of entanglement comes close to Lee's 'con-fusion'. It entails an impossibility to distance oneself from the artwork. This is not necessarily bound up with human-like figurations. The blue colour of that river is as powerful as a figure resembling a human being. That colour *works*; this is how an artwork becomes an object that *works*, hence, becomes a subject that speaks back. This is why I have devoted this entry to the ambiguity of work; an object becoming a subject, a noun becoming a verb. This is why we should stop talking about artworks and instead, keep saying, thinking, and reflecting on, 'the *work* of art'. That phrase accepts both sides of the original noun, altering it as we speak, or look, or listen.

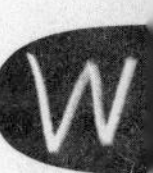

X-Ray

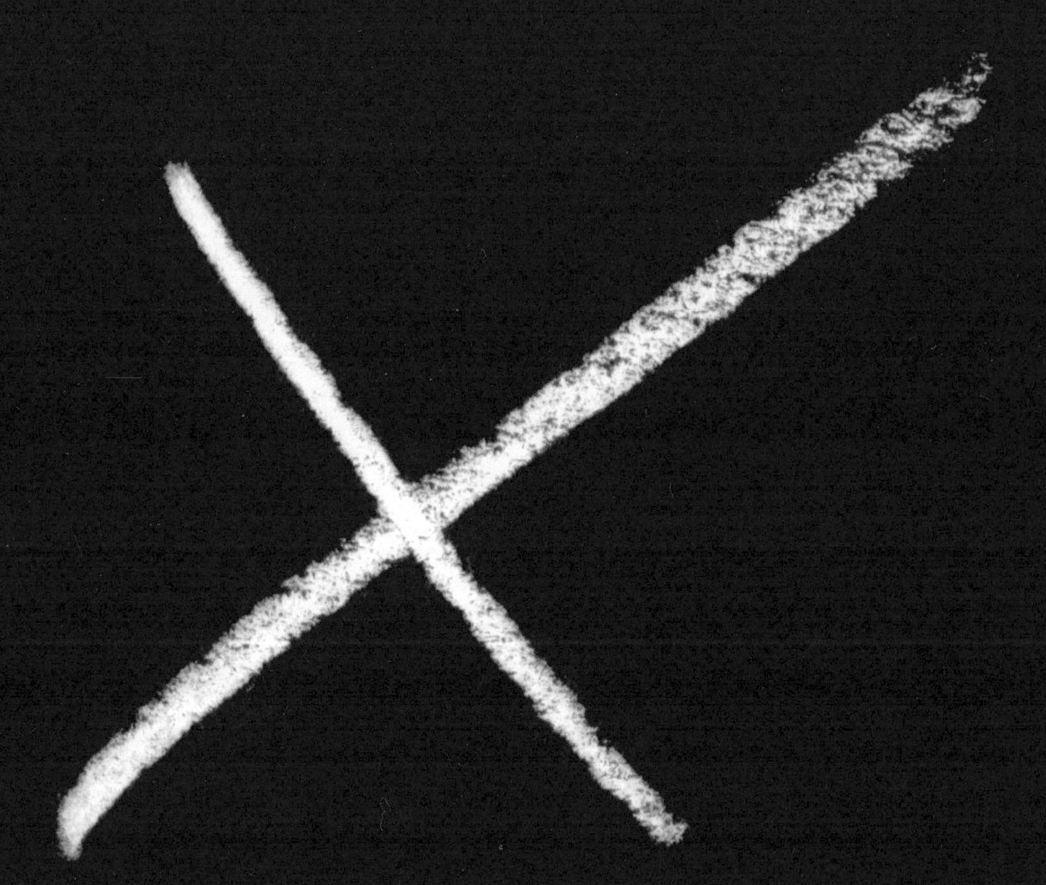

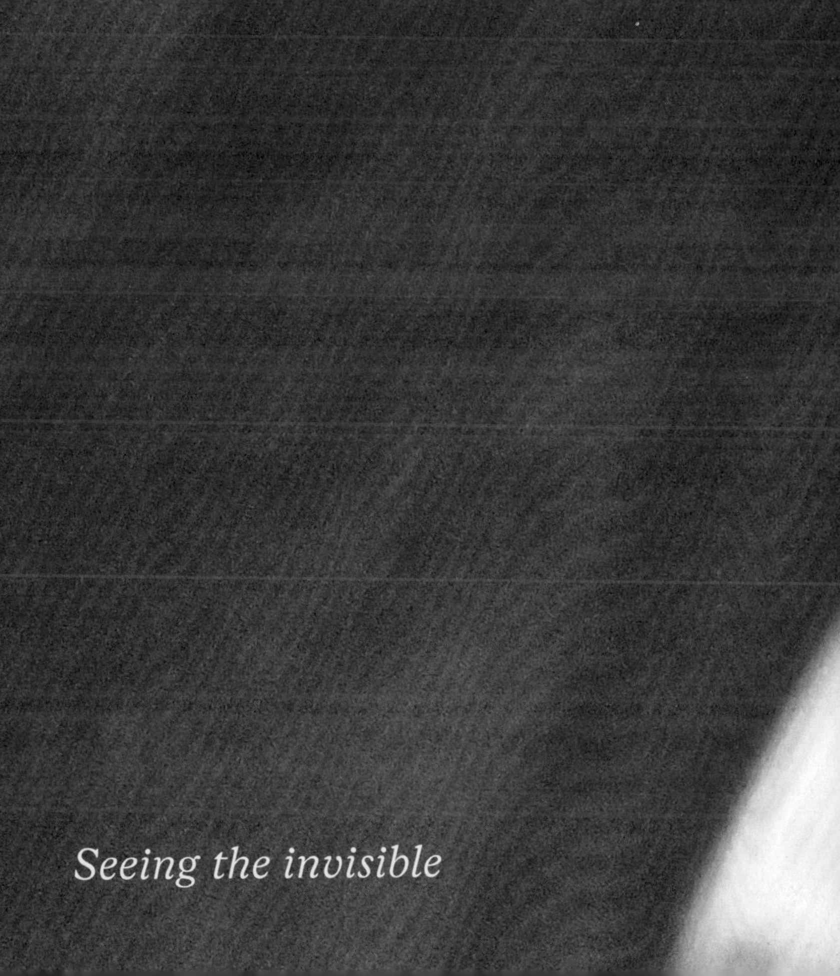

Seeing the invisible

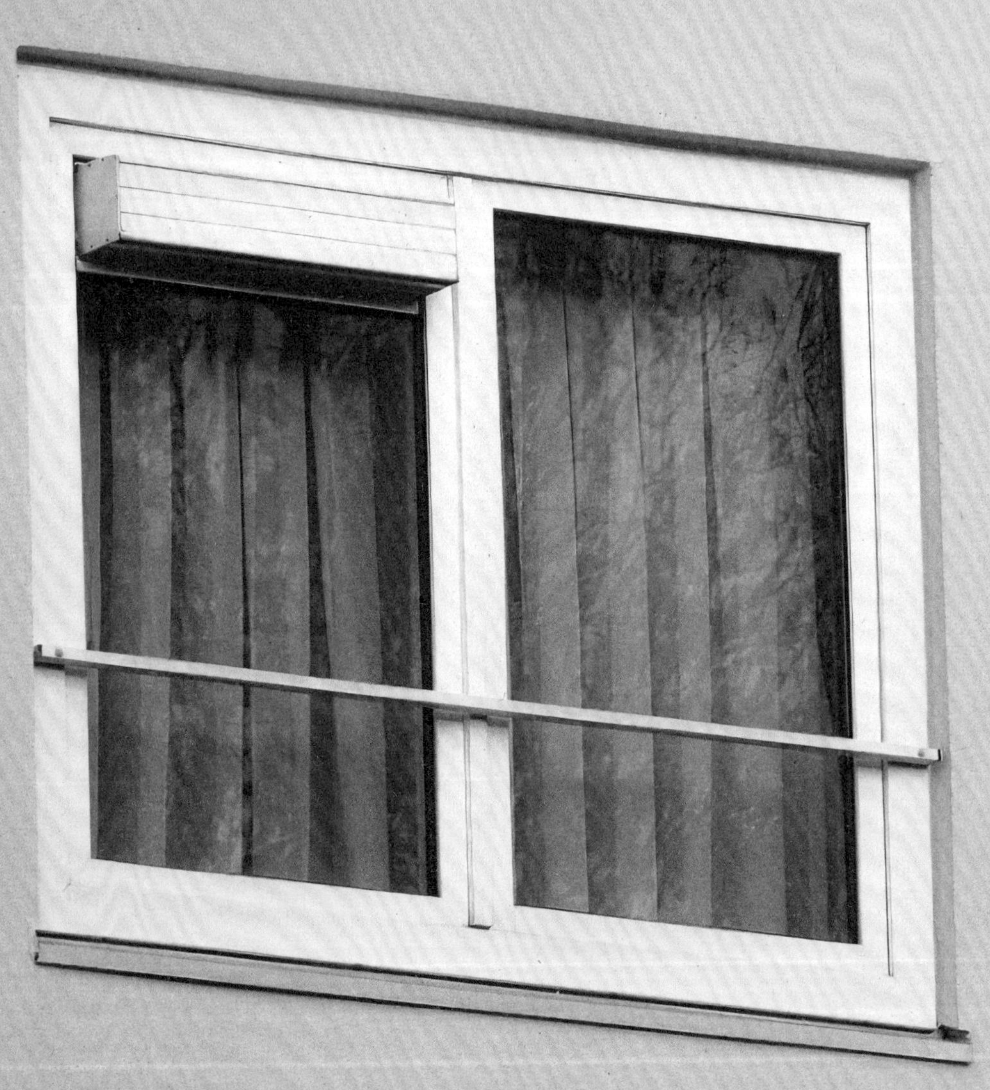

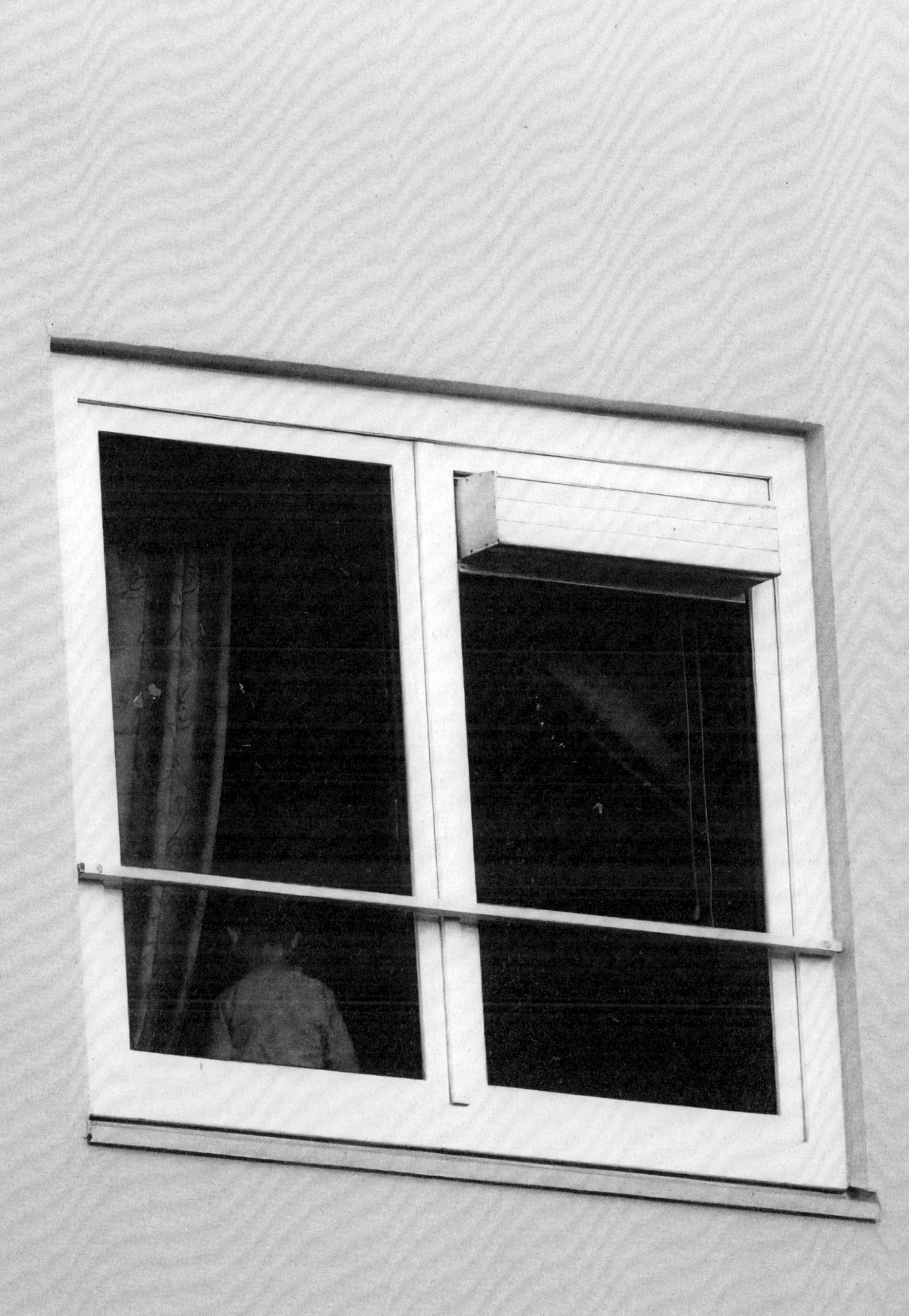

One of my frightening childhood experiences occurred when my younger sister broke her arm. I don't remember how; she must have fallen. But my parents panicked, of course, and took her straight to the hospital. When they came back, several apprehensive hours later, my sister had her arm in a cast, but looked rather cheerful. 'Does it hurt?' I asked. 'Not anymore', she answered. But Father was carrying a big scroll under his arm. He unpacked it, and there was a large plastic-looking sheet, mostly black, with some pieces of white. He explained that this was called an X-ray, a photograph of the bone of the broken arm. I was flabbergasted. So far, I had no idea what an X-ray was. When he explicated the point, the fact that a photograph of the inside of her arm had been made; that the white pieces were the bone of her arm, clearly broken as if it was a wooden stick. I was deeply impressed. It did look scary, but 'don't fear', he said; the broken pieces will grow together and, in a few months, her arm will be whole again. However, my emotion concerned not only the idea that the bone was actually broken, as the image demonstrated, but more, the unbelievable fact that the broken bone could be seen, shown, in a photograph.

For weeks, I kept turning and tossing in my bed, awaking with the question how she could sleep, now that the arm would inevitably be painful so that she was bound to lay on one side only. But also, that scary, spooky image of her bone, in pieces. How could I, how dared I, look inside her body? It felt so indiscreet. Father had also told us that the German-Dutch medical scholar Wilhelm Röntgen had invented the technique. That name, and the term derived from it, I had vaguely heard before. Röntgen had called the images X-rays because there was no known name attached to the technology. And clearly, calling it after himself was beyond his personal modesty. For me, the relevance of the X-ray was the possibility of seeing the invisible. As if the body, its flesh, had become transparent. This was, for the child I was, a discovery that would stay with me for the rest of my learning life.

One recent moment in that process of learning was when I had the chance to read a book-in-production by media scholar Nanna Verhoeff of Utrecht University, the third chapter of which she had titled 'crossing'. Published by Amsterdam University Press, the book examines intersections and interactions of screens in the public urban space. The book's title, *Urban Screens: Situations, practices, Concepts*, clearly lays out its programme of analytical study and teaching cultural analysis. She came up with a newly coined concept, *XR*, as one of a range of abbreviations including AR (Augmented Reality), VR (virtual reality), and MR (Mixed Reality). In that row of concepts XR came to mean 'crossing realities'. She sought to 'explore the shapes and forms of *crossing* as the main principle at the heart of XR', and as she wrote in the preface, in order to understand how the practice of crossing enables us 'to use crossing as a concept to examine how urban screens can make different "realities" intersect'. The letter X, here, acquires the additional meanings of movement and merging, which can only further enrich the 'Röntgenish' meaning of making the invisible visible. For that earlier meaning, the idea of transparency is key, along with the recognition that seeing the invisible is, in fact, impossible. Only thanks to Röntgen's experiments and discoveries has the medical establishment been enabled to transgress that limit of what the eye can see. The medical community can see, or make visible, what cannot be seen, and thus help detect breaks and tumours—dangerous situations inside the body.

In the previous entry, I have insisted, in interaction with Michael Ann Holly's publications, on the priority of 'work' in our interaction with images. In an earlier book, although translated into English ten years after its first publication in German, philosopher Emmanuel Alloa contributed to Holly's claim concerning the work of art by more insistently including the spectator as a worker. Alloa's book, like Holly's newest one, also makes phenomenology, that branch of philosophy that takes the experience of readers and viewers into account, the core of our interactions with images and other visual experiences. Alloa's main title is 'Looking *Through* Images'. The preposition 'through' alludes to the 'diaphanousness' of images: their inherent 'transparency' where light is indispensable for the image to become attached to a medium. That preposition brings back the memory of our looking through the skin and flesh of the wounded child to thus see the invisible inside of her body.

Because of that preposition 'through', the indicator of the

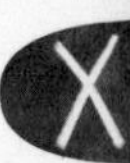

possibility of traversing visually the layers of substance that stand between the outside and the inside, Alloa's book is, in fact, a decisive step forward in the theorization of mediality. Rejecting the idea of the supposed stillness of images, he insists that images do something: they *appear*; and that appearance is their 'work', to recall Holly's core concept put forward under W. It is their active appearance that demonstrates the importance of appearing, which is an activity only feasible in interaction with the 'seer', the spectator who allows and accepts, and actively sees the image in its appearance. It is not a matter of 'reading' and thus solving the riddle (what does this image mean?); the appearance and thus the meaning of what appears, comes into plain sight. That coming is a movement, an occurrence in a moment; *time* returns. Only on that condition can we *see* it. Seeing, thus, requires the participation that seeing the appearance demands. This view rejects the idea that the artwork is an object, a still 'thing'. Instead, it is the interactive, dialogic nature of the visuality that includes both 'object' and viewer, that makes visuality possible at all.

MAKING THE INVISIBLE VISIBLE

This thrust of making the invisible visible was and is the purpose of Indian artist Nalini Malani's art-making, according to her many pronouncements on this. All through her lifelong passionate working, she has been pursuing that goal. And for me, this is what 'art' is about. It is its *work*. The invisibility of problems, traumas, losses, injustices, and other problematic confrontations with the world and its people, can only be remedied if the invisible can yield, as if through X-rays, to visibility. This has also been, all along, my motivation to make videos. One of the first videos I (co-)made was devoted to a situation I could not endorse; the unfair hostility of European governmental measures against so-called 'illegal' immigrants. Although it was always obvious to me that no one, no person, can be 'illegal', I did encounter situations where this question of (il-)legality did come up. One was a temporary neighbour in Paris, when I was teaching there for a semester. And to the extent that this issue appeared, simply when I met that neighbour in the courtyard of our building, as a European citizen I could not abide by it. As a consequence, I began to make videos as a medium to analyze the impossibility of that term, 'illegal', as well as other social issues. That first film I made, titled *A Thousand and One Days*, alluding to the classical Arabic literature, still helps me to understand and endorse my resistance against the idea of 'illegal' people. This impossibility is invisible; it is just 'the law', as if the law is shielded from personhood and the responsibility that belongs to it, and from visibility.

Art and the resulting 'work' are an integral part of the socio-political issues that problem raises. Making the invisible visible, as the equivalent of X-raying, can help. My sister's broken arm got rid of some of its mystery when the X-ray showed the actual broken piece of bone, and her recovery helped. However, that the break had become visible, although it couldn't really be seen from the outside, expanded my experience of seeing considerably. This has made me wonder about what I see, if I see it, and if not, what else is there to see? The double question of what it is I see and what it is I cannot see has remained with me ever since. Alloa's insistence that it is the (active) appearance that decides what seeing is and what we see, seems to me a most fruitful way of thinking-seeing. Only when the appearance shows its face and we, as viewers, respond to that appearance, seeing becomes possible, productive, and sensually effective; visually but also auditively, olfactorily, and tactily. That the senses collaborate, so that the appearances can work together, produces a rich, multi-sensorial, synesthetic experience that helps the invisible to become visible. This is how seeing becomes an indispensable, active verb. This multi-sensorial appearance and its active, interactive dialogue response is what makes visuality a relevant, albeit not mono-sensorial, 'medium'.[62]

To understand better how culture works, we must move beyond the standard idea of fixating or, as some critically-thinking media specialists have it, 'classifixating', in other

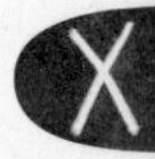

---

62 For an extensive discussion of intermediality, see my article 'Citational Aesthetics' (2023).

words, boxing in specific images and their works in genre-categories. This is an ironic concept coined by Van der Tuin and Verhoeff in a 'dictionary' of concepts 'for the creative humanities' as the authors call it, from 2022. That invented term *classifixation* describes actions that determine what images mean, instead of allowing them to appear in various ways, with various meanings. The best way to consider the meaning of images is by allowing them to appear in any way they want, and responding in kind. Of course, the phrase 'they want' suggests an intention that images as such cannot have. But both their makers and their curators, installers, and other 'framers', as well as their viewers as 'second persons', contribute to the possibilities of appearing. Classifixation fixates instead of liberating thought. If, rather, we wish to let images have their say, do their work in their appearing, it is necessary to respond to them, as viewers, in ways that facilitate variation, freedom, and activity. Of course, no image can be 'still' in the usual sense, if we allow this. As we should. This appearing-based moving activity of the 'work of art' and its reciprocal interaction with viewers leads to a specific conception of aesthetics that, in loyalty to what counts most in that interaction, I like to call 'moving'.

MOVING AESTHETICS

Instead of condemning image to stillness, we and the images are better off if we consider them according to Gilles Deleuze's 'Sahara aesthetics'. This is a concept according to the idea of constant moving and changing, of the impossibility of classi-fixation and instead, of accepting the impossibility to fix down the aesthetic as well as the meaning of what we see. If this aesthetics is moving, that verb/qualifier does not simply mean that it entails physical movement, but also, at the same time, of being emotionally moving. And that implies that the spectators are also participating in this double movement; being moved does not leave them still.

I now associate the X-ray, the visibilization of the invisible, with another experience of seeing, which seems almost the opposite. Whereas the X-ray compelled seeing the inside of the body, I also once experienced seeing nothing with my eyes wide open, while being inside the working artwork. This was my first visual encounter with the famous 'mist rooms' of Belgian artist Ann Veronica Janssens—also a favourite artist, about whose work I have written a book, titled *Endless Andness*. My enthusiasm about the visual experience of her work began with the astounding moment of seeing nothing at all. But whereas the idea of 'not seeing' is usually associated with darkness, the dense, impenetrable mist packed into the space whose limits I could not even guess was so bright that it seemed made out of kitsch fantasies of heaven. The kind of clouds angels sit on, little fat putti with egg-shell skin and bodies too appealing to be decently angelic. The clouds of Renaissance and Baroque painting. Except that such clouds have shapes and this mist did not. Or rather, whatever shape it might have had was invisible to me. Shapes can only be seen from the outside, and I was inside the heavenly cloud. Imprisoned in nothingness. No X-ray to help me here.[63]

After a while, ever so slowly it seemed—but time was arrested as much as sound—vague lines came through. The event of their coming to visibility was just that: an event, occurring in time; a movement, an appearance. The change in the space consisted of a gradual, partial receding of the absolute opacity of the white that surrounded me and that stuck to my skin, challenging my sense of my own boundaries. That whiteness seemed a reversed X-ray. When this receding took place, I became aware of my own dissolution. Thus, the after-effect of the event retrospectively turned the initial experience into an unsettling one, which it had not been until then. Here, another event happened, a deeply narrative one in that it had the retroversive capacity to change the state of what, before, I would have called 'my mind'.

Now, I couldn't call it that any longer. For the anxiety I did not feel at first but which was created by contrast and after

63 *Endless Andness* (2013) focuses on the political power of the coherence the artist brings to the 'endlessly' additive work she puts forward. It is one volume of a trilogy of books on the political power of art as activating. The other two are *Thinking in Film* (2013), devoted to film and video maker Eija-Liisa Ahtila and *Of What One Cannot Speak* (2010) on sculptor Doris Salcedo.

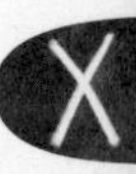

the fact, was an anxiety 'of the heart'. According to Baroque philosopher Blaise Pascal: 'Le *cœur* a ses raisons que la raison ne connaît pas.' The heart as the seat of a domain of reason that reason does not know, or that it actively ignores: this was what I discovered. The mind-body or the body-mind acts on its own. What happened when I felt the earlier possibility of fear was a 'retroversion'. Retroversion is a narrative figure. We know such figures from novels, not from visual art, be it figurative, abstract, or conceptual. Retroversion is a narrative device that requires a narrative agent, a narrator, to manipulate the linearity of time. Readers are given access to a universe of events that run through time in different directions, criss-crossing where time thickens. Hence my choice of the octopus as the key metaphor of time, as I briefly introduced it under T. Retroversion empowers the reader or viewer; it gives access to unknown worlds. It opens our lives to manifold possibilities that console us in our grief of being bound, hands and feet, by time's tyranny. In Janssens' mist room I was without sight and blissfully coming into sight at the same time.[64]

The access to the visibility of the lines was also the emergence through the limitless cloud, of the ceiling, plinths, and corners of the room; appearing out of an X-ray of the space. An emergence barely identifiable; fragile, in permanent danger of annihilation. Only now could I begin to see—helped by the knowledge that it was likely—that I was indeed in a room. I could see its square forms and its proportions. But lingering on my retina—on my skin, for retina and skin were by now abandoning their ongoing struggle for mutual independence—was the sensation of a moment earlier, when no space other than the absolute was present for me. What was happening with and within me during that slow appearance was an experience of *duration* as an implausibly important element of perception; *an X-ray of time*. This was a unique moment of meaning-making.

Not only were the boundaries of my body—my skin as protection and site of vulnerability and access—less obvious than I had always assumed them to be. Not only was being inside the heavenly cloud incompatible with seeing it. Not only was vision a slowly granted and slowly developed privilege. The

---

64 Pascal's writings have been posthumously published for the first time in 1670 with the title *Pensées* (Thoughts) by the éditions de Port Royal. Also see Pascal, *The Harvard Classics* (1910).

duration of perception was also uneven in its rhythm, unstable in its linearity, dense and pervasive in its impact, and wavering in its location, siding, now with the subject, me, then with the object, the unstable lines I was beginning to see. But then again, those notions—subject, object—and the distinction they proclaim, lost their own boundaries, their separate identities. They became as vague and blurred as the mist.

All this time I could not walk. I was nailed to the floor, fearful even of shuffling my feet forward, as the blind might feel when deprived of their aids. Walking, even when safety can be expected, is impossible without the help of perception. Pondering this, I heard a hissing sound. It seemed close by, but of course I could not gauge its distance from me. I could not see its source, or interpret its meaning. Perhaps it was there for a purpose; perhaps also it was part of the installation. But then, perhaps it was arbitrary, belonging to the air-conditioning system of the building. Who was to say where 'the work' began and ended, where its performance stitched its seams to its environment? The sound was not loud, but in the total silence of the fog-cushioned space it constituted an unsettling interruption. Like the emergence of lines, the hissing constructed the preceding silence at the very moment the silence was broken; a sonic X-ray.

The room of mist is now a stage on which I play a role I have never played before. What kind of visuality is at stake here? As a result of previous visual experiences—of painting, of installations of paintings in spite of their installations, but also of the world around our bodies and around the visual object that we see and perceive as 'works of art'—the mobilized body, conjured into participation *qua* body, is the same body whose eyes are doing the looking, responding to the appearing. Hence, in contrast to the disembodied gaze, which is a-temporal and does not even know it has a body let alone a body involved in looking, the mode of looking which is not only desirable for this space but also the only one possible, the only one that leads to seeing, is a *participatory* look. Seeing *through* the mist is an instance of that crossing for which the letter X also stands; the diaphanous moment of 'looking through images', to recall Alloa's title.

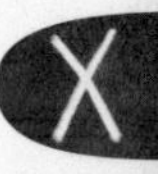

Thus, the 'work of art' drives the point home that the debate on how to gain knowledge is not over. This intellectual posture, this embodied look, is not only epistemologically indispensable, necessary for knowledge to become possible. It concerns being; it is ontological. The notion of *performance* seems most appropriate for characterizing it. While I am sitting in, or standing on the stage of Janssens' mist, this concept suddenly thickens, on the waves of bizarrely intensified and messy duration. Since the adventure described above, which was my first encounter with Janssens' extraordinary work, I have entered into many different versions of that mist installation. They are not always cloud-white, but can have different colours, challenging the limits between one colour and the next. The effects are different, but what remains constant is the experience that, in addition to the unsettling of our certainties, also, seeing is touching. Both seeing and touching are experiential, sensual sensations. Such a conception of seeing has been discussed in view of Deleuze's and others' theories of 'haptic' seeing. It was developed by Deleuze and Guattari in *A Thousand Plateaus*.[65]

Haptic, from the Greek *aptô* ('touching') is characterized by three primary features. It solicits proximity, inviting viewers to caress the image with the eyes; it is formless, and lines change their function, from delimiting fields to moving between points. All these features are key to Janssens' mist rooms, whether these are primarily white or adding changes of colours to the event, so that in addition to form, transitions from one colour to another become also ungraspable. Janssens inflects these features of haptic seeing while maintaining them in near-hyperbolic force. Proximity in her work does not lead to the impressionist fusion of foreground and background. Instead, the works' work hinders that fusion, maintaining the intense experience of the incommensurability of distance and proximity. Formlessness shifts gears as well. The spectator is part of it, as becomes clear when, vaguely, someone else emerges from the mist, as another appearance. This can be a disconcerting sensation. Finally, while the blurry lines remain moving between points, as haptic lines do, their movement precludes access to any points whatsoever. Instead of clarity, something happens that is of the order of the heart: what we

---

65 Deleuze and Guattari, *A Thousand Plateaus* (1987), 614 and following.

call moving. This is what we learn at such moments. I would like to insist that this word always contains a double movement: physical or perceptual and emotional. 'Touching' would be the right word for this, thanks to its ambiguity.

I said above that this experience was like a reversed X-ray. To be inside that which one sees is an extreme experience, as much as was that seeing inside my sister's body. But it can be considered, also, crucial for what seeing is. In the space, the object seen and the subject seeing are together, surrounded by and immersed in a space we don't even notice because it is so obvious.

It is only an assumption, unwarranted, that seeing is an autonomous act of distinguishing subject from object; the subject in power, the object available for the visual taking. This is wrong; a colonializing conception of seeing, based on an untenable but tenacious conception that has tyrannized scholarship with a harsh opposition between subjective and objective, a polarization that privileges the latter. In visual art, the subject-object opposition has been historically enhanced by the insistent practice of linear perspective. Significantly, the mist rooms have no perspective whatsoever.

And if formerly self-evident space is indissolubly bound up with seeing, this dimension has an inevitable counterpart. Janssens' mist works also breach the self-evident nature of time passing. These works foreground the humbling need to learn to walk again, small slow step by small slow step, because nothing can be taken for granted. Instead of visual mastery, here there is a sense of danger, of insecurity in relation to the act of seeing. This is already a strong feeling, bodily experienced. And the slowdown the experience enforces stands for the need, more in general, to take the time or give the time to really see, in an active response to the appearance. The X-ray of the body and the slow entrance into the space are crossing. But even if these transformations of sensation change our bodily awareness profoundly, the touch comes in most strongly when other visitors enter the space and my own line of sight crosses theirs. We must conclude, then, that acts of seeing are performances of tentative encounters. Fragile, touching, moving, crossing. But never one-sided, passive, still.

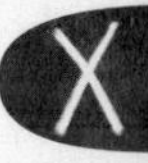

You
and Yes, Yesterday, Yoke, Youth, Yours, or Yummy vs Yuck

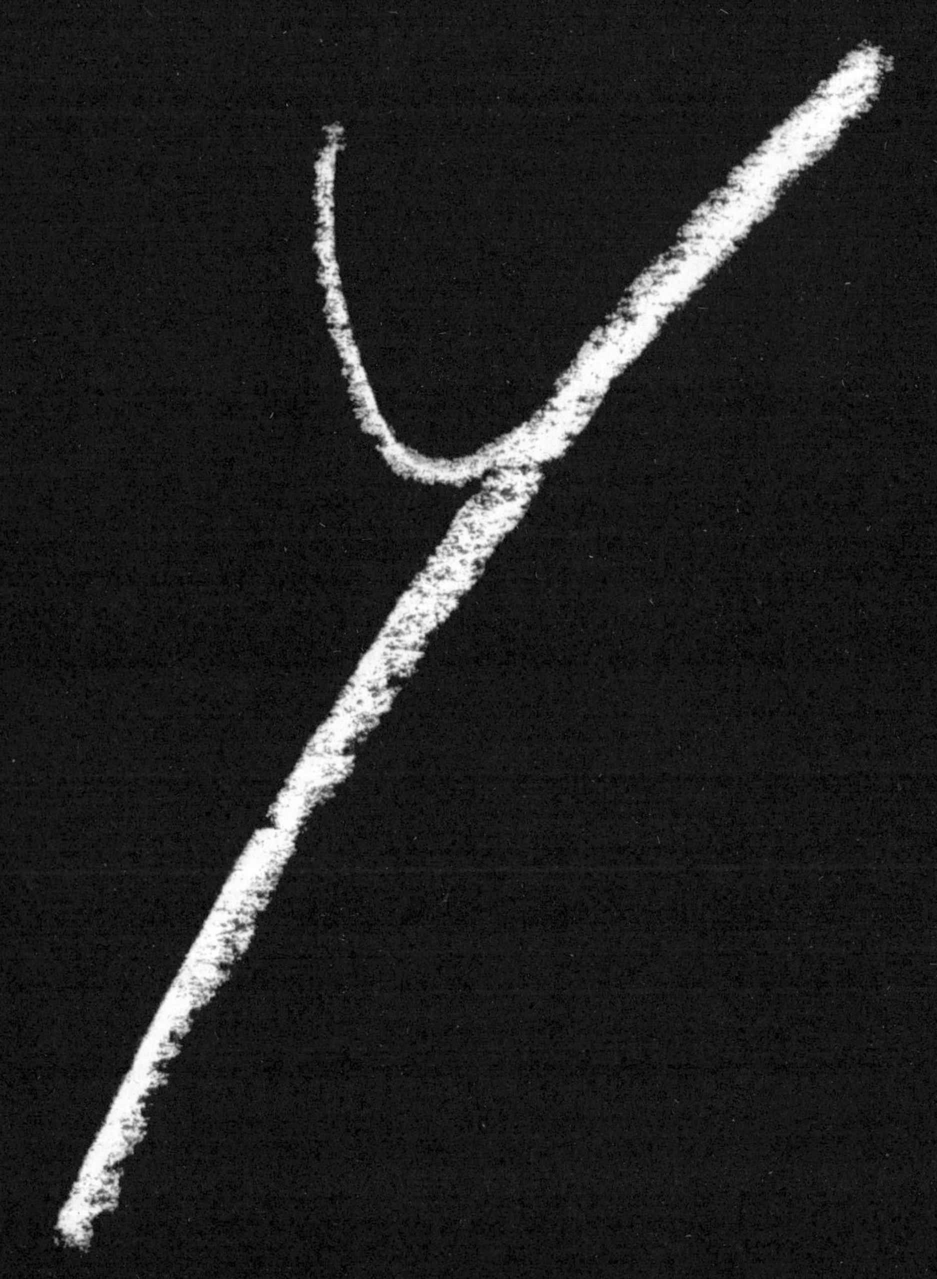

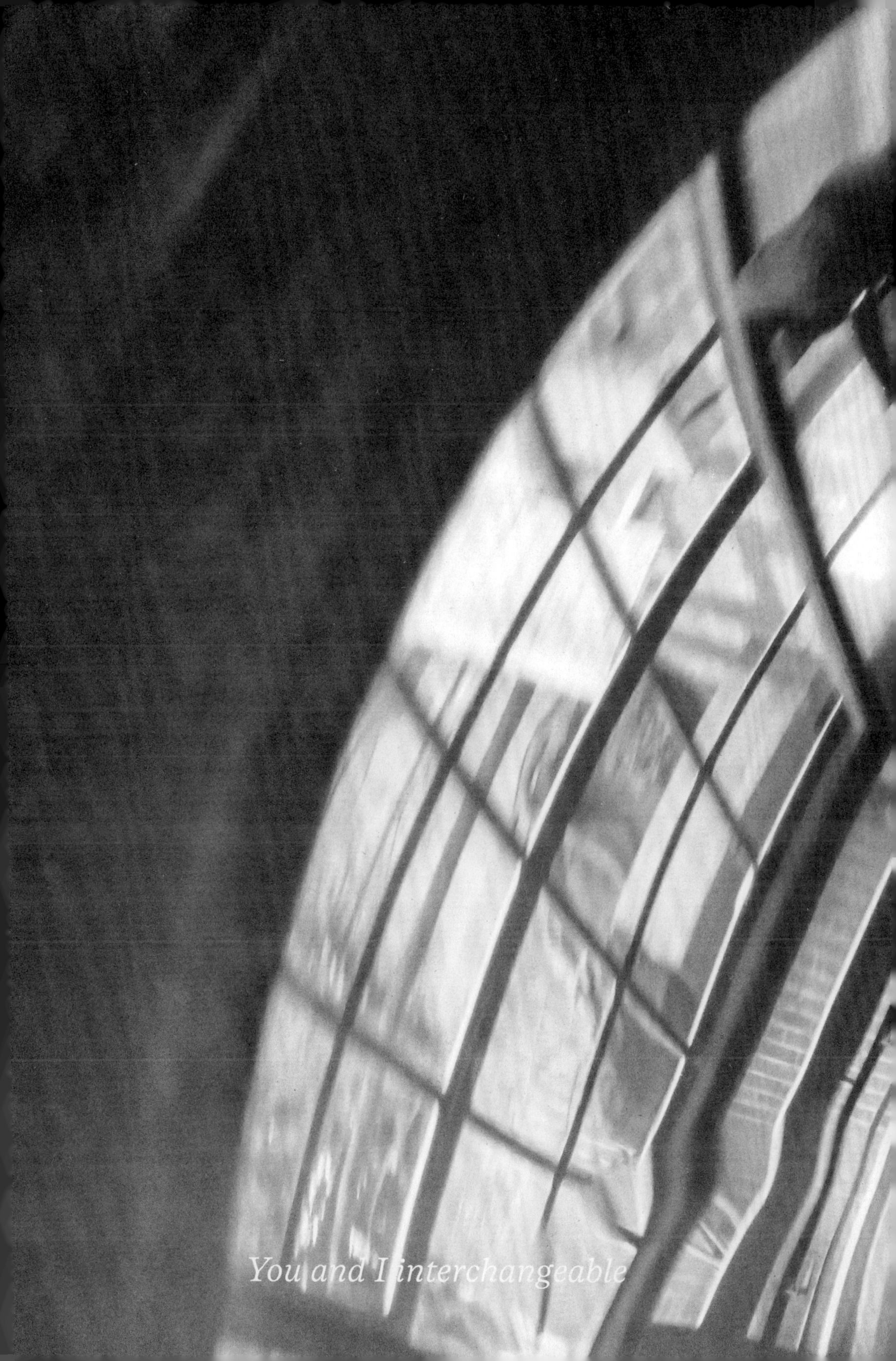

You and I interchangeable

The explicit address to the 'second person' is less obvious in narrative and visual artworks than the speech by a 'first person', the 'I', usually seen as the narrator or artist. In literary text and artworks, the 'first person' is considered the primary speaker, the artist, author, or their fictional substitute, called the narrator, who addresses others. The point, here, is *address*. When talking about, describing, or depicting others, we consider the discourse a 'third-person' one. In third-person narratives, the figures 'about' whom the narrator speaks, or whom the artist depicts, seem to be the object; the ones who have no say in what is being presented. The primary speakers may gossip about them, slander, or, instead, praise them. Or just tell about events in which 'they' participate.

The concept of 'object' is fitting for that position. By being discarded from the communication, that 'third person' is fixated into a thing. In contrast, the voice that speaks as an 'I', the so-called first person, is the subject. This makes the subject-object distinction a hard one. I have never been comfortable with that distinction; I could never believe in it. For me, it was always crucial to be able to say 'I' in order to express my opinions and visions of what, according to such divisions, would be the 'third person', the object about whom we speak, but without turning those third persons into objects. That subject-object distinction never sat well with me. This was partly due to the home situation, where the parental authority was rather strong, and where, as a small girl, I didn't get much of a chance to say what I wanted; to take on the 'first-person' position. As I have written above, whenever I had an opinion to express, as I tended to have, I was usually shut up, silenced, for being too headstrong, stubborn, pig-headed, priggish, and as a consequence of those judgments, never to be taken seriously, or even believed. On silencing as shutting up, see under S. So, the status of 'you', of the second person, was more or less withheld from me. At least, in the exchange between first and second, which is the essence of language. The key is exchange, which presupposed equality.

The inequality built into those judgment-induced dismissals has been a lifelong frustration for me. I always felt that as a 'you', a second person, I was never taken seriously enough. One first person would be addressing me, but without allowing the exchange between the two positions of first and second person, which is the key to communication. I was a 'you' only in the sense that I was given orders and prohibitions, rather than having conversational exchanges between the two positions. The grammatical terms that have 'person' as their primary noun and a number as their qualifier, foregrounds the personhood of each of the participants in the conversation, or interaction. Stubborn as I was, I tended to claim the 'first-personhood' as a right to speak, after being addressed as the 'you'. The way I was frequently silenced made that urge even more important for my sense of self. The right to turn the binary around, and take the first-person position up in response to the address directed to me as a 'you', seemed crucial to being a person at all.

However, I was often told off, silenced, as the young one who had no serious right to speak up. But I couldn't let that happen. The fact that, as they told me, I was too young, to cite another Y term, in other words, that my youth disqualified me as a speaker, deprived me from any sense of authority as in 'having something to say'. But it only made me more adamant to express my thoughts. To put it simply: from my position as a 'you', I demanded to be recognized as a potential 'I', a first person, addressing the previous first person now as a 'you', a second person, on a basis of equality. This later became the principle of dialogue. And dialogue, the only way equality could work in communication, has therefore become the core principle of my life, as a teacher, a mother, a scholar, a colleague, a friend.

Second-personhood, or to be taken seriously as a 'you' who becomes an 'I' in the follow-up of response, is crucial to human life. It defines it. I have written about this in various vignettes, such as F, for friendship, where I presented the conception of philosopher Lorraine Code, who fundamentally revised the antique notion of teaching through the concept of the lover, transforming it into a friend. And a bit more on this under Q. But beyond my personal frustration, I have also developed second-personhood as the 'you' of narrative and visual art. During my French studies I got to know the novel *La modification* by Michel Butor, the only second-person novel we knew of at the

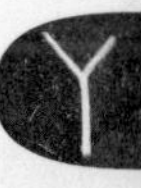

time, and I didn't quite feel convinced by it. In my reading, it was a first-person novel disguised as a second-person one. The problem seemed to be that it was more a formal 'translation' than a truly 'you'-oriented narrative. The main reason of that was that it never shifted, never was there an exchange.

In my 1999 book *Quoting Caravaggio*, wherein I articulated a sense of time based on mutuality between present and past, I devoted an entire chapter to 'you-ness', so to speak, which I termed 'second-person narrative'. There, I unfolded the complexity of the exchange in relation to my attempt to move beyond the traditional word-image opposition, and in connection to that one, the space-time distinction. Neither of these oppositions *works*, in the sense of the activity of art discussed under W. Almost reaching the end of this alphabetic series of merging personal memories and subsequent conceptual thoughts, it seems appropriate to revise once more the traditional conceptions of art and thought *together*, as I have attempted to do in my 2022 book under the heading of its main title, *Image-Thinking*.

THE STICKINESS OF IMAGES

With my habit, or hobby, of inventing non-existing words, phrases or concepts, in that chapter of the 1999 book I use the qualifier 'sticky' for images that compel more time than the usual rush through galleries. Two of the artists I invoke, or let's say, address there, are American painter David Reed (1946), and Norwegian artist Jeannette Christensen (1958). I have extensively written about both, albeit in very different framings and projects, but they both appear in the chapter mentioned. What they have in common, in spite of their totally different modes and media of making art that works, is that the resulting works *work*. They work by holding the viewer, compelling durational looking, even if the art of the one, Reed, is technically still, and that of Christensen is often moving, in the sense that it changes over time.[66]

---

66 On the work of Reed, see my article 'Second-Person Narrative' (1996), 179–204, and the relevant passages in *Quoting Caravaggio* (1999), as shown in the book's index. On Christensen, in addition to the same book, also my book *Fragments of Matter* (2009) on her work.

One series of sculptural objects by Christensen has made the point of temporality emphatically clear. Instead of sculpting with marble, Christensen has made that series out of the sweet dessert substance called Jell-O, made from gelatine, for example. She created human-size straight beds looking like benches, which begin as brilliantly smooth surfaces, intensely red. But they deteriorate, mould, over time, in a few weeks. They even end up smelling nasty, which made me concerned for the gallery guards sitting in close proximity to them, for entire days. The yummy dessert becomes frankly yuck, if I may play again on the letter Y. This insertion of two words that are usually attributed to children, those young ones with their informal use of words, is not as arbitrary as it may seem. For, it brings up again the meagre, semi-poor food our too-densely populated household provided, and for which, as the near-permanent cook of the house, I was held responsible, but often only got to eat the left-overs, given the time the cooking took. My cooking duty had enormous temporal implications. Christensen's Jell-O benches with their decay over time, use, as their primary material, something that in my youth I barely ever got to eat, since dessert was a rare luxury. This connects the issue of food and near-poverty to that of materiality and the time that eats it up. Sometimes, liquid stains come out of the gelatin, shaping as beautiful abstract objects (1999). There, two colours from the material separate into red and yellow, outside of the artist's intention, and make abstract-looking stains on the floor. She also makes art that deteriorates in a different way, such as polaroid photographs that, over time, fade and lose colour and sharpness. Or things that have movement built into them, as sculptures that rise up and lay down again, thanks to a ventilator inside them. (171 of the 1999 book) She also makes exasperatingly slow videos, that look more like photos or paintings (inspired by Vermeer). The slowness, the Vermeer-ish stillness is suddenly interrupted when the model turns her face to the viewer. This is the moment when, as a viewer, *you* are implicated, addressed, called in. In one of Christensen's exhibitions I was myself asked to participate in this. Of course, this was a moment of raising my awareness of the *work* of art even more strongly.

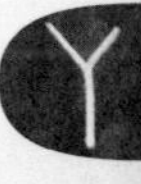

David Reed suspends that other binary, between flatness
and spatial three-dimensionality. His paintings are known as
abstract, because no human figures are depicted. Reed is a fundamentally Baroque painter. It is in the Baroque tradition that
he finds the kind of 'second-personhood', the *you*, that enables
him to narrate outside of the realm of figuration, but in a more
intensely second-person narrative way. But if the qualifier
'abstract' is used in the sense assigned to that term in other
contexts, namely, to mean the opposite of concrete, tangible,
then, I would argue, Reed's art is emphatically *not* abstract.
For, it is neither disembodied nor rationalistic; instead, it is
extremely sensuous. Nor is Reed's work expressionist; on the
contrary, Reed appears to oppose the whole idea of abstract
expressionism, with its two problematic words. His work has
nothing of the tangible layering of brush strokes that is the
most distinctive mark of a certain brand of abstract expressionism. Nowhere is there the mark of the artist's hand.

Instead, Reed's work is making an astounding composition
of folds and curls, with straight lines seeming to interrupt
that play. And colour is its primary element. The connection
to Caravaggio's art, even without a single figurative element,
does appear to be strong. This is mainly due to its appeal to the
exchange between 'I' and 'you', which seems irresistibly erotic.
On this, my detailed ('close') analysis of Caravaggio's *John
the Baptist* on pages 186–198 in my 1999 book may be helpful.
This view of the Old Master painting in connection to Reed's
work has been taken up again in my short film *It's About Time!*,
where a painting by Reed shifts over Caravaggio's *John the
Baptist*, next to which the film's actor playing Aeneas is sitting,
imitating the pose of the latter. The tripartite combination of
the cinematic-narrative event, the Old Master painting which
may well be that artist's most emphatically 'you' address, and
the contemporary pseudo-abstract painting makes the point
of Reed's transgression of the flatness/volume and the still/
moving binaries emphatic. But that transgression is subservient to the main point: the importance of the second person.
For Reed's multi-sensuous appeal to the viewer that turns his
paintings into sticky images, is the point here.[67]

67 Here is the link to that film on time in which Reed's painting is at work:
youtu.be/DK-5lbK4t5M.

In spite of the total absence of figuration, the paintings of Reed emanate a very strong, lush attraction. In this respect they address the viewer as a 'you'. The work of the brush strokes with the shapes and colours is so powerful, indeed, moving, that as viewers one feels compelled to respond to it, emotionally as well as sensuously. It is as if the surface of the canvas is not, cannot be, flat. Somehow, the artist is capable of making the folds and curls not only strongly attractive, but moving, in the double sense. This is mainly due to their three-dimensionality effect. They come forward, so forcefully that the desire to touch, caress them, becomes almost over-whelming. This effect is enhanced by the different surfaces, which suggest a variety of materials.

In this way, the non-figurative surfaces come very close to the material effects in Caravaggio's paintings. Visual erotics, as distinct from expressionism, is not based on the inscription of the 'I' in the work, but on the inscription of the strongest possible dynamic between the 'I' and the 'you' grounded in a sense-based attraction that is not limited to vision, nor to one of the two persons. Instead of imagining tactile roughness as a trace of the maker's hand, one wants to caress or even lick the surfaces. But, while leaving self-expression behind, Reed's work holds on to the passionate abstraction that is characteristic of the preceding generation. For a partial engagement with, and distancing from, a narrative outside of figuration, he has to look elsewhere.

This erotic tactility joins and then breaks away from yet another predecessor: Francis Bacon. In his totally different mode, both figurative and pastose, Bacon also locates narrativity in the contact between painting and viewer rather than in the image. Ernst van Alphen develops a pragmatics of vision as a narratology of Bacon's painting: 'I have proposed a narrative reading in which Bacon's works represent a pragmatics of vision as the narrative of perception.' And he aptly describes the resulting narrative as follows:

> This narrative would then have a double status. On the one hand, it would be diegetic: the events acted

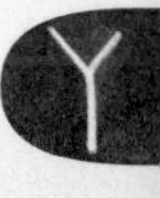

out by the figures in the representations are events
of perception. On the other hand, this diegetic narrative *about* perception would be doubled in relation to
the viewer. The narrative could be called apostrophic
and metonymic: it touches the viewer.[68]

Whereas Reed's paintings, with their non-figurative forms
and non-pastose mode, have nothing visibly in common with
Bacon's work, the essence of Bacon's engagement with the
viewer through a pragmatic, you-oriented narrativity is the
most important feature of the work of both painters.

There is even a comparable temporal shift at work in these
painters' narrative modes: just as Reed's surface kicks the eye
back, then attracts it again, so Bacon insisted on having his
paintings framed behind glass, thus hampering the visibility
of their impasto. As Van Alphen contended in a personal
communication, this is Bacon's way of forcing the viewers, who
are bounced back by the glass' reflections, to come closer and
thereby to see better. I have argued something similar about
American artist (painter and poet) Ken Aptekar's glass-covered
paintings, about which I have also written in that 1999 book.
Yet, whereas Bacon's narrative, as Van Alphen explains, tells
a story of eroticism as the loss of self, Reed's, in contrast,
promotes an embrace of the self, not in self-absorption but
in the exchange of 'I' and 'you'. In that sense, Reed, better
than any other artist I know, has fully grasped the essence of
personhood.

HOW TO BECOME
A SECOND PERSON?

... especially if you seem doomed to remain either a third
person or no person at all? The most obvious way would be to
be selected. In class, when the teacher posed a question and
invited the students to raise their hand if they knew the answer,
sometimes a few, sometimes none, and sometimes a large number of hands were raised. The teacher would look at all those

68 Alphen van, *Francis Bacon and the Loss of Self* (1998).

with raised hands, and then select one, pointing to her, and addressing that person: 'Yes, you?' Those were moments that the student was installed as a second person in an exchange, about to be allowed to speak and thus, become, for just a little while, a first person. Whenever I was selected, I would try to not only answer the question but also explain my answer, taking as much time in the first-person position as would be acceptable. Sometimes the teacher would interrupt me, cut off my lengthy explanation, clearly and rightly annoyed by my attention-craving, but occasionally she did let me speak. In retrospect, I now see how important it was for me to be, finally, a speaking first person. But I could only become that thanks to the second-person I had been when the question was raised.

However, being selected is not an arbitrary event. It is only when the first person has confidence that you are the best choice, that this can happen. I was never good at sports, and a bit medium-sized, and so, I was never selected for a basketball team. I was not artistically gifted, so my clumsy drawings where not chosen for the once-a-year exhibition in the drawing class. And for the fashion show, I was not well-dressed enough, with the second-hand clothes inherited from my older sister. All those competitions were based on selection, but the agent of choosing was the first person, the teacher. Hence, apart from the intellectual competition when the teacher raised a question of which I had either learned, or read about, so that I could come up with an answer, my chance to take my turn rarely came. However, second-personhood does not only depend on such competitive selections. As we have seen above, not only people but also texts or artworks can take on first-personhood, and thus address all those 'yous' that constitute their public, readers, viewers or other interacting people. And through that *work*, as I keep calling it, the former object can become an active subject, a first person, and thus address *you*. And if you, then, become a second person, allowed to speak in the exchange and thereby become temporarily a first person, your response to the speech or expression of the work or text becomes a first-person statement. This is how, as a reader or viewer, you actually become not simply a second person, but

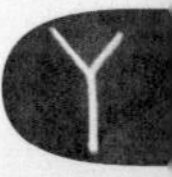

a speaker; someone who has something to say, whether or not you really speak and, for example, become an art or literature critic.

There are other situations where, as a child, I remember taking up the exchange launched by the first person. The way the boys condemned me to loneliness after school by not only refusing to let me into their group, but even threatening me with violence, as I described under L, was one of those moments of meaning-making. I made new meaning through taking their negative address seriously. I refused their refusal, and took up the second-personhood they bestowed on me. So, instead of always running away in fear, I began to respond, to answer, and thus, to participate in the exchange their nastiness was in fact setting up. Hence, when I took up the courage to respond, I became a true second person, one allowed into the exchange of which personhood consists. When I now juxtapose that situation to the artworks I have briefly invoked above, I can see how the work of art can indeed be compared to the teasing, the tormenting, the ganging up by those boys. Not that it is the same, of course. But the crucial moment is when you feel touched, either pleasantly or nastily. The guards in Christensen's exhibition may have been annoyed by the yucky smell of the rotting Jell-O, or amused by their privilege to be witnesses to the passing of time—Christensen's favourite title—of which the smell was a symptom. As were the abstract images created by the puddles of the liquid coming out of the rotting stuff. The passing of time is the work of her art.

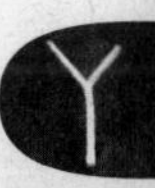

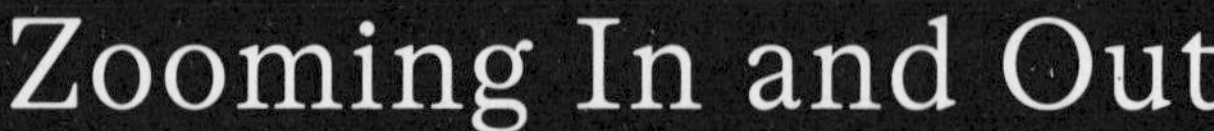
Zooming In and Out

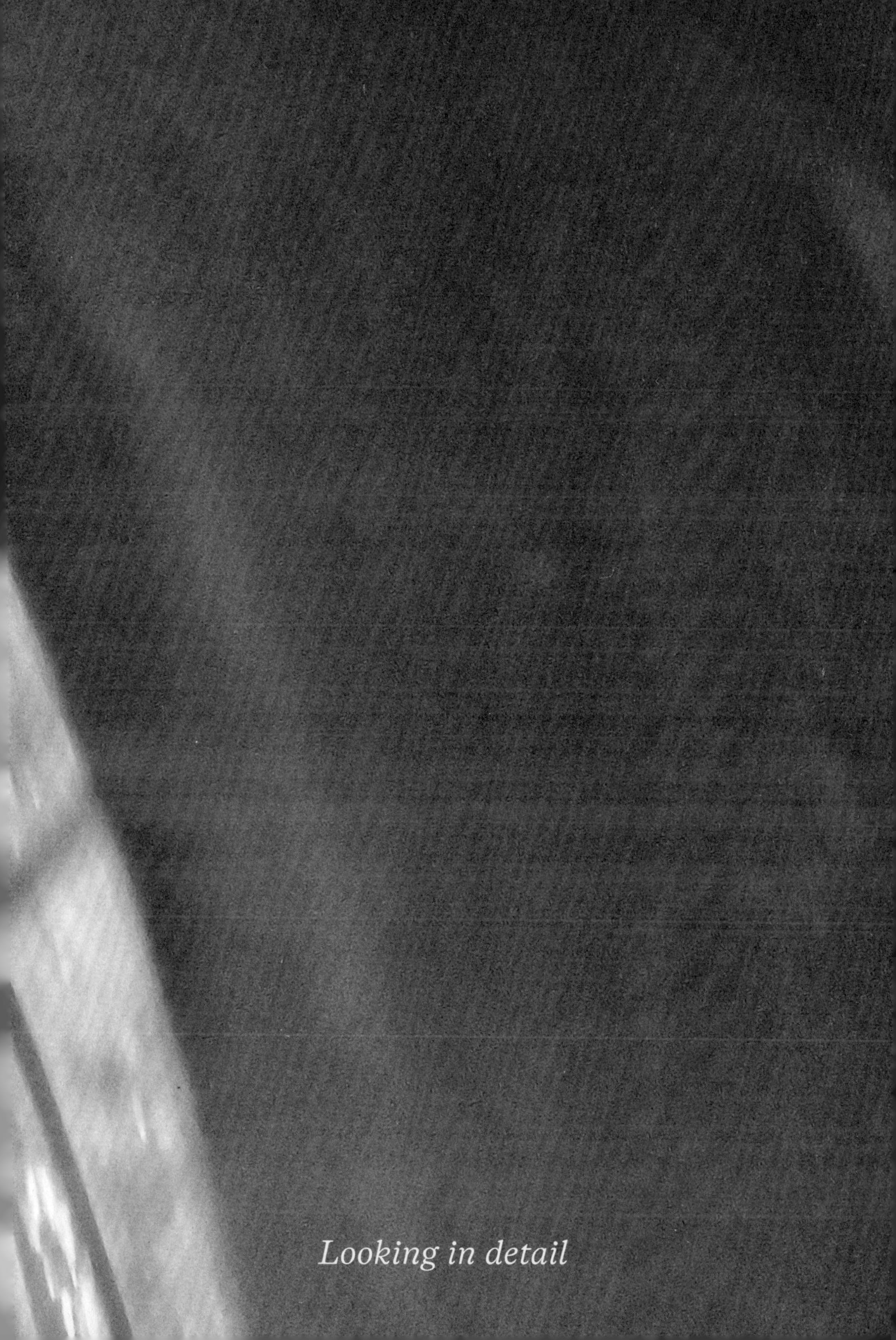

Looking in detail

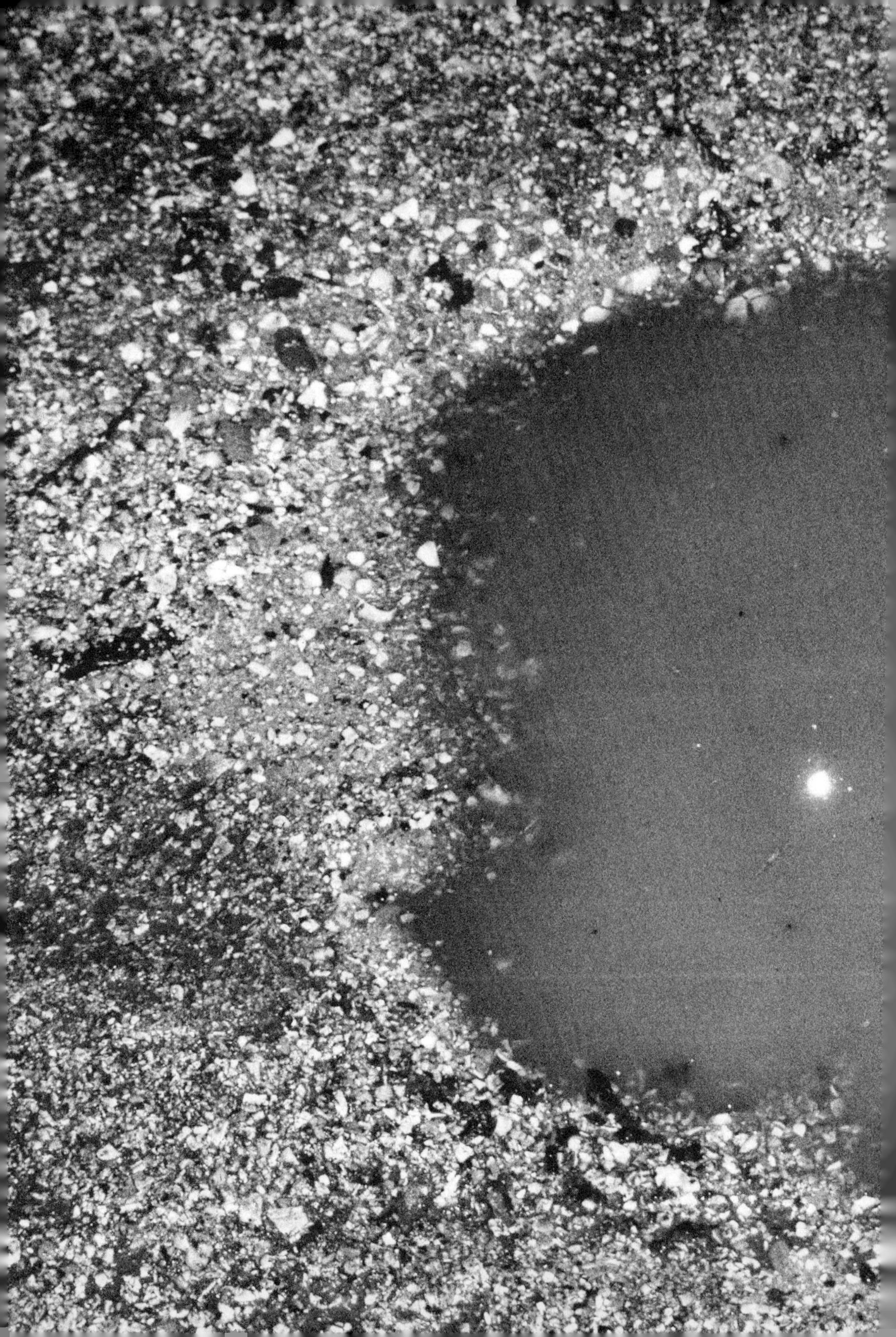

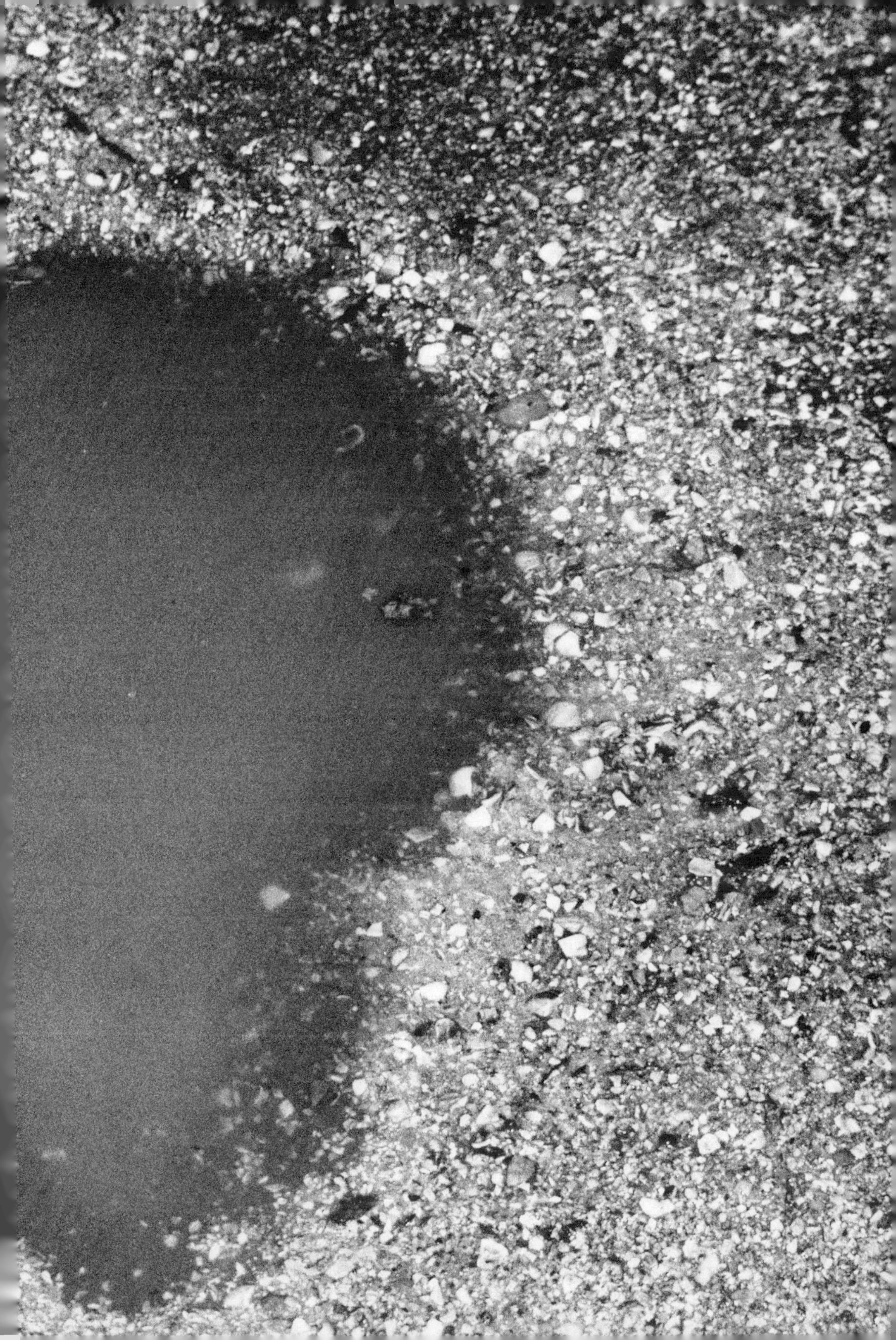

ZOOMING IN, FOR BETTER SEEING

Daisies and mini-dandelions among all that green grass of the lawn: this was how, as a child, from, let's say, age five on, I developed the habit of looking at my surroundings. Part of our garden was a lawn, and monotonous as the grass looked, when I sharpened my eyes, I saw those tiny flowers. They were rather sparse and minuscule, but I soon discovered that precisely their small size and scarcity made them stand out, made them 'step into view'. I especially valued the daisies, few as they were. I loved their white petals and yellow hearts. I picked and gathered them in a small vase or a simple water glass. It was a skill I had to develop quickly, since the daisy season was short, and I had to pluck the flowers as low as possible on their stems. If not, they could not be immersed in water and would fade away ultra-quickly.

The dandelions required a severe selection, for they tended to be larger and thus overrule the daisies. But there were different kinds, one of which was almost as small as the daisies. Moreover, we were told that the white liquid in their stems was poisonous, which made picking them a bit scary. But in my memory, the point of this dealing with the tiny flowers was less to pick them than to see them; to discern those small things where they did not seem to belong, since the green grass constituted the blanket laid over the earth. Their exceptionality was what fascinated me. I have strong memories of short excursions outside, in the garden, or on the banks of the ditch, to gather daisies. As the naughty girl I was, I even sometimes sneaked into someone else's garden to 'steal' some daisies. It became a kind of game to search for them and then see them, take them, and put them in a small vase at home. They never lasted long. But the point was to discern them.

The tiny flowers interested me more than the lilies, roses, and other large flowers in borders around lawns. Lawns surrounded by borders always bored me. The most surprising effect of those excursions in search of tiny flowers was a generalizing tendency. Instead of only focusing on the tiny flowers, the effect was the development of a habit of looking for small, exceptional things, which would disrupt the monotony of lawns, sidewalks, the sandhills of the dunes, and beaches. At least, I consider that habit, which became a key part of my life and behaviour, as a consequence of the tiny-flower-picking of my earliest years. I began to constantly look out for small things, especially on the sidewalk, where I walked daily. I saw weird-looking leftovers of chewing gum, tiny tree branches, little pieces broken from toys, hairpins, children's scooters or tricycles. And as much as Mother had warned me that picking up such things was dirty, and would put my health at risk, I couldn't help myself. Sometimes I even put the thrown-away chewing gum, if it looked still pink enough, into my mouth. True, I was a bit sloppy as a child, even a bit dirty (unhygienic) and tended to take unnecessary risks. But what stayed with me was an attentiveness to the smallest, tiniest things.

This also happened while I was reading. Even the reading-when-walking home from school did not prevent me from zooming in on the tiniest details of the books I was holding as much as of the sidewalks. I noticed the damage done to the book covers, the stickers from the library catalogue system, the font, the images inside, sometimes handwritten comments or even drawings: I looked for it, and saw it all. And seeing it rejoiced me. But then, also, in the texts themselves; the small details of descriptions, storytelling, and character presentation began to haunt me. This, I now think, determined my later intellectual attitude, and my lifelong passion for 'close reading'. I started to be sensitive to the smallest details. If a character was busy with some action, fine; but I not only paid attention to the phases of their actions but also to their clothing (in images or descriptions), their ways of talking, words chosen, and whatever their movements were. That attention to all things small became a permanent personality feature, something like an obsession. In my memory I was aware of its strangeness, but felt it was important.

And that aspect came in good stead. Once I started to look closely at literary texts, later on, it was a 'natural' tendency to keep focused on the smallest aspects. Zooming in became my way of life. So, when early on, at the age of about eight, I bought a simple photo camera from my savings, in order to take pictures of the little ones when I took them out in a stroller, I zoomed in, not just on their faces, but even very closely, on their eyes. One little sister had dimples in her cheeks with peach-soft skin. I loved that. But how to take a photograph of just dimples, and render the softness of a baby skin? This is impossible. That very impossibility only made me more fanatic. I wasted several precious negatives on this effort. I could get close, but then the photo came out as blurry. Of course, it was the effort that excited me, more than the result, which always failed. I wish I had kept those photographs, but I have no idea where they would be now.

The word 'zooming in' I didn't know. I was only sharply aware that tiny things mattered. And that, of course, turned me into a close reader, even if I never bought the idea that later became standard: that close reading did not involve context, historical or social, or framing; or whatever it came to be termed later. I always felt the opposite was the case. The closeness of the reading constituted the context. It involved me, the reader—what, under Y, I called the second person ready to act for a short time as a first person—and thereby made a flexible, always-changing context. Under the always helpful guidance of the work of Jonathan Culler, I began to call it 'framing', rather than context. In my later book *Travelling Concepts in the Humanities: A Rough Guide*, from 2002, I devoted a chapter to this transformation of context to framing. The relevance of that change is the fact that framing is a verb, an activity, whereas context is supposed to be a mute 'thing', which needs to be read, interpreted, before it can be meaningful. The submersion of the daisies within the predominant grass turned the grass into a frame and made the daisies stand out, as if the grass and its green colour gave the white petals and yellow hearts a special beauty. This insight helped me to see better, to attribute meaning to the tiny things I saw. Zooming in, thus, became crucial, not only for my (close) reading but also for seeing itself. I think this has become a key tool in my later filmmaking.

The failed attempt to photograph my little sister's dimples was a first step that later became a principle of viewing, looking, seeing, and in relation to others, showing. This recalls Wittgenstein's final sentence of the *Tractatus*, 'Whereof one cannot speak, thereof one must be silent', which he later revised into 'Of what one cannot speak, one can always show' (quoted from memory). For me, it was not the speaking about but the looking leading to seeing that mattered. This became the root of my shift from close reading to close seeing; from literature to visual art. In fact, the traditional distinction, even opposition between those two media didn't seem to matter. The 'zooming in' and its framing did not seem to be media-bound. The rejection of the opposition between words and images turned me into a controversial art critic. I didn't care; for me what mattered was to see and read the details, the small things that mattered for the *work* of art.

ZOOMING OUT, FOR SEEING MORE

The opposite of 'zooming in' would be, of course, zooming out. But that verb with its preposition does not mean a departure, a going away. According to dictionaries, it would suggest a change of camera lens that makes the view seem farther away. For reading literature, there has been a reaction against close reading, which literary scholar Franco Moretti has termed 'distant reading'. He was fed up with the detailing of texts and instead, sought to sum up massive amounts of texts and see what they had in common. This, obviously, is not my kind of reading, with all due respect for the great scholar he is. His many books provide insights into social issues, such as *Signs taken for Wonders*, on the social meanings of literary forms. So, my reluctance to endorse his 'distancing' reading method must not be taken as disrespect for his work. However, 'zooming out' is not necessarily connected to that.[69]

Zooming out is, instead, considered a way of distancing the view, making the elements in the image seem smaller, and farther away. But this is not the only meaning of the verb-plus-preposition. Just as zooming in is a way of approaching, detailing the view, zooming out is an attempt to embrace more, to create a wider view. This is not necessarily an attempt to put what we see at a distance, but to make it possible to see

69 See especially Moretti, *Signs Taken for Wonders* and *Distant Reading* (1983).

more at any one time. Instead of the daisies, the large grass lawn would become the content of what we see. Including trees at the far end, at the edge of a forest, for example. In filmmaking, this helps to include many more figures, objects, spaces within a single image, and thus to see more elements simultaneously. 'Embracing' would be the right verb for this. But then, the verb 'zooming', whether it is in or out, implies a movement. It is not so much the accumulation of visible elements, but the move from close to distant or vice versa, which brings the cinematic into the orbit of the look. Hence, zooming out encompasses more, makes our vision wider, but it also makes the move from close to far as a cinematic form.

In the alphabetically ordered book on the art of John Sparagana mentioned in my Introduction, the three Z words that open the final chapter are zealous, zestful, and zoned. The first one, the qualifier 'zealous', indicates an enthusiasm, a supportive attitude, which is what I find very relevant for a reading or viewing outlook. My childhood addiction to reading came out of such an approach. This was also the way I attempted to answer the teacher's questions. But in relation to zooming out, the zealousness is inspired by a desire to see, encompass, detect more, rather than just those little things we call details. In that sense it can almost be at risk of becoming an occupational, colonialist mode of looking. But the zestfulness of the participants in the game, play, or story, is what makes it a positive, enthusiastic, and moving, in the double sense, event. The third word I put out there, 'zoned', has the opposite effect. It restricts; the issue is to delimit or limit parts of the environment, devoting it to a particular function. A beautiful, natural landscape can be 'zoned' for an industrial purpose.

When I began to make films, the zooming verbs became of the highest actuality. Zooming in for seeing better, in more detail, leads to the kind of takes called 'close-ups'. Isolating and aggrandizing something in view of filming in detail: this became very important on several occasions. In *Madame B*, (2012–2014) the faces of the figures addressed one another. Particularly, the three men, Charles, Rodolphe, and Léon, all three played by the same brilliant French actor Thomas

Germaine, had to be distinctive enough to be plausible as different characters. This was especially important because they had distinct ages, hair colours, expressions, and mentalities. The committed Charles, the cynical predator Rodolphe ('I am sure she'll fall for it, but how to get rid of her afterwards?') and the naive, young clerk Léon look so different, as if even their noses seem to have different shapes, although that is impossible, since we filmed the three roles in the same week. For this effect to occur, not only did we need a marvellous actor and an equally dazzling make-up artist, but even their voices, the interiors of the house, and the clothing had to make a distinction. It worked so well that even an art-historian friend, so used to looking in detail, did not notice, when viewing the film, that the three men were played by the same actor. Zooming in on the face made the con-fusing possible.[70]

Something comparable happened in the film on Descartes, *Reasonable Doubt,* from 2016. Here, the same actor as in *Madame B*, Thomas Germaine, plays the main character. Here, there is no multiple figuration, but the zooming in on his face made it possible to distinguish the great philosopher from the somewhat hysterical, even slightly mad man. In one image you clearly see the doubting, insecure look, the facial expression of the 'reasonable doubt', as the title of the film has it. When you see that photograph, made by the brilliant Polish photographer Przemo Wojciechowski, you, as the addressed viewer, have doubts about it: is this the father of Western rationality, or some crazy guy? Zooming in on that face is the way to understand, not simply a potential madness, but the uncertainty of what an image in close-up shows us.[71]

The act of zooming out, which implies a movement of the lens, aggrandizes what you see and turns, for example, a lawn into an immense prairie. But here, the habits of looking are deceptive. We assume that you can see that entire large view in a single glance. But no; this is not what happens. The viewer, who thinks the zooming out turns the view into a large single image, cannot, can never, see the entire image in a single look. Instead, the eye of the viewer roams around the entire view. Looking takes time and movement. This is the lesson we must

70 Bal, *Image-Thinking* (2022), 341.

71 This is wonderfully clear in a photograph on page 190 of *Image-Thinking* (2022).

learn from the result of zooming out. No image can be taken in with one look. And this, I want to suggest, is how looking becomes seeing, and how looking-seeing is always already cinematic, in the sense of moving.

Zooming Out

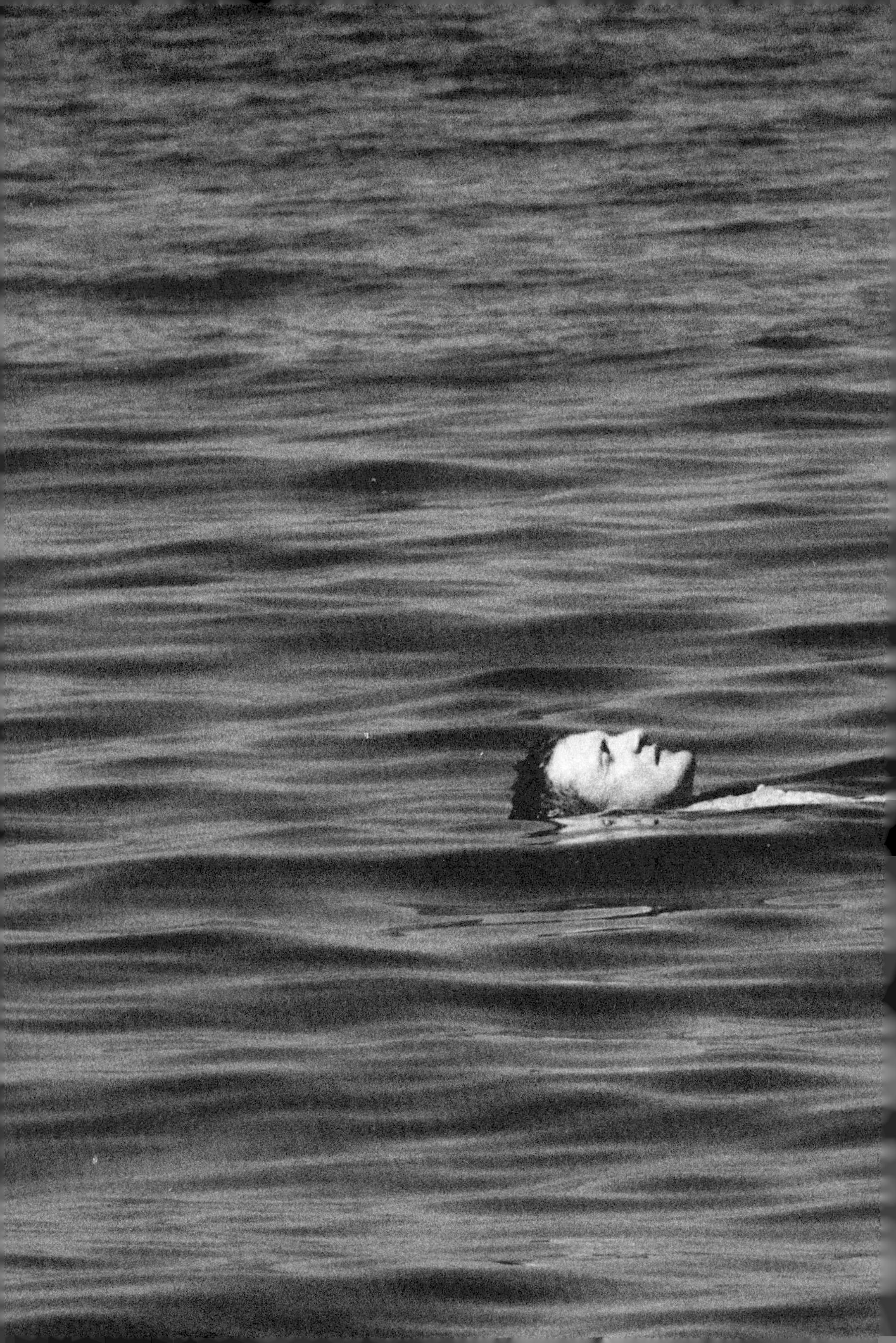

AFTERWORD

When I approached the last few vignettes according to the alphabet, and Kyoo Lee—editor of the journal *PhiloSOPHIA*, in which I had published the first few entries—asked me to start again with A once the 26 would be finished, I was wondering what I could evoke next. So, I keep it at just one fake new beginning, the A, for 'afterword'. I will just mention a few things that, in this book, indicate how it may be used by readers. In a sense, the first A word: 'Anachronism', is significant for all students and scholars, researchers and artists; for anyone interested in the Humanities. Anachronism is crucial for our work in that it lays down what has become a key issue in my later work: the conceptualization of 'pre-posterous history', the view of history as it matters simultaneously in and with the present. Instead of the usual arrogance to assume we can reconstruct the past, and that from there on, time is linear, my plea is for a view of time that is mutual. This mutuality also appears in the second vignette, on the B of 'becoming', which begins with my awareness, at age four, that I did not want to become a housewife, or, as my father called it, a 'home-maker'. What else, instead? I had no idea. But not that subservient imprisonment. This was the beginning of my self-consciousness of the future, of what I wanted to do with my life. That this moment was the start of my feminist conviction has been central in my later life as well. The intellectual and later, artistic itinerary I ended up following was not at all foreseeable at that moment. The meaning I made then was simply a loud and clear *no*! That refusing attitude has stayed with me forever. I have always had the tendency to feel strongly what I did not want, did not accept, did not approve of.

I consider this book as an anthology of moments when ideas, insights, convictions, not only began to make sense but also led to later ideas useful for my work as a researcher, teacher, and all the other things I have done. The moments when meanings occurred to me were always both dynamic, 'moving', and socially relevant. That combination is the spine of everything I have done, and still do. The vignettes articulate refusals, but also values, such as the G for 'generosity', the F for 'friendship', and the D for 'details'. The latter concept has been a lasting value in my approach to texts, images, people, and the world. Details prevent the kind of over-hasty generalizations that flatten the objects instead of making them stand out as uniquely valuable. This is why I remain attached to 'close reading' as a way of giving the objects we study the opportunity to 'speak back' instead of being subjected to the ambition, even the vanity of the scholar. This does not mean that the wider context is irrelevant, as early adepts of close reading assumed. On the contrary. The way I consider details connect, or as I call it, encounter, those small aspects or elements with the broader context in which the artworks work.

It is not necessary to go over all the vignettes and the letters of the alphabet with which their key words begin. The vignettes are explicit enough about this. The point is not, not at all, to dictate which words produce enriching meanings, and what those meanings mean. Instead, the book aims to demonstrate how acts of memory—in this case, my own, personal memories, which I produce—generate tools for a fruitful life later on, not in a linear fashion but through semi-arbitrary associations. This is why 'becoming' is a better conception of meaning than anything that fixates what words, things, or works of art, can mean. The ironic term 'classifixation' says it clearly enough: meanings emerge at specific moments, in encounters with people and situations, but they don't ever stay stable. The fact that memories are acts, that meanings move, and that art works, makes classifixation impossible and instead provides a view of the world, of culture, and of art that is live, that *moves*. The best way to use this book is to consider, and reconsider, every time anew, where the meanings come from, and how they stay alive as moving, and thereby assist our thinking.

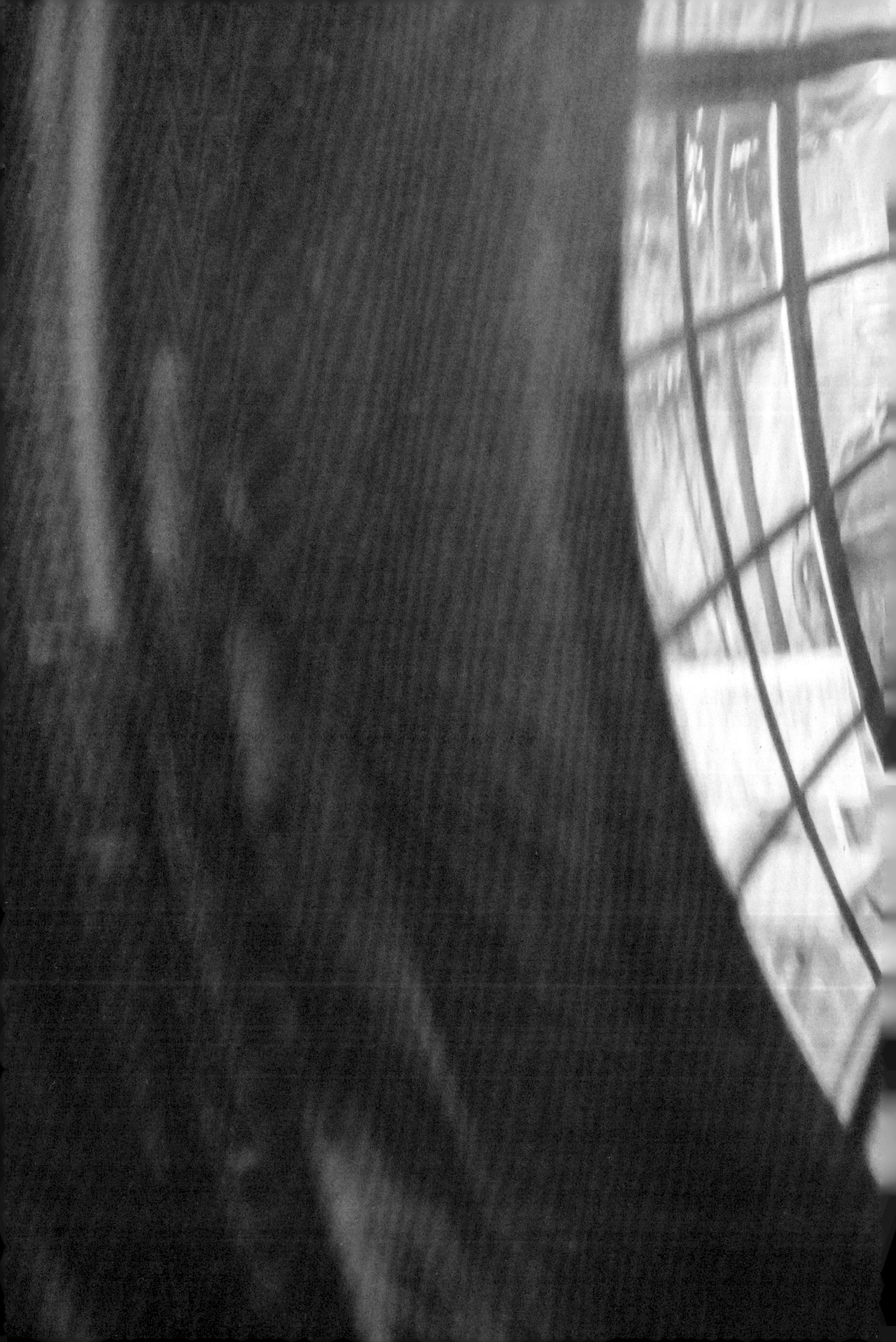

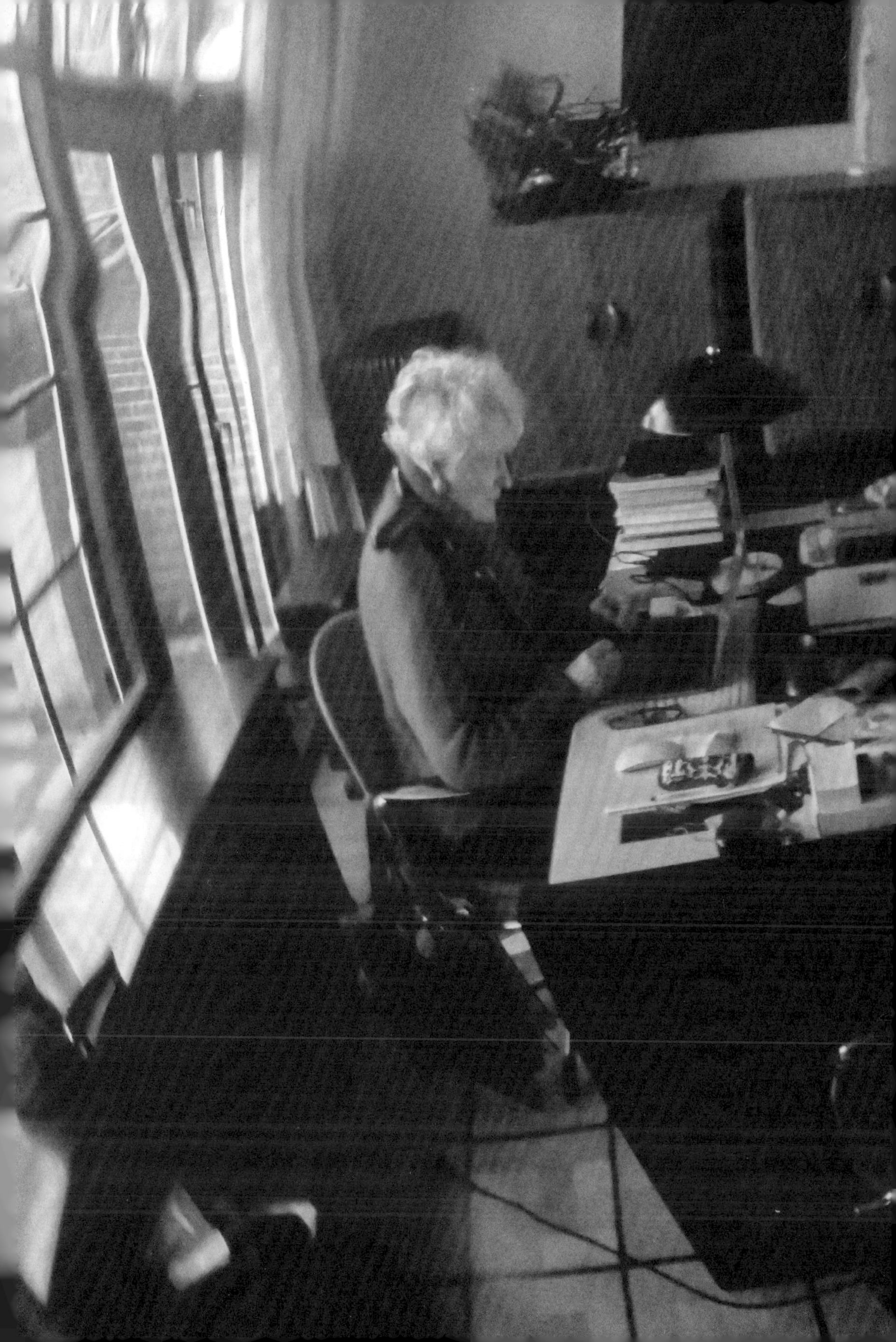

BIBLIOGRAPHY
Moments of Meaning-Making

Adorno, Theodor W. In Rolf Tiedemann, ed. *Can One Live After Auschwitz? A Philosophical Reader*. Trans. Rodney Livingstone et al. Stanford: Stanford University Press, 2003.

——'The Essay as Form'. In Rolf Tiedemann, ed. *Notes to Literature*, 1. Trans. Shierry Weber Nicholson. New York: Columbia University Press, 1991, 3–23.

Alloa, Emmanuel. *Partages de la perspective*. Paris: Fayard, 2020.

Alphen, Ernst van. *Caught by History: Holocaust Effects in Contemporary Art, Literature, and Theory*. Stanford: Stanford University Press, 1998.

——*Francis Bacon and the Loss of Self*. London: Reaktion Books, 1998.

Appadurai, Arjun. 'Globalization and the research imagination'. Hoboken: Blackwell Publishers, 1999.

——'Grassroot Globalization and the Research Imagination'. *Public Culture*, 12: 1, 2000, 1–19.

Attridge, Derek. *The Singularity of Literature*. London: Routledge, 2004.

Aydemir, Murat, Noa Roei, Aylin Kuryel, eds. *The Future of Cultural Analysis: A Critical Inquiry*. Amsterdam: Amsterdam University Press, 2025.

Bakhtin, Mikhail. In Michael Holquist, ed. *The Dialogic Imagination: Four Essays by M.M. Bakhtin*. Trans. Caryl Emerson and Michael Holquist. Austin: University of Texas Press, 1981.

Balibar, Étienne. *Nous, citoyens d'Europe? Frontières, États, peuples*. Paris: La découverte, 2001.

Baxandall, Michael. *Patterns of Intention: On the Historical Explanation of Pictures*. New Haven and London: Yale University Press, 1985.

Benjamin, Walter. 'The Task of the Translator'. In Hannah Arendt, ed. *Illuminations*. Trans. Harry Zohn. New York: Schocken, 1968, 69–82.

Bergson, Henri. *Matter and Memory*. Trans. N. M. Paul and W. S. Palmer. New York: Zone Books, 1991.

——*Creative Evolution*. Trans. A. Mitchell. Lanham: University Press of America, 1983.

Boer, Inge E. *Uncertain Territories: Boundaries in Cultural Analysis*. Amsterdam and New York: Rodopi 2006.

Buydens, Mireille. *Sahara: L'esthétique de Gilles Deleuze*. Paris: Vrin, 2005.

Cartier-Bresson, Henri. *Les Européens. Photographies*. Paris: Verve, 1955.

Code, Lorraine. *What Can She Know? Feminist Theory and the Construction of Knowledge*. Ithaca and London: Cornell University Press, 1991.

Davoine, Françoise. *Wittgenstein's Folly: Philosophy, Psychoanalysis and Language Games*. Trans. William J. Hurst. London and New York: Routledge, 2024.

——*Mother Folly: A Tale*. Trans. Judith G. Miller. Stanford: Stanford University Press, 2014.

Deleuze, Gilles, Felix Guattari. *A Thousand Plateaus: Capitalism and Schizophrenia*. Trans. Brian Massumi. London: Athlone Press, 1987.

——*Rhizome: Introduction*. Paris: Editions de Minuit, 1976.

Derrida, Jacques. *Speech and Phenomena and Other Essays on Husserl's Theory of Signs*. Trans. David B. Allison and Leonard Lawlor. Evanston: Northwestern University Press, 1973.

Didi-Huberman, Georges. *Images in Spite of All: Four Photographs from Auschwitz*. Trans. Shane B. Lillis. Chicago: University of Chicago Press, 2008.

Dumas, Marlene. *Sweet Nothings: Notes and Texts 1982–2014*. London: Tate Publishing, 2015.

Fanon, Frantz. *The Wretched of the Earth*. Trans. C. Farrington. London: Penguin Classics, 2001.

Felman, Shoshana. 'Psychoanalysis and Education: Teaching Terminable and Interminable'. *Yale French Studies*, 63, 1982, 21–44.

——'To Open the Question'. *Yale French Studies*, 55/56, 1977, 5–10.

Flaubert, Gustave. *Madame Bovary*. Paris: Club de l'Honnête Homme, 1971.

Gatens, Moira, Genevieve Lloyd. *Collective Imaginings. Spinoza, Past and Present*. New York and London: Routledge, 1999.

Genette, Gérard. *Figures III*. Paris: Le Seuil, 1972.

Gennep, Arnold van. *The Rites of Passage*. Chicago: University of Chicago Press, 1960.

Haraway, Donna. *Staying with the Trouble: Making Kin in the Chthulucene*. Durham: Duke University Press, 2016.

Holly, Michael Ann. *Somewhere Between Art History and Phenomenology: At the Still Point of the Painted World*. Edinburgh: Edinburgh University Press, 2025.

——*Past Looking: Historical Imagination and the Rhetoric of the Image*. Ithaca: Cornell University Press, 1996.

Huber, Monika. *Archive OneThirty*. Berlin and München: Deutscher Kunstverlag, 2023.

Illouz, Eva. *Why Love Hurts: A Sociological Explanation*. Cambridge: Polity Press, 2012.

——*Cold Intimacies: The Making of Emotional Capitalism*. Cambridge: Polity Press, 2007.

Kubler, George. 'The Shape of Time Reconsidered'. *Perspecta*, 19, 1982, 112–121.

——*The Shape of Time: Remarks on the History of Things*. New Haven: Yale University Press, 1962.

Klee, Paul. In Jürgen Spiller, ed. *The Thinking Eye*. The Notebooks of Paul Klee, 1. Trans. Ralph Manheim. San Francisco: Wittenborg Art Books, 2013.

Lee, Kyoo. *Reading Descartes Otherwise: Blind, Mad, Dreamy, and Bad*. New York: Fordham University Press, 2012.

Lutters, Jeroen. *The Trade of the Teacher. Visual Thinking with Mieke Bal*. Amsterdam: Valiz, 2018.

Lyotard, Jean-François. *Discourse, Figure*. Trans. Antony Hudek and Mary Lydon. Minneapolis: The University of Minnesota Press, 2020.

Man, Paul de. *The Resistance to Theory*. Theory & History of Literature, 33. Minneapolis: University of Minnesota Press, 1986.

Marx, William. *Vivre dans la bibliothèque du monde*. Paris: Collège de France/Fayard, 2020.

Millà, Martina. *Nalini Malani: No em sents*. Barcelona: Fundació Joan Miró, 2020.

Mitchell, W. J.T. 'Present Tense: An Iconology of the Epoch'. *Critical Inquiry*, 47, Winter 2021, 370–406.

Mondzain, Marie José. *Confiscation des mots, des images et des temps. Pour une autre radicalité*. Paris: Les livres qui libèrent, 2017.
—*Image, Icon, Economy: The Byzantine Origins of the Contemporary Imaginary*. Stanford: Stanford University Press, 2005.
—*Le Commerce des regards*. Paris: Le Seuil, 2003.

Moretti, Franco. *Signs Taken for Wonders: Essays in the Sociology of Literary Forms*. Trans. Susan Fischer, David Forgacs, and David Miller. London: Verso Editions, 1983.

Pascal, Blaise. In Charles William Eliot, ed. *The Harvard Classics: Pascal, Blaise. Thoughts; Letters; minor works*, 48. New York: PF Collier & Son, 1910.

Peirce, Charles Sanders. 'Logic as Semiotic: The Theory of Signs'. In Robert E. Innis, ed. *Semiotics: An Introductory Anthology*. Bloomington: Indiana University Press, 1984, 4–23.

Popper, Karl. *The Logic of Scientific Discovery*. New York: Harper and Row, 1968.

Rajchman, John. *Constructions*. Cambridge: MIT Press, 1998.

Rodowick, D.N. *Reading the Figural, or, Philosophy After the New Media*. Durham and London: Duke University Press, 2001.

Rousseau, Jean-Jacque. *Discourse on the Origin and Basis of Inequality Among Men*. Trans. G.D.H. Cole. London: Penguin Classics, 1985.
— 'Another View of Abstraction'. *Journal of Philosophy and the Visual Arts*, 5: 16, 1995, 16–25.

Saloul, Ihab. 'Postmemory and Oral History: Inter-generational Memory and Transnational Identity in Exile'. In Gil Pasternak, ed. *Visioning Israel-Palestine: Encounters at the Cultural Boundaries of Conflict*. London: Bloomsbury, 2020, 244–263.

Silverman, Kaja. *The Threshold of the Visible World*. New York: Routledge, 1996.

Skryzak, Richard. *Vanité et art vidéo*. Paris: L'Harmattan, 2024.

Spitzer, Leo. In David Bellos, ed. *Le récit de Théramène: Essays on Seventeenth-century French Literature*. Trans. David Bellos. Cambridge and New York: Cambridge University Press, 1983.

Spivak, Gayatri Chakravorty. *A Critique of Postcolonial Reason: Toward a History of the Vanishing Present*. Cambridge: Harvard University Press, 1999.

Tamm, Marek, Peeter Torop, eds. *The Companion to Juri Lotman: A Semiotic Theory of Culture*. London: Bloomsbury, 2022.

Tuin, Iris van der, Nanna Verhoeff. *Critical Concepts for the Creative Humanities*. London: Rowman and Littlefield, 2022.

Verhoeff, Han. *'Adolphe' et Constant: Une étude psychocritique*. Paris: Klincksieck, 1976.

Verhoeff, Nanna. *Urban Screens: Situations, Practices, Concepts*. Amsterdam: Amsterdam University Press, 2025.

—— *After the Beginning: Westerns Before 1915*. Amsterdam: Amsterdam University Press, 2006.

Wolf, Christa. *Cassandra: A Novel and Four Essays*. Trans. Jan Van Heurck. New York: Farrar, Straus and Giroux, 1988.

Books
(incl. Short Books and Brochures)

Beyond the Habitual: Louise Bourgeois as Builder, Narrator, Theorist. Oltre l'abituale: Louise Bourgeois come construttrice, narratrice, teorica. Trans. Sara Benaglia and Gianni Romano. Milano: Postmedia Books, 2024.

The Milliner's Daughter: The Art Practice of Ydessa Hendeles. Co-authored with Ernst van Alphen, with contributions by Emily Cadger, Markus Müller and Gaëtane Verna. Cologne: Verlag der Buchhandlung Walther und Franz König, 2024.

Un rêve culturel: L'Europe au pluriel. Paris: Collège de France | Fayard, 2023.

Image-Thinking: Artmaking as Cultural Analysis. Refractions: At the Borders of Philosophy and Art History, 1. Edinburgh: Edinburgh University Press, 2022.

Figuraciones: Cómo la literatura crea imagines. Trans. María José García Rodríguez. Murcia: Editum, 2021.

Narratology in Practice. Toronto: University of Toronto Press, 2021.

Kunst uit noodzaak. Arhem: ArtEZ Press, 2020.

Exhibition-ism: Temporal Togetherness. The Contemporary Condition, 15. Berlin: Sternberg Press, 2020.

Don Quijote: Sad Countenances. Växjö: Trolltrumma, 2019.

——Bilingual edition English/Spanish: *Don Quijote: Tristes figuras; Don Quijote: Sad Countenances.* Murcia: Cendeac (Ad Litteram), 2020.

Het geel van Marcel Proust: Over denkbeelden en beelddenken. Nijmegen: VanTilt, 2019.

Allo-Portraits: On the Impossibility of Likeness in the Face of Movement. Brochure for the exhibition *Rendez-vous with Frans Hals.* Haarlem: Frans Hals Museum, 2018.

Semiotics of Narrative: Essays in Visual Analysis. Edited and translated by Lian Duan. Chengdu: Sichuan University Press, 2018.

Emma & Edvard Looking Sideways: Loneliness and the Cinematic. Oslo: Munch Museum; Brussels: Mercatorfonds; New Haven: Yale University Press, 2017.

In Medias Res: Inside Nalini Malani's Shadow Plays. Ostfildern: Hatje Cantz, 2016.

Tiempos trastornados: análisis, historias y políticas de la mirada. Trans. Remedios Perni Llorente. Madrid: AKAL, 2016.

Lexikon der Kulturanalyse. Aka texts, 3. Trans. Brita Pohl. Vienna: Verlag Turia + Kant, 2016.

——Spanish: *Lexicón de análisis cultural.* Trans. Remedio Perni Llorente. Madrid: AKAL, 2021.

Endless Andness: The Politics of Abstraction According to Ann Veronica Janssens. London: Bloomsbury, 2013.

Thinking in Film: The Politics of Video Installation According to Eija-Liisa Ahtila. London: Bloomsbury, 2013.

Of What One Cannot Speak: Doris Salcedo's Political Art. Chicago: The University of Chicago Press, 2010.

——Spanish: *De lo que no se puede hablar: el arte política de Doris Salcedo.* Trans. Marcelo Cohen and Miguel Á. Hernández Navarro. Bogotá: Universidad Nacional de Colombia, Sede Medellín/Panamericana, 2014.

Fragments of Matter: Jeannette Christensen. Bergen: Bergen National Academy of the Arts, 2009.

2MOVE: Video, Art, Migration. Co-authored with Miguel Á. Hernández Navarro. Murcia: Cendeac, 2008.

Sleeping Beauty. Co-authored with John Sparagana. Chicago: University of Chicago Press, 2008.

Loving Yusuf: Conceptual Travels from Present to Past. Chicago: University of Chicago Press, 2008.

——Turkish: *Yusuf Nasıl Sevilir.* Trans. Gülden Güllü. Istanbul: Dergah Yayınları, 2020.

Balthus: Works and Interviews. Barcelona: Ediciones Polígrafa, 2008.

——French: *Balthus: Oeuvres, Écrits, Entretiens.* Trans. Jean-François Allain. Barcelona: Ediciones Polígrafa, 2008.

——Spanish: *Balthus: Obras y entrevista.* Trans. Marta Pérez Sánchez. Barcelona: Ediciones Polígrafa, 2008.

A Mieke Bal Reader. Chicago: University of Chicago Press, 2006.

Travelling Concepts in the Humanities: A Rough Guide. Toronto: University of Toronto Press, 2002.

——French: *Concepts itinérants. Comment se déplacer dans les sciences humaines.* Trans. Cécile Dutheil de la Rochère. Dijon: les presses du réel, 2023.

——Polish: *Wędrują Pojęcia W Naukach Humanistycznych.* Trans. Marta Bucholc. Warsaw: Narodowe Centrum Kultury, 2012.

——Spanish: *Conceptos viajeros en las humanidades: Una guía de viaje.* Trans. Yaiza Hernández Velázquez. Murcia: Cendeac, 2009.

——Adapted version of introduction trans. into Serbian as 'Putujući koncepti u humanistici: Vodič za pionire-Uvod'. Trans. Irena Šentevska. *TkH* 16, 2008, 79–89.

Kulturanalyse. Trans. Joachim Schulte. Frankfurt am Main: Suhrkamp, 2002 and 2006.

Louise Bourgeois' Spider: The Architecture of Art-writing. Chicago: University of Chicago Press, 2001.

——Spanish: *Una casa para el sueño de la razón: Ensayo sobre Bourgeois.* Trans. Rafael Sánchez Cacheiro and Ángel Paniagua. Murcia: Cendeac, 2006.

——Ch. 7 trans. into Russian. Trans. Petr and Olga Serebriany. In *Novy Mir Isskustva*, 23, 2001, 24–28.

Ann Veronica Janssens: Lichtspiel. Trans. Karen Lauer. Munich: Kunstverein München/Berliner Künstlerprogramm/DAAD, 2001.

Looking In: The Art of Viewing. Introduction by Norman Bryson. Amsterdam: G+B Arts International, 2001.

——Ch. 'Dispersing the Image' trans. into Polish as 'Rozsiewanie obrazu.' Trans. Łukasz Zaremba. In: Andrzej Mencwel, ed. *Almanach Antropologiczny.* Warsaw: University of Warsaw Press, 2010.

Ecstatic Aesthetics: Metaphoring Bernini. Critical Issues, 4. Sydney: Artspace Visual Art Centre, 2000; reprinted in Claire Farago and Robert Zwijnenberg, eds. *Compelling Visuality: the Work of Art In and Out of History.* Minneapolis: University of Minnesota Press, 2003, 1–30, and in *Ec-Stasy: Baroque and Beyond.* Brisbane: Queensland Art Museum, 2017, 71–94.

Verwikkelingen. Over recht en literatuur. OKW-voorjaarslezing. Den Haag: NOW, 2001.

Quoting Caravaggio: Contemporary Art, Preposterous History. Chicago: University of Chicago Press, 1999 and 2001.

Introduction trans. into Czech in Eva Skopalová, Václav Janoščík, eds. *Návrat do bud ucn sti.* Prague: UMPRUM (Academy of Arts, Architecture and

Design), 2019, 135–164.

Jeannette Christensen's Time. Bergen: Center for the Study of European Civilization, 1998.

Hovering between Thing and Event: Encounters with Lili Dujourie. München: Kunstverein München; Brussels: Xavier Hufkens; London: Lisson Gallery, 1998.

——German: *Schweben zwischen Gegenstand und Ereignis: Begegnungen mit Lili Dujourie.* Trans. Silvia Friedrich Rust. München: Kunstverein München/ Wilhelm Fink Verlag, 1998.

Images littéraires, ou comment lire visuellement Proust. Montréal: XYZ Editeur; Toulouse: Presses Universitaires de Toulouse, 1997.

——English: *The Mottled Screen: Reading Proust Visually.* Trans. Anna-Louise Milne. Stanford: Stanford University Press, 1997.

——Macedonian: *Шарен Екран: Визуелно Читање На Пруст.* Trans. Slavica Srbinovska. Skopje: Sigmapress, 2005.

Double Exposures: The Subject of Cultural Analysis. London and New York: Routledge, 1996.

——Ch. 3 trans. into Serbian in Angelina Čanković Popović, Anomalija, 1. Novi Sad: Museum of Contemporary Art, 2005, 15–26.

——Ch. 5 trans. into German as 'Erste Person, zweite Person, dieselbe Person: Zum Verhältnis von Ausstellen und Beschreiben aus narratologischer Sicht'. Trans. Kerstin Kazzazi. In Sigrid Nieberle, Elisabeth Strowick, eds. *Narration und Geschlecht: Texte – Medien – Episteme.* Cologne: Böhlau Verlag, 2006, 283–314.

——Ch. 1 trans. into German as 'Sagen, Zeigen, Prahlen'. In *Heft: Formen der Artikulation*, 02, 2009, 313–358.

On Meaning-Making: Essays in Semiotics. Sonoma: Polebridge Press, 1994.

Als de dood: theorie, metaforen en het avontuur van wetenschap. Inaugural address for professorship on literary theory, Universiteit van Amsterdam, 1993.

Reading 'Rembrandt': Beyond the Word-Image Opposition. Cambridge and New York: Cambridge University Press, 1991 and 1994 (paperback); reprint Amsterdam University Press, 2006.

——Dutch (abridged and reworked): *Verf en verderf: lezen in 'Rembrandt'.* Amsterdam: Prometheus, 1990.

——Introduction trans. into Hungarian as 'Látvány és narratíva egyensúlya'. Trans. Gabriella Hartvig. In Beáta Thomka, ed. *Narratívák 1: Képelemzés.* Budapest: Kijárat, 1998, 155–182.

——Adapted version of ch. 1 trans. into Hungarian as 'Túl a szó-kép oppozíción'. In *Enigma*, 14/15, 1998, 132–164.

——Ch. 2 trans. into Hebrew as 'תילאוזי סנואה לש הקרטוי-מסה חקידוטו'. In *Ha'Midrasha*, 12, 2009, 109–61.

On Story-Telling: Essays in Narratology. Sonoma: Polebridge Press, 1991.

——Ch. 5 trans. into Hungarian as 'A leírás mint narráció'. Trans. Melinda Huszanagics. In Beáta Thomka, ed. *Narratívák 2: Történet és fiktió.* Budapest: Kijárat, 1998, 135–171.

——Ch. 4 reprinted in Mieke Bal, ed. *Narrative Theory: Critical Concepts in Literary and Cultural Studies*, 1. London and New York: Routledge, 2004, 263–296.

Over haar lijk: waarheid, wetenschap en cultuurverschil. Amsterdam: Ad. Dekker, 1990.

Macht, mythe en misverstand of het recht om verkeerd te lezen: over Richteren 19 en het interpretatieprobleem. Amsterdam: Katholieke Theologische Universiteit Amsterdam, 1989.

Death and Dissymmetry: The Politics of Coherence in the Book of Judges. Chicago: University of Chicago Press, 1988.

Murder and Difference: Gender, Genre and Scholarship on Sisera's Death. Trans. Matthew Gumpert. Bloomington and Indianapolis: Indiana University Press, 1988 and 1992.

——French: *Meurtre et différence: Méthodologie sémiotique de textes anciens.* Montréal: XYZ Editeur, 1995.

Verkrachting verbeeld: seksueel geweld in cultuur gebracht. Utrecht: HES, 1988.

Lethal Love: Literary-Feminist Readings of Biblical Love Stories. Bloomington and Indianapolis: Indiana University Press, 1987.

Over literatuur. Co-authored with Jan van Luxemburg and Willem Weststeijn. Muiderberg: Coutinho, 1987, 1990, 1996, 1999, and 2002 (revised).

——Indonesian: *Tentang Sastra.* Jakarta: Intermasa, 1989.

Femmes imaginaires: L'Ancien Testament au risque d'une narratologie critique. Utrecht: HES; Montréal: HMH; Paris: Nizet, 1986.

En Sara in haar tent lachte: patriarchaat en verzet in bijbelverhalen. Co-authored with Fokkelien van Dijk and Grietje van Ginneken. Utrecht: HES, 1984.

——German: *Und Sara lachte...: Patriarchat und Widerstand in biblischen Geschichten.* Münster: Morgana Frauenverlag, 1988.

Het Rembrandt effect: visies op kijken. Utrecht: HES, 1987.

Inleiding in de literatuurwetenschap. Co-authored with Jan van Luxemburg and Willem Weststeijn. Muiderberg: Coutinho, 1981, 1982 (revised), 1983 (revised), 1985, 1987 (revised), 1988, and 1992.

——Indonesian: *Pentantar Ilmu Sastra.* Jakarta: Penerbit PT Gramedia, 1985.

De theorie van vertellen en verhalen. Muiderberg: Coutinho, 1978, 1980 (revised), 1985 (revised), 1987, and 1990 (revised and expanded).

——Spanish: *Teoría de la narrativa: Una introducción a la narratología.* Trans. Javier Franco. Madrid: Catédra, 1985 and 1988.

——English (revised and expanded): *Narratology: Introduction to the Theory of Narrative.* Trans. Christine van Boheemen. Toronto: University of Toronto Press, 1985, 1988, 1992, 1994, 1997 (revised and expanded), 1999, 2002, 2004, 2006, 2007, 2009 (revised and expanded), 2012, 2014, and 2017 (revised).

——Chinese: *Xushuxue: Xushi Lilun Daolun.* Trans. Tan Junqiang. Bejing: China Social Sciences Publishing House, 1995, 2003 (revised and expanded), 2015 (revised and expanded), and reprinted in 2017 by Beijing Normal University Press (Beijing shifan daxue chubanshe).

——Korean: Trans. YongHwan Han and DeokHwa Kang. Seoul: Moonye Publishing, 1999.

——Serbian: *Naratologija-teorija price i pripovedanja.* Trans. Rastislava Mirković. Belgrade: Narodna Knjiga, 2000.

——Polish: *Narratologia. Wprowadzenie do teorii narracji.* Trans. Ewa Kraskowska and Ewa Rajewska. Kraków: Wydawnictwo Uniwersytetu Jagiellonskiego, Eidos, 2012.

——Romanian: *Naratologia: Introducere în teoria naraţiunii*, with an introduction by Monica Bottez. Trans. Sorin Pârvu. Iaşi: Institutul European, 2008.

——Ch. 'Story: Aspects' trans. into Czech as 'Fokalizace'. Trans. Miroslava Kotáska. In *Aluze: Revue pro Literaturu, Filozofi a Jiné*, 2/3, 2004, 147–154.

Narratologie: Essais sur la signification narrative dans quatre romans modernes. Paris: Klincksieck, 1977; Utrecht: HES, 1984.

Complexité d'un roman populaire. Paris: La Pensée Universelle, 1974.

Book Chapters and Articles

'Cultural Analysis: Critical Encounters in Time, Space, and Thought'. In Murat Aydemir, Noa Roei, Aylin Kuryel, eds. *The Future of Cultural Analysis: A Critical Inquiry*. Amsterdam: Amsterdam University Press, 2025, 25–38.

'Plat? Een polemische vraag tussen twee- en driedimensionaliteit'. In Raoul Locht, ed. *Jaarboek Kunstenaars 2025*. Oosterhout: Stichting Kunstweek, 2025, 248–249.

'El análisis cultural cómo un método'. In Aldo Ocampo González, ed. *Diálogos imaginativos y re-significaciones críticas sobre Cine, Neurodiversidad y Análisis Cultural, Emergencias culturales, performatividad, e imaginación política*. Santiago de Chile: CELEI, 2024, 21–32.

'Allo-portraits: Á propos de l'impossibilité de reproduire un visage en mouvement'. In Leszek Brogowski, Gwénola Druel, Anna Szyjkowska-Piotrowska, eds. *L'insaisissable du visage. Envoutement esthétique et regard éthique*. Rennes, Presses Universitaires de Rennes, 2024, 25–42.

'Arte en la historia: resistiendo la invisibilidad social'. *Quintana: Revista do deparamento de historia del arte*, 23, 2024, doi.org/10.15304/quintana.23.9912.

'Untimeliness, Inter-ship, Mutuality'. In Tomasz Dobrogoszcz, Agata Handley, Krzysztof Majer, Tomasz Fisiak, eds. *The Woman Artist: Essays in Memory of Dorota Filipczak*. Lodz: Lodz University Press, 2024, 27–45.

'Why Matter Matters: Doris Salcedo's Material Memorial Movements'. In Ihab Saloul, Patrizia Violi, Anna Lorusso, Cristina Demaria, eds. *Questioning Traumatic Heritage: Spaces of Memory in Europe and South America*. Amsterdam: Amsterdam University Press, 2024, 39–60.

'Precarity as Threshold and Grounds of Comparison'. In Jacopo Masi, Rui Carlos Fonseca, Patrícia Lourenço, Bruno Henriques, eds. *Dedans, dehors et à travers: perspectives littéraires et comparatistes sur le seuil/In, Out and Through: Literary and Comparative Perspectives on Thresholds*. Paris: Honoré Champion, 2024, 189–211.

'The Cinematic in Literature'. In Neil Murphy, W. Michelle Wang, Cheryl Julia Lee, eds. *The Routledge Companion to Literature and Art*. London: Routledge, 2024, 60–71.

'Driving the Plot Through Colour'. In Neil Murphy, W. Michelle Wang, Cheryl Julia Lee, eds. *The Routledge Companion to Literature and Art*. London: Routledge, 2024, 384–396.

'The Architecture of Loneliness: Introduction'. Co-authored with Ernst van Alphen. In Mieke Bal, ed. *The Architecture of Loneliness*. Amsterdam: Valiz, 2024, 11–17.

'A Cultural Dream: Europe in the Plural'. *Journal of Visual Culture*, 22: 3, 2024, 295–318.

'Imaging'. In Michael Marden, Giovanbattista Tusa, eds. *Contemporanea: A Glossary for the Twenty-First Century*. Cambridge: MIT Press, 2024, 37–50.

'Dialogar, encontrar, imaginar entre las sociedades y las culturas'. *Revista de la Universidad de la Habana*, 2024, 299.

'Citational Aesthetics: For Intermediality as Interrelation'. In J. Bruhn, Asun López-Varela Azcárate, Miriam de Paiva Vieira, eds. *The Palgrave Handbook of Intermediality*, 1. New York: Springer International Publishing, 2023, 461–492.

'Con-Temporary: Thinking and Feeling Together'. *AN-ICON. Studies in Environmental Images*, 2: 1, 2023, 11–28, doi.org/10.54103/ai/19939.

'Images that Speak'. In Valery Vino, ed. *Aesthetic Literacy Vol III: an endgame*. Melbourne: mongrel matter, 2023, 68–80.

'Utopia Here and Now: Resisting Othering/Utopie hier und Jetzt: der Andersheit widerstehen'. In Andreja Hribernik et al., eds. *Blueprint for a Museum*. Graz: Kunsthaus Graz, Verlag für moderne Kunst, 2023, 76–124.

'Psychopoetic Encounters: Figurations of Difficulty'. *Word and text: A Journal of Literary Studies and Linguistics*, 2023, 15–36, jlsl.upg-ploiesti.ro/site_engleza/documente/documente/Arhiva/Word_and_Text_2023/02_Bal.pdf.

'Foreword: Turning Toward a Turn'. In Hayden White. *The ethics of Narrative Volume 2: Essays in History, Literature, and Theory 2007–2017*. Ithaca and London: Cornell University Press, 2023, vii–xiv.

'Migratory Aesthetics: Proximity and Mutuality'. In Amanda Minervini, Amelie Björck, Omri Grinberg, Amrita Ghosh, eds. *ReFiguring Global Challenges: Literary and Cinematic Explorations of War, Inequality, and Migration*. Leiden and Boston: Brill, 2023, 13–32.

'Encounters'. In Claudia Mattos Avolese, ed. *Motion:Migration. 35th world congress*. Comité International de l'Histoire de l'Art and Vasto, 2023, 32–53.

'Em- or Sym- or Con–: Feeling with Others'. In Frauke Berndt, Isabel Karremannn, Klaus Müller-Wille, eds. *Figures of Pathos: Festschrift in Honor of Elisabeth Bronfen*. Würzburg: Königshausen & Neumann GmbH, 2023, 23–35.

'Creating Coherence'. *Future Book(s): Sharing Ideas on Books and (art) publishing*. In Pia Pol, Astrid Vorstermans, eds. Amsterdam: Valiz, 2023, 190–193.

'Préface. Déballer le genre de la fiction théorique, pour le bien de tous et des fous'. In Françoise Davoine. *Mère Folle: Récit*. Toulouse: Éditions Érès, Arcanes, Collection Hypothèses, 2023, 9–17.

'Art's Agency: On Being Flabbergasted'. In Sara Alonso Gómez, Isabel J. Piniella Grillet, Nadia Radwan, Elena Rosauro, eds. *No Rhetoric(s): Versions and Subversions of Resistance in Contemporary Global Art*. Zürich: Diaphanes, 2023, 105–131.

'How to Say It? Symbiosis as Inter-Ship'. In Peggy Karpouzou, Nikoleta Zampaki, eds. *Symbiotic Posthumanist Ecologies in Western Literature, Philosophy and Art*. Berlin: Peter Lang, 2023, 79–98.

'Woman as Anti-Suicide Bomb: Women Trapped between Past and Future'. In Robin Truth Goodman, ed. *Feminism as World Literature*. London: Bloomsbury, 2023, 147–163.

'Religion as Pre-Text, Art as Counter-Text'. In Tarek R. Dika, Martin Shuster, eds. *Religion in Reason: Metaphysics, Ethics, and Politics in Hent de Vries*. London and New York: Routledge, 2023, 249–269.

'No ver más sino mejor: para enseñar una mirada políticamente productiva'. *Polyphōnia. Revista de Educación Inclusiva*, 6: 1, 2022, 12–30.

'Encuentros Cercanos: Inter-relaciones'. In Domingo Sánchez Mesa, Jordi Alberich Pascual Martínez, eds. *Transmedialización & Crowdsourcing: los placeres de la intermedialidad y la colaboración en los relatos de la cultura digital*. Valencia: Tirant Editorial, 2022, 27–42, editorial.tirant.com/es/libro/transmedializacion--crowdsourcing-jordi-alberich-pascual-9788419071545.

'Prólogo: Lo personal es político y lo político es Personal'. In Lidia Mateo Leivas. *Imaginarios de la clandestinidad: Complicidad, memoria y emoción en nueve tramas*. Trans. Jesús Espino Nuño. Madrid: Akal, 2022, 7–14.

'Hetero-Chronical Experiments Between Life and Death: Vanitas Revolts Against Time Management'. In Victoria von Flemming, Julia Catherine Berger, eds. *Vanitas als Wiederholung*. Berlin: De Gruyter, 2022, 207–236.

'Afectivamente efectivo: el afecto como estrategia artístico-política'. In Silvana Mandolessi, Martín Zícari, Reindert Dhondt, eds. *Afectos y violencias en la cultura latinoamericana*. Madrid and Frankfurt am Main: Iberoamericana-Vervuert, 2022, 51–80.

'Meaning-Making in the European Semiosphere'. *Chinese Semiotic Studies*, 18: 3, 2022, 363–389.

'Préface/Prefacio: Ceci n'est pas un livre/esto no es un libro'. In Hubert Damisch. *Goya, Le Mythe de l'assimilation/el mito de la assimilación*. Madrid: Akal, 2022, 5–19.

'Meaning Making with Mistakes'. In Caleb Kelly, Jakko Kemper, Ellen Rutten, eds. *Imperfections: Studies in Mistakes, Flaws, and Failures*. London: Bloomsbury, 2022, 51–82.

'Epilogue'. In Mathieu de Bakker, Bauke van den Berg, Jacqueline Klooster, eds. *Emotions and Narrative in Ancient Literature and Beyond. Studies in honour of Irene de Jong*. Leiden: Brill, 2022, 743–746.

'Dis-remembered and mis-remembered: a confrontation with failures of cultural memory'. In Michał Haake, Piotr Juszkiewiecz, eds. *Image, History and Memory: Central and Eastern Europe in a Comparative Perspective*. London and New York: Routledge, 2022, 7–21.

'Refugees and Representation: An Impossible Necessity'. *Humanities*, 11: 29, 2022, mdpi.com/2076-0787/11/1/29.

'Oh no! Indispensable but Insufficient: Resistance Between Activist and Activating Art/'Oh non! Indispensable mais insuffisant: la résistance entre art activiste et art activant'. In Bernard Fibicher, ed. *Resistance Anew: Artworks, Culture & Democracy*. Lausanne: JRP|editions & les Presses du réel, 2022, 16–39 and 16–43.

'From "Madame Bovary c'est moi" to "Emma is Us": Focalization as Political Tool'. In Kornélia Horváth, Judit Mudriczki, Sarolta Osztroluczky, eds. *Diversity in Narration and Writing: The Novel*. Cambridge: Cambridge Scholars Publishing, 2022, 10–31.

'Timely Commitments'. *Linguistics and Literary Science of the Macedonian Academy of Sciences and Arts (OLLN)*, 2021, 5–36.

'Lying as Truth: Cervantes as Co-Author of Don Quijote'. In Bill Balaskas, Carolina Rito, eds. *Fabricating Publics: The Dissemination of Culture in the Post-Truth Era*. London: Open Humanities Press, 2021, 167–188.

'Art and/as Thought'. *Hybrids: A Textured Future*. Amsterdam: Futures Photography, 2021, E-2-E8.

'Collective Subjectivity in the Essay Film'. *Ekphrasis: Images, Cinema, Theory, Media*, 26, 2, 2021, 10–26.

'How the Concept of Performativity Travels: Between People and Media'. *Methis, Studia Humaniora Estonica*, 22: 27/28, 2021, doi.org/10.7592/methis.v22i27/28.18440.

'Munch Bringing Thinking Home'. In Janicke Stensvaag Kaasa, Jakob Lothe, Ulrike Spring, eds. *Nordic Travels*. Oslo: Novus Press, 2021, 25–48, novus.no/products/lothe-jakob-ed-nordic-travels?_pos=1&_sid=be093ffdb&_ss=r.

'Ghosts of Dead Authors'. In Mette Høeg, ed. *Literary Theories of Uncertainty*. London: Bloomsbury, 2021, 110–135.

'Bodies Dead or Alive? Intermediality, Ambiguity, and the Politics of Dying'. In Andrew Hass, ed. *Sacred Mode of Being in a Postsecular World*. Cambridge: Cambridge University Press, 2021, 183–204.

'Fiction as Weapon'. *Estetica. studi e ricerche*, XI: 1, 2021, 45–62.

'Moments of Meaning-Making: Autobiographical Reflections in Fragments'. *PhiloSOPHIA: A Journal of transcontinental feminism*. I A–C, 226–246, vol. 10.2, Spring 2021; II, D–F, 158–177 in vol. 11; III, G–I, 117–147 in vol. 12, 2022; IV, J–L, 160–182 in vol. 13, 2023, V, M–O, 73–96 in vol. 14, 2024.

'Advocacy of shock: How to bring art to life (and its visitors with it)'. In Marianne Achiam, Michael Haldrup, Kirsten Drotner, eds. *Experimental Museology: Institutions, Representations, Users*. London and New York: Routledge, 2021, 100–116.

'Gegenseitigkeit (Ann Veronica Janssens)'. In Hanna Sohns, Johannes Ungelenk, eds. *Berühren Lesen*. Berlin: August Akademie, 2021, 62–69.

'Foreword: Mediations of Method'. In Lars Elleström, ed. *Beyond Media Borders: Intermedial Relations among Multimodal Media*, 1/2. Basingstoke: Palgrave Macmillan, 2021, v–ix.

'Migration: Migratory Aesthetics for New Visions'. In Waugh, Marc Botha, eds. *Future Theory: A Handbook of Critical Concepts*. London: Bloomsbury, 2021, 175–201.

'Ruch: kinowość w malarstwie i literaturze'. *Artium Quaestiones*, xxxi, 2020, 277–312.

'Art Making as Analysis: Thought-Images and Image-Thinking'. *Theoretical Studies in Literature and Art*, 41: 4, 2020, 1–10.

'Time and Form: The "Unthought Known"'. In Gabriele Genge, Ludger Schwarte, Angela Stercken, eds. *Aesthetic Temporalities Today: Present, Presentness, Re-Presentation*. Bielefeld: Transcript Image, 2020, 113–128.

'Contaminations: Toward an Empathic Museology'. In Bernd Herzogenrath, ed. *Practical Aesthetics*. London: Bloomsbury, 2020, 237–245.

'Improving Public Space: Trauma Art and Retrospective-Futuristic Healing'. In Arleen Ionescu, Maria Margaroni, eds. *Arts of Healing: Cultural Narratives of Trauma*. London: Rowman & Littlefield Ltd, 2020, 73–98.

'It's About Time! Trying an Essay Film'. *Text Matters*, 10, 2020, 27–48.

'Movement, Precarity, Affect'. In Radek Przedpełski, S.E. Wilmer, eds. *Deleuze, Guattari and the Art of Multiplicity*. Edinburgh: Edinburgh University Press, 2020, 83–96.

'Annunciation: The Moving Image as an Act of Witnessing.' In Hana Gründler, Alessandro Nove, Itay Sapir, eds. *The Announcement: Annunciations and Beyond*. Berlin and Boston: Walter de Gruyter GmbH, 2020, 197–218.

'Narrative Polyphonie: Kakophonie oder Zitastismus?' In Silvan Moosmüller, Boris Previšic, eds. *Polyphonie und Narration*. RABE – Series of Alternative Contributions to Narrative Research, 7. Trier: Wissenschaftlicher Verlag, 2020, 111–122.

'Challenging and Saving the Author, for Creativity/Sfidare e salvare l'autore, per creatività'. *Vesper. Rivista di architettura, arti e Teoria/Journal of Architecture, Arts & Theory*, 2, 2020, 132–149, DOI 10.1400/283006.

'Looking with Women'. In Julia Donner, Hanna Johansson, Emma Lilja, eds. *Ikkunalla. Näkymiä sukupueleen, titaal ja aikaan. Kirsi Saarikankaan juhlakirja*. Taidehistoriallisia tutkimuksia, Konsthistoriska studier, 51, 2020, 14–27.

'La pensée-ciné: le retour d'Emma'. In Barbara Vinken, Pierre-Marc de Biasi, Anne Herschberg Pierrot, eds. *Flaubert et les sortilèges de l'image*. Berlin and Boston: De Gruyter, 2020, 5–21.

'Allo-Portraits: Collaboration Between Mirror and Mask'. Luca del Baldo. *The Visionary Academy of Ocular Mentality: Atlas of the Iconic Turn*. Berlin: De Gruyter, 2020, 36–43.

'Thinking in Film'. In Jill Bennett, Mary Zournazi, eds. *Thinking in the World: A Reader*. London: Bloomsbury Academic, 2020, 173–201.

'Facing the Face: To be or not to be Don Quijote'. *World Literature Studies*, 11, 2019, 69–83.

'Fotografia po kinie' (Photography after Cinema) and 'Watpliwoc jako przyczyna' (Doubt as Reason). In Maja Gomulska, Wiktoria Kozioł, Gabriela Sułkowska, eds. *Tradycja Kartezjanska po zwrocie afectywnym. Mieke Bal: Reasonable Doubt*. Kraków: Uniwersytetu Jegiellonskiego, 2019, 9–14 and 147–176.

'Für den Moment'. In Sigrid Adorf, Kathrin Heinz, eds. *Zeichen/Momente: Vergegenwärtigungen in Kunst und Kulturanalyse*. Trans. Otmar Lichtenwörther. Bielefeld: Transcript, 2019, 95–111.

'Close Encounters, Producing Mutual "Integration"'. In Burcu Dogramaci, Birgit Mersmann, eds. *Handbook of Art and Global Migration*. Berlin and Boston: De Gruyter, 2019, 79–101.

'Temporal Turbulence: In Praise of Anachronism'. In Andrea Bubenik, ed. *The Persistence of Melancholy in Arts and Culture*. New York and London: Routledge, 2019, 144–162.

'Learning Listening'. *Practices of Listening, Soap Box A Graduate Journal for Cultural Analysis*, 1: 1, 2019, 187–193.

'Narrative Here-Now'. In Marina Grishakova, Maria Poulaki, eds. *Narrative Complexity: Cognition, Embodiment, Evolution*. Lincoln: University of Nebraska Press, 2019, 247–269.

'An Aesthetic of Interruption: Stagnation and Acceleration'. Co-authored with Jeannette Christensen. *ASAP Journal*, 4: 1, 2019, 85–112.

'The Point of Narratology: Part 2'. *INDECS*, 17: 2, 2019, 242–258.

'Affectively Effective: Affect as an Artistic-Political Strategy'. In Ernst van Alphen, Tomáš Jirsa, eds. *How to Do Things with Affects: Affective Triggers in Aesthetic Forms and Cultural Practices*. Leiden and Boston: Brill | Rodopi, 2019, 179–199.

'Cuadro-por-cuadro: entre el análisis visual y la producción de imagines'. *Los cuerpos de la imagen*, Colección diecisiete: teoría crítica, psicoanálisis, acontecimiento, 8, 2018, 119–159.

'Y-cidad: los múltiples sentidos de "y"'. *Versants*, 65: 3, 2018, 187–207.

'Narrando comida, haciéndonos urbanos: *Glub* y la estética de lo cotidiano'. *Mitilogías hoy: revista de pensamiento, crítica y estudios literarios latinoamericanos*, 2018, 245–265.

'Abolish the Peer Review System'. *Media Theory*, 3 September 2018, mediatheoryjournal.org/mieke-bal-lets-abolish-the-peer-review-system/.

——Italian: 'Aboliamo il sistema peer review'. *Lavoroculturale.org*, 4 December 2019.

'Activating Temporalities: The Political Power of Artistic Time'. *Open Cultural Studies*, 2: 1, 2018, 84–102, doi.org/10.1515/culture-2018-0009.

'In the Absence of Post-'. In Divya Dwivedi, Henrik Skov Nielsen, Richard Walsh, eds. *Narratology & Ideology: Negotiating Context, Form, and Theory in Postcolonial Narratives*. Columbus: Ohio State Press, 2018, 231–250.

'Towards a Relational Inter-Temporality'. In Eva Wittcocx, Ann Demeester, Peter Carpreaau, Melanie Bühler, Xander Karskens, eds. *The Transhistorical Museum: Mapping the Field*. Amsterdam: Valiz, 2018, 48–63.

'Violence Re-Viewed'. In Rebecca Jagoe, Sharon Kivland, eds. *On Violence*. London: Ma Bibliothèque, 2018, 213–223.

'Is There an Ethics to Story-Telling?' In Hanna Meretoja, Colin Davis, eds. *Story-Telling and Ethics: Literature, Visual Arts and the Power of Narrative*. New York and London: Routledge, 2018, 37–54.

'Prólogo'. In Alberto Montoya Hernández. *Acompañar la locura. En las encrucijadas de un Sancho Panza*. México City: Circulo psicoanalítico Mexicano, 2017, 17–27.

'Speaking Doesn't Happen Without Vision'. *Qui Parle?*, 26: 2, 2017, 355–357.

'Telling Food, Going Urban: Glub and the Aesthetics of Everyday Life'. In Blanca Montalvo, ed. *How Are Things Being Told?* Proceedings of the 3d International Conference 'art, Science, City', Malaga, 23–24 November 2017, 23–36.

'Sneaky Snakes: Seduction, the Biblical imagination, and Activating Art'. In Yvonne Sherwood, ed. *The Bible and Feminism: Remapping the Field*. Oxford: Oxford University Press, 2017, 589–607.

'Im Angesicht der De-Figuration [Facing de-facement]. Zwölf Fragmente zu Repräsentation'. In Anna Babka, Katrin Lasthofer, eds. *Representation Revisited*. Vienna: Turia + Kant, 2017, 57–86.

'Stains Against Violence: Nalini Malani's Strategies for Durational Looking'. *Journal for Contemporary Painting*, 4: 1, 2017, 59–80.

'Sensing the Present: "Conceptual Art of the Senses"'. Co-authored with Rachel E. Burke. *Text Matters*, 7: 7, 2017, 27–43.

'Dare to Doubt'. *The Philosophical Salon of the LA Review of Books*, 2017, thephilosophicalsalon.com/dare-to-doubt/.

'Intership: Anachronism between Loyalty and the Case'. In Thomas Leitch, ed. *The Oxford Handbook of Adaptation Studies*. New York and Oxford: Oxford University Press, 2017, 179–196.

'Intimacy, Modesty, Silence: Documentary Filmmaking in the Face of Trauma'. In David LaRocca, ed. *The Philosophy of Documentary Film: Image, Sound, Fiction, Truth*. Lanham: Rowman & Littlefield; London: Lexington Books, 2017, 261–286.

'Migracja: estetyki migracyjne na rzecz'. Trans. Anna Kowalcze-Pawlik. In Ryszard Nycz, Roma Sendyka, Tomasz Sapota, eds. *Migracyjna pamięć, wspólnota, toższamość*. Warszawa: Institut Badań Literackich Pan Wydawnictwo, 2016, 53–91.

'El tiempo que se toma', *Contra Narrativas, Revista de Estudios Visuales*. Murcia, November 2016, um.es/artlab/index.php/revista/the-time-it-takes-el-tiempo-que-tarda/.

'Reasonable Doubt: Kijken naar denkbeelden'. *Tijdschrift voor biografie*, 5: 4, 2016, 56–65.

'Breaking the Narrative: The *Madame B* Project and Historical Loyalty'. In Anna Babka, Marlen Bidwell-Steiner, Wolfgang Müller-Funk, eds. *Narrative im Bruch. Theoretische Positionen und Anwendungen*. Vienna: V&R unipress/Vienna University Press, 2016, 255–270.

'Scale as a Political Tool: Louise Bourgeois' *Cells* as a Mode of Living. On the Occasion of the Munich Exhibition'. *Kunst Chronik*, 69, 7 July 2016, 349–362.

'Movement and the Still Image'. *Espacio, Tiempo y Forma*, VII: 4, 2016, 15–44.

'Afekt jako siła kulturowa'. Trans. Anna Turczyn. In Elżbieta Wichrowska, Anna Szczepan-Wojnarska, Roma Sendyka, Ryszard Nycz, eds. *Historie afektywne I polityki pamienci*. Warsaw: Institut Badan, literackich pan wydawnictwo, 2016, 33–46.

'Zagubienie: gruntowna przemiana kwestii naszego "my"'. Trans. Tomasz Bilczewski and Anna Kowalcze-Pawlik. In Elzbiet Wichrowskia, Anna Szczepan-Wojnarskia, Roma Sendyka, Richard Nycz, eds. *Historie afektywne I polityki pamienci*. Warsaw: Institut Badan, literackich pan wydawnictwo, 2016, 501–548.

'From Documentary to Fiction and Back'. Co-authored with Michelle Williams Gamaker. [...] (*Ellipses*), 1, 2016, ellipses.org.za/project/from-documentary-to-fiction-and-back/.

'Long Live Anachronism'. In Lia Brozgal, Sara Kippur, eds. *Being Contemporary: French Literature, Culture, and Politics Today*. Liverpool: Liverpool University Press, 2016, 281–304.

'Lostness, Tents, and Faces: When Home Fails Us'. In Cecile Sandten, Kathy-Ann Tan, eds. *Home: Concepts, Constructions and Contexts*. Trier: Wissenschaftlicher Verlag Trier, 2016, 113–140.

'Photography After Cinema'. In Mariama Attah, Ben Burbridge, eds. *Photoworks: Photography, Art, Visual Culture, 22: Women*. Brighton: Photoworks, 2015, 8–9.

'Preface'. In Helinä Hukkataival. *Helinä Hukkataival: Space Between Ritual and Carnival*. Heidelberg: Kehrer Verlag, 2014, 1–8.

'In Medias Res: Visiting Nalini Malani's Retrospective Exhibition, New Delhi, 2014'. *Qui Parle: Critical Humanities and Social Sciences*, 24: 1, Fall/Winter 2015, 31–62.

'Eccentricity in Order to Re-centre: La Maison Rouge'. *Journal of Curatorial Studies*, 4, 2015, 214–236.

'Reflection: Memory and Storytelling in Proust'. In Dmitri Nikulin, ed. *Memory: A History*. Oxford: Oxford University Press, 2015, 220–227.

'Curaduría intercultural'. *Errata: La geopolítica del arte contemporáneo*, 14, 2015, 132–153.

'Power to the Imagination!' *Krisis*, 2, 2015, 68–76.

'An island of madness: the social force of mental fortresses – a visual essay'. Co-authored with Michelle Williams Gamaker. *Transnational Cinemas*, 6: 2, 2015, 1–15, doi.org/10.1080/20403526.2015.1071040.

'The Last Frontier: Migratory Culture, Video, and Exhibiting without Voyeurism'. In Annie E. Coombes, Ruth B. Phillips, eds. *The International Handbooks of Museum Studies: Museum Transformations*, 4. London: John Wiley & Sons, Ltd., 2015, 415–438.

'In Your Face: Migratory Aesthetics.' In Sten Pulz Moslund, Anne Ring Petersen, Moritz Schramm, eds. *The Culture of Migration: Politics, Aesthetics and Histories*. London: I.B. Tauris, 2015, 147–170.

'Zin zien'. *Vooys*, 33: 2, 2015, 17–27.

'Im Wirbel der Zeiten. Lob des Anachronismus.' In Günter Blamberger, Sidonie Kellerer, Tanja Klemm, Jan Söffner, eds. *Sind alle Denker Traurig? Fallstudien zum melancholischen Grund des Schöpferischen in Asien und Europa*. Cologne: Morphomata, 2015, 63–92.

'Documenting What? Auto-Theory and Migratory Aesthetics'. In Alexandra Juhasz, Alisa Lebow, eds. *A Companion to Contemporary Documentary Film*. Oxford: Wiley Blackwell, 2015, 124–144.

'Always Too Long: My Short Film Experience'. *Empedocles: European Journal for the Philosophy of Communication*, 5: 1/2, 2015, 13–18.

'Travel Companions'. In Siobhan Kattago, ed. *The Ashgate Research Companion to Memory Studies*. Farnham: Ashgate, 2014, 145–162.

'De la novella a la película: El Proyecto de Madame B'. In *Madame B. Exploraciones en el capitalism emocional*. Medellín: Universidad Nacional de Colombia, sede Medellín, 2014.

'Moving Images: Two-Way'. In Kathryn Brown, ed. *Interactive Contemporary Art: Participation in Practice*. London: I.B. Tauris, 2014, 17–26.

'Masterly Maxims'. *PMLA*, 129: 3, May 2014, 491–497.

'Intercultural Curating'. In Michael Kelly, ed. *Encyclopedia of Aesthetics*, 2. New York and Oxford: Oxford University Press, 2014, 238–242.

'Peface.' In Françoise Davoine. *Mother Folly: A Tale*. Stanford: Stanford University Press, 2014, xiii–xxiv.

'Mores leren.' In Agnes Andeweg, Lies Wesseling, eds. *Wat de verbeelding niet vermag! Essays bij het afscheid van Maaike Meijer*. Nijmegen: Van Tilt, 2014, 23–29.

'Pensar em Filme'. *Celeuma*, 2: 3, December 2013, doi.org/10.11606/issn.2318-7875.v2i3p12-29.

'Raconter en images: Flaubert aujourd'hui'. *Lendemains*, 38: 149, 2013, 64–78.

'First Memories and Second Thoughts'. In Jo Carruthers, Mark Knight, Andrew Tate, eds. *Literature and the Bible: A Reader*. London and New York: Routledge, 2013, 306–312.

'Imaging Madness: Inter-ships'. *In/Print*, 2: 1, 2013, 52–70.

'Scenography of Death: Figuration, Focalization, and Finding Out'. Co-authored with Michelle Williams Gamaker. *Performance Research*, 18: 3, June 2013, 179–186.

'Buñuel's Critique of Nationalism: A Migratory Aesthetic?' In Rob Stone, Daniel Gutiérrez-Albilla, eds. *A Companion to Luis Buñuel*. Oxford: Wiley-Blackwell's, 2013, 116–137.

'Affect and the Space We Share: Three Forms of Installation Art'. In Pablo Baler, ed. *The Next Thing: Art in the Twenty-First Century*. Madison: Fairleigh Dickinson University Press, 2013, 67–80.

'Not so Stupid'. *Parallax*, 19: 3, 2013, 50–69.

'Deliver Us from A-Historicism: Metahistory for Non-Historians'. In Robert Doran, ed. *Philosophy of History After Hayden White*. London: Bloomsbury, 2013, 67–88.

——Spanish (edited): 'Libranos del ahistoricismo: metahistoria para no historiadores'. *Blanco sobre blanco: miradas y lecturas sobre artes visuales*, May 2015, 10–28.

'Art Moves'. *ARKEN Bulletin Migration: Contemporary Art from India*, 6, 2013, 25–29.

'Intercultural Story-Telling'. In Alexandra Strohmaier, ed. *Kultur – Wissen – Narration: Perspektiven transdisciplinärer Erzählforschung für die Kulturwissenschaften*. Vienna and Graz: [transcript], 2013, 289–306.

'Heterochrony in the Act: The Migratory Politics of Time'. In Ivan Stevonic, ed. *Symmeikta: Collection of Papera Dedicated to the 40th Anniversary of the Institute for Art History*. Belgrade: Faculty of Philosophy, University of Belgrade, 2012, 579–596.

'Lexicon for Cultural Analysis'. In Anna Babka, Daniela Finzi, Clemens Ruthner, eds. *Die Lust an der Kultur/Theorie. Transdisziplinäre Interventionen Für Wolfgang Müller-Funk*. Vienna and Berlin: Turia + Kant Verlag, 2012, 49–81.

'Extranjerías, or How to Exit Cultural Autism'. In *Knowledge Politics and Intercultural Dynamics: Actions, Innovations, Transformations*. Barcelona: United Nations University, 2012, 7–26.

'Zabójcze zwierciadla'. In Anna Matysiak, ed. *Antropologia. Kultury wizualnej*. Warsaw: Wydawnictwa Uniwersytetu Warszawsiego, 2012, 703–710.

'*Madame B*.: l'analyse cinématographique d'un roman'. *Flaubert: Revue Critique et génétique. Flaubert* [En ligne], *Traductions/Adaptations, mis en ligne*, 7 December 2012, doi.org/10.4000/flaubert.1837.

'S-Words'. *Journal of Visual Culture*, 11: 2, 2012, 145–148.

'Curatorial Acts'. *Journal of Curatorial Studies*, 1: 2, 2012, 179–192.

'La maison: pour l'hospitalité'. In Jean-François Vallée, Jean Klucinskas, Gilles Dupuis, eds. *Transmédiations: traversées culturelles de la modernité tardive*. Montréal: Les Presses de l'Université de Montréal, 2012, 25–40.

'Facing: Intimacy Across Divisions'. In Geraldine Pratt, Victoria Rosner, eds. *The Global and the Intimate: Feminism in Our Time*. New York: Columbia University Press, 2012, 119–144; longer version in Lu Liande, Ernst van Alphen, eds. *Literature, Aesthetics and History*. Bejing: Forum of Cultural Exchange Between China and the Netherlands, 2015, 42–74.

'Introduction'. Co-authored with Michelle Williams Gamaker. *Le Coq-Héron*, 211: 4, December 2012, 117–118, doi.org/10.3917/cohe.211.0111.

'Folie et déraison créatrice'. *Le Coq-Héron*, 211: 4, December 2012, 119–126, doi.org/10.3917/cohe.211.0117.

'Imaging Pain'. In Asbjørn Grønstad and Hendrik Gustafsson, eds. *Ethics and Images of Pain*. New York: Routledge, 2012, 115–143.

'L'interdisciplinarité: travailler avec des concepts'. In Frédéric Darbellay, ed. *La circulation des savoirs. Interdisciplinarité, concepts nomades, analogies, métaphores*. Bern and Berlin: Peter Lang, 2012, 25–58.

'Spatialising Film'. In Jan Fredrik Hovden, Karl Knapskog, eds. *Hunting High and Low: Festschrift for Jostein Gripsrud*. Oslo: Scandinavian Academic Press, 2012, 160–182.

'Perpetual Contest'. In Jan N. Bremmer, Marco Formisano, eds. *Perpetua's Passions: Multidisciplinary Approaches to the* Passio Perpetuae et Felicitatis. Oxford: Oxford University Press, 2012, 134–49; revised version in Ihab Saloul, Jan Willem van Henten, eds. *Martyrdom: Canonisation, Contestation and Afterlives*. Amsterdam: Amsterdam University Press, 2020, 105–128.

'Cultural Analysis – The Joseph Plays'. Co-authored with Maaike Bleeker, Bennett Carpenter, and Frans-Willem Korsten. In Jan Bloemendal, Frans-Willem Korsten, eds. *Joost van den Vondel (1587–1669): Dutch Playwright in the Golden Age*. Leiden: Brill, 2012, 317–40.

'Towards a Babel Ontology'. Co-authored with Michelle Williams Gamaker. *European Journal of Women's Studies*, 18: 4, 2011, 439–447.

'Introduction'. In Mieke Bal, Miguel Á. Hernández-Navarro, eds. *Art and Visibility in Migratory Culture: Conflict, Resistance, and Agency*. Amsterdam: Rodopi, 2011, 9–20.

'Heterochrony in the Act: The Migratory Politics of Time'. In Mieke Bal, Miguel Á. Hernández-Navarro, eds. *Art and Visibility in Migratory Culture: Conflict, Resistance, and Agency*. Amsterdam: Rodopi, 2011, 211–238.

'Losing It: The Politics of the Other (Medium)'. *Journal of Visual Culture*, 10: 3, 2011, 372–396. Reprinted in Cathleen Chaffee, ed. *Eija-Liisa Ahtila: Ecologies of Drama*. Buffalo: Albright-Knox Art Gallery, 2015, 56–73.

'Earth Aches: The Aesthetics of the Cut'. In Juan A. Gaitan, ed. *Cornerstones*. Rotterdam: Witte de With Publishers/Sternberg Press, 2011, 212–227.

'An Inter-Action: Rembrandt and Spinoza'. Co-authored with Dimitris Vardoulakis. In Dimitris Vardoulakis, ed. *Spinoza Now*. Minneapolis: University of Minnesota Press, 2011, 277–306.

'Baroque Matters'. Helen Hills, ed. *Rethinking the Baroque*. Surray: Ashgate, 2011, 183–202.

'A Thousand and One Voices'. In Mads Anders Baggesgaard, Jakob Ladegaard, eds. *Confronting Universalities: Aesthetics and Politics under the Sign of Globalisation*. Aarhus: Aarhus University Press, 2011, 269–304.

'*Mektoub*: When Art Meets History, Philosophy, and Linguistics'. In Allen F. Repko, Williams H. Newell, Rick Szostak, eds. *Case Studies in Interdisciplinary Research*. Thousand Oaks: SAGE, 2011, 91–122.

'Deborah'. In Daniel Patte, ed. *The Cambridge Dictionary of Christianity*. Cambridge: Cambridge University Press, 2010, 313.

'True Lies: on Ana Torfs's *Du mentir-faux*, or Some Dilemmas of History'. In Rune Ottosen, Solveig Steigen, eds. *HiO–report 12: Framing War with Facts and Fiction in the Cultural Field*. Oslo: Oslo University College, 2010, 28–51.

'The Quoted Artist'. *Italian Journal*, 20: 3, 2010, 40–43.

'Religion and Powerlessness: Elena in *Nothing Is Missing*'. In Meerten B. ter Borg, Jan Willem van Henten, eds. *Powers: Religion as a Social and Spriritual Force*. New York: Fordham University Press, 2010, 209–239.

'Exhibition Practices'. *PMLA*, 125: 1, 2010, 9–23.

'After-Images: Mère folle'. *Nomadikon: About Images*, 7, 2010.

'Exhibition as a Syntax of the Face'. *Manifesta Journal: Journal of Contemporary Curatorship*, 9, 2009/2010, 13–22.

'Arte para lo Político'. Trans. Roberto Riquelme. *Estudios Visuales*, 7, 2009, 39–65.

'Becoming of the World versus Identity Politics'. *Nordlit: Tidsskrift i litteratur og kultur*, 24, 2009, 9–30, uit.no/getfile.php?PageId=977&FileId=1453.

'The Commitment to Face'. In Begüm Özden Firat, Sarah De Mul, Sonja van Wichelen, eds. *Commitment and Complicity in Cultural Theory & Practice*. Basingstoke: Macmillan, 2009, 120–136.

'¿Arte Narrativo? Reflexiones discontinuas'. In Manuel Borja-Villel, Yolanda Romero, eds. *10.000 francos de recompensa (El museo de arte contemporáneo vivo o muerto)*. Trans. Antonio León Correa et al. Barcelona: Actar, 2009, 121–138.

'Working with Concepts'. *European Journal of English Studies*, 13: 1, 2009, 13–23; also in *Slovo a smysl/Word & Sense*, 11/12, 2009, 202–212.

'Response: Ariel Dorfman's Quest for Responsibility'. *Art Bulletin*, 41: 1, 2009, 44–50.

'Lesbarkeit der Kultur'. In Hans-Peter Schmidt, Daniel Weidner, eds. *Bibel als Literatur*. Munich: Wilhelm Fink Verlag, 2008, 281–282.

'Visual Analysis'. In Tony Bennett, John Frow, eds. *The SAGE Handbook of Cultural Analysis*. London: SAGE Publications, 2008, 163–184.

'Heterochronotopia'. In Murat Aydemir, Alex Rotas, eds. *Migratory Settings*. Amsterdam and New York: Rodopi, 2008, 35–56.

'Research Practice: New Words on Cold Cases'. In Michael Ann Holly, Marquard Smith, eds. *What is Research in the Visual Arts: Obsession, Archive, Encounter*. Williamstown: Sterling and Francine Clark Art Institute, 2008, 196–211.

'Migratory Aesthetics: Double Movement'. *EXIT*, 32, 2008, 150–161.

——Spanish: 'Estéticas migratorias: Movimiento doble'. *EXIT*, 32, 2008, 138–149.

'Mélanges'. In Eric de Haard, Wim Honselaar, Jenny Stelleman, eds. *Literature and Beyond: Festschrift for Willem G. Weststeijn on the Occasion of his 65th Birthday*. Amsterdam: Pegasus, 2008, 65–91.

'Migratory Terrorism'. In Jaap Kooijman, Patricia Pisters, Wanda Strauven, eds. *Mind the Screen: Media Concepts According to Thomas Elsaesser*. Amsterdam: Amsterdam University Press, 2008, 297–309.

'"You Do What You Have To Do": A Response To Joseph Früchtl'. *Krisis: Journal for Contemporary Philosophy*, 1, 2008, 59–69, krisis.eu/content/2008-1/2008-1-08-bal.pdf.

——Serbian: '"Radiš ono što moraš": Odgovor Josefu Früchtlu'. *TkH*, 16, 2008, 95–103.

'Exhibition as Film'. In Robin Ostow, ed. *(Re)Visualizing National History: Museums and National Identities in Europe in the New Millennium*. Toronto: Univerisity of Toronto Press, 2008, 15–47, reprinted in 2014.

——Serbian: *'Изложба као филм'*. Trans. Novica Petrovic. *Collection of Department of History of Modern Art Faculty of Philosophy of Belgrade*, 5, 2009, 137–156.

——Reprinted in Sharon Macdonald, Paul Basu, eds. *New Interventions in Art History: Exhibition Experiments*. Hoboken: Blackwell Publishing Ltd, 2007, 71–93.

'Gemengde Gevoelens'. *Denkwerk: Cahier EAJ*. The Hague: Department of Justice, 2008, 118–133.

'Phantom Sentences'. In Robert S. Kawashima, Gilles Philippe, Thelma Sowley, eds. *Phantom Sentences: Essays in Linguistics and Literature Presented to Ann Banfield*. Bern: Peter Lang, 2008, 17–42.

'Loving Yusuf: A Story of Taboos'. *Hecate: An Interdisciplinary Journal of Women's Liberation*, 33, 2, 2007, 14–30.

'Autotopography: Louise Bourgeois as builder', and 'Postscript: Mieke Bal in Conversation'. *Reading Room: A Journal of Art and Culture*, 1, 2007, 40–59 and 101.

'A Thousand and One Voices'. *Amsterdam International Electronic Journal for Cultural Narratology*, 4, Autumn 2007, cf.hum.uva.nl/narratology/a07_bal.htm.

'Far Encounters: Looking Desire'. In Kristie S. Fleckenstein, Sue Hum, Linda T. Calendrillo, eds. *Ways of Seeing, Ways of Speaking*. West Lafayette: Parlor Press LLC, 2007, 179–202.

'What If? The Language of Affect'. In Gilliam Beer, Malcolm Bowie, Beate Perrey, eds. *In(ter)discipline: New Languages for Criticism*. London: Modern Humanities Research Association and Maney Publishing, 2007, 6–24.

——Polish: 'Język afektu'. Trans. Maciej Maryl. *Teksty Drugie*, 1/2, 2007, 165–189.

'Lost in Space, Lost in the Library'. In Sam Durrant, Catherine Lord, eds. *Essays in Migratory Aesthetics*. Amsterdam and New York: Rodopi, 2007, 23–36.

'From Cultural Studies to Cultural Analysis'. *Kritische Berichte: Zeitschrift für Kunst und Kulturwissenschaften*, 35: 2, 2007, 34–44.

'Elena: An episode of my work Nothing is Missing'. In Krist Gruijthuijsen, ed. *We All Laughed at Christopher Columbus*. Berlin: Revolver, 2007, 183–210.

'Lost in Space: The Violence of Language'. In Kata Kulavkova, ed. *Interpretations: European Research Project for Poetics and Hermeneutics, vol. 1, Violence and Art*. Skopje: Macedonian Academy of Sciences and Arts, 2007, 53–68.

'Exhibition as Film.' In Sharon MacDonald, Paul Basu, eds. *Exhibition Experiments*. Oxford: Blackwell Publishing, 2007, 71–93.

'Editorial: Acts of Translation'. Co-authored with Joanne Morra, and 'Translating Translations'. *Journal of Visual Culture*, 6, April 2007, 5–11 and 109–124.

'Migratory Aesthetics'. In Renee Ridgway, Katarina Zdjelar, eds. *Another Publication*. Rotterdam: Piet Zwart Institute, 2007, 13–19.

'Women's Rembrandt'. In Griselda Pollock, Joyce Zemans, eds. *Museums After Modernism: Strategies of Engagement*. Oxford: Blackwell, 2007, 40–69.

'The Pain of Images'. In Mark Reinhardt, Holly Edwards, Erina Duganne, eds. *Beautiful Suffering: Photography and the Traffic in Pain*. Chicago: University of Chicago Press, 2007, 93–115.

——Spanish: 'El arte contemporáneo y el mundo: El dolor de las imágines'. In *Cuerpo y mirada, huellas del siglo XX: Edición a cargo de Aurora Fernández Polanco*. Madrid: Museo nacional Centro de Arte Reina Sofía, 2007, 145–181.

——French: 'Beautiful Suffering: La douleur des images'. Trans. Morad Montazami. In Giovanni Careri, Bernhard Rüdiger, eds. *Face au réel: Éthique de la forme dans l'art contemporain*. Lyon: Archibooks, École nationale des beaux-arts de Lyon, and École des hautes études en sciences sociales, 2008, 275–299.

'From Sub- to Suprasemiotic: The Sign as Event'. In Sunil Manghani, Arthur Piper, Jon Simons, eds. *Images: A Reader*. London: SAGE Publications, 2006, 115–118.

'Loops and Gaps: Video as Entrance into the Unknown'. *Amsterdam International Electronic Journal for Cultural Narratology*, 3, Autumn 2006, cf.hum.uva.nl/narratology/a06_bal.html.

'Facing Severance'. *Intermédialités*, 8, 2006 189–210; reprinted in *Traverser/Crossing, Intermédialités*, 20, Autumn 2012/Spring 2013, 197–218.

'Nothing is Missing'. *Intermédialités*, 8, 2006, 189–224.

'Lepljive podobe: krčenje časovne dimenzije v umetnosti trajana', *Likovne Besede*. Ljubljana: Union of the Slovene Fine Artists Associations, Summer 2006, 39–51.

'Affekt als kulturelle Kraft: Einleitung'. In Antje Krause-Wahl, Heike Oehlschlägel, Serjoscha Wiemer, eds. *Affekte: Analysen ästhetisch-medialer Prozesse*. Bielefeld: Transcript Verlag, 2006, 7–19.

'Metaphoring: Making a Niche of Negative Space'. In Maria Margaroni, Effie Yiannopoulou, eds. *Metaphoricity and the Politics of Mobility*. Amsterdam and New York: Rodopi, 2006, 159–180.

'Dreaming Art'. In Griselda Pollock, ed. *Psychoanalysis and the Image: Transdisciplinary Perspectives*. Oxford: Blackwell, 2006, 30–59.

'Faithfully Submitted: The Logic of the Signature in Marcel Proust's *A la recherche*'. In Sonja Neef, José van Dijck, Eric Ketelaar, eds. *Sign Here! Handwriting in the Age of New Media*. Amsterdam: Amsterdam University Press, 2006, 150–163.

'Erste Person, zweite Person, dieselbe Person: Zum Verhältnis von Ausstellen und Beschreiben aus narratologischer Sicht'. In Sigrid Nieberle, Elisabeth Strowick, eds. *Narration und Geschlchte. Texte – Medien – Episteme*. Cologne, Weimar, and Vienna: Böhlau Verlag, 2006, 283–314.

'Aestheticizing Catastrophe'. In Michael P. Steinberg, Monica Bohm-Duchen, eds. *Reading Charlotte Salomon*. Ithaca and London: Cornell University Press, 2006, 167–193.

——Italian: 'Estetizzare la catastrofe', *Trasparenze*. 2021, 7, sanmarcodeigiustiniani.it/trasparenze-nuova-serie/.

'The Commitment to Look', *Journal of Visual Culture*, 4, 2005, 145–162.

——Spanish: 'El compromiso con el mirar'. Trans. Diego Gómes Venegas. *Canal. Cuadernos de estudios visuales y mediales*, 2/3, 2018/2019, 13–54.

'Hva om? Å utforske det som ikke er naturlig'. Trans. Harald Nortun. In Anne Beate Maurseth, Erik Østerud, eds. *Estetiske teknologier 1700–2000*, 2. Oslo: Scandinavian Academic Press, 2005, 157–171.

'Food, Form, and Visibility: *GLUB* and the Aesthetics of Everyday Life.' *Postcolonial Studies*, 8, 1, 2005, 51–77; reprinted in *Enigma Objekta: Zbornik teorijskih tekstova*, eds. Gordan Karabogdan, Nikica Klobučar. Zagreb: I. T. GRAF, 2005, 9–23; and in Günter Bamberger, Dietrich Boschung, eds. *Kulturelle Figurationen: Genese, Dynamik und Medialität*. München: Morphomata, 2011, 175–196.

'Introduction'. In Mieke Bal, ed. *The Artemisia Files: Artemisia Gentileschi for Feminists and Other Thinking People*. Chicago: University of Chicago Press, 2005, ix–xxv.

'Grounds of Comparison'. In Mieke Bal, ed. *The Artemisia Files: Artemisia Gentileschi for Feminists and Other Thinking People*. Chicago: University of Chicago Press, 2005, 129–168.

'To Read a Picture'. In Julian Wolfreys, ed. *The J. Hillis Miller Reader*. Edinburgh: Edinburgh University Press, 2005, 82–88.

'Interdisciplinary Approaches to Narrative'. In David Herman, Manfred Jahn, Marie-Laure Ryan, eds. *Encyclopedia of Narrative Theory*. London and New York: Routledge, 2005, 250–252.

'Fifteen Stories of Cleopatra'. In *Cléopâtre dans le miroir de l'Art Occidental*. Musée Rath, Genève: 5 Continents Editions srl, Milan, 2005, 293–305.

'Visual Narrativity'. In David Herman, Manfred Jahn, Marie-Laure Ryan, eds. *Encyclopedia of Narrative Theory*. London and New York: Routledge, 2005, 629–633.

'L'éthique de la description'. In Vincent Jouve, Alain Pagès, eds. *Les Lieux du réalisme. Pour Philippe Hamon*. Paris: Éditions L'improviste/Presses de la Sorbonne Nouvelle, 2005, 146–157.

'The Violence of Gender'. In Philomena Essed, David Theo Goldberg, Audrey Kobayashi, eds. *A Companion to Gender Studies*. Oxford: Blackwell, 2005, 530–543.

'Light Writing: Portraiture in a Post-Traumatic Age'. *Mosaic: A Journal for the Interdisciplinary Study of Literature*, 27: 4, December 2004, 1–19.

'Figuration'. *PMLA*, 119: 5, 2004, 1289–1292.

'Akte des Schauens: Proust und die visuelle Kultur'. Trans. Maria Imhof and Kirsten Kramer. In ed. Wolfram Nitsch, Riner Zaiser, eds. *Marcel Proust und die Kunste*. Frankfurt am Main and Leipzig: Insel Verlag, 2004, 90 –111.

'Over-writing as Un-writing: Descriptions, World-Making, and Novelistic Time'. In Mieke Bal, ed. *Narrative Theory: Critical Concepts in Literary and Cultural Studies*, 1. London and New York: Routledge, 2004, 341–388; and in Franco Moretti, ed. *The Novel*. Princeton: Princeton University Press, 2006, 571–610.

'Exposing the Public'. In Malte Hagener, Johann N. Schmidt, Michael Wedel, eds. *Die Spur durch den Spiegel: Der Film in der Kultur der Moderne*. Berlin: Bertz-Verlag, 2004, 51–64; reprinted in Sharon Macdonald, ed. *A Companion to Museum Studies*. Oxford: Blackwell, 2006, 525–542.

'Cultuur en traditie'. In Peter van Zilfhout, ed. *Denken over cultuur*. Heerlen: Open Universiteit Nederland, 2003, 225–255.

'Embracing the Horizon'. In *Arcadia: International Journal of Literary Studies*, 38: 2, 2003, 414–418.

'De droom als theater: de droomduiding in het licht van hedendaagse cultuurstudies'. In Mieke Taat, ed. *De droomduiding herdacht: essays over cultuuronderzoek en psychoanalyse*. Amsterdam: Uitgeverij Boom, 2003, 93–107.

'Mieke Bal's Reply to the Responses to Her Article "Visual Essentialism and the Object of Visual Culture" [*Journal of Visual Culture*, 2: 1, 2003, 5–32]'. *Journal of Visual Culture*, 2: 2, 2003, 260–268.

——Spanish: 'Respuesta las respuestas'. Trans. Carolina Díaz, David García Casado, and María Teresa Tellechea. *Estudios Visuales*, 2, December 2004, 97–107.

'Allo-Portraits'. In David Blostein, Pia Kleber, eds. *Mirror or Mask: Self–Representation in the Modern Age*. Berlin: VISTAS Verlag, 2003, 11–43.

'Meanwhile: Literature in an Expanded Field'. *Journal of the Australasian Universities Language and Literature Association*, 99, May 2003, 1–22; revised version in Isabel Hoving, Frans-Willem Korsten, Ernst van Alphen, eds. *Africa and Its Significant Others: Forty Years of Intercultural Entanglement*. Amsterdam and New York: Rodopi, 2003, 183–198.

'Anthropometamorphose: Sich verzweigende Pfade und Kristalle in Louise Bourgeois' Philosophie der Temporalität/Anthropometamorphosis: Forking Paths and Crystals in Louise Bourgeois' Philosophy of Temporality'. In Beatrice E. Stammer et al., eds. *Louise Bourgeois – Intime abstraktionene/Louise Bourgeois: Intimate Abstractions*. Berlin: Akademie der Künste, 2003, 116–144.

——Polish: 'Antropometamorfoza: rozwidlające się ścieżki I kryształw filozofii czasu Louise Bourgeois'. Trans. Dorota Kozińska. *Teksty Drugie*, 2/3, 2003, 314–329.

'Her Majesty's Masters'. In Michael F. Zimmermann, ed. *The Art Historian: National Traditions and Institutional Practices*. Williamstown: Sterling and Francine Clark Art Institute, 2003, 81–109.

'Critique of Voice: The Open Score of her Face'. In Nancy Pedri, ed. *Travelling Concepts III: Memory, Narrative, Image*. Amsterdam: ASCA Press, 2003, 91–114; revised version in Lazar Fleishman, Christine Gölz, Aage A. Hansen-Löve, eds. *Analysieren als Deuten: Wolf Schmid zum 60. Geburtstag*. Hamburg: Hamburg University Press, 2004, 31–51.

'From Cultural Studies to Cultural Analysis: "A Controlled Reflection on the Formation of Method"'. In Paul Bowman, ed. *Interrogating Cultural Studies: Theory, Politics and Practice*. London: Pluto Press, 2003, 30–40.

'Le public n'existe pas'. In Catherine Perret, Elizabeth Caillet, eds. *L'art contemporain et son exposition*, 2. Paris: L'Harmattan, 2002.

'Norman Bryson, British Historian of Art and Visual Culture'. In Chris Murray, ed. *Key Writers on Art:*

The Twentieth Century. London and New York: Routledge, 2003, 62–68.

'Visual Essentialism and the Object of Visual Culture'. *Journal of Visual Culture*, 2: 1, 2003, 5–32.

——Spanish: 'El esencialismo visual y el objeto de los estudios visuales'. Trans. Carolina Díaz, David García Casado, and María Teresa Tellechea. *Estudios Visuales*, 2, December 2004, 11–49.

——Hungarian: 'Vizuális esszencializmus és a vizuális kultúra tárgya'. Trans. Marianne Csáky. *Enigma*, 41, 2004, 86–116.

'Autotopography: Louise Bourgeois as Builder'. *Biography: An Interdisciplinary Quarterly*, 25: 1, 2002, 180–202; reprinted in Sidonie Smith, Julia Watson, eds. *Interfaces: Women, Autobiography, Image, Performance*. Ann Arbor: University of Michigan Press, 2002, 163–185; also reprinted in *Reading Room: A Journal of Art and Culture*, 1, 2007, 40–59.

'Descrizioni, costruzione di mondi e tempo della narrazione'. In Franco Moretti, ed. *Il romanzo*, 2, *Le forme*. Milan: Einaudi, 2002, 189–224.

'Atti di sguardo: Proust, il romanzo e la cultura visiva'. In Franco Moretti, ed. *Il romanzo*, 4, *Temi, luoghi, eroi*. Milan: Einaudi, 2003, 279–291.

'The Genius of Rome: Putting Things Together'. *Journal of Visual Culture*, 1: 1, 2002, 25–45.

'Der Rembrandt der Frauen'. In Matthias Bickenbach, Axel Fliethmann, eds. *Korrespondenzen: Visuelle Kulturen zwischen Früher Neuzeit und Gegenwart*. Cologne: DuMont Literatur and Kunst Verlag, 2002, 27–54.

'Yesterday Isn't What It Used to Be'. *Documents*, 21, Fall 2001/Winter 2002, 11–23.

'Dreaming Art'. *Umění/Art, Journal of the Institute for Art History of the Academy of Sciences of the Czech Republic*, 5, 2001, 370–383.

'Prosthetic Poetics'. In Nathalie Roelens, Wanda Strauven, eds. *Homo Orthopedicus: Le corps et ses prothèses à l'époque (post)moderniste*. Paris, Budapest and Turin: L'Harmattan, 2001, 139–166.

'*Mise en scène*: Zur Inszenierung von Subjektivität'. Trans. Sonja Neef. In Josef Früchtl, Jörg Zimmermann, eds. *Ästhetik der Inszenierung: Dimensionen eines künstlerischen, kulturellen und gesellschaftlichen Phänomens*. Frankfurt am Main: Suhrkamp Verlag, 2001, 198–221.

'Jeannette Christensen'. *Likovne besede*, 57/58, Winter 2001, 98–102.

'Legal Lust: Literary Litigations'. *Writing against Legal Racism: Law and Literature Explorations*, special issue of *The Australian Feminist Law Journal*. December 15, 2001, 1–22.

'Postmodern Theology as Cultural Analysis', In Graham Ward, ed. *The Blackwell Companion to Postmodern Theology*. Oxford: Blackwell, 2001, 3–23.

'Pour une histoire pervertie'. In Nicolas Goyer, Walter Moser, eds. *Résurgences baroques: Les trajectoires d'un processus transculturel*. Brussels: Éditions de la Lettre Volée, 2001, 61–88.

'La répétition, la tête dans les nuages/Rehearsal, Head in the Clouds'. In Laurence Gateau, ed. *Action, on tourne/Action, We're Filming*. Nice: Villa Arson, 2001, 34–73.

'Voix/voie narrative: La voix métaphorée'. *Cahiers de narratologie*, 10: 1, 2001, 9–36, DOI: 10.4000/narratologie.6906.

'Mission Impossible: Postcards, Pictures, and Parasites'. In Hent de Vries, Samuel Weber, eds. *Religion and Media*. Stanford: Stanford University Press, 2001, 241–268.

'Introduction: Travelling Concepts and Cultural Analysis'. In Joyce Goggin, Sonja Neef, eds. *Travelling Concepts: Text, Subjectivity, Hybridity*. Amsterdam: ASCA Press, 2001, 7–25.

'Performance and Performativity'. *Lier en boog*, 16, 2001, 108–124; expanded version in Jörg Huber, ed. *Kultur-Analysen (Interventionen* 10). Zurich: Instituts für Theorie der Gestaltung und Kunst an der Hochschule für Gestaltung und Kunst and Edition Voldemeer, 2001, 197–241.

'Enfolding Feminism'. In Elisabeth Bronfen, Misha Kavka, eds. *Feminist Consequences: Theory for the New Century*. New York: Columbia University Press, 2001, 321–352.

'Auf die Haut/Unter die Haut: Barockes steigt an die Oberfläche'. In Peter J. Burgard, ed. *Barock: Neue Sichtweisen einer Epoche*. Cologne, Weimar, and Vienna: Böhlau Verlag, 2001, 17–51.

'Pour une interprétation intempestive'. In Régis Michel, ed. *Où en est l'interprétation de l'oeuvre d'art?* Paris: Musée du Louvre and École Nationale Supérieure des Beaux-Arts, 2000, 239–267.

'Three-Way Misreading'. *Diacritics*, 30: 1, 2000, 2–24; reprinted in *Purushottama Bilimoria, Dina Al-Kassim*, eds. *Postcolonial Reason and Its Critique: Deliberations on Gayatri Spivak's Thoughts*. Oxford University Press India, 2014.

'Heteroglossia' and 'Narratology'. In Lorraine Code, ed. *Encyclopedia of Feminist Theories*. London and New York: Routledge, 2000, 244–245 and 357–359.

'Poetics, Today'. *Poetics Today*, 21: 3, 2000, 479–502.

'Fantasy and the Mirror of Nature'. In Klaus Krüger, Alessandro Nova, eds. *Imagination und Wirklichkeit: Zum Verhältnis von mentalen und realen Bildern in der Kunst der frühen Neuzeit*. Mainz: Verlag Philipp von Zabern, 2000, 183–194.

'Ecstatic Aesthetics: Metaphoring Bernini'. In Claire Farago, Robert Zwijnenberg, eds. *Compelling Visuality: The Work of Art in and out of History*. Minneapolis and London: University of Minnesota Press, 2003, 1–30; reprinted in Andrea Bubenik, ed. *Ecstasy: Baroque and Beyond*. Brisbane: The University of Queensland Art Museum, 2017, 71–93.

'Religious Canon and Literary Identity'. *European Electronic Journal for Feminist Exegesis*, 2, 2000; reprinted in Erik Borgman, Bart Philipsen, Lea Verstricht, eds. *Literary Canons and Religious Identities*. Aldershot: Ashgate, 2004, 9–32.

'Visual Narrativity'. In Graham Coulter-Smith, ed. *The Visual-Narrative Matrix: Interdisciplinary Collisions and Collusions*. Southampton: Southampton Institute, 2000, 7–16.

'Sticky Images: The Foreshortening of Time in an Art of Duration'. In Carolyn Bailey Gill, ed. *Time and the Image*. Manchester: Manchester University Press, 2000, 79–99; Fragments in Amelia Groom, ed. *Documents of Contemporary Art: Time*. Cambridge and London: MIT Press, 2013, 62–64.

'Memory Acts: Performing Subjectivity'. *Performance Research*, 5: 3, 2000, 102–114.

'The Spirit as Parasite'. *Western Humanities Review*, 53: 4, 1999/2000, 315–335.

'Crossroad Theory and Travelling Concepts: From Cultural Studies to Cultural Analysis'. In Jan Baetens, José Lambert eds. *The Future of Cultural Studies: Essays in Honour of Joris Vlasselaers*. Leuven: Leuven University Press, 2000, 3–21.

'Snow White in the Wrong Story: Cultural Analysis, Aesthetics, and Catastrophic Culture'. In Jostein Gripsrud, ed. *Aesthetic Theory, Art and Popular Culture*. Kristiansand: Nordic Academic Press, 1999, 33–57.

'Selbstporträt in einem facettierten Spiegel'. In Gerda Buxbaum, Christina Lammer, eds. *Schneewittchen: über den Mythos kalter Schönheit. Ein Eiskristallbuch.* Tübingen: Konkursbuchverlag Claudia Gehrke, 1999, 105–117.

'Narrative Inside Out: Louise Bourgeois' "Spider" as Theoretical Object'. *Oxford Art Journal*, 22: 2, 1999, 101–126.

'Basic Instincts and Their Discontents'. In M. Heusser et al., eds. *Text and Visuality: Word and Image Interactions* 3. Amsterdam and Atlanta: Rodopi, 1999, 13–32.

'Introduction'. In Mieke Bal, Jonathan Crewe, Leo Spitzer, eds. *Acts of Memory: Cultural Recall in the Present.* Hanover: University Press of New England, 1999, vii–xvii.

'Memories in the Museum: Preposterous Histories'. In Mieke Bal, Jonathan Crewe, Leo Spitzer, eds. *Acts of Memory: Cultural Recall in the Present.* Hanover: University Press of New England, 1999, 171–190.

——Portuguese: 'Memórias no museu. Histórias absurdas para os dias de hoje'. In Fernanda Mota Alves, Luísa Alfonso Soares, Christiana Vasconcelos Rodrigues, eds. *Estudias de memória. Teoria e análise cultural.* Lisbon: Universidade de Lisboa, 2016, 359–378.

'Geelzucht en Schone Letteren'. *De Witte Raaf*, 77, January/February 1999, 1–3.

'All in the Family: Familiarity and Estrangement According to Marcel Proust'. In Marianne Hirsch, ed. *The Familial Gaze.* Dartmouth: University Press of New England, 1999, 223–247.

'Ruumiiseen sisällytetty Tila'. In Kirsi Saarikangas, ed. *Kuvasta tilaan.* Tampere: Vastapaino, 1999, 299–333.

'Frame Her If You Can!' *Art Bulletin of Nationalmuseum Stockholm*, 5, 1998, 137–152.

'Quoting Caravaggio'. In *Center 18: Record of Activities and Research Reports, June 1997–May 1998.* Washington, D.C.: National Gallery of Art, Center for Advanced Study in the Visual Arts, 1998, 45–48.

'Seeing Signs: The Use of Semiotics for the Understanding of Visual Art'. In Mark A. Cheetham, Michael Ann Holly, Keith Moxey, eds. *The Subjects of Art History: Historical Objects in Contemporary Perspectives.* New York: Cambridge University Press, 1998, 74–93.

'Close Reading Today: From Narratology to Cultural Analysis'. In Walter Grünzeig, Andreas Solbach, eds. *Grenzüberschreitungen: Narratologie im Kontext/ Transcending Boundaries: Narratology in Context.* Tübingen: Gunter Narr Verlag, 1998, 19–40.

'A Meagre One Thousand Words for Stefan Germer'. *Texte zur Kunst*, 31, September 1998, 43–45.

'Reading Bathsheba: From Mastercodes to Misfits'. In Ann Jensen Adams, ed. *Rembrandt's 'Bathsheba Reading King David's Letter'.* Cambridge and New York: Cambridge University Press, 1998, 119–146.

——Chinese: Trans. Molin Wang and Lian Duan. *Art Observation monthly*, 6, June 2012, 121–130.

'Semiotics as a Theory of Art'. Co-authored with Norman Bryson. In Michael Kelly, ed. *Encyclopedia of Aesthetics*, 4. Oxford and New York: Oxford University Press, 1998, 263–267; revised and expanded second edition 2014.

'Narrative and the Visual and Literary Arts' and 'Charles Sanders Peirce'. In Michael Kelly, ed. *Encyclopedia of Aesthetics*, 3. Oxford and New York: Oxford University Press, 1998, 328–331 and 448–451; revised and expanded second edition 2014.

'Back to the Future: Art and Its History'. *Semiotica*, 119: 3/4, 1998, 287–308.

'Alter Ego: Le regard hétéropathique dans *A la recherche du temps perdu*'. In J. Leblanc, ed. *Texte: Iconicité et Narrativité.* Toronto: Trinity College, 1998, 107–125.

'Introduction to *Reading "Rembrandt": Beyond the Word-Image Opposition*'. In William H. Newell, ed. *Interdisciplinarity: Essays from the Literature.* New York: The College Entrance Examination Board, 1998, 363–387.

'Space, Inc.' In E.W.B. Hess-Lüttich, Jürgen E. Müller, Aart van Zoest, eds. *Signs & Space/Raum & Zeichen.* Proceedings of International Conference on the Semiotics of Space and Culture in Amsterdam. Tübingen: Gunter Narr Verlag, 1998, 199–223.

'Semiotics and Art History: A Discussion of Context and Senders'. Co-authored with Norman Bryson. In Donald Preziosi, ed. *The Art of Art History: A Critical Anthology.* Oxford and New York: Oxford University Press, 1998, 242–256.

'Shifting Visions: History and the Contemporary Collection'. In *The Curator, the Museum, the Collection.* International Committee of Museums of Modern Art (CIMAM) Annual Meeting Barcelona 1997. Barcelona: Fundación 'la Caixa', 1997, 27–37.

'Vers une narratologie visuelle: poétique du détail dans la narration: L'exemple de Proust'. In María Concepción Pérez, ed. *Los Géneros Literarios: Curso Superior de Narratología Narratividad-Dramaticida.* Seville: University of Seville, 1997, 17–30.

'Documenta X: Le parcours'. *Omnibus* hors-série, October 1997, 8–40.

'Narratologie et dialogue'. In Daniel Luzzati et al., eds. *Le dialogique.* Bern: Peter Lang, 1997, 259–268.

'Looking at Love: An Ethics of Vision'. *Diacritics*, 27: 1, 1997, 59–72.

'Narcissus' Vision and Semiotic Space'. *European Journal for Semiotic Studies*, 9: 1, 1997, 139–157.

'Een jongetje van zes en een plaatje van een moeder'. In J.J. Pott, V. Vasteling, R. van de Vall, K. Vintges, eds. *Liber amicarum: over kunst, literatuur en filosofie.* Meppel: Boom, 1997, 96–107.

'In het museum: hedendaags exhibitionisme'. In Jan C.A. van de Lubbe, Aart J.A. van Zoest, eds. *Teken en betekenis.* Haarlem: Aramith, 1997, 126–40.

'Focalization'. In Susana Onega, José Angel García Landa, eds. *Narratology: An Introduction.* London and New York: Longman, 1996, 115–28; originally published in Mieke Bal. *Narratology: Introduction to the Theory of Narrative.* Trans. Christine van Boheemen. Toronto: University of Toronto Press, 1985, 100–114.

'Reading Art?' In Griselda Pollock, ed. *Generations and Geographies in the Visual Arts: Feminist Readings.* London and New York: Routledge, 1996, 25–41.

——Italian: 'Leggere l'arte'. In Andrea Pinotti, Antonio Somaini, eds. *Teorie dell'immagine: Il dibattito contemporaneo.* Milan: Raffaelo Cortina Editore, 2009, 209–240.

——Croatian: Krešimir Purgar, ed. *Vizualni studiji: umjetnost i mediji u doba slikovnog obrata.* Trans. Miloš Đurđević. Zagreb: CVS-centar za vizualne studije, 2009.

——Chinese; Trans. Suhong Chu and Lian Duan. *Art Observation monthly*, 10, 123–130.

——Estonian: 'Lugeda kunsti'. Trans. Ingrid Ruudi. *Kunstiteaduslikke Uurimusi*, 20: 1/2, 2011, 213–228.

——French: 'Lire l'art?' In Emmanuel Alloa, ed. *Penser l'image III.* Dijon: Les Presses du réel, 2017, 43–74.

'Proust et l'image primitive'. *Gradiva: Revue Européenne d'anthropologie littéraire*, 1: 1, 1996, 59–70.

'Un objet d'obsession: la photo d'outre-tombe'. *Vives lettres*, 1: 2, 1996, 75–91.

'Lacan in dialoog: Kaja Silverman en film'. In Nathalie Kok, Kees Nuijten, eds. *In dialoog met Lacan*. Meppel: Boom, 1996, 195–216.

'Le verre grossissant'. *Etudes littéraires*, 28: 3, 1996, 13–28.

'Second-Person Narrative'. *Paragraph*, 19: 3, 1996, 179–204.

'Semiotic Elements in Academic Practices (Critical Response)'. *Critical Inquiry*, 22, Spring 1996, 569–585.

'The Discourse of the Museum'. In Reesa Greenberg, Bruce Ferguson, Sandy Nairne, eds. *Thinking about Exhibitions*. London and New York: Routledge, 1996, 201–218.

——Polish: 'Dyskurs muzeum'. In Maria Popczyk, ed. *Muzeum Sztuki: Antologia*. Krakow: Universitas, 2005, 345–365.

'Signs in Painting'. *The Art Bulletin*, 78: 1, 1996, 6–9.

'The Gaze in the Closet'. In Teresa Brennan, Martin Jay, eds. *Vision in Context: Historical and Contemporary Perspectives on Sight*. London and New York: Routledge, 1996, 139–154.

'Franco Adami: *Tableau*'. *Fine Arts Magazine*, 19: 1, 1996, 106–111.

'Cultural Studies and Philosophy'. *Parallax*, 1: 1, 1995, 110–113.

'Reading the Gaze: The Construction of Gender in "Rembrandt"'. In Stephen Melville, Bill Readings, eds. *Vision & Textuality*. London: MacMillan, 1995, 147–173.

——Serbian: 'Citanje pogleda: konstrukcija roda u Rembranta'. Trans. Miroslava Andjelkovic and Rastko Jovanovic. In Branislava Andjelkovic, ed. *Uvod u feministicke teorije slike*. Belgrade: Belgrade Center for Contemporary Art, 2002, 161–186.

'Bird Watching: Visuality and Lesbian Desire in Marcel Proust's *A la recherche du temps perdu*'. *Thamyris/Intersecting*, 2: 1, 1995, 45–66.

'Lire l'un avec l'autre: Chardin et Proust'. In Leo Hoek, Kees Meerhoff, eds. *Rhétorique et image: textes en hommage à A. Kibédi Varga*. Amsterdam and Atlanta: Rodopi, 1995, 179–197.

'Plaidoyer pour un personnage plat: à propos d'une page de Proust'. In Gérard Lavergne, ed. *Le personnage Romanesque: Cahiers de narratologie*. Nice: Association des Publications de la Faculté des Lettres de Nice, 1995, 11–28.

'Zichtbaar ont-zettend: Proust en het fotografisch oog'. In J. Plessen et al., eds. *Marcel Proust Vereniging Jaarboek*. Amsterdam: Marcel Proustvereniging and Bosbespers, 1993/1994, 77–93.

'De Turner-turn: over de ritueelgekte in de literatuurwetenschap in de jaren tachtig', *Antropologische verkenningen*, 13: 4, 1994, 56–68.

'Verhalende teksten', 'De vertelsituatie', 'Effecten', and 'Interpretatie'. In Lizette Duyvendak, ed. *Inleiding Letterkunde*, 1, *Literatuuranalyse*. Heerlen: Open Universiteit, 1994, 237–262, 263–290, 319–342, and 343–364.

'Instantanés', *C.R.I.N.*, 28, 1994, 117–130.

'*The Rape of Lucrece* and the Story of W'. In A.J. Hoenselaars, ed. *Reclamations of Shakespeare*. Amsterdam: Rodopi, 1994, 75–104.

'Een gebruiksaanwijzing in gebruik: narratologie van onderzoek naar onderwijs'. *De Nieuwe Taalgids*, 87: 4, 1994, 352–355.

'Head Hunting: "Judith" on the Cutting Edge of Knowledge'. *Journal for Studies on the Old Testament*, 19: 63, 1994, 3–34; reprinted in Athalya Brenner, ed. *A Feminist Companion to Esther, Judith and Susanna*.

Sheffield: Sheffield Academic Press, 1995, 253–286.

'Kiekjes'. In Rob de Jong, David Rijser, Jan de Ruijter, eds. *Virtute e canoscenza*. Amsterdam: Barlaeus Gymnasium, 1994, 63–72.

'Identification et apprentissage de la compassion: Proust et la photographie'. In Suzanne van Dijk, Christa Stevens, eds. *(En)jeux de la communication romanesque: Hommage à Françoise van Rossum-Guyon*. Amsterdam and Philadelphia: Rodopi, 1994, 241–256.

'Dead Flesh, or the Smell of Painting'. In Norman Bryson, Michael Holly, Keith Moxey, eds. *Visual Culture: Images and Interpretations*. Middletown: Wesleyan University Press, 1994, 365–383.

'Telling Objects: A Narrative Perspective on Collecting'. In John Elsner, Roger Cardinal, eds. *The Cultures of Collecting*. London: Reaktion Books, 1994, 97–115.

——Japanese: Tokyo: Kenkyusha Ltd., 1998, 123–145. Reprinted in Donald Preziosi, Claire Farago, eds. *Grasping the World: The Idea of the Museum*. Aldershot: Ashgate, 2004, 84–102.

——Slovak: 'Objecty, ktoré rozprávajú: naratívne hl'adisko zbierania'. In Mária Orišková, ed. *Efekt múzea: predmety, praktiky, publikum: Antológia textov anglo-americkej kritickej teórie múzea*. Bratislava: AFAD Press, 2006, 171–189.

'Weliswaar, maar: de binaire oppositie voorbij'. *Simulacrum*, 3: 1, 1994, 9–12.

'Scared to Death'. In Mieke Bal, Inge E. Boer, eds. *The Point of Theory*. Amsterdam: Amsterdam University Press/New York: Continuum, 1994, 32–47; revised version published as 'Scared to Death: Metaphor, Theory, and the Adventure of Scholarship'. In David Jasper, Mark Ledbetter, eds. *In Good Company: Essays in Honor of Robert Detweiler*. Atlanta: The Scholars Press, 1994, 11–32.

——Polish: 'Śmiertelna zgroza'. Trans. Krzysztof Kłosiński. *Teksty Drugie*, 6, 2008, 95–114.

'A Body of Writing: Judges 19'. In Athalya Brenner, ed. *A Feminist Companion to Judges*. Sheffield: Sheffield Academic Press, 1993, 208–230.

'Light in Painting: De-seminating Art History'. In Peter Brunette, David Wills, eds. *Deconstruction and the Visual Arts: Art, Media, Architecture*. Cambridge and New York: Cambridge University Press, 1993, 49–64.

'Heroism and Proper Names, or the Fruits of Analogy'. In Athalya Brenner, ed. *A Feminist Companion to Ruth*. Sheffield: Sheffield Academic Press, 1993, 42–70.

'Letteren, vrouwenstudies, psychoanalyse: een driehoeksverhouding met relatieproblemen'. *Allure*, 1, 1993, 89–106.

'The Elders and Susanna'. *Biblical Interpretation*, 1: 1, 1993, 1–19.

'Metaphors He Lives By'. *Semeia*, 61, 1993, 185–207

'His Master's Eye'. In David M. Levin, ed. *Modernity and the Hegemony of Vision*. Berkeley: University of California Press, 1993, 379–404.

'Give and Take'. In Craig Barrow, Katherine Frank, John Phillips, Reed Sanderlin, eds. *Gender, Race, Identity*. Chattanooga: Southern Humanities Press, 1993, 3–9.

'First Person, Second Person, Same Person: Narrative as Epistemology'. *New Literary History*, 24: 2, 1993, 293–320.

'Cultuur en macht: leereenheid 12'. In Auke van Breemen, Johannes Fabian, eds. *Denken over cultuur: gebruik en misbruik van een concept*. Heerlen: Open Universiteit, 1993, 327–347.

'Avec son regard de maître'. *Protée*, 20: 3, 1992, 54–68.

'Prema kritickoj naratologiji'. In Vladimir Biti, ed. *Suvremena teorija pripovijedanja*. Zagreb: Globus, 1992, 54–68, 313–340.

'Telling, Showing, Showing Off: A Walking Tour'. *Critical Inquiry*, 18, Spring 1992, 556–594.

'Over Her Dead Body'. In Iqbal Kaur, ed. *Literature and Gender*. New Delhi: D.K. Publishers Ltd., 1992, 3–24.

'Narratology and the Rhetoric of Trashing'. *Comparative Literature*, 44: 3, 1992, 293–306.

'The Predicament of Semiotics'. *Poetics Today*, 13: 3, 1992, 543–552.

'Rape: Problems of Intention'. In Elizabeth Wright, ed. *Feminism and Psychoanalysis*. Oxford: Blackwell, 1992, 367–371.

'De hang naar houvast'. *Opzij*, 20: 2, 1992, 52–59.

'Who Cares? Where Stories Come From and What They Do'. In Ad van Berlo, Yvonne Kiwitz-De Ruijter, eds. *Information in a Healthy Society/Health in the Information Society*. Knegsel: Akontes Publishing, 1992, 276–281.

'Reply'. Co-authored with Norman Bryson. *The Art Bulletin*, 74: 3, 1992, 528–531.

'De grenzen van wetenschappelijkheid'. *Forum der Letteren*, 33: 4, 1992, 275–283.

'The Point of Narratology'. *Poetics Today*, 11: 4, 1990, 727–753.

——Swedish: 'Vitsen med narratologi'. *Tidskrift för litteraturvetenskap*, 2/3, 1993, 3–25.

'A Body of Writing'. *Crossroads/Continuum*, 1: 2, 1991, 110–126.

'Semiotics and Art History'. Co-authored with Norman Bryson. *The Art Bulletin*, 73: 2, 1991, 174–208.

——Russian: 'Semiotika i iskusstvoznanie'. Trans. E. Revzina and G. Revzina. *Voprosy Iskusstvoznania*, 9: 2, 1996, 521–551.

——Serbian: 'Semiotika i istorija umetnosti'. Trans. Ksenija Stevanovic and Dragana Kitanovic. *Prelom*, 1: 1, 2001, 161–192.

——Croatian: 'Semiotika i povijest umjetnosti'. In Ljiljana Kolešnik, ed. *Umjetničko djelo kao društvena činjenica: Perspektive kritičke povijesti umjetnosti*. Zagreb: Institut za povijest umjetnosti, 2005, 51–104.

'The Politics of Citation'. *Diacritics*, 21: 1, 1991, 25–45.

'Mooie boel: een driehoeksverhouding in lagen'. In Rien T. Segers, ed. *Visies op cultuur en literatuur: opstellen naar aanleiding van het werk van J.J.A. Mooij*. Amsterdam and Atlanta: Rodopi, 1991, 157–162.

'Murder and Difference: Uncanny Sites in an Uncanny World'. *Journal of Literature and Theology*, 5, 1, 1991, 11–19.

'"Door zuiverheid gedreven": het troebele water van *Het land van herkomst* van E. du Perron'. In Ernst van Alphen, Maaike Meijer, eds. *De canon onder vuur: Nederlandse literatuur tegendraads gelezen*. Amsterdam: Van Gennep, 1991, 122–1421.

'Une ou deux choses…'. *Protée*, 19: 1, 1991, 51–60.

'Lots of Writing'. *Semeia*, 54, 1991, 77–102; also published in *Poetics Today*, 15: 1, 1994, 89–114; reprinted in Athalya Brenner, ed. *Ruth and Esther: A Feminist Companion to the Bible*. Sheffield: Sheffield Academic Press, 1999, 212–238.

'Experiencing Murder: Ritualistic Interpretation of Ancient Texts'. In Kathleen M. Ashley, ed. *Victor Turner and the Construction of Cultural Criticism: Between Literature and Anthropology*. Bloomington and Indianapolis: Indiana University Press, 1990, 3–20.

'Dealing/With/Women: Daughters in the Book of Judges'. In Regina M. Schwartz, ed. *The Book and the Text: The Bible and Critical Theory*. Oxford: Blackwell, 1990, 16–39.

——German: 'Frauen-Handlung: Töchter im Buch Richter'. Trans. Daniel Weidner. In Hans-Peter Schmidt, Daniel Weidner, eds. *Bibel als Literatur*. Munich: Wilhelm Fink Verlag, 2008, 283–304.

'The Rape of Narrative and the Narrative of Rape: Speech Acts and Body Language in Judges'. In Elaine Scarry, ed. *Literature and the Body. Selected Papers from the English Institute*. Baltimore: Johns Hopkins University Press, 1988, 1–32; paperback reprint 1990.

'Dis-semination: "Rembrandt" and the Navel of the Text'. *Literature, Interpretation, Theory*, 2, 1990, 145–166.

'De-disciplining the Eye'. *Critical Inquiry*, 16: 3, 1990, 506–531.

'Showcase'. In Raymond Corbey, Paul van der Grijp, eds. *Natuur en cultuur*. Baarn: Ambo, 1990, 209–219.

'Over haar lijk: waarheid, wetenschap en cultuurverschil'. In Agnes Verbiest, Anne van de Zande, eds. *Een zee van golven: vijf jaar Annie Romein-Verschoorlezingen*. Nijmegen: Vita, 1995, 18–48.

'Visual Poetics: Reading with the Other Art'. In Martin Kreiswirth, Mark A. Cheetham, eds. *Theory Between the Disciplines: Authority, Vision, Politics*. Ann Arbor: University of Michigan Press, 1990, 135–150.

'Reading as Empowerment: The Bible from a Feminist Perspective'. In Barry N. Ohlsen, Yael S. Feldman, eds. Approaches to *Teaching the Hebrew Bible as Literature in Translation*. New York: Modern Language Association of America, 1989, 87–92.

'Visual Readers and Textual Viewers'. *Versus*, 52/53, 1989, 133–150.

'On Looking and Reading: Word and Image, Visual Poetics, and Comparative Arts'. *Semiotica*, 76: 3/4, 1989, 283–320.

'Language and Its Motivations' and 'The Effects of Language'. In Stichting Praemium Erasmianum. *Three Cultures: Fifteen Lectures on the Confrontation of Academic Cultures*. Rotterdam: Universitaire Pers Rotterdam, 1989, 31–42 and 57–70.

'Literature and Its Insistent Other'. *Journal of the American Academy of Religion*, 57: 2, 1989, 373–383.

'Geheimpjes uit het rovershol: een reactie op Evelyn Kellers analyse van wetenschappelijke taal'. *Tijdschrift voor vrouwenstudies*, 38: 10, 1989, 271–286.

'Beste mensen'. In Hanna van Dorsen et al., eds. *En zij lachte en het lichtte: scepsis als grondslag voor het zien van vrouwen*. Voorburg: Protestantse Stichting tot Bevordering van het Bibliotheekwezen en de Lectuurvoorziening in Nederland, 1989, 13–18.

'Eine Notlüge'. In Renate Jost, Mieke Korenhof, Eva Renate Schmidt, eds. *Feministisch gelesen*, 2. Stuttgart: Kreuz Verlag, 1988, 47–54.

'Communicatie of eenzijdige macht: Susanna en de ouderlingen in de bijbel en bij Rembrandt'. In L. Feenstra, R.O. Fock, N.H.H. Beyer, eds. *Communicatie*. Meppel and Amsterdam: Boom, 1989, 58–87.

'Literatuurwetenschap interdisciplinair'. *Spektator*, 18: 5, 1988/89, 336–339.

'Rivalität zwischen Männern – Grund der Unterdrückung von Frauen'. In Renate Jost, Mieke Korenhof, Eva Renate Schmidt, eds. *Feministisch gelesen*, 1. Stuttgart: Kreuz Verlag, 1988, 60–66.

'Tricky Thematics'. *Semeia*, 42, 1988, 133–155.

'Introduction: Visual Poetics'. *Style*, 22: 2, 1988, 177–182.

'Speech, Murder, Tricks, and Gender: Judges 4 and 5'. *Recherches sémiotiques/Semiotic Inquiry*, 7: 2, 1987, 127–151.

'Myth à la lettre: Freud, Mann, Genesis and Rembrandt, and the Story of the Son'. In Shlomith Rimmon-

Kenan, ed. *Discourse in Psychoanalysis and Literature*. London: Methuen, 1987, 57–89; reprinted in Athalya Brenner, ed. *A Feminist Companion to Genesis*. Sheffield: Sheffield Academic Press, 1993, 343–378.

'Force and Meaning: Rembrandt and the Interdisciplinary Struggle of Psychoanalysis, Semiotics and Aesthetics'. *Semiotica*, 63: 3/4, 1987, 244–317.

'Virginity: Toward a Feminist Philology'. *Dispositio: Revista Hispanica de Semiotica Literaria*, 12, 1987, 30–32, 65–82.

'Naar zijn beeld en gelijkenis, of de identiteit van en tussen vertelinstanties'. *Forum der Letteren*, 28: 1, 1987, 43–52.

'Tekst en geschiedenis: reflecties over de sociale kleur van literatuur'. In Lida Coumou et al., eds. *Verbeelden: themaboek 10*. Groningen: Z.U.V., 1987, 9–24.

'Tuer sur parole: Pour une narratologie dynamique'. In Maryse Souchard, ed. *Sémiotique et analyse textuelle: Description, paraphrase, métalangage*. Winnipeg: Collège Saint Boniface, 1987, 234–277; also in *Protée*, 15: 3, 1987, 80–103.

'The Language of Subjectivity'. In Th. D'haen, ed. *Linguistics and the Study of Literature*. Amsterdam: Rodopi, 1986, 201–217.

'Tell-Tale Theories'. *Poetics Today*, 7: 3, 1986, 555–564.

'Quelle est la faute de l'abbé Mouret? Pour une narratologie diachronique et polémique'. *Australian Journal of French Studies*, 23: 2, 1986, 149–168.

'De tekenen des tijds en de tijd als teken'. In Aart van Zoest, ed. *De macht van de tekens: opstellen over maatschappij, tekst en literatuur*. Utrecht: HES, 1986, 71–84.

'De Bijbel als volksliteratuur'. In Ria Lemaire, ed. *Ik zing mijn lied voor al wie met mij gaat. Vrouwen in de volksliteratuur*. Utrecht: HES, 1986, 45–71; also in Ria Lemaire, ed. *Eu canto a quen comigo camiña*. Santiago de Compostela: Edicións Laiovento, 1998, 43–70.

'The Bible as Literature: A Critical Escape'. *Diacritics*, 16, Winter 1986, 71–79.

'Inconsciences de Chéri: Chéri existe--t-il?' In Bernard Bray, ed. *Colette, nouvelles approches critiques*. Paris: Nizet, 1986, 15–25.

'Sexuality, Sin and Sorrow: The Emergence of the Female Character (A Reading of Genesis 1–3)'. *Poetics Today*, 6, 1/2, 1985, 21–42; also in Susan Suleiman, ed. *The Female Body in Western Culture: Contemporary Perspectives*. Cambridge: Harvard University Press, 1986, 317–338; and in Elizabeth A. Castelli, ed. *Women, Gender, Religion: A Reader*. New York: Palgrave, 2001, 149–173.

'Ruth o come ammettere l'amore: Preliminari a proposito d'un particolare'. In Partizi Magli, ed. *Le donne e i segni: Scrittura, linguaggio, identità nel segno della differenza femminile*. Ancona: Il lavoro editoriale, 1985, 131–151.

'Semiotiek in de literatuur. Communiceren, vertellen, liegen: de narratieve semiotiek van Bernstein'. In Suzette Haakma, ed. *Semiotiek*. Utrecht: Studium Generale, 1985, 40–54.

'Why I? Discussing the Subject in/of Semiotics'. *Poetics Today*, 5: 4, 1984, 857–965.

'The Rhetoric of Subjectivity'. *Poetics Today*, 5: 2, 1984, 337–376.

'Pour une théorie critique de la subjectivité narrative'. *Lalies*, 4, 1984, 107–148.

'Réfléchir la réflexion: Du nom propre à la mise en abyme'. *Annali dell'Istituto Universitario Orientale*, 44, 1984, 7–48.

'Preface and Introduction'. *Poetics*, 13: 4/5, 1984, i–ii and 279–298; also in *Style*, 18: 3, 1984, 239–260.

'Mise en Abyme and Metatextuality: Sexual Politics in the Book of Ruth'. In W. van Peer, J. Renkema, eds. *Pragmatics and Stylistic*. Leuven and Amersfoort: Acco, 1984, 71–94.

'Verteltheorie'. In A.G.H. Bachrach et al., eds. *Moderne encyclopedie van de wereldliteratuur*, 10. Haarlem: De Haan, 1984, 106–108.

'Sexuality, Semiosis and Binarism: A Narratological Comment on Bergren and Arthur'. *Arethusa*, 16: 1/2, 1983, 117–135.

'The Semiotics of Symmetry, or the Use of Hermeneutic Models'. *Versus*, 35–36, 1983, 7–36.

'Hoe eng is de poort? Het boek Ruth vanuit een feministische visie'. *Schrift*, 85, 1983, 30–39.

'Over interpretatie'. *Tijdschrift voor vrouwenstudies*, 4: 13, 1983, 121–134.

'Naar een kritisch gebruik van genre-begrippen'. *Schrift*, 90, 1983, 234–240.

'The Narrating and the Focalizing: A Theory of the Agents in Narrative'. *Style*, 17: 2, 1983, 234–269.

'Verteltheorie als instrument voor ideologiekritiek'. In C. Halkes, ed. *Feministische theologie*. Nijmegen: Studium Generale, 1982, 266–280; revised version published in *Spektator*, 13: 4, 1983, 266–280.

'Théorie de la description: L'exemple de *Madame Bovary*'. In P.M. Wetherhill, ed. *Flaubert: La dimension du texte*. Manchester: Manchester University Press, 1982, 175–236.

'Mimesis and Genre Theory in Aristotle's *Poetics*'. *Poetics Today*, 3: 1, 1982, 171–80.

'Delila's onschuld: narratologie, psychoanalyse en ideologiekritiek'. *Tijdschrift voor vrouwenstudies*, 3: 9, 1982, 34–73.

'Wilde dieren, of de verscheurde eenheid: over "De Sirenen" van Maria Dermoût'. Co–author ed with Ernst van Alphen. In J. Hoogteijling, F. C. de Rover, eds. *Over verhalen gesproken*. Groningen: Wolters-Noordhoff, 1982, 97–124; reprinted in Ernst van Alphen, ed. *De toekomst der herinnering: essays over moderne Nederlandse literatuur*. Amsterdam: Van Gennep, 1993, 128–156.

'Structuralism, History and the Semiotics of the Subject: Recent Developments in French Literary Theory'. *Amsterdammer Beiträge zur neueren Germanistik*, 15, 1982, 55–78.

'On Meanings and Descriptions'. *Studies in Twentieth Century Literature*, 6: 1/2, 1981/1982, 100–148.

'Notes on Narrative Embedding' and 'The Laughing Mice, or, On Focalization'. Poetics Today, 2: 2, 1981, 41–59 and 203–212.

'Aristoteles semioticus: een aantekening bij een voetnoot bij 47a'. *Spektator*, 10: 6, 1981, 490–495.

'Methoden in de literatuurwetenschap'. *Tijdschrift voor vrouwenstudies*, 2: 7, 1981, 394–417.

'Logica en realisme: kanttekeningen bij J. A. Dautzenberg, "De logische opbouw van de verhaaltheorie"'. *Forum der Letteren*, 22: 2, 1981, 204–206.

'Teksttypen en taalhoudingen'. In Mieke Bal, ed. *Literaire genres en hun gebruik*. Muiderberg: Coutinho, 1981, 7–31.

'Narrativité et manipulation'. *Degrés*, 8, 1980/81, 24–25, C1–C24.

'Descriptions: Etude du discours descriptif dans le texte narratif'. *Lalies*, 1, 1980, 99–129.

'L'iconicité narrative'. *Zagadnienia Rodzajôw Literackich*, 23: 1, 1980, 11–18.

'Tradition et renouvellement: Enseigner la littérature, à quoi bon?' *Le Français dans le monde*, 20: 154, 1980, 59–64.

'Huisje, boompje, beestje: over beschrijvingen in verhalende teksten'. *Spektator*, 9: 4, 1980, 304–334.

'Structure narrative et signification: Le cas de *Wuthering Heights*'. Co-authored with Aart van Zoest. *Neophilologus*, 64: 3, 1980, 333–346.

'Flaubert'. In A.G.H. Bachrach et al., eds. *Moderne encyclopedie van de wereldliteratuur*, 3. Haarlem: De Haan, 1980, 243–246.

'Wat zijn personages en wat doen we ermee?' In Mieke Bal, ed. *Mensen van papier: over personages in de literatuur*. Assen: Van Gorcum, 1979, 1–13.

'De homo semioticus en zijn interpretatie van de werkelijkheid'. *Hollands Maandblad*, 20: 374, 1979, 15–22.

'Over lachende muizen en naïeve zieners'. *Forum der Letteren*, 20: 4, 1979, 471–476.

'Mise en abyme et iconicité'. *Littérature*, 29, 1978, 116–128.

'Over narratologie, narrativiteit en narratieve tekens'. *Spektator*, 7: 9, 1978, 528–448.

'Gebruiksaanwijzing bij het bestuderen van de verhaaltheorie van Greimas'. Internal publication, Instituut voor Algemene literatuurwetenschap, Rijksuniversiteit Utrecht, 1978.

'Wanbegrip is nog sterieler'. *Forum der Letteren*, 18: 4, 1977, 301–304.

'Strukturalistische verhaalanalyse: een poging tot systematisering'. *Forum der Letteren*, 18 : 2, 1977, 105–119.

'L'analyse structurale du récit'. *Le Français dans le monde*, 17 July 1977, 6–14.

'Narration et focalisation: Pour une théorie des instances du récit'. *Poétique*, 29, 1977, 107–127.

'L'enseignement de la narratologie'. *Rapports*, 47: 2, 1977, 59–64.

'Du nouveau sur Colette'. *Rapports*, 41: 4, 1974, 12–23.

'Un roman dans le roman: Encadrement ou enchâssement?' *Neophilologus*, 47: 1, 1974, 2–21.

'Fonction de la description romanesque'. *Revue des langues vivantes*, 40 : 2, 1974, 132–149.

'Fonction narrative de la description'. *Actes de la journée de travail sur Madame Bovary*, February 1973, 7–14.

'Colette devant la critique'. *Rapports*, 41: 2, 1971, 56–63.

Catalogue Essays

'Halting the News'. In Monika Huber. *Archive OneThirty*. Berlin and München: Deutscher Kunstverlag, 2023, 10–17.

'Con D de Diálogo/De de diálogo' and 'D is for Dialogue'. In Xunta de Galicia, ed. Manuel Vilariño. *After the Whale. Un diálogo con Museo*. A Coruña: Museo de Belas Artes da Coruña, 2022, 53–70 and 171–177.

'Inter-ships with Nalini Malani: The Foreshortening of Time'. In *Nalini Malani: My Reality is Different*. London: National Gallery Global, 2022, 86–99.

Twelve entries in Tor Eystein Øverås, ed. *Edvard Munch: Infinite*. Oslo: Munch, 2022. 'Self-Portrait with a Bottle of Wine', 40; 'Self-Portrait Between the Clock and the Bed', 58; 'Girl at the Piano', 70; 'Death and the Child', 108; 'The Drowning Child', 114; 'The Wedding of the Bohemian', 158; 'Half-Nude in a Blue Skirt', 186; 'The Death of Marat', 190; 'The Hands', 216; 'Kissing Couples in the Park', 242; 'Galloping Horse', 360; 'Uphill with a Sledge', 362.

——A selection of these entries was published in Italian in *Edvard Munch. Opera scelte*. Oslo: Munch Museet, 2023, 59, 72, 90, and 106.

'Quand rien ne fonctionne, du nouveau peut surgir' and 'When Nothing Fits, Newsness May Happen'. In Angela Bullock. *Paradigme perpendiculaire*. Trans. Vincent Raynaud. Nantes: Musée d'arts de Nantes, 2022, 21–28 and 31–37.

'Thinking, Seeing, Taking Away: Lidó Rico's Strategies of Activating Sculpture/Pensar, ver, quitar: las estrategias de Lidó Rico para activar la escultura'. In *Lidó Rico, Tu vuelo, mis alas*. Murcia: Sala Verónicas, 2021, 6–53.

'Paisajes de ideas, experiencias, transformaciones: Espacios transformados, ideas instaladas, tiempos transtornados, conceptos actudados/Landscapes of ideas, Experiences, Alteratios: Spaces Transformed, Ideas Installed, Times Messed Up, Concepts Enacted'. In *Que nos roban la memoria: Concha Jerez/ Our Memory is Being Stolen: Concha Jerez*. Madrid: Museo Nacional Centro de Arte Reina Sofía, 2020, 201–261.

'Contaminaciones: leer, imaginar, visualizar'. In Miguel Ángel Hernández Navarro, ed. *Mieke Bal: Contaminaciones: leer, imaginar, visualizar*. Murcia: Comunidad Autónoma de la Región de Murcia, Consejo de Educación y Cultura, Instituto de las Industrias Culturales y las Artes, CENDEAC, Centro Párraga, 2020, 11–22.

'Corps Noir'. In Ann Veronica Janssens. *Hot Pink Orange*. Humlebæk: Louisiana Museum of Modern Art; London: South London Gallery, 2020, 128–137.

'Grenzen als Raüme, Verhandlung und die Wechselseitigkeit der "otherness"/Borders as spaces, Negotiation, and the Mutuality of Otherness'. In *Getting Across*. München: Goethe Institut, 2019, 44–53/51.

'Linea Recta, Linea Perplexa: Moving Through Entangled Time With Nalini Malani/Linea Recta, Linea Perplexa: Muoversi in un tempo intricato con Nalini Malani'. In Marcella Beccaria, ed. *Nalini Malani: The Rebellion of the Dead. Retrospective 1969–2018/ Nalini Malani: La rivolta dei morti. Retrospettiva 1969–2018*, II. Rivoli and Torino: Castello di Rivoli Museo d'Arte Contemporanea; Ostfilden: Hatje Cantz, 2018, 60–109.

'Trzy rodzaje ruchu na granicy/Triple Movement on the Threshold'. In Agnieszka Kulazinska, ed. *Watering Hole: Agnieszka Kalinowska*. Gdansk: Centre for Contemporary Art Łaźnia, 2018, 115–163.

'Insaississable: Les Peintures de nuages de Benoît Maire/Ungraspable: Benoît Maire's Cloud Paintings'. In Alice Motard, ed. *Benoît Maire*. Bordeaux: CAPC Musée d'art contemporain, 2018, 33–59.

'Matter Matters'. Co-authored with Anne Leonard. In Geof Oppenheimer, ed. *The Hysterical Material*. Chicago: Smart Museum of Art/Soberscove Press, 2018, 24–35.

'Distintas formas de movimiento/Movement in Different Forms'. In Jesús Segura. *Time Lag*. Cartagena: Museo Regional de Arte Moderno Cartagena, 2018, 33–52.

'Exposing Broken Promises: Nalini Malani's Multiple Exposures/La mise à nu des promesses brisées: les "Expositions" multiples de Nalini Malani'. In Sophie Duplaix , ed. *Nalini Malani: The Rebellion of the Dead. Retrospective 1969–2018/ Nalini Malani: La rivolta dei morti. Retrospettiva 1969–2018*, I. Paris: Centre Georges Pompidou; Ostfilden: Hatje Cantz, 2017, 36–79.

'Deceptions: "yes, but", "re-", "huh?", "post-", "oh yes!"'.
In Roxana Marcoci, ed. *Louise Lawler: Receptions*.
New York: Museum of Modern Art, 2017, 42–49.

'Art's Winderness'. In Shimon Attie. *Facts on the Ground*.
New York and Tel-Aviv: Nazraeli Press, 2016.

'The Time It Takes'. In Marquard Smith, ed. *How to
Construct a Time machine*. London: MK Gallery 2015,
34–49.

——Spanish/English (revised): 'El tiempo que toma'.
Contra Narrativas, 0, 2018, 8–21.

'Hacer arte como una forma de análisis visual'. In
Gabriela Olmos, Benjamin Mayer Foulkes, eds.
Mieke Bal, retrospectiva fílmica. Mexico City: Cine
Tonalá, 2015, 9–11.

Seven entries in Maria Kappel Blegvad, Zev Tiefenbach,
eds. *Something Strange This Way*. Ostfildern:
Hatje Cantz, 2014. 'Archive', 89; 'Immersion', 115;
'Madness', 116; 'Nightmare', 119–122; 'Time', 135;
'Time Machine', 135; 'White Cube', 141–142.

——Japanese trans. 'Archive', 85; 'Immersion', 113–4;
'Madness', 114–5; 'Nightmare', 120–1; 'Time', 135;
'White Cube', 143. Tokyo: Seigensha Art Publishing,
2017.

'Time on Show: Heterochrony in the Work of Stan
Douglas'. In Fiona Bradley, ed. *Stan Douglas*.
Edinburgh: Fruitmarket Gallery, 2014, 68–147.

'Modus vivendi oder das unvollendete Geschäft der
Geschichte' and 'Modus Vivendi, or History's
Unfinished Business'. In Sabine Folie, Ilse Lafer,
eds. *Ulrike Grossarth: Wäre ich von Stoff, ich würde
mich färben/ Ulrike Grossarth: Were I made of Matter,
I would Color*. Vienna, Generali Foundation, 2014,
35–51 and 295–308.

'The Beholder's Eye/Im Auge des Betrachters'. Jodi
Bieber. *Real Beauty*. Goch: Pagina Verlag, 2014, 77–84.

'Stasis: How to See'. Trine Søndergaard. *Stasis*,
Ostfilfern: Hatje Cantz, 2013, 7–24; revised and
expanded second edition 2019.

'Fins a cert límit: traçar la línia, o no/Hasta cierto
límite: dibujar la línea, o no/Only so far: Drawing
the Line, or Not'. In *Davant l'horitsó*. Barcelona:
Fundació Joan Miró, 2013, 197–223; shortened
and adapted version *Islas y horizontes: Obras de la
collección Es Baluard*. Palma: Museu d'art modern
i cotemporani Es Baluard, 2016, 27–34 (Spanish),
126–130 (Catalan), 176–80 (English).

'Allo-Portraits: Inventing Deconstruction'. In Christian
Gether, ed. *Frida Kahlo: A Life in Art*. Arken: Arken
Museum of Modern Art, 2013, 56–67.

'Photograph'. In *James Coleman*. Madrid: Museo
Nacional Centro de Arte Reina Sofía, 2012, 246–253.

'Landscapes of Madness'. Co-authored with Michelle
Williams Gamaker. In Mia Hannula, ed. *Landscapes
of Madness*. Turku: Aboa Vetus & Ars Nova, 2011.

'Serendipity: The Miracle of Being Where You Are',
'Serendipity: Le miracle d'être où l'on est', and
'Serendipiteit: Het mirakel van te zijn waar je bent'.
In *Ann Veronica Janssens: Serendipity*. Brussels Wiels,
2011, 11–32, 33–56, and 57–80.

'Waiting for the Political Moment'. In *Doris Salcedo,
Plegaria Muda*. Munich: Prestel, 2011, 79–86

——Portuguese: 'À espera do momento politico'. Lisbon:
CAM – Fundaçao Calouste Gulberkian. Swedish:
'I väntan på det politiska ögenblicket'. Stockholm:
Moderna Museet, 2011, 87–104.

'Fighting, Cutting, Crossing Him Out: Stripes Against
volume'. In Laurie Kluitmans, Arnisa Zeqo, eds.
*He Disappeared into Complete Silence: Rereading of
a Single Artwork by Louise Bourgeois*. Eindhoven:
Onomatopee, 2011, 73–82.

'Liikkuva kuva todistaa/The Moving Image as
Witness'. In *Eija-Liisa Ahtila: Marian Ilmestys – The
annunciation*. Helsinki: Crystal Eye, 2011, 73–82;

——Spanish/English: *El entorno ecológico y temporal
de las películas de Eija-Liisa Ahtila*. Santiago de
Compostela: Museo de Arte Contemporáneo, 2017,
43–112.

'Memory as Lace'. In *Seet van Hout: Red Greenhouse*.
Rheine: Edition & Verlag Kloster Bentlage, 2011,
31–35.

'La última frontera' and 'The Last Frontier'. In *La última
frontera/The Last Frontier*. Murcia: Fundación José
García Jiménez, 2011, 16–24 and 100–108.

'Timely Remains'. In *Jussi Niva: Timely Remains*.
Helsinki: Parvs Publishing, 2010, 66–117 and 118–169.

'Intertwined Dualities' and 'Verflochtene Dualitäten'.
In Sabine Folie, Doris Krystof, eds. *Ana Torfs:
Album/Tracks A + B*. Düsseldorf: Kunstsammlung
Nordrhein-Westfalen, 2010, 176–177 and 119–121.

'Eija-Liisa Ahtila'. In *100 Video Artists/100 Videoartistas*.
Madrid: EXIT Publicaciones, 2010, 46–49.

'Conversazioni sussurrate'and 'Whispered
Conversations'. In *Betty Woodman*. Brescia: Galleria
Massimo Minini, 2009, 18 and 19.

'Synesthesie: geur, klank, en andere zintuiglijke
ervaringen'. In *Annelies Planteijdt*. Nijmegen: Galerie
Marzee, 2009, 5–92.

'Marcel and Me: Woodman through Proust/Marcel y
yo: Woodman a través de Proust'. Trans. Francisco
Carpio. In Isabel Tejeda, ed. *Francesca Woodman
Retrospective*. Murcia: Espacio AV, 2009, 114–141.

'Re-: Killing Time'. In Hans D. Christ, Iris Dressler,
eds. *Stan Douglas: Past Imperfect Works 1986–2007*.
Staatsgallerie Stuttgart and Würtembergischer
Kunstverein Stuttgart. Stuttgart: Hatje Cantz, 2007,
64–93.

——Farsi: ‏وقت تقو: نمايش احساسات/ بازداري از نمايش‏
‏احساسات‎. *Global Media Journal*, January 2009,
gmj.ut.ac.ir/maghale.aspx?id=54.

'"Anthropometamorphosis": Forking Paths and
Crystals in Louise Bourgeois' Philosophy of
Temporality/"Antropometamorfosis": Caminos
que se bifurcan y cristales en la filosofía de la
temporalidad de Louise Bourgeois'. In *Louise
Bourgeois: La Sage Femme*. Murcia: Murcia Cultural,
2007, 20–41.

'Earth Aches: The Aesthetics of the Cut'. In Doris
Salcedo. *Shibboleth*. London: Tate Modern
Publishing, 2007, 40–63.

'Forms of Movement' and 'Formas de Moviemento'.
Transl. Nuria Navarro. In Jesús Segura. *Stereo*.
Murcia: Murcia Cultural, 2007, 9–16 and 143–148.

'Light Politics'. In Madeleine Grynsztejn, ed. *Take Your
Time: Olafur Eliasson*. San Francisco Museum of
Modern Art. New York and London: Thames and
Hudson, 2007, 153–182.

'Inside the Polis' and 'Im Innern der Polis'. Trans.
Martina Fuchs. In *Ann Veronica Janssens: An
den Frühling*. Museum Morsbroich Leverkusen.
Cologne: DuMont Literatur und Kunst Verlag, 2007,
165–201 and 43–81.

'Water en los zand: drie vormen van beweging'. In *Land
of water: tijdschrift voor de toekomst*. Enkhuizen:
Zuiderzeemuseum, 2007, 86–95.

'Invisible Art, Hypervisibility, and the Aesthetics of
Everyday Life'. In Martina Weinhart, Max Hollein,
eds. *Nichts/Nothing*. Frankfurt: Schirn Kunsthalle
Frankfurt, 2006, 81–104.

'Los cuerpos barrocos y la ética de la percepción'.
In *Andres Serrano: El dedo en la llaga*. Madrid:
ARTIUM de Alava, 2006, 17–44.

'De-Centering: The Fragility of Mastery/
Descentramiento: La fragilidad de la maestría'. In
Bartomeu Marí, ed. *Peter Friedl: Work 1964–2006*.
Barcelona: Museu d'Art Contemporani de
Barcelona, 2006, 79–110.
——French: 'Le dé-centrage, ou la fragilité de la
maîtrise.' In Bartomeu Marí, ed. *Peter Friedl: Travail
1964–2006*. Barcelona: Museu d'Art Contemporani
de Barcelona, 2006, 81–112.
——German: 'Dezentrierung: Die Fragilität des
Meisterns'. In Dirk Snauwaert, ed. *Über Peter Friedl*.
Brussels: Wiels, 2013, 15–62.
——Republished in *On Peter Friedl*, on the occasion of
the exhibition *Peter Friedl: Report 1964–2022*. Berlin:
KW Institute for Contemporary Art, 2022, 11–55.
'Spin'. In Dominic van den Boogerd, ed. *Wild at Heart*.
Amsterdam: Stichting Ateliers 63, 2006, 47–51.
'À l'est d'Eden/East of Eden/Ten oosten van Eden', In
B.P.S.2 Projects, ed. *Marthe Wéry: Les couleurs du
monochrome*. Tournai: Musée des Beaux-Arts, 2005,
35–104 and 119 –127.
'Fifteen Stories of "Cleopatra"'. In *Cléopâtre dans le
miroir de l'art d'Occident*. Genève: 2004 .
'Bodily Light (Lichaamslicht)'. Summary of the speech
at the opening of the presentation by Ann Veronica
Janssens and Mike Tyler in De Verbeelding Pavilion
in Zeewolde, 6 July 6 2002. In *Look and Feel: Art,
Landscape, Nature 2002–2003*. Zeewolde: De
Verbeelding – Art, Landscape, Nature, 2004, 56–60.
'Setting the Stage: The Subject Mise-en-scène/Eine
Bühne schaffen: das Thema Mise-en-scène'.
In Peter Pakesch, ed. *Videodreams: Zwischen
Cinematischem und Theatralischem/Between the
Cinematic and the Theatrical*. Cologne: Verlag der
Buchhandlung Walther König, 2004, 28–49; revised
and expanded version in Stan Douglas, Christopher
Eamon, eds. *Art of Projection*. Stuttgart: Hatje Cantz,
2009, 167–181; also revised in Alina Serban, Mirela
Duculescu, eds. *The Seductiveness of the Interval*.
Catalogue of the Romanian Pavillion 53rd Venice
Biennal, 2009.
'Matter and Memory/Materie en geheugen'. In *Seet van
Hout: Rood draad – Red Thread*. Staphorst: Hein
Elferink, 2004, 6–25.
'What If... Exploring "Unnaturality"'. In *World Rush:
_4 Artists*. Melbourne: National Gallery of Victoria,
2004, 30–37.
'Antropometamorfoza: rozwidlające się ścieżki i
kryształy filozofii czasowości Louise Bourgeois'
and 'Anthropometamorphosis: Forking Paths
and Crystals in Louise Bourgeois' Philosophy of
Temporality'. Trans. Dorota Kozińska. In Jolanta
Pieńkos, ed. *Louise Bourgeois: Geometria pożądania/
Geometry of Desire*. Warsaw: Zachęta Państwowa
Galeria Sztuki i Autorzy, 2003, 31–37 and 253–261.
'Strings Attached'. In Anne Karin Jortveit, Andrea
Kroksnes, eds. *Devil-may-care: The Nordic Pavillion
at the 50th Venice Biennial 2003*. Oslo: Office for
Contemporary Art Norway, 2003, 116–125.
'Women as the Topic'. Annette Dixon, ed. In *Women
Who Ruled: Queens, Goddesses, Amazons in
Renaissance and Baroque Ar*. London: Merrell,
in association with the University of Michigan
Museum of Art, 2002, 61–96.
'The Dissolution of the World'. In *Martijn Schuppers –
Early Monograph: Paintings 1994–2002*. Amsterdam:
Cato Publishers, 2002, 14–21.
'Companion Portraits: A Collaborative Project by
Rembrandt van Rijn and Ken Aptekar'. New York:
Pamela Auchincloss Project Space, May 2001, 1–4.

'George Deem and Peter Angelo Simon: Timely
Conversation'. In *George Deem and Peter Angelo
Simon: Paintings and Photographs in Conversation*.
Evansville: Evansville Museum of Arts and Science,
2001, 4–40.
'Beckoning Bernini'. In *Louise Bourgeois: Memory and
Architecture*. Madrid: Museo Nacional Reina Sofía,
2000, 75–85.
'Ann Veronica Janssens: Light in Life's Lab/Ann
Veronica Janssens: Labo de Lumière'. Trans. Daniel
Vander Gucht. In Laurent Jacob, ed. *Ann Veronica
Janssens: Une image différente dans chaque oeil/A
Different Image in Each Eye*. Liège: Espace 251 Nord,
1999, 73–102.
'Zwarte Piet's *Bal Masqué*'. In *Zwarte Piet: Anna
Fox*. London: Black Dog Publishing, 1999, 1–11;
reprinted in Val Williams, ed. *Anna Fox: Photographs
1983–2007*. Brighton: Photoworks, 2007, 107–119;
revised version in *Travelling Concepts in the
Humanities*; revised and extended version in Mark
Salber Phillips, Gordon Schochet, eds. *Questions
of Tradition*. Toronto: University of Toronto Press,
2004, 110–151; Dutch revised version 'Cultuur en
traditie' in P. van Zilfhout, ed. *Denken over cultuur*.
Heerlen: Open Universiteit Nederland, 2003,
225–55.
'Points of Departure: Portraits of the Body's Cover-
up'. In *Jeannette Christensen/Kim Soo-Ja*. Feldbach:
Kunsthalle Feldbach (Steirischer Herbst), 1999,
4–23.
'David Reed's *#275*: A Story of Erotic Vision'. In *David
Reed Paintings: Moving Pictures*. San Diego: Museum
of Contemporary Art San Diego, 1998, 36–49.
'Looking at the Other Side with Lili Dujourie'. In *The
Fascinating Faces of Flanders: 58/98 Two Hours Wide
or Two Hours Long*. Antwerp: City of Antwerp, 1998,
188–92.
'Larger than Life: Reading the Corcoran Collection'. In
Ken Aptekar: Talking to Pictures. Washington, D.C.:
Corcoran Gallery of Art, 1997, 5–12.
'De verbeelding van vrouwen'. In *Cahier Charlotte van
Pallandt*. Scheveningen: Museum Beelden aan Zee,
1995, 39–56.
'Verbeelding: verschijningsvormen van narcisme/
Imagination: manifestations of narcissism'. In
Edwin Janssen. *Narcissus en de poel des verderfs/
Narcissus and the Pool of Corruption*. Rotterdam:
Museum Boijmans Van Beuningen, 1994, 33–50.

Edited Books, Special Issues, Interviews

'Mieke Bal: viaje de ida y vuelta de la teoría de la cultura al video arte'. Interview by Professor Domingo Sánchez-Mesa Martíenez, University of Granada, 17 September 2024, youtube.com/watch?v=WnFcKaQx-Oc.

The Architecture of Loneliness: Reflections on Displacement and Welcoming. Amsterdam: Valiz, 2024.

Victoria Hawco, Makenzie Salmon, Mieke Bal. 'In Conversation with Mieke Bal. An Interdisciplinary Exploration of Cultural Spheres (or Inter, Inbetween and Cultural Mediations)'. *Scaffold*, 22 December 2023, ojs.library.carleton.ca/index.php/J-ICSLAC/article/view/4434/3404.

Jeroen Lutters. *The Trade of the Teacher. Visual Thinking with Mieke Bal*. Amsterdam: Valiz, 2018.

Emma & Edvard. Co-edited with Rachel E. Burke. *Text Matters*, 7, 2017, 27–160.

Art *Moves: Performativity in Time, Space and Form/ El Arte (se) Mueve: Performatividad en el Tiempo, el Espacio y la Forma*. Dossier of *Espacio, Tiempo y Forma*, VII: 4, 13–373, revistas.uned.es/index.php/ETFVII/issue/view/869.

Art and Visibility in Migratory Culture. Co-edited with Miguel Hernández-Navarro. Thamyris/Intersecting: Place, Sex and Race, 23. Amsterdam and New York: Rodopi, 2011.

The Rhetoric of Sincerity. Co-edited with Ernst van Alphen and Carel Smith. Stanford: Stanford University Press, 2009.

Acts of Translation. Co-edited with Joanne Morra. *Journal of Visual Culture*, 6: 1, April 2007.

Inge E. Boer. *Uncertain Territories: Boundaries in Cultural Analysis*. Co-edited with Bregje van Eekelen and Patricia Spyer. Amsterdam and New York: Rodopi, 2006.

The Artemisia Files: Artemisia Gentileschi for Feminists and Other Thinking People. Chicago: University of Chicago Press, 2005.

Inge E. Boer. *Disorienting Vision: Rereading Stereotypes in French Orientalist Texts and Images*. Amsterdam and New York: Rodopi, 2004.

Narrative Theory: Critical Concepts in Literary and Cultural Studies, 4. London and New York: Routledge, 2004.

Cultural History: Straddling Borders. John Neubauer zum 70. Geburtstag. Co-edited with Jan van Luxemburg. *Arcadia: International Journal of Literary Studies*, 38: 2, 2003.

The Practice of Cultural Analysis: Exposing Interdisciplinary Interpretation. Stanford: Stanford University Press, 1999.

Acts of Memory: Cultural Recall in the Present. Co-edited with Jonathan Crewe and Leo Spitzer. Hanover: University Press of New England, 1999.

ASCA Brief: Intellectual Traditions in Movement. Co-edited with Thomas Elsaesser, Burcht Pranger, Beate Roessler, Hent de Vries, and Willem Weststeijn. Amsterdam: ASCA Press, 1998.

ASCA Brief: Visions and Voices of Otherness. Co-edited with Thomas Elsaesser, Burcht Pranger, Hent de Vries, and Willem Weststeijn. Amsterdam: ASCA Press, 1997.

Passagen 2000: The City, Pace and Space. Co-edited with David Vanderburgh. *Parallax*, 12, July/September, 1999.

Territorialism and Desire. Co-edited with Mario Caro. *European Journal for Semiotic Studies*, 9: 1, 1997.

Dire l'indicible: Une écriture moderne de la vision. Co-edited with Monique Moser-Verrey. *Etudes littéraires*, 28: 3, 1996.

ASCA Brief: Issues in Cultural Analysis. Co-edited with Thomas Elsaesser, Burcht Pranger, Patricia Spyer, Hent de Vries, and Willem Weststeijn. Kampen: Kok Pharos, 1996.

The Point of Theory. Co-edited with Inge E. Boer. Amsterdam: Amsterdam University Press; New York: Continuum, 1994.

Anti-Covenant: Counter-Reading Women's Lives in the Hebrew Bible. Sheffield: Sheffield Academic Press and the Almond Press, 1989.

Visual Poetics. *Style*, 22: 2, 1988.

Psychopoetics at Work. *Style*, 18: 3, 1984.

Psychopoetics: Theory. *Poetics*, 13: 4/5, 1984.

Literaire genres en hun gebruik. Muiderberg: Coutinho, 1981.

Mensen van papier: over personages in de literatuur. Assen: Van Gorcum, 1980.

Artworks

NB: Unless otherwise indicated, all videos are preserved, updated, and available in the collection of EYE Film Museum, Amsterdam.

An overview article on the thrust of Mieke Bal's artwork in its relationship with her scholarship appeared in December 2020 in *Artium Quaestiones*, a journal from the University of Poznań, Poland. The special issue, edited by Filip Lipiński, is titled *The Cinematic Turn in Art Practice and Theory*, and the opening article 'Cinematic Art (History) and Mieke Bal's Thinking in Film', 5–38. The issue contains another article on her artwork, in Polish.

In March 2022, the book *Image-Thinking* appeared in which Mieke Bal extensively analyzed the relationship between this practice of art making and my academic work.

Fiction

Refugeedom: Lonely but not Alone. With Lena Verhoeff. Abstract Essay film. 24.43', colour, Dolby sound, voice-over but no dialogue, 2022–2023.

INDEX
Personal Names
Including Biblical, Mythical, and Fictional Characters

A B C

I

N P

O Q T

R S

W

D E F G H
K L M
J X Y Z
V

SHORT BIOGRAPHIES

<u>Author</u> Mieke Bal

Author of almost fifty books—the fiftieth being in its final stages—and supervisor of 81 finished PhDs, the cultural theorist, critic, video artist, and curator Mieke Bal (1946, NL) writes from an interdisciplinary perspective on cultural analysis, literature, and art, focusing on gender, migratory culture, the critique of capitalism, and the political agency of art. In 2022–2023 she was elected to hold the Chair 'The Invention of Europe through Languages and Cultures' at the Collège de France in Paris. From 2002 on, she has also been making films, as a different, more in-depth, more contemporary and interactive mode of cultural analysis. Since then, writing, filmmaking, and curating go together. In her book *Image-Thinking* (2022) she developed her ideas about how to integrate academic and artistic thinking. She made a number of experimental documentaries, mostly about migratory situations, and 'theoretical fictions', films, and installations in which cultural-heritage fiction helped developing difficult ideas. Recently she made the 16-channel video-installation *Don Quijote: Sad Countenances* (2019) and a short essay film *It's About Time! Reflections on Urgency* (2020). Her latest short film, made with Lena Verhoeff, *Refugeedom: Lonely but not Alone*, premiered in May 2023 in the SPEME programme on traumatic memory.

miekebal.org

<u>Photography</u> Lena Verhoeff/Artist Statement

'I am in the process of developing myself as an experimental creator exploring identities, in photography, video, and other media. My interest in humans is strongly reflected in my work. I aim to play with the various layers of the human being and capture this in a variety of ways. There are countless forms of behaviour and personalities, and I want to show these to others and exchange thoughts about them.

Often, things are not what they seem; there is so much more to see and notice behind what people are at first glance. From a young age, I've been deeply curious about people's differences and unique traits. I want to delve deeper into the stories behind individuals. This often results in abstract imagery combined with sound, through which I aim to evoke emotions in the viewer. I leave space for personal interpretation but also focus on a trigger point for the audience. My interest in layering is also visible in the abstraction of my work. I am continually fascinated by how moving or still images are merely snapshots, which I can direct and enhance through sound. With this, I create audiovisual pieces, but I also let images speak for themselves as in the photographs here.'

@Lenaverhoefffff

Graphic Design

Lotte Lara Schröder is a designer who often deploys her image-world into her designs. She describes her practice as the making of 'manuals' in which she visualizes (complex) natural/financial/social systems through various materials and techniques such as drawing, collages, and sound.

termsofcircumstance.org

Publisher

Valiz is an independent international publisher that addresses contemporary developments in art, design, urban affairs, and visual culture.

valiz.nl

COLOPHON

Author Mieke Bal
Photography Lena Verhoeff
Copy-editing Leo Reijnen
Proofreading and index Irene de Craen
Book design Lotte Lara Schröder
Typefaces ABC Otto & BFF.otf
Paper inside Holmen Trnd, 70 grs 2.0
Paper cover Sulphate Board, 240 grs
Lithography Wilco Art Books, Amsterdam
Printing and binding Wilco Art Books, Amersfoort
Publisher Astrid Vorstermans, Valiz,
Amsterdam, 2025

This publication has been generously supported by: 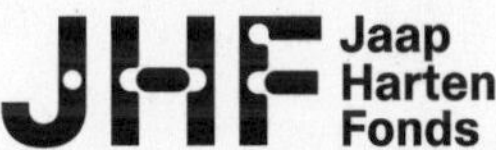

This publication has been printed on FSC-certified paper by an FSC-certified printer. The FSC, Forest Stewardship Council promotes environmentally appropriate, socially beneficial, and economically viable management of the world's forests. fsc.org

INTERNATIONAL DISTRIBUTION
NL/LU: Centraal Boekhuis, www.centraal.boekhuis.nl
BE: EPO, www.epo.be
Europe/Asia (except GB/IE): Idea Books, www.ideabooks.nl
GB/IE: Central Books, www.centralbooks.com
USA/Canada/Latin America: D.A.P., www.artbook.com
Australia: Perimeter Books, www.perimeterbooks.com
Individual orders: www.valiz.nl; info@valiz.nl

ISBN 978-94-93246-43-0
Printed and bound in the EU, 2025

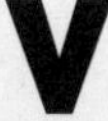